Contesting Islamophobia

Contesting Islamophobia

*Anti-Muslim Prejudice in Media,
Culture and Politics*

Edited by
Peter Morey, Amina Yaqin and Alaya Forte

I.B. TAURIS
LONDON · NEW YORK · OXFORD · NEW DELHI · SYDNEY

I.B. TAURIS
Bloomsbury Publishing Plc
50 Bedford Square, London, WC1B 3DP, UK
1385 Broadway, New York, NY 10018, USA
29 Earlsfort Terrace, Dublin 2, Ireland

BLOOMSBURY, I.B. TAURIS and the I.B. Tauris logo are
trademarks of Bloomsbury Publishing Plc

First published in Great Britain 2019
Paperback edition first published 2021

Copyright © Peter Morey, Amina Yaqin, Alaya Forte and contributors, 2019

Peter Morey, Amina Yaqin and Alaya Forte have asserted their right under the Copyright, Designs and Patents Act, 1988, to be identified as Editors of this work.

For legal purposes the Acknowledgements on p. xii constitute
an extension of this copyright page.

Cover design: Adriana Brioso
Cover image © English Defence League march in Birmingham, April 2017.
Joe Giddens/PA Archive/PA Images

All rights reserved. No part of this publication may be reproduced or transmitted in any form or by any means, electronic or mechanical, including photocopying, recording, or any information storage or retrieval system, without prior permission in writing from the publishers.

Bloomsbury Publishing Plc does not have any control over, or responsibility for, any third-party websites referred to or in this book. All internet addresses given in this book were correct at the time of going to press. The author and publisher regret any inconvenience caused if addresses have changed or sites have ceased to exist, but can accept no responsibility for any such changes.

A catalogue record for this book is available from the British Library.

A catalog record for this book is available from the Library of Congress.

ISBN: HB: 978-1-7883-1163-2
PB: 978-0-7556-4121-5
ePDF: 978-1-7883-1613-2
eBook: 978-1-7883-1614-9

Series: Library of Modern Religion

Typeset by Deanta Global Publishing Services, Chennai, India

To find out more about our authors and books visit
www.bloomsbury.com and sign up for our newsletters.

Contents

List of Figures	vii
Notes on Contributors	viii
Acknowledgements	xii
Foreword: The Roots of Modern Islamophobia *John L. Esposito*	xiv
Introduction: Contesting Islamophobia in Theory and Practice *Peter Morey*	1

Part One Islamophobia, Politics and History

1	American Foreign Policy, Self-Fulfilling Prophecy and Muslims as Enemy Others *Nathan Lean*	29
2	Donald Trump at the Intersection of Nativism, Islamophobia and Anti-Muslim Sentiment: American Roots and Parallels *Peter Gottschalk*	47
3	Islamophobia: The Muslim Problem? A Discussion between Dibyesh Anand, Myriam Francois and Jim Wolfreys *Chaired by Peter Morey*	70

Part Two Islamophobia and Representation

4	Islamophobia and the War of Representations: Martin Amis's 'The Last Days of Muhammad Atta' *Nath Aldalala'a and Geoffrey Nash*	87
5	'A Sly and Stubborn People': *Game of Thrones*, Orientalism and Islamophobia *Roberta Garrett*	103
6	Islamic Feminism in a Time of Islamophobia: The Muslim Heroines of Leila Aboulela's *Minaret* and Elif Shafak's *Forty Rules of Love* *Amina Yaqin*	123

Part Three Youth Contesting Islamophobia

7	Countering Islamophobia in the Classroom *Sarah Soyei*	147
8	Resisting Islamophobia: Muslim Youth Activism in the UK *Tania Saeed*	165
9	Young Muslims in Germany and Their Use of New Media to Counter Islamophobia *Asmaa Soliman*	185

Part Four Art beyond Islamophobia

10 Adjusting the 'Islamic' Focus: Exhibitions of Contemporary Pakistani Art in Britain in the Post-9/11 Decade *Madeline Clements* 205
11 Super Moozlim Battles Islamophobia *Leila Tarakji* 227
12 *Homegrown*: The Story of a Controversy *Nadia Latif interviewed by Peter Morey and Amina Yaqin* 248

Index 263

Figures

7.1	The Spread of False Information. Image courtesy of Equaliteach	153
7.2	'Facts' versus Research. Image courtesy of Equaliteach	156
7.3	Muslim Flip-chart. Image courtesy of Equaliteach	157
10.1	*Infinite Justice*, Aisha Khalid (2001). Image courtesy of Green Cardamom © Vipul Sangoi	215
10.2	*Infinite Justice* (detail), Aisha Khalid (2001). Image courtesy of Green Cardamom © Vipul Sangoi	216
10.3	*Please Do Not Touch, Stay Out and Enjoy the Show*, Hamra Abbas (2004). Image courtesy of Green Cardamom © Vipul Sangoi	217
10.4	*Please Do Not Touch, Stay Out and Enjoy the Show* (detail), Hamra Abbas (2004). Image courtesy of Green Cardamom © Vipul Sangoi	217
10.5	*Politically Incorrect,* Imran Qureshi (2006). Image courtesy of Green Cardamom © Vipul Sangoi	218
11.1	'Calling all Bigotry Busters'	240
11.2	'Stamp Out Racism'	241

Contributors

Nath Aldalala'a is Associate Professor of International Relations and Cultural Studies at Shandong University, China. He is a specialist in international relations of the Middle East and American foreign policy. He has a special interest in post-9/11 writings, on which he has published a number of articles, specifically those that focus on security and global terrorism.

Dibyesh Anand is the head of the Department of Politics and International Relations at the University of Westminster in London. He is the author of the books *Geopolitical Exotica: Tibet in Western Imagination* (2007) and *Hindu Nationalism in India and the Politics of Fear* (2011) and has published on varied topics including Tibet, the China–India border dispute, Hindutva and Islamophobia, identity politics in Tanzania and nationalism.

Madeline Clements is Research Lecturer in English Studies at Teesside University. She is the author of *Writing Islam from a South Asian Muslim Perspective* (2015). She has published and reviewed widely, particularly in the area of post-colonial literary fiction. Her current research interest is in the politics of South Asian Muslim art and literature. Her articles and reviews have appeared in a range of publications, including the *Times Literary Supplement*.

Myriam Francois is a writer, broadcaster and academic with a focus on current affairs. Her writing has been featured in the *Guardian*, *CNN*, the *New Arab*, *Jadaliyya* and *ABC*, among others. She is the presenter of two BBC One documentaries, *The Muslim Pound* (2016) and *A Deadly Warning: Srebrenica Revisited* (2015).

Roberta Garrett is Senior Lecturer in Literature at the University of East London. She has published widely on gender representation in film and literature, being the author of *Postmodern Chick-Flicks: The Return of the Woman's Film* (2007) as well as numerous articles and book chapters. She co-edited (with Tracey Jensen and Angela Voela) *We Need to Talk about Family: Essays on Neoliberalism, The Family and Popular Culture* (2016) and is currently completing a book entitled *Writing the Modern Family: Neoliberalism and Representation of Parenting in Contemporary Novels and Memoirs*.

Peter Gottschalk is Professor of Religion at Wesleyan University. His research focuses on the dynamics of cultural interpretation and conflict in the context of Islam, Hinduism and the West. He is the author of *Beyond Hindu and Muslim: Multiple Identity in Narratives from Village India* (2000); collaborated with Mathew N. Schmalz in editing *Engaging South Asian Religions: Boundaries, Appropriations and Resistance* (2011) and in creating an interactive website called *A Virtual Village* (2001); and co-wrote, with Gabriel Greenberg, *Islamophobia: Making Muslims the Enemy* (2007).

Nadia Latif is an Anglo-Sudanese theatre and film director based in London. She has spent the last decade working exclusively in new writing, at theatres including the Royal Court, the Bush, the Almeida and the Royal Shakespeare Company.

Nathan Lean is the research director at Georgetown University's project on 'Pluralism, Religious Diversity and Islamophobia' at the Prince Alwaleed bin Talal Center for Muslim–Christian Understanding. He is the author of numerous books; among them is the award-winning *The Islamophobia Industry: How the Right Manufactures Fear of Muslims* (2012). His fourth volume, *The Changing Middle East: Power and Politics in an Age of Revolution*, was published in early 2015. His writings on Islamophobia have been featured in the *Los Angeles Times*, the *New York Daily News*, the *Washington Post*, the *Christian Science Monitor*, *CNN* and *Salon* among others.

Geoffrey Nash's work focuses on Western writing that addresses the Middle East and the Islamic world. His expertise encompasses Arab American and European writing on the Middle East. He has a particular interest in Orientalism and the Orientalists, travel writing, Arab anglophone fiction and Islamic themes in contemporary British fiction. Among his recent publications are the edited volume *Postcolonialism and Islam* (2013) and his book *Writing Muslim Identity* (2012).

Tania Saeed is Assistant Professor in the Mushtaq Ahmad Gurmani School of Humanities and Social Sciences at the Lahore University of Management Sciences (LUMS), Pakistan. She has published in peer-reviewed journals and edited collections and is the author of *Islamophobia and Securitization: Religion, Ethnicity and the Female Voice* (2016). Her research focuses on issues of security, education and social justice in the context of the UK and Pakistan.

Asmaa Soliman is Project Coordinator for Knowledge Transfer in the Akademie für Islam in Wissenchaft und Gesellschaft (AIWG) at the Goethe-Universität Frankfurt am Main. She has previously worked for several media companies and research projects in Germany, Egypt and the UK, mostly on religion, Islam and intercultural dialogue. In 2015 she was awarded a PhD for her thesis on Muslim youth culture in Germany. She has written about Muslims in Europe and is involved in the work of numerous NGOs.

Sarah Soyei is Head of Partnerships at EqualiTeach. She has worked in the field of equality and diversity training and consultancy for over ten years and has overseen the development of educational programmes delivered to over 200,000 people. These have included work commissioned by the British government, EHRC, the Football Foundation, over twenty local authorities and private sector organizations such as *Partnerships in Care*. She has delivered presentations at the House of Commons, London's City Hall and several national and international conferences.

Leila Tarakji is a doctoral candidate in the Department of English at Michigan State University and a recipient of the University Distinguished Fellowship. Her research is committed to the development of Muslim American literary studies and its role within a broader field of ethnic literary studies. Her most recent work considers how contemporary poetry records the transnational circuits that define Muslim American cultural memories and affective histories.

Jim Wolfreys is Senior Lecturer in French and European Politics at King's College London. He is an expert in French politics, fascism, political corruption, the French labour movement and the history of revolution. He is co-author (with Peter Fysh) of *The Politics of Racism in France* (2003) and has just completed a new book, entitled *Republic of Islamophobia: The Rise of Respectable Racism in France* (2018). He has published widely in books and journals as well as in newspapers and periodicals, such as the *Guardian*, *Jacobin*, *Prospect* and *Contretemps*.

The Editors

Peter Morey is Professor of 20th Century English Literature at the University of Birmingham. He specializes in colonial and post-colonial literature, culture and theory, with a particular interest in issues of narrative and power. He has authored and edited numerous books, including *Framing Muslims: Stereotyping* *and Representation after 9/11* (2011) (with Amina Yaqin). He has also held research grants and led projects studying contemporary intercultural relations and Islamophobia. His new book, *Islamophobia and the Novel*, was published in 2018.

Amina Yaqin is Senior Lecturer in Urdu and Postcolonial Studies at SOAS, University of London. She has published widely on Urdu poetry, fiction and autobiography. Her research interests include colonial and post-colonial literary and cultural studies and British Islam. She is co-author (with Peter Morey) of *Framing Muslims: Stereotyping and Representation after 9/11* (2011) and co-editor of *Culture, Diaspora and Modernity in Muslim Writing*. She was Co-Director of the AHRC-funded International Research Network 'Framing Muslims' from 2007 to 2010 and project partner on 'Muslims, Trust and Cultural Dialogue', funded by RCUK (2012–15).

Alaya Forte is a PhD candidate at SOAS, University of London, where she is researching the political representation of Muslim women in British local and national politics. She has a BA in Arabic and Islamic Studies from the University of Exeter (UK), a degree in Politics from the University of Nice (France) and an MA in Gender Studies from SOAS. She is also a researcher for the 'Muslims, Trust and Cultural Dialogue' project, where she is exploring British Muslims' involvement in the arts and cultural sphere.

Acknowledgements

The seeds of this book were planted at the Beyond Islamophobia conference, held at SOAS, University of London, in 2014. Academics, activists and artists from around the world gathered to share experiences of Islamophobia and the fruits of their research into this global form of prejudice, and to consider the means by which anti-Muslim prejudice might be challenged. The conference was part of the RCUK-funded 'Muslims, Trust and Cultural Dialogue' project, and we would first like to give thanks to the combined UK funding councils for their generous support during that project. Thereafter, this volume took its present shape owing to the dedication of its contributors who have risen to the challenge of reflecting on the ways in which Islamophobia might be contested in the various walks of life where it is most prevalent. Our gratitude is owed to those who have written for us, allowed their discussions to be transcribed and permitted us to interview them. We hope the resulting volume captures something of the dynamism with which individuals and groups are banding together to better understand and fight this form of prejudice.

Intellectually, we are indebted to those who have charted this area before us, no one more tellingly than the late Edward Said. His work in describing how Islam is 'covered' – in the sense of both being heavily reported by Western media forms and, in the process, being smothered by limited, stereotypical framing – provides the foundation for all the work we have done in this field. In his attempts to expose the one-sidedness of Western views of Islam – and especially Arabs – Said was followed by the redoubtable and much-missed Jack Shaheen, whose work on Arab stereotypes in cinema remains the benchmark for all accounts of media representations of Muslims. Their legacy can be seen in the present volume's concern to bring together perspectives from disciplines such as history, sociology, literature, art and media studies. This is important since it is by means of a broad array of discourses, touching on all walks of life, that our views of the world and its inhabitants are shaped for good or ill.

We are extremely fortunate to have had the support of John L. Esposito, the leading figure in the understanding of Muslims and anti-Muslim prejudice in the world today. The foreword he has provided is only one of the ways he has helped us since his attendance at that initial conference. As such he is to be heartily thanked. Several others represented in this volume have, likewise, been generous with their time and advice, so that any shortcomings the reader finds here must be held against the editors, rather than our contributors who form a roster of some of the leading figures in their respective fields.

We would like to also thank our respective institutions – the University of Birmingham and SOAS, University of London. Peter Morey would also like to acknowledge the support he received from the University of East London, where he spent many years and where he was employed while running the 'Muslims, Trust and Cultural Dialogue' project. We wish to acknowledge the many colleagues and students who have supported and believed in this project over the years and who have contributed to its intellectual nurturing. We would particularly like to thank Sarah Pett and Kai Easton for their invaluable support and friendship.

A huge debt of gratitude is owed to Professor Muhammad Abdel Haleem and the Centre for Islamic Studies at SOAS for their help in covering the book production costs. Thanks are also due to Sophie Rudland and her colleagues at I. B. Tauris for immediately seeing the publishing potential of our initial idea and for their patience and guidance as we slowly pulled it together. We must also save a word of praise and gratitude for Rachel Goodyear, whose meticulous and proactive copyediting allowed us to smarten up a rather rough first draft and make it publishable.

Foreword: The Roots of Modern Islamophobia

John L. Esposito

The roots of Islamophobia in America and Europe are long and run deep, providing the context for attitudes towards Islam and Muslims, government policies and mass and social media coverage.

In 1981 Edward Said presciently warned the following:

> For the general public in America and Europe today, Islam is 'news' of a particularly unpleasant sort. The media, the government, the geopolitical strategists, and – although they are marginal to the culture at large – the academic experts on Islam are all in concert: Islam is a threat to western civilization. Now this is by no means the same as saying that only derogatory or racist caricatures of Islam are to be found in the West. … What I am saying is that negative images of Islam are very much more prevalent than any others, and that such images correspond not with what Islam 'is' … but to what prominent sectors of a particular society take it to be. Those sectors have the power and the will to propagate that particular image of Islam, and this image therefore becomes more prevalent, more present, than all others.[1]

Yet it took until 1997 to create a term that effectively names this phenomenon of negative responses to Islam and Muslims. In November 1997, the British Runnymede Trust's report *Islamophobia: A Challenge for Us All*, launched in the UK, defined Islamophobia as 'the dread, hatred and hostility towards Islam and Muslims perpetrated by a series of closed views that imply and attribute negative and derogatory stereotypes and beliefs to Muslims'.[2] It results in the following: exclusion from economic, social and public life; discrimination in the blatant form of hate crimes and subtler forms of disparagement; the perception that the religion of Islam has no common values with the West is inferior to the West and is a violent political ideology rather than a source of faith and spirituality, unlike the other Abrahamic religions, Judaism and Christianity.[3]

The naming of this reality continues to gain momentum. The term 'Islamophobia' has generated increased scholarly and popular understanding and communication as well as multiple responses aimed at addressing its negative consequences.

Islamophobia's contemporary resurgence

In recent years, Islamophobia has grown exponentially, triggered by many events: the Iranian Revolution, hijackings, hostage-taking and acts of terrorism in the 1980s and 1990s, attacks against the World Trade Center and Pentagon on 9/11 and subsequent terrorist attacks by Al Qaeda and ISIS in Europe. As a result of these events and the responses to them, the same period has seen a significant influx of Muslims into the West.

Given these realities, Muslims have faced many challenges. For example, a report by the Public Religion Research Institute describes how 'no religious, social, or racial and ethnic group [is] perceived as facing greater discrimination in the U.S. than Muslims'.[4]

The beginning of the modern cycle of Islamophobia is often located at the time of the Iranian Revolution, which deposed the Western-backed Shah and saw the installation of an Islamic Republic in 1979. Iran's Islamic Revolution stunned global leaders and became the lens through which many in the West first learnt about Islam. Governments, experts and media alike scrambled to understand how the mighty Shah of Iran could be overthrown by a mass movement whose leader was an aged Ayatollah Khomeini, living in exile in a Paris suburb. The example of Iran and the threat of Khomeini's call for the export of its revolution fuelled fears of the spread of radical Islamic fundamentalism in the Middle East and beyond.

Another strand in the tale concerns the decline of the Soviet Union in the 1980s. Its eventual collapse in 1991 increased fears that 'radical Islamic fundamentalism' would prove to be the next global threat. Statements by authoritarian Muslim government leaders, Western policy makers and media commentators reinforced fears of the 'Red Threat' of communism being replaced by the 'Green Threat' of Islam. The portrayal of Islam as a triple threat (political, civilizational and demographic) serves to trivialize the complexity of political, social and religious dynamics in the Muslim world and paints a simplistic picture that can be used to support what Samuel Huntington's seminal article and subsequent book characterized as an imminent 'Clash of Civilizations' between Islam and the West.[5] With its simplistic view of separate 'civilizations' in perpetual conflict, Huntington's international bestselling book reinforced fears of Islam as *the* major source of threat to the West and had – and continues to have – enormous influence internationally.

In the period immediately pre- and post-9/11 a slew of selective and biased analyses of Islam and events in the Muslim world by prominent journalists, commentators and some politicians worked to foster a sense of global crisis that fuelled an even more extreme demonization of Muslims. Examples of this scaremongering include articles with titles such as 'Don't Look for Moderates in the Islamic Revolution',[6] 'A Holy War Heads Our Way'[7] and 'Prince Charles Is Wrong – Islam Does Menace the West'.[8] Will Cummins in the *Telegraph* asserted, 'It is the black heart of Islam, not the black face, to which millions object.'[9] Robert Kilroy-Silk, one-time British politician and talk-show host, wrote in the *Daily Express* that 'Muslims everywhere behave with equal savagery. They behead criminals, stone to death female – only female – adulteresses, throw acid in the faces of women who refuse to wear the chador, mutilate the genitals of young girls and ritually abuse animals.'[10] And Jean-Marie Le Pen, then president of France's far-right National Front party, warned, 'These elements have a negative effect on all of public security. They are strengthened demographically both by natural reproduction and by immigration, which reinforces their stubborn ethnic segregation, their domineering nature. This is the world of Islam in all its aberrations.'[11] It is hardly surprising that a climate of fear and violence fed rising Islamophobia.

The impact of 9/11 on popular culture

The 9/11 attacks in America on the World Trade Center in New York and Pentagon in Washington, DC – both symbols of US economic and military power – reinforced by Al Qaeda attacks in London, Madrid and Bali, proved a watershed moment, prompting what the George W. Bush administration, with strong support from Britain's prime minister, Tony Blair, would call a war against global terrorism. The events of 9/11 exacerbated and fed the growth of Islamophobia in the West. In 2002, the European Monitoring Centre on Racism and Xenophobia published the *Summary Report on Islamophobia in the EU after 11 September 2001*, which documented increased and widespread acts of discrimination and racism against Muslims in fifteen EU member countries and warned them of Islamophobia and anti-Semitism becoming acceptable in European society.¹² In a follow-up report in 2004, the Runnymede Trust concluded that Islamophobia was a pervasive feature of British society. It also characterized media reporting on Muslims and Islam as biased and unfair.[13]

Far-right, anti-immigrant political parties and political commentators in Europe have demonized Islam and Muslims; the net result has been a virulent form of cultural racism. Similarly, in the United States, the Council on American–Islamic Relations documented an increase of reported hate crimes between 2004 and 2005, with a 29.6 per cent increase in the total number of complaints of anti-Muslim harassment, violence and discriminatory treatment.[14] The international scope of Islamophobia was recognized and addressed by the United Nations, when Kofi Annan, then its secretary general, addressed a 2004 UN conference on 'Confronting Islamophobia: Education for Tolerance and Understanding'. Annan underscored the global need to acknowledge and address this new form of increasing bigotry:

> [when] the world is compelled to coin a new term to take account of increasingly widespread bigotry – that it is a sad and troubling development. Such is the case with 'Islamophobia'. ... Since the September 11 attacks on the United States, many Muslims, particularly in the West, have found themselves the objects of suspicion, harassment and discrimination. ... Too many people see Islam as a monolith and as intrinsically opposed to the West.[15]

The media as an enabler of Islamophobia

The mass media's market-driven sales emphasis, epitomized by the phrase 'if it bleeds, it leads', is reflected in a penchant for explosive, headline events and an overemphasis on violence, terrorism and the more sensational anti-Islam and anti-Muslim statements of political leaders, media commentators and a host of 'preachers of hate'. Minimal coverage of the broader context, the attitudes and behaviours of a majority of mainstream Muslims, has resulted in an imbalance in American and European mass media news coverage. The media analyst organization Media Tenor International discovered that out of nearly 975,000 news stories from US and European media outlets, networks significantly reduced coverage on events in the Middle East and North Africa (MENA) to the actions of Muslim militants. A comparison of media coverage in 2001 with that in 2011 demonstrated the shocking disparity of coverage. In 2001, 2 per cent of all news stories in Western media presented images of Muslim militants, while just over 0.1 per cent presented stories of the vast majority of ordinary Muslims. By 2011, 25 per cent of the stories presented a militant image, while only 0.1 per cent presented images of ordinary Muslims: no improvement at all in the balance of coverage over the ten-year period.[16] The year 2015 witnessed an all-time high in the level of negative reporting. In the United States, UK and Germany nine out of ten articles were negative. Over 80 per cent of the coverage of religious protagonists on television was negative. Moreover, even coverage of mainstream Muslims tended to be negative (more than 50 per cent of reports).[17] Finally, in its 2016 Davos report, 'Reviewing Tone and Coverage of Islam: Global TV 2005–2016', Media Tenor reported that at least two-thirds of coverage of Muslims was extremely negative.[18]

For over a decade, there has been an explosion of social media websites and anti-Muslim diatribes with international and domestic consequences. This has been accompanied by the emergence of an organized Islamophobia network and its engineered campaigns orchestrated by ideological, agenda-driven anti-Muslim polemicists and their funders. Major reports based on US Internal Revenue Service returns have shed a light on support funding and its sources. The Center for American Progress report, *Fear, Inc.* (August 2011), documented that $42.6 million flowed from seven foundations over ten years to support Islamophobic authors and websites.[19] A Council on American–Islamic Relations report in 2013, *Legislating Fear: Islamophobia and Its Impact in the United States*, identified $119,662,719 in total revenue between 2008 and 2011.[20]

Islamophobia in American and European elections

American and European political elections have been a major driver or trigger of Islamophobia, as seen in the 2008 and 2012 Obama presidential elections and results in American and European elections in 2016 and 2018, as well as the significant performance of anti-immigrant and anti-Muslim parties and political leaders. In 2016, the presidential candidate (and soon-to-be president) Donald Trump declared, 'Islam hates us' and called for a Muslim travel ban as well as the monitoring or even the forced closure of American mosques. During Republican presidential primaries, Newt Gingrich, Rick Santorum, Ben Carson, Ted Cruz and Marco Rubio weighed in warning of the dangers of the implantation of sharia, calling for a freeze on Muslim immigration and refugee programmes and questioning whether a Muslim could be president or serve in the cabinet.

Trump's Muslim travel ban (officially known as Presidential Executive Order: Protecting the Nation from Foreign Terrorist Entry into the United States), designed to halt the refugee resettlement process and bar all immigration from seven Muslim-majority countries, mobilized a cross section of Americans and organizations at airport protests. Uri Friedman called it 'a phantom menace', pointing out the following:

> Nationals of the seven countries singled out by Trump have killed zero people in terrorist attacks on U.S. soil between 1975 and 2015. ... Over the last four decades, 20 out of 3.25 million refugees welcomed to the United States have been convicted of attempting or committing terrorism on U.S. soil, and only three Americans have been killed in attacks committed by refugees – all by Cuban refugees in the 1970s.[21]

In contrast to Donald Trump and the Republican Party's victory in 2016, in Europe the gains of anti-Muslim and anti-immigrant parties were less spectacular. However far-right, anti-immigrant and anti-Muslim parties and politicians have championed a white nationalist supremacist message, calling for a halt in immigration and even the expulsion of Muslim refugees from the UK, Germany, France, the Netherlands and elsewhere.

Conclusion

Mainstream American and European Muslims have too often been equated inaccurately with terrorists and branded as people who reject democracy. In fact, major polls by Gallup and Pew report that majorities of Muslims desire democracy and freedom, are loyal citizens and reject religious extremism and terrorism. Failure to recognize and appreciate these facts continues to feed a growing Islamophobia that threatens the safety, security and civil liberties of many Muslims in the West and discourages those in the West from joining in partnership with the majority of Muslims to fight the extremist fringe. It is time to distinguish between the religion of Islam and the behaviour of a fraction of Muslims who commit acts of terrorism. President Barack Obama's reminder for Americans should also be true for Americans and Europeans today as they face Al Qaeda, ISIS and other terrorist groups: 'The United States is not – and never will be – at war with Islam ... . Bin Laden was not a Muslim leader; he was a mass murderer of Muslims. Indeed, al Qaeda has slaughtered scores of Muslims in many countries, including our own.'²²

Contesting Islamophobia provides in one volume a much-needed view of the history and spread of Islamophobia, its major characteristics as well as its diversity of expression in differing contexts. Terrorist attacks by Al Qaeda and especially ISIS both in Muslim countries and in the West in recent years as well as the exponential growth of Islamophobia and xenophobia and their expression in American and European politics make *Contesting Islamophobia* a 'must read' for policy makers, journalists and scholars as well as concerned citizens in America, Europe and Muslim countries alike.

Notes

1. Edward Said, *Covering Islam* (London: Vintage, 1997), p. 144.
2. *Islamophobia: A Challenge for Us All* (London: Runnymede Trust, 1997). Available at www.runnymedetrust.org/companies/17/74/Islamophobia-A-Challenge-for-Us-All.html (accessed 1 February 2018).
3. Runnymede Trust, *Islamophobia*.
4. Robert P. Jones, Daniel Cox, Betsy Cooper and Rachel Lienesch, *Anxiety, Nostalgia, and Mistrust: Findings from the 2015 American Values Survey* (Washington, DC: Public Religion Research Institute, 2015). Available at www.prri.org/wp-content/uploads/2015/11/PRRI-AVS-2015.pdf (accessed 1 February 2018).
5. See Samuel P. Huntington, *The Clash of Civilizations and the Remaking of World Order* (New York: Simon and Schuster, 1996).
6. Peter Rodman, 'Don't look for moderates in the Islamic Revolution', *International Herald Tribune*, 4 January 1995.
7. Fergus M. Bordewich, 'A holy war heads our way', *Reader's Digest* (1995), pp. 76–80.
8. Patrick Sookhdeo, 'Prince Charles is wrong – Islam does menace the west', *Daily Telegraph*, 19 December 1996.
9. Will Cummins, 'The Tories must confront Islam instead of kowtowing to it', *The Telegraph*, 18 July 2004. Available at www.telegraph.co.uk/comment/personal-view/3608563/The-Tories-must-confront-Islam-instead-of-kowtowing-to-it.html (accessed 1 February 2018).
10. Robert Kilroy-Silk, *Daily Express*, 15 January 1995. As cited in John L. Esposito and Ibrahim Kalin (eds), *Islamophobia: The Challenge of Pluralism in the 21st Century* (Oxford: Oxford University Press, 2011), p. xxii.
11. Adar Primor, 'Le Pen ultimate', *Haaretz*, 18 April 2002. Available at www.haaretz.com/1.5196268 (accessed 1 February 2018).

12 Muhammad Anwar, 'Muslims in Britain: Issues, policy and practice', in Tahir Abbas (ed.), *Muslim Britain: Communities under Pressure* (London: Zed Books, 2005), pp. 31–46.
13 Runnymede Trust, *Islamophobia: Issues, Challenges and Action* (London: Runnymede Trust, 2004).
14 *The Status of Muslim Civil Rights in the United States 2005* (Washington, DC: Council on American–Islamic Relations, 2005). Available at www.cair.com/images/pdf/CAIR-2005-Civil-Rights-Report.pdf (accessed 1 February 2018).
15 Kofi Annan, 'Secretary-general, addressing headquarters seminar on confronting Islamophobia, stresses importance of leadership, two-way integration, dialogue', *United Nations*, 7 December 2004. Available at www.un.org/press/en/2004/sgsm9637.doc.htm (accessed 1 February 2018).
16 'A new era for Arab–Western relations', *Media Tenor*, 2001. As cited in John L. Esposito, '2013 AAR presidential address: Islam in the public square', *Journal of the American Academy of Religion* 82/2 (June 2014), p. 301.
17 Media Tenor, 'A new era for Arab–Western relations'.
18 Media Tenor, *Reviewing Tone and Coverage of Islam: Global TV 2005–2016* (2016). Available at www.mediatenor.cz/wp-content/uploads/2015/02/ADR_2015_LR_WEB_PREVIEW.pdf (accessed 1 February 2018).
19 Wajahat Ali, Eli Clifton, Matthew Duss, Lee Fang, Scott Keyes and Faiz Shakir, *Fear, Inc.: The Roots of the Islamophobia Network in America* (Washington, DC: Center for American Progress, 2011). Available at www.americanprogress.org/issues/religion/report/2011/08/26/10165/fear-inc/ (accessed 1 February 2018).
20 *Legislating Fear: Islamophobia and Its Impact in the United States* (Washington, DC: Council on American–Islamic Relations, 2013). Available at www.cair.com/images/islamophobia/Legislating-Fear.pdf (accessed 1 February 2018).
21 Uri Friedman, 'Where America's terrorists actually come from', *The Atlantic*, 30 January 2017. Available at www.theatlantic.com/international/archive/2017/01/trump-immigration-ban-terrorism/514361/ (accessed 1 February 2018).
22 'President Obama's address to the nation to announce that the United States has killed Osama Bin Laden, the leader of Al Qaeda', 2 May 2011. Available at https://obamawhitehouse.archives.gov/blog/2011/05/02/osama-bin-laden-dead (accessed 29 March 2018).

Works cited

Ali, Wajahat, Eli Clifton, Matthew Duss, Lee Fang, Scott Keyes and Faiz Shakir, *Fear, Inc.: The Roots of the Islamophobia Network in America* (Washington, DC: Center for American Progress, 2011). Available at www.americanprogress.org/issues/religion/report/2011/08/26/10165/fear-inc/ (accessed 1 February 2018).

Annan, Kofi, 'Secretary-general, addressing headquarters seminar on confronting Islamophobia, stresses importance of leadership, two-way integration, dialogue', *United Nations*, 7 December 2004. Available at www.un.org/press/en/2004/sgsm9637.doc.htm (accessed 1 February 2018).

Anwar, Muhammad, 'Muslims in Britain: Issues, policy and practice', in Tahir Abbas (ed.), *Muslim Britain: Communities Under Pressure* (London: Zed Books, 2005), pp. 31–46.

Bordewich, Fergus M., 'A holy war heads our way', *Reader's Digest* (1995), pp. 76–80.

Council on American–Islamic Relations, *Legislating Fear: Islamophobia and its Impact in the United States* (Washington, DC: Council on American–Islamic Relations, 2013). Available at www.cair.com/images/islamophobia/Legislating-Fear.pdf (accessed 1 February 2018).

Council on American–Islamic Relations, *The Status of Muslim Civil Rights in the United States 2005* (Washington, DC: Council on American–Islamic Relations, 2005). Available at www.cair.com/images/pdf/CAIR-2005-Civil-Rights-Report.pdf (accessed 1 February 2018).

Cummins, Will, 'The Tories must confront Islam instead of kowtowing to it', *The Telegraph*, 18 July 2004. Available at www.telegraph.co.uk/comment/personal-view/3608563/The-Tories-must-confront-Islam-instead-of-kowtowing-to-it.html (accessed 1 February 2018).

Esposito, John L., '2013 AAR presidential address: Islam in the public square', *Journal of the American Academy of Religion* 82/2 (June 2014), pp. 291–306.

Esposito, John L. and Ibrahim Kalin (eds), *Islamophobia: The Challenge of Pluralism in the 21st Century* (Oxford: Oxford University Press, 2011).

Friedman, Uri, 'Where America's terrorists actually come from', *The Atlantic*, 30 January 2017. Available at www.theatlantic.com/international/archive/2017/01/trump-immigration-ban-terrorism/514361/ (accessed 1 February 2018).

Huntington, Samuel P., *The Clash of Civilizations and the Remaking of World Order* (New York: Simon and Schuster, 1996).

Jones, Robert P., Daniel Cox, Betsy Cooper and Rachel Lienesch, *Anxiety, Nostalgia, and Mistrust: Findings from the 2015 American Values Survey* (Washington, DC: Public Religion Research Institute, 2015). Available at www.prri.org/wp-content/uploads/2015/11/PRRI-AVS-2015.pdf (accessed 1 February 2018).

Media Tenor, *Reviewing Tone and Coverage of Islam: Global TV 2005–2016* (2016). Available at www.mediatenor.cz/wp-content/uploads/2015/02/ADR_2015_LR_WEB_PREVIEW.pdf (accessed 1 February 2018).

Obama, Barack, 'President Obama's address to the nation to announce that the United States has killed Osama Bin Laden, the leader of Al Qaeda', 2 May 2011. Available at https://obamawhitehouse.archives.gov/blog/2011/05/02/osama-bin-laden-dead (accessed 29 March 2018).

Primor, Adar, 'Le Pen ultimate', *Haaretz*, 18 April 2002. Available at www.haaretz.com/1.5196268 (accessed on 1 February 2018).

Rodman, Peter, 'Don't look for moderates in the Islamic Revolution', *International Herald Tribune*, 4 January 1995.
Runnymede Trust, *Islamophobia: A Challenge for Us All* (London: Runnymede Trust, 1997). Available at www.runnymedetrust.org/companies/17/74/Islamophobia-A-Challenge-for-Us-All.html (accessed 1 February 2018).
Runnymede Trust, *Islamophobia: Issues, Challenges and Action* (London: Runnymede Trust, 2004).
Said, Edward, *Covering Islam* (London: Vintage, 1997).
Sookhdeo, Patrick, 'Prince Charles is wrong – Islam does menace the west', *Daily Telegraph*, 19 December 1996.

Introduction: Contesting Islamophobia in Theory and Practice

Peter Morey

It seems to be open season on Muslims. With hostile statements from press and politicians, physical attacks and discrimination spiking, Islamophobia, or 'anti-Muslim prejudice' as it is sometimes known, is all around us.

We live in an age where the established civilities of everyday discourse are challenged by the proliferation of new media, where opinions, prejudices and threats can be blurted out instantaneously. While they are by no means the only victims of a culture where abuse can travel around the globe in the time it takes to hit a 'post' button, Muslims now comprise perhaps the most recognizable targets. Indeed, in the first decade and a half of the twenty-first century, Islamophobia has emerged as the dominant mode of prejudice in contemporary Western societies. In North America and across the nations of Europe, concerns about Muslims are central to political debates and policies. As part of the response to international conflicts, acts of terrorism, and state violence by Western nations, the figure of the Muslim has come under increased scrutiny. Muslims and Islam have emerged as the focal point of anxieties about citizenship, loyalty and liberal values. They have been the object of heightened levels of criticism, intolerance and abuse: their cultures homogenized and vilified and their religion depicted as backward and warlike.[1]

In addition to the rise of a number of right-wing, anti-Islam political groups across Europe and North America, recent years have seen an explosion in anti-immigrant, and specifically anti-Muslim, popular rhetoric. At the same time, the political attraction of scapegoating grows as populations feel the inequitable effects of the neoliberal economics that led to the 2008 financial crash and also shaped the austerity programmes that responded to it.[2] The successful Labour Party candidate in the London mayoral elections of 2016, Sadiq Khan, had to fight off a campaign by his Conservative opponents to smear him with the presumed guilt-by-association his Muslim background was felt to carry;[3] the

'Brexit' vote in Britain saw a spike in anti-Muslim hate crime,[4] and the 2016 US presidential election was won by Donald Trump, a candidate running on an explicitly Islamophobic platform, who later cemented his credentials by retweeting Islamophobic videos posted online by the extreme-right Britain First party, causing an international spat.[5]

We ought to recognize the devastating impact of terrorist attacks, carried out in the name of Islam by individuals and groups who choose to affiliate with the so-called Islamic State or ISIS forces battling across Syria, Iraq and Libya. However, what concerns us here is the way in which responses to such criminal acts have come to be orchestrated in particular ways. For example, after the November 2015 terror attacks in Paris, Islamophobia in the West reached a new peak of hysteria.[6] In response to the murder, by so-called Islamic State operatives, of 129 innocent citizens enjoying a relaxing Friday night in the heart of one of Europe's most famous cities, Muslims were attacked and abused, their places of worship vandalized and their loyalties called into question.[7] This is a pattern that has been repeated in other cities and in response to other terrorist outrages. Equally troubling was the assertion of a collective guilt in which all Muslims were somehow implicated. Commentators and politicians queued up to make fresh demands on beleaguered communities whose despair at the violence was at least equal to their own. Muslims were routinely invited into news studios to be grilled about their supposed responsibilities for terrorism. In the UK, *The Sun* newspaper splashed on its front page the shocking claim that one in five British Muslims had 'sympathy for jihadis' (the inaccurate story was later forcibly retracted), while the *Daily Express* cited research conducted by a right-wing American think tank to claim that, worldwide, '42 million Muslims support ISIS'.[8] In North America, twenty-three states in the United States closed their borders to migrants fleeing the depredations of ISIS, and Republican presidential hopeful Jeb Bush suggested only Christian refugees should be accepted, while Trump called for all mosques to be closed down, a database of US Muslims to be established and Muslims to be barred from entering the United States – the latter initiative becoming one of the keystone policies of the early days of his presidency.[9]

This political mainstreaming of more aggressive attitudes towards Muslims is reflected by a change in the tone in which these things are discussed. Sometimes there are echoes of the most extreme rhetoric from Europe's dark past. In the UK the *Daily Mail* ran a cartoon depicting mainly Muslim refugees as rats swarming to gain admittance to the country, which observers were quick to recognize as echoing a similar cartoon mocking Jews being denied entry into Austria in 1939.¹⁰ Not long after, Trevor Kavanagh and Katie Hopkins – two stalwarts favoured by the right-wing press – respectively wrote of 'the Muslim problem' and advocated a 'final solution' to it.¹¹ On one level, such anti-Muslim press sentiment was not unusual. In 2011, the UK government minister Baroness Sayeeda Warsi, identifying the new intolerance, went as far as to declare that Islamophobia seemed to have 'passed the dinner-table test' of social respectability, being the only form of prejudice now indulged and approved in the so-called liberal societies of the West.¹² More recently she has written, 'The dislike of all things Muslims is no longer a fringe practice. … The fact that as a country we have allowed this scourge of Islamophobia to grow should worry us all.'¹³

Something of this mood was captured in the public attitudes survey carried out by the HOPE not hate organization in England in 2017. While finding that acceptance of immigration had held up, the survey also showed a worrying rise in Islamophobia. Fifty-two per cent of respondents saw Islam as 'posing a threat to the West', while 42 per cent were more suspicious of Muslims following that summer's terror attacks in London, and a quarter believed that 'Islam is a dangerous religion that incites violence'.¹⁴ This is not an exclusively British or American phenomenon. The latest European Islamophobia Report data on anti-Muslim racism for 2016, which included twenty-seven European countries from Russia to Portugal, shows widespread and worsening animosity and enmity towards Muslims in all sectors of public life (education, employment, politics and the media, both online and offline) with Muslim women emerging as the most vulnerable direct victims of Islamophobia.¹⁵ It is hard to collect figures, however, as very few governments actually record hate crimes against Muslims. Police forces in England and Wales only started recording anti-Muslim hate crimes as a specific category on 13 October 2015, while many other countries rely on grass roots and civic organizations for reporting of Islamophobic incidents.¹⁶

Such views do not grow in a vacuum, and the daily drip-feed of news stories in which Muslim acts and attitudes appear aberrant and threatening adds to the negative atmosphere.¹⁷ Now, in an era of social media where unregulated stories, spin and propaganda swirl all around us, the repetition of Islamophobic perspectives by mainstream media sources marks a serious turn in the propagation of prejudice against Muslims. Resurgent anti-black racism has been a feature of the contemporary political landscape – especially in the United States – but in recent years it has joined forces with the fear of an Islamized world, particularly at a time of low religious literacy. A Pew Research Center survey conducted in Spring 2016 in ten European countries showed that these perceptions vary according to countries: over half the population surveyed in Hungary (72 per cent), Italy (69 per cent), Poland (66 per cent) and Greece (65 per cent) said they view Muslims unfavourably, with roughly a third holding *very* unfavourable opinions in Italy (36 per cent), Hungary (35 per cent) and Greece (32 per cent). The research also goes to show 'even in countries with more positive views, such as Germany, Sweden and the Netherlands, at least half believe Muslims do not want to integrate into the larger society'.[18]

This volume aims to cut through the current impasse not only by offering a snapshot of the forms, historical roots and geographical locations of Islamophobia, but also by suggesting ways in which it is being contested and alternative forms of Muslim self-fashioning growing. What emerges is a picture of Islamophobia as demonstrating a particular kind of paranoia that discriminates against Muslims precisely by *not* discriminating – in terms of differentiating – between doctrinal differences, nor between the many intractable geopolitical crises that feed cultural suspicion and that have to do with unequal patterns of development and of historical and current Western policies at least as much as Muslim atavism. It brings together chapters outlining the history, characteristics and spread of Islamophobia in Britain, the United States and parts of Europe, with those indicating how Islamophobia is being contested 'on the ground' by artists, educators, and activists. In our increasingly interlinked world, it is only to be expected that anti-Muslim agitators in one part of the world should reach out to, and become entwined with, their fellows in other countries. Such links have helped shape the face of contemporary Islamophobia as a prejudice with unique reach. They also mean that a Muslim diaspora which now spans the globe can be 'Othered', made into a convenient scapegoat for any and all failings by national governments struggling with the legacies of domestic inequalities and rapacious global economics. Yet, at the same time, that very global interconnectedness means that tactics to fight back against Islamophobia can be quickly shared.

When we consider the very diverse meanings of the term 'Islamophobia' we are immediately brought face-to-face with what AbdoolKarim Vakil has called the 'conceptual stretching' of the term. 'Islamophobia' has meant different things to those enunciating the phrase in different contexts and at different times.[19] The rate at which the term has taken off over the last twenty or so years has meant that actual definitions have struggled to keep up, being many and varied. Chris Allen's book, called simply *Islamophobia*, attempts to trace the contested coinage of the term and some of its potential definitions, and also to point out how more precise usage in the future might clarify and enable questioning of and resistance to anti-Muslim prejudice.[20] The nature of Islamophobia and its relation to pre-existing prejudices such as anti-Semitism was recognized in the 1997 Runnymede Trust report, *Islamophobia: A Challenge for Us All*, which also offered the most precise account of its key features: 'The dread, hatred and hostility towards Islam and Muslims perpetrated by a series of closed views that imply and attribute negative and derogatory stereotypes and beliefs to Muslims.'[21]

Indeed, the relationship of Islamophobia to preceding forms of prejudice, such as anti-Semitism, has been the subject of much critical debate. Some see strong connections between Islamophobia and anti-Semitism – emphasizing similarities in the Jewish and Muslim experiences of racialization[22] – while others emphasize key distinctions. For instance, in a recent intervention, Michael Dobkowski has insisted on distinguishing anti-Semitism, which, with its basis in an ancient, mythologized prejudicial system, constitutes an ideology, from Islamophobia, which he sees as a 'reflexive prejudice' that is more like a 'troubling social trend'.[23] For him, those baseless conspiracy theories that have circulated around Jews through the ages underline anti-Semitism as an irrational fear, whereas actual violence in the name of Islam – one of the world's most powerful religions – means that Islamophobia does have a rational basis. Dobkowski's interpretation is slippery and problematic, but not unusual. At one point, he suggests that Islamophobia is 'more akin to racism, sexism, ageism and the like' and cannot be compared to anti-Semitism that 'at its core ... is a form of Manichaeism'.[24] There are many possible objections to these views. Dobkowski's conflation of violence with rational fear appears oblivious to the state violence done to Muslims in many parts of the world – not least in Israel. Is this violence somehow legitimated by being contained within, and inflicted by, the nation state? The equation of Islamophobia with sexism and ageism is absurd: sexists or ageists do not advocate the expulsion of women or old people from their societies as active threats to their culture. And finally, while anti-Semitism certainly has a long and dishonourable intellectual lineage, Islamophobia too has ancient roots. In its modern form, it has its own 'playbook' of accusation and totalization, a sophisticated and wealthy network of backers and a sort of retrospective Manichaean narrative placing Muslims always outside the boundaries of 'the West' through the selective use of history. In short, each of Dobkowski's assertions can be met with its at least equally plausible opposite.

The limitations of such views are based on too static a view of history, something that can also be claimed of Matti Bunzl's more benign reading, which argues that anti-Semitism in its ideational guise was a product of the era of the nation state, whereas Islamophobia is a post-national, transcontinental phenomenon, 'marshaled to safeguard the future of European civilization'.[25]

Bunzl's rather rigid schema now seems somewhat premature in its dismissal of the significance of nationalism to contemporary prejudice; he is writing before the 2008 economic crash, the resurgence of autocrat-led populist nationalism across Europe and the partial repudiation of the European project by these forces, and the blanket suspicion of migrants and visible Others. Yet his view at least has the virtue of understanding the relationship between history and prejudice, and he recognizes the potency of the charge that Muslims can never be good, integrated Europeans. The most comprehensive account of recent thinking can be found in James Renton and Ben Gidley's 2017 collection *Antisemitism and Islamophobia in Europe: A Shared Story?* For them anti-Semitism and Islamophobia are neither the same nor totally different, but 'relational' and evolving over time. The example they offer is the concept of the 'Semite', the idea – widely held at one time – that Muslim and Jew were linked by a 'joint linguistic and racial heritage'.[26] This construction fell from favour after the First World War and the beginnings of the conflict over Israel–Palestine. After the end of Empire, the fulfilment of the Zionist vision and increasing late twentieth-century economic and political conflicts with 'Muslim' nations, 'Islam becomes a largely political subject and European Jews cease to be Oriental'.[27] This account serves as a useful reminder that, when dealing with Islamophobia, we are following a moving target.

Of course, there are critics, with the late Fred Halliday being among them, who have felt that 'Islamophobia' is a misnomer for a phenomenon that targets Muslims themselves, rather than their religion.[28] Dobkowski too posits a distinction between being 'anti-' something – opposed to it – and having a fear or 'phobia'.[29] Moreover, concerns have been raised that the loose bandying of the word could serve simply as a blanket with which to stifle legitimate criticisms of aspects of Muslim society and culture.[30] Yet, there is now enough evidence – not least in the outpourings of the highly organized and networked groups in the United States that Nathan Lean refers to as constituting an 'Islamophobia industry' – to indicate that it is often Islam itself, in a bowdlerized, crude and reductive version, that is held up as an ideological adversary for secular Western society.[31] Islamophobia is, by definition, 'anti-Muslim'. The important thing is that those hostile to Muslims will generally homogenize their targets on the basis that there is something involuntary in Muslims' adherence to their religion: that Islam as a system of thought precludes the exercise of individual reason and conscience. As it operates, this is a new version of the tendency to homogenize Jews as conspiratorial and collectively opposed to their host society. The names change, but the tactics of prejudice remain stubbornly consistent.

In addition to looking at Islamophobia as a mode of prejudice that might be practised by individuals or groups against other individuals or groups, we also need to reflect on the enabling context for such prejudice. This involves considering contemporary global geopolitics, their complex prehistories and the manner in which inequalities of power sometimes find articulation in shrill discourses of essential difference that seek to justify certain actions by state and international actors. For example, while concerned to delineate the shifting historical relationship between the West and the Muslim world, Deepa Kumar concludes that Islamophobia has been constructed and promoted by elites for political reasons, a process we can still trace today in the fulminations of politicians, journalists and bloggers in search of an enemy to blame or a distraction from other problems. During the War on Terror, for example, it was necessary to create a 'spectacle of fear' around Muslims and Islam to bolster support for an illegal imperialist foreign policy.[32] Going further, Stephen Sheehi has argued that 'Islamophobia' is the term used to describe what is actually an 'ideological campaign against Muslims'. In contrast to many critics, such as Ziauddin Sardar, Nabil Matar and others who have traced a long history for Islamophobia, going back beyond twentieth-century popular culture stereotypes into the medieval era, Sheehi dates modern Islamophobia very particularly to that moment in the 1990s when America became the sole world superpower, with the will and means to impose its political and economic model on the rest of the world. For him, 'Islamophobia is the latest ideological construct deployed to facilitate American power'.[33] Sheehi traces a line of Islamophobia from the Clinton White House, through George W. Bush and his 'War on Terror', all the way to Barack Obama with his Janus-faced rhetoric on Muslim countries, continued unconditional support for the state of Israel and unease with the politically explosive Muslim part of his heritage. (Sheehi's critique has echoes of Salman Sayyid's reading of Islamophobia in Britain as tied to the moment of Muslim political self-assertion and an anxiety about the tenuous nature of Western hegemony.)[34]

Indeed, we might also say that Islamophobia – like all prejudices – actually reveals more about those holding the prejudices than it does about its objects. A demonic Islamic enemy is all the better for accentuating those – always contested – values by which we fetishize 'our' own difference and superiority. Claims that Muslims and their Holy Book are backward or barbaric are always predicated on the assumption that 'we' in the West have a monopoly on modernity and normality, even when Western state terrorism continues to vie with other kinds in intensity and human cost. This is also the basis of that so-called liberal

Islamophobia, wherein critics homogenize Islam as illiberal in order to parade their own liberal credentials, often in terms that imply that the Western model of social development is the only one of value and that it now faces an existential threat from alien values in our midst.[35] Such figures often justify their diatribes by reference to that freedom of expression that Muslims are taken to oppose. However, in their disregard for the social consequences of ostracizing already marginalized and economically disadvantaged groups, liberal Islamophobes demand only that speech is free, never that it is exercised thoughtfully or with sensitivity for others. The result of entrenched and aggressive posturing among Islamophobes, and some Muslims too, is a terrain where understanding has a hard time finding room to grow.

At the same time there is often a strange second-hand, urban myth quality about some of the blanket assertions made about Muslims. The widespread nature of negative views of Muslims reported by pollsters across a broad range of nations and contexts indicates that such negative views are often carried by modes of representation and reinforced by repetition, rather than based on first-hand experience. This explains the prevalence of anti-Muslim prejudice even in those parts of the Western world where there are hardly any Muslims. Slovakia's prime minister Robert Fico, who took over the EU presidency in the second half of 2016, declared that 'Islam has no place' in the country,[36] while in Hungary, often presented as a case of 'Islamophobia without Muslims',[37] Prime Minister Viktor Orbán has repeatedly spoken of Europe's Christian identity as being under threat. In the United States, Gottschalk and Greenberg speak of Islamophobia as a 'distant phobia', 'arising from distant social experiences that mainstream American culture has perpetrated in popular memory, which are in turn buttressed by a similar understanding of current events'.[38]

To be sure, there are international variations in the antecedents, development and manifestation of Islamophobia. In the United States we find career Islamophobes such as Robert Spencer, Pamela Geller and Daniel Pipes whose crude polemics depend on depicting Islam as a threatening monolith and an ideological foe. Their interventions can now be seen as part of a right-wing historical revisionism that attempts to selectively downplay the significance of aspects of America's immigrant history in shaping its modern plural culture, in the cause of white nationalism. Although they are also now globally networked, European Islamophobes tend to evoke post-war immigration as a dilution of essential national and societal characteristics and a precursor – through the misguided policies of multiculturalism – to separatism. There is often a reductive and insidious tendency for bilious opinion to pass as the respectable exercise of free expression – as in the work of controversialists, such as the French author Michel Houellebecq or the Italian journalist Oriana Fallaci, where Islam and Muslims are lumped together as alien, undermining the secular project of modern Europe, to create a mongrelized space which Fallaci calls 'Eurabia'.[39] In Europe, with its history of colonial contact with Muslim peoples, one might expect a more nuanced, historicized understanding of regional and doctrinal variations. However, just as it can be argued that Europe has never properly come to terms with the loss of its pre-war imperial power, so too new generations have come through often furnished with only a limited understanding of that longer history, and hence more susceptible to the casual prejudice peddled by the press and politicians. In the rise of populist nationalism, seen in recent years, old style racism is bolstered by an idea of 'our culture under threat', as attempts are made to double down on newcomers deemed unwilling or unable to appreciate the achievements of Western nations, and whose presence might even undermine those achievements. The sense that 'we' have lost control of our borders and need to reassert control in the face of economic migrants and terrorists was felt strongly both in the British 'Brexit' vote and in the election of President Donald Trump in 2016 while also providing the focal point for debates about responses to the Syrian refugee crisis across the nations of Europe.

* * *

Because of its obvious relationship to the pursuit and effects of global geopolitics, Islamophobia has most often been addressed as a problem in policy, social or political science circles. The express intention of this volume is to set those perspectives in dialogue with others, from culture and the humanities. This is partly out of the conviction that culture represents an untapped source for creating understanding – as art and literature, for example, allow for the possibility of fellow-feeling with those who are different – and also because of the ability of artists and writers themselves to articulate visions of good (and bad) societies, creating from the raw materials of their cultures new perspectives and giving voice to new solidarities. More than that, the matter of representation is at the heart of debates about multiculturalism and Islamophobia for reasons mentioned previously: the concentration of Muslim communities in the West is overwhelmingly in urban metropolises, whereas Islamophobia itself is spread much more broadly. In *Framing Muslims*, Amina Yaqin and I tried to outline some of the limiting frames around Muslims and to show how these were shared between the discourses of politics, journalism and popular culture. In that book we described a nexus of 'Muslim issues', generally having to do with self-segregation, violence and patriarchal tyranny, which are repeated in popular and journalistic narratives over and over again.[40] These form the basic modes of articulation for contemporary Islamophobia, which then feed into the level of policy in forms of legislation to 'address' the identified issues. This process might also remind us of John L. Esposito's examples – in his introduction to *Islamophobia: The Challenge of Pluralism in the 21st Century* – where he describes how totally diverse phenomena such as rioting in the Parisian *banlieues*, protests against the Danish cartoons, conflicts over the hijab and so on are all seen as 'Muslim issues'. Local factors, such as poverty or civil rights, are hidden and Islam is identified as the spark for these troubles, even though religion has little role to play in any of them.[41] The contributions to this book focus on this overarching framework with an international and interdisciplinary range that allows the reader a comparative perspective on an important modern phenomenon.

Islamophobia is often seen as a unified and monolithic discourse that is actively imposed on passive objects. However, it is actually a discourse constantly in the making and riven with anxieties and contradictions. To take only one example, in Europe Islamophobia appears more virulently in those far-right and neo-fascist groups that are also strongly anti-Semitic. In the United States, by contrast, while clearly a latter-day articulation of that melancholic racism that laments the white Anglo-Saxon hegemony of yesteryear to which Trump pandered so successfully, Islamophobia is seen not only among old style racists and neo-Nazis but also in parts of the evangelical Christian Right who often proclaim unqualified support for the state of Israel. Once more, we can witness the expedient shifts that take place over time, as one 'enemy' is replaced by another. Complicating the picture further is the fact that, as Bunzl points out, the far-right in Europe ended the twentieth century largely renouncing their previous anti-Semitism to concentrate instead on the demonization of Muslim migrants.[42] Yet another recent twist has seen the unsurprising re-emergence of anti-Semitism as both part of the project of a 'purified' Europe for the extreme Right and among some Muslims themselves for whom Jews and Israel represent a colonizing Western vanguard in the Middle East. This is a complex example of the way prejudices creak under the weight of their own contradictory views of the world. Islamophobes misunderstand causes and consequences, just as much as do those Islamists for whom Western society is uniformly evil. We would suggest that an understanding of the conflicted nature of Islamophobia might lead us towards the possibility of moving beyond it.

One of the main messages of this book is that while contesting Islamophobia requires action from all of us, Muslims are already doing it for themselves. For example, those Muslim women who feel that their faith requires them to veil nowadays have a range of options, with garments – including sports gear – to help them participate fully in public activities. The phenomenon of modest fashion has become a highly lucrative growth industry and, while any kind of Islamic visibility still marks the garment wearer out for abuse from racists, such products assist women in taking part in a range of activities that might otherwise be problematic for them.[43] Much of the marketing and consumption of such products takes place online. In the same way, as some of our contributors point out, the internet and social media are transforming the way Muslims interact with each other and with the wider world, even colouring Islamic interpretations and practices, as Gary Bunt has noted.[44] Thus, while the mainstream media's attitudes towards Islam may be somewhat hostile, the spaces of new media and the internet currently provide a channel for the articulation of proactive Muslim self-fashioning at least as much as of Islamophobic stereotypes. As work in these areas grows, we will gain a greater understanding of how contemporary Muslim identities are developing independently of, as well as in dialogue with, the images projected by others.

***

The present volume has been divided into sections in order to point up different aspects of Islamophobia and the struggle against it. In the first, 'Islamophobia, Politics and History', contributors chart the relationship and utility of anti-Muslim prejudice to state actors, something that has a significant historical lineage, particularly in the United States. In his consideration of the staggering success of Donald Trump in capturing the presidency in 2016, Peter Gottschalk traces the roots of the rhetoric of nativism and Islamophobia that Trump employed to the longer American history from which it emerges. He sees successive waves of nativist prejudice – viewing new minorities as a threat to the emerging nation – going back to the foundation of the United States. Its early targets were Catholic and, in the late nineteenth century, Jewish immigrants. In both cases, as with Muslims, national loyalty was questioned in terms which drew on both practices and beliefs that were felt to be incompatible with the dominant Protestant trajectory of the new nation, and on a more basic racism that equated these newcomers with African Americans who were deemed to be less civilized and evolved. Shuttling between the present and these historical precursors, Gottschalk shows how Trump relied on conventional racist staples such as homogenization of the Other, the challenge to a presumed Christian norm, national security as under threat and even – somewhat ironically – the protection of women, to bolster his rhetoric about the threatening Muslim enemy. He suggests that Muslims face greater challenges in the search for acceptance owing to the contemporary projection of a secularized 'Judaeo-Christian' American identity from which they are always excluded.

Focusing on politics, Nathan Lean, in his chapter, describes the link between American foreign and domestic policies and Islamophobia. Eschewing conventional ideas that Islamophobia is a post-9/11 phenomenon, Lean takes the story back to the Cold War era after the Second World War, when American concerns about Soviet influence in the Middle East led to an obsessive focus on the region and its predominantly Muslim peoples. These inhabitants were understood through reductive Orientalist stereotypes, which made their disciplining and control a matter of American strategic interest. Subsequently, in the 1970s and 1980s, concerns about energy supplies made the same region a focus for American meddling. In the twenty-first century, the War on Terror further augmented Islamophobia, now backed by a network of interests and individuals with a tentacular reach into government and the security industry. Lean describes how the institutionalized fear of Muslims is now a self-perpetuating, multimillion-dollar business. It is this 'hegemonic political structure, with ossified institutions, gargantuan budgets and an insatiable thirst for exerting cultural and economic influence' that perpetuates the climate of fear in which Islamophobia grows. Remedying this requires nothing less than 'a systematic rethinking of the overarching power structures that govern our world today'.

In conversation with contemporary Islamophobia in its historical and comparative national contexts at the 2017 Bradford Literature Festival, Dibyesh Anand, Myriam Francois and Jim Wolfreys dissected what is now called, in some quarters, 'the Muslim Problem', considering the utility of scapegoating communities for politicians who, in an age of neoliberalism and increasing inequality, are unable otherwise to manufacture consent for their policies. In the edited transcription presented here, they consider the mutation of a certain form of 'muscular' liberalism, which will now countenance anti-Muslim prejudice as a guarantor of commitment to other minority rights around issues such as gender and sexuality. Taking specific examples from the recent histories of India and France, as well as Britain, they link the repudiation of multiculturalism – itself always a contested phenomenon – to the rise of populist 'strong men' leaders, whose machismo is elevated as symbolic of nations determined to deal with recalcitrant minorities. Thus, in India, Nehruvian secularism – which fostered the vision of a multi-religious society – has given way to the aggressive Hindu nationalism associated with Narendra Modi and the BJP. In France, Islamophobia was given mainstream legitimacy by Nicolas Sarkozy and continues to play out in increasingly absurd local government diktats about leisure provision and school meals. Ultimately, in an era when anti-Muslim prejudice is promoted in the press, incorporated as enforcement obligations on public bodies and enthusiastically taken up by politicians, to cooperate with rather than contest such narratives is to be complicit with them.

In the second section of the book we look at Islamophobia and its representation in literature and on screen. Writing about Martin Amis – and specifically his short fiction 'The Last Days of Muhammad Atta' – Geoffrey Nash and Nath Aldalala'a consider one particular instance wherein literature might be seen to trade on Islamophobic generalizations. In the aftermath of 9/11, Amis and others defended literary fiction as a flowering of that liberal secularism associated with the West, now seen as being under threat from the forces of religious irrationalism. Coupled with his widely publicized intemperate statements about Muslims in general, Amis's story is seen by Nash and Aldalala'a to peddle reductive stereotypes wherein the notions of Islam and terror are conflated. Curiously, however, Amis himself confesses his lack of interest in interrogating what he elsewhere calls the 'dependent mind' of the religious fanatic, instead casting Atta as a nihilistic psychopath who merely pays lip service to Islamic faith. Yet rather than using this diagnosis to place a distance between the aberrant Atta and mainstream Muslim belief, Amis is more interested in playing out retribution for the 9/11 mass murders and concludes his story by condemning Atta to a cycle of eternal recurrence. Thus, rather than contesting Islamophobia, Amis merely confirms it via the conflation of Muslim masculinity and a seemingly overpowering death drive that is the fruit of emotional and sexual repression.

Popular cultural forms have long been understood as vehicles for the rehearsal and contestation of aspects of contemporary ideology. In her chapter on George R. R. Martin's phenomenally successful fantasy novel series collectively known as *Game of Thrones*, and the even more successful HBO television adaptation, Roberta Garrett identifies aspects of plotting and characterization that echo Orientalist and Islamophobic tropes. Despite Martin's liberal credentials, Garrett sees in the novels' depiction of the alien lands of Esteros the same reductive homogenizing characterization that one finds in conventional stereotypical

Hollywood representations of Arabs and Muslims. Against them is ranged a set of more deeply realized characters from the series' version of Europe, Westeros, led by the 'white saviour' figure of Daenerys Targaryen, whose well-meaning interventions recall the condescending pseudo-feminist rationale used to bolster the Bush administration's foreign adventures, supposedly in aid of oppressed Muslim womanhood, and result in the same kind of chaotic social breakdown and counter-insurgency that accompanied the later days of US involvement in Afghanistan and Iraq. Garrett maintains that, although Daenerys is an attractive, empowered figure who has garnered an extensive female following enthused by her sense of justice, in her dealings with her Eastern dominions she nonetheless betrays the standard cultural prejudices of present day neo-imperialism.

In the world of global writing, Elif Shafak and Leila Aboulela are two of the most high-profile Muslim women writers producing fiction today. They offer very different outlooks on the role of faith, politics and personal female agency, as reflected in their respective novels *The Forty Rules of Love* and *Minaret*. Amina Yaqin considers these novels' protagonists as exemplars of two supposed modes of female agency, reading them in response to feminist reworkings of Qur'anic injunctions about gender relations. She sees Shafak's heroine as embodying a degree of agency, inasmuch as she rejects conventional domesticity to pursue a path laid out by Sufi models of love and spiritual enlightenment. However, in view of the novel's double time frame – which juxtaposes the contemporary relationships with the thirteenth-century friendship of the poet Rumi and his companion Shams – Yaqin suggests that the modern protagonist does not so much display female autonomy as stand as a decontextualized symbol of the validity of Sufism in an age when the West is primed to accept this more 'friendly face' of Islam. In *Minaret*, by contrast, Najwa is never able to find consolation for the loss of her family, either in the adoption of pious modes of dress and behaviour or in the romantic relationships she tentatively cultivates. Although their depictions contest Islamophobic stereotypes, in the end neither female protagonist really manages to shake off the burdens of the past to exercise true autonomy.

The third section of the book explores youth cultures contesting Islamophobia. Although Islamophobia cuts across all ages, the more flexible thinking of the young often provides fertile terrain for contestation. In her personal account of 'Countering Islamophobia in the Classroom', Sarah Soyei describes the pervasiveness of Islamophobic views among the young people she encounters in her work with the educational organization EqualiTeach. These views are often sown by the mass of negative press coverage that currently circulates around Muslims, but they can also be augmented by peer pressure and outside influences in the home. In her chapter, Soyei describes the strategies by which Islamophobia can be contested in schools, describing exercises that encourage students to debate and test out received opinions and to discuss attitudes in a safe environment moderated, but not dictated, by a teacher or facilitator. She emphasizes the importance of allowing students the space to speak – something which in itself instils important civic values as well as building confidence. The onus is also on schools to treat Islamophobic incidents seriously, and catalogue and address them. Soyei advocates an inclusive definition of the term 'Islamophobia' that makes its identification easier and will provide victims with avenues of recognition and redress that might not otherwise be open to them. Soyei's work, with some of the youngest members of society, underlines the importance of contesting Islamophobia at as early an age as possible.

In her chapter, Tania Saeed offers some examples of direct attempts by young Muslims to contest Islamophobia. She takes a sample of female Muslim students in British universities, exploring their experience of, and attitudes to, Islamophobia. She compares the local conditions in which such individuals attempt to challenge and overturn prejudicial attitudes through interpersonal dialogue with the larger strategies developed by student Islamic societies and the National Union of Students (NUS) to contest the British government's Prevent programme. This programme requires that universities take responsibility for 'having due regard' to the need to prevent students succumbing to violent extremism: a duty for which they are ill-equipped and which has resulted in wrongful referrals and even detention. Inevitably, the burden of Prevent has fallen most heavily on Muslims, and Saeed describes how campaigns such as 'Students Not Suspects' have attempted to fight back, questioning what they see as the flawed underlying tenets and biased implementation of the programme. Saeed argues that the variety of tactics young Muslims have evolved can help challenge the limiting frame that requires them always to respond to others' agendas. She sees hope in direct acts of contestation by young Muslims against this wider narrative, confronting the prevailing security discourse on Muslim identity with its own repressive double standards.

Looking at media contributions from young Muslims, Asmaa Soliman finds that in contemporary Germany the Habermasian ideal of a neutral, accessible and democratic public breaks down when it comes to Muslims. She argues that the key to countering Islamophobia lies in reclaiming the power of self-definition and constructing alternative identities that challenge mainstream representations, thereby creating what Nancy Fraser and Michael Warner have called 'counterpublics'. Illustrating the concept and practice of counterpublics are two case studies of Muslim activists from Germany who challenge negative perceptions through blogging and online media platforms. Nuri Senay has founded *muslime.tv*, an online website that shows short documentary videos about Muslim life in Germany, while Kübra Gümüşay is known for her blog *Ein Fremdwörterbuch* ('A Dictionary of Foreign Words'), which provides an insight into her personal life as a young Muslim woman living in Germany. Three elements can be found in these platforms: disappointment with an exclusive, restrictive and Islamophobic mainstream public; the circulation of definitions that challenge these representations and the construction of an opposition to standard discourses about Muslims. In addition to confronting the German public with its Islamophobic bias, such online platforms serve as sources of information about Islamophobic incidents that are otherwise often ignored.

The imaginative space of the arts offers ground on which to interrogate and challenge prevailing ideas and biases. In the final section 'Art beyond Islamophobia', we see not only the potential of visual culture to challenge stereotypical perceptions but also, in the final chapter, the consequences of refusing to accept a pre-scripted public discourse that sees Muslims as a problem. Exploring two exhibitions of Pakistani diaspora art in Britain in the years after 9/11, Madeline Clements considers the extent to which artworks and their staging have confirmed or challenged Islamophobic stereotypes. She argues that such exhibitions potentially offer alternative, more equal or at least ambiguous grounds on which non-Muslim audiences and Muslim-background artists may come to know one another. The gallery space can become a site for the refashioning of viewer–object relationships in ways that expose the impact of contemporary Islamophobia and emphasize global interests and mutual vulnerability. Yet there is always the danger that this art may be co-opted and filtered through a lens which instrumentalizes it as part of a set of responses to political problems around extremism, fundamentalism and terrorism, burdening art and artists with a restrictive and unwelcome 'culturally representative' baggage. Clements argues that attention to the materiality of the art itself – which often employs traditional South Asian forms such as textiles and the Mughal miniature, at the same time updating and transvaluing them – furnishes us with a broader, more contextualized understanding of Pakistani art than Islamophobic political agendas normally allow.

Leila Tarakji argues for the efficacy of the comic strip form in providing Muslim role models and combating Islamophobia. She considers the case of G. Willow Wilson's Muslim American incarnation of *Ms Marvel*, Kamala Khan, as a reclamation of Muslim identity in one of the most quintessentially American of cultural forms. Tarakji argues that the traditional outsider status of superheroes, together with their hybrid identities, makes them an appropriate vehicle for considering the ambiguous position of Muslims in America. Through the challenges Kamala faces – which have to do with reconciling the requirements of faith with the secular, hedonistic youth culture that surrounds her – the position of the young Muslim woman growing up in America is played out. The tenets of faith are, in Wilson's work, less a sign of strangeness than the moral framework within which the Muslim *Ms Marvel* operates; they motivate her good works and, at the same time, show how Muslim values align with American ones such as tolerance and respect. As well as providing a role model, *Ms Marvel* is used to call out bigotry in others, thereby showing the potential for popular culture directly to contest Islamophobia.

We often think of Islamophobia as manifest in aggressive speech and actions. But what about the underlying assumptions by which it is legitimized? How are we to understand the deep cultural triggers that produce it, especially when Muslims try to speak in their own voices? In the realm of the arts, these issues tend most often to crystallize around questions of freedom of speech. In conversation with Amina Yaqin and Peter Morey, Nadia Latif, director of the play *Homegrown*, commissioned and later unceremoniously cancelled by the National Youth Theatre, describes her experiences with a production that caught the national headlines and seemed to say much about the contemporary fear of Muslims. Latif describes the National Youth Theatre (NYT) commission – based on the presumed ability of Latif and her co-creator, Omar El-Khairy, to speak authoritatively about the radicalization of young Muslims – and their decision to subvert this agenda by producing a free-form, experimental play, designed for performance in a school and showcasing the range of influences and voices circulating around the issue. She describes the unsettling experience of being forced to switch venues, and having the police ask to see the script, before the NYT pulled the plug. A shifting range of reasons from child safety to quality concerns were cited to justify the cancellation. However, rather than blaming a conscious decision to censor the play, Latif identifies a more general climate of patronage but at the same time mistrust of minority ethnic artists in an industry still controlled by middle-aged white males. Here, it would seem that Islamophobia dovetails with existing cultural hierarchies and practices to exclude anything that strays too far from a tightly controlled 'script'.

This example might serve as a salutary reminder that censorship is not the sole prerogative of religious zealots. Secularists can be equally determined in the imposition of their views. The question of how some of the deepest assumptions about the relationship of culture and religion have come to be shaped in ways that see these two interconnected (but not identical) phenomena as antithetical is worthy of greater consideration. In addition to a surface Islamophobia, we might identify a more latent, but nonetheless ingrained, set of assumptions about the development of the West, modernity and even 'civilization', which takes to task a shifting series of religious adversaries – from Catholicism during the Reformation, through Judaism to Islam – in an attempt to delineate itself more clearly. As Susan Buck-Morss reminds us, if the word 'civilization'

> is to have any signifying value within global conditions of multiple cultural diasporas, then it will have to live up to its universal claim. There is only one 'civilization', the human one, and there is much *un*civilized human behavior within it. No collective can claim to be civilized as an ontological fact. Yet we hear from every side that saving one's own civilization justifies any and all uncivilized means used against one's enemies.[45]

A full investigation of the shifting definitions of 'Islam' and 'the West' stands beyond the scope of the present volume. Nonetheless, it is to be hoped that the range of essays in this book might serve as a reminder that the normalization of Islamophobia as a mode of common sense depends upon the selective identification – we might say fetishization – of certain characteristics that are historically contingent and constantly evolving. Faced with ever-louder voices that would deny that evolution in the interests of the ahistorical fixity of the clash of civilizations, it is incumbent on us all to point to areas where the demonization of others runs up against its own limiting narrowness. If, as the Runnymede report famously claimed, Islamophobia is 'a challenge for us all', then the fight against it also requires a united effort by those who favour real justice and equality.

Notes

1 Sabrina Siddiqui, 'Anti-Muslim rallies across US denounced by civil rights groups', *Guardian*, 10 June 2017; Matt Zapotosky, 'Hate crimes against Muslims hit highest mark since 2001', *Washington Post*, 14 November 2016; Linda Sarsour, 'A Muslim woman was set on fire in New York. Now just going out requires courage', *Guardian*, 13 September 2016.
2 Myriam Francois, 'Why is David Cameron using British Muslims as the scapegoat for his government failings?', *New Statesman*, 19 June 2015.

3   Jack Blanchard, Julia Rampen and Dan Bloom, 'David Cameron sparks fury with "racist" attack on Sadiq Khan', *Daily Mirror*, 20 April 2016; Simon Hattenstone, 'David Cameron accused of racial profiling in London mayoral letter', *Guardian*, 28 March 2016; Miqdaad Versi, 'Like Sadiq Khan, Muslims in public life are being branded as extremists', *Independent*, 4 March 2016. Available at www.independent.co.uk/voices/like-sadiq-khan-in-public-life-are-being-branded-as-extremists-a6912056.html (accessed 3 March 2017).

4   Catrin Nye, 'Islamophobic tweets "peaked in July"', *BBC News*, 18 August 2016. Available at www.bbc.co.uk/news/world-europe-37098643 (accessed 3 March 2017). 'Race and religious hate crimes rose 41% after EU vote', *BBC News*, 13 October 2016. Available at www.bbc.co.uk/news/uk-politics-37640982 (accessed 3 March 2017).

5   Moustafa Bayoumi, 'Donald Trump has made it clear: In his America, Muslim citizens don't exist', *Guardian*, 8 November 2016. 'Donald Trump retweets far-right group's anti-Muslim videos', *BBC News*, 29 November 2017. Available at www.bbc.co.uk/news/world-us-canada-42166663 (accessed 1 December 2017). Antonia Blumberg, 'A brief history of Donald Trump stoking Islamophobia', *Huffington Post*, 29 November 2017. Available at www.huffingtonpost.co.uk/entry/donald-trump-islamophobia-history_us_5a1eeea2e4b01edb1a819c9e (accessed 1 December 2017).

6   'Anti-Islam hate crimes triple in London after Paris attacks', *BBC News*, 4 December 2015. Available at www.bbc.co.uk/news/uk-england-london-34995431 (accessed 3 March 2017).

7   'France: Abuses under state of emergency', *Human Rights Watch*, 3 February 2016. Available at www.hrw.org/news/2016/02/03/france-abuses-under-state-emergency (accessed 21 September 2017).

8   Tom Newton Dunn, '1 in 5 Brit Muslims' sympathy for jihadis', *The Sun*, 23 November 2015. Will Worley, '*Sun* forced to admit "1 in 5 British Muslims" story was "significantly misleading"', *Independent*, 26 March 2016. Available at www.independent.co.uk/news/media/ipso-sun-british-muslims-story-headline-significantly-misleading-a6953771.html (accessed 3 March 2017). Tom Parfitt, 'More than 42 MILLION Muslims "support ISIS" – As experts warn the figure will grow', *Daily Express*, 1 July 2015.

9   Ed O'Keefe, 'Jeb Bush: US assistance for refugees should focus on Christians', *Washington Post*, 15 November 2015; Alan Rappeport, 'Donald Trump says he would be open to closing US mosques to fight ISIS', *New York Times*, 22 October 2015; Evan Annett, 'Trump's original immigration ban: How it was introduced, and how the courts shut it down', *Globe and Mail*, 23 February 2017.

10 Ryan Grenoble, 'The *Daily Mail* anti-refugee cartoon is straight out of Nazi Germany', *Huffington Post*, 18 November 2015. Available at www.huffingtonpost.com/entry/daily-mail-nazi-refugee-rat-cartoon_us_564b526ee4b06037734ae115 (accessed 1 September 2017).

11 Trevor Kavanagh, 'Now Philip Hammond is finally out he must shut the door behind him and take control over our laws, our trade and especially immigration', *The Sun*, 13 August 2017. Available at www.thesun.co.uk/news/4235655/now-philip-hammond-is-finally-out-he-must-shut-the-door-behind-him-and-take-control-over-our-laws-our-trade-and-especially-immigration/ (accessed 1 September 2017). See also Kathryn Snowdon, 'Trevor Kavanagh's *The Sun* column slammed for failing to apologise for "The Muslim Problem" comment', *Huffington Post*, 17 August 2017. Available at www.huffingtonpost.co.uk/entry/trevor-kavanagh-the-sun-muslim-problem_uk_599567cde4b0acc593e55936 (accessed 1 September 2017). 'Katie Hopkins reported to police after "final solution" Manchester attack tweet', *Guardian*, 23 May 2017.
12 David Batty, 'Lady Warsi claims Islamophobia is now socially acceptable in Britain', *Guardian*, 20 January 2011.
13 Sayeeda Warsi, *The Enemy Within: A Tale of Muslim Britain* (London: Allen Lane, 2017), p. 157.
14 Available at http://hopenothate.org.uk/research/fear-and-hope-2017/ (accessed 1 September 2017). See also Phil McDuff, 'England is now more pro-immigrant – But it's more Islamophobic too', *Guardian*, 31 August 2017; Steven Hopkins, '"Deeply worrying" fears around Muslims and Islam revealed in damning report', *Huffington Post*, 30 August 2017. Available at www.huffingtonpost.co.uk/entry/fear-and-hope-report_uk_59a538b2e4b041393a205e00 (accessed 1 September 2017).
15 Enes Bayrakli and Farid Hafez, 'The state of Islamophobia in Europe', in *European Islamophobia Report 2016*. Available at www.islamophobiaeurope.com/wp-content/uploads/2017/03/Introduction_2016.pdf (accessed 20 September 2017).
16 I am grateful to Alaya Forte for this data.
17 Miqdaad Versi, 'Why the British media is responsible for the rise in Islamophobia in Britain', *Independent*, 4 April 2016. Available at www.independent.co.uk/voices/why-the-british-media-is-responsible-for-the-rise-in-islamophobia-in-britain-a6967546.html (accessed 3 March 2017).
18 Richard Wike, Bruce Stokes and Katie Simmons, 'Negative views of minorities, refugees common in EU', *Pew Research Center*, 11 July 2016. Available at www.pewglobal.org/2016/07/11/negative-views-of-minorities-refugees-common-in-eu/ (accessed 20 September 2017). I am indebted to Alaya Forte for these figures.
19 AbdoolKarim Vakil, 'Is the Islam in Islamophobia the same as the Islam in anti-Islam; or, When is it Islamophobia time?', in S. Sayyid and AbdoolKarim Vakil (eds), *Thinking through Islamophobia: Global Perspectives* (London: Hurst & Co., 2010), p. 37.
20 Chris Allen, *Islamophobia* (London and New York: Routledge, 2010).

21 Quoted in Esposito and Kalin, *Islamophobia*, pp. xxii–xxiii.
22 See, for example, Nasar Meer (ed.), *Racialization and Religion: Race, Culture and Difference in the Study of Antisemitism and Islamophobia* (London: Routledge, 2014).
23 Michael Dobkowski, 'Islamophobia and anti-Semitism: Shared prejudice or singular social pathologies', *Crosscurrents* 65/3 (2015), pp. 321–33, 330–1.
24 Dobkowski, 'Islamophobia and anti-Semitism', p. 330.
25 Matti Bunzl, *Anti-Semitism and Islamophobia: Hatreds Old and New in Europe* (Chicago, IL: Prickly Paradigm Press, 2007), p. 45.
26 James Renton and Ben Gidley (eds), *Antisemitism and Islamophobia in Europe: A Shared Story?* (London: Palgrave Macmillan, 2017), p. 9.
27 Renton and Gidley, *Antisemitism and Islamophobia in Europe*, p. 12.
28 Fred Halliday, '"Islamophobia" reconsidered', *Ethnic and Racial Studies* 22/5 (1999), pp. 892–902.
29 Dobkowski, 'Islamophobia and anti-Semitism', p. 329.
30 Kenan Malik, *From Fatwa to Jihad: The Rushdie Affair and its Legacy* (London: Atlantic Books, 2009), p. 131.
31 Nathan Lean, *The Islamophobia Industry: How the Right Manufactures Fear of Muslims* (London: Pluto Press, 2012).
32 Deepa Kumar, *Islamophobia and the Politics of Empire* (Chicago, IL: Haymarket Books, 2012), p. 154.
33 Stephen Sheehi, *Islamophobia: The Ideological Campaign against Muslims* (Atlanta, GA: Clarity Press, 2011), p. 40.
34 Salman Sayyid, *A Fundamental Fear: Eurocentrism and the Emergence of Islamism*, 2nd edn (London and New York: Zed Books, 2003).
35 Polly Toynbee, 'In defence of Islamophobia: Religion and the state', *Independent*, 23 October 1997; Bruce Bawer, *While Europe Slept: How Radical Islam is Destroying the West from Within* (New York: Broadway Books, 2006).
36 Hardeep Matharu, 'Slovakian Prime Minister says "Islam has no place in this country" – Weeks before it takes over EU presidency', *Independent*, 22 May 2016. Available at www.independent.co.uk/news/world/europe/islam-has-no-place-in-this-country-says-slovakian-prime-minister-weeks-before-it-takes-over-eu-a7052506.html (accessed 20 September 2017).
37 Michał Buchowski and Katarzyna Chlewińska, 'Tolerance of cultural diversity in Poland and its limitations', in *Accept Pluralism* (Florence: European University Institute, 2012), pp. 32–3.
38 Peter Gottschalk and Gabriel Greenberg, *Islamophobia: Making Muslims the Enemy* (Lanham, MD: Rowman and Littlefield, 2008), p. 5.
39 See, for example, Michel Houellebecq, *Submission: A Novel* (New York: Farrar, Straus and Giroux, 2015); Tunku Varadarajan, 'Prophet of decline: An interview with Oriana Fallaci', *Wall Street Journal*, 23 June 2005.

40 Peter Morey and Amina Yaqin, *Framing Muslims: Stereotyping and Representation after 9/11* (Cambridge, MA: Harvard University Press, 2011), pp. 44–78.
41 Esposito and Kalin, *Islamophobia*, p. xxvi.
42 Bunzl, *Anti-Semitism and Islamophobia*, pp. 16–24.
43 See Reina Lewis, *Muslim Fashion: Contemporary Style Cultures* (Durham, NC and London: Duke University Press, 2015); see also Emma Tarlo, 'Hijab online: The fashioning of cyber Islamic commerce', *Interventions* 12/2 (2010), pp. 209–25.
44 Gary R. Bunt, *iMuslims: Rewiring the House of Islam* (London: Hurst & Co., 2009).
45 Susan Buck-Morss in Bunzl, *Anti-Semitism and Islamophobia*, p. 97.

Works cited

Allen, Chris, *Islamophobia* (London and New York: Routledge, 2010).
Annett, Evan, 'Trump's original immigration ban: How it was introduced, and how the courts shut it down', *Globe and Mail*, 23 February 2017.
Batty, David, 'Lady Warsi claims Islamophobia is now socially acceptable in Britain', *Guardian*, 20 January 2011.
Bawer, Bruce, *While Europe Slept: How Radical Islam is Destroying the West From Within* (New York: Broadway Books, 2006).
Bayoumi, Moustafa, 'Donald Trump has made it clear: In his America, Muslim citizens don't exist', *Guardian*, 8 November 2016.
Bayrakli, Enes and Farid Hafez, 'The State of Islamophobia in Europe', in *European Islamophobia Report 2016*. Available at www.islamophobiaeurope.com/wp-content/uploads/2017/03/Introduction_2016.pdf (accessed 20 September 2017).
BBC News, 'Anti-Islam hate crimes triple in London after Paris attacks', *BBC News*, 4 December 2015. Available at www.bbc.co.uk/news/uk-england-london-34995431 (accessed 3 March 2017).
BBC News, 'Donald Trump retweets far-right group's anti-Muslim videos', *BBC News*, 29 November 2017. Available at www.bbc.co.uk/news/world-us-canada-42166663 (accessed 1 December 2017).
BBC News, 'Race and religious hate crimes rose 41% after EU vote', *BBC News*, 13 October 2016. Available at www.bbc.co.uk/news/uk-politics-37640982 (accessed 3 March 2017).
Blanchard, Jack, Julia Rampen and Dan Bloom, 'David Cameron sparks fury with "racist" attack on Sadiq Khan', *Daily Mirror*, 20 April 2016.
Blumberg, Antonia 'A brief history of Donald Trump stoking Islamophobia', *Huffington Post*, 29 November 2017, Available at www.huffingtonpost.co.uk/entry/donald-trump-islamophobia-history_us_5a1eeea2e4b01edb1a819c9e (accessed 1 December 2017).

Buchowski, Michał and Katarzyna Chlewińska, 'Tolerance and cultural diversity discourses in Poland', in *Accept Pluralism* (Florence: European University Institute, 2012).

Bunt, Gary R., *iMuslims: Rewiring the House of Islam* (London: Hurst and Company, 2009).

Bunzl, Matti, *Anti-Semitism and Islamophobia: Hatreds Old and New in Europe* (Chicago, IL: Prickly Paradigm Press, 2007).

Dobkowski, Michael, 'Islamophobia and anti-Semitism: Shared prejudice or singular social pathologies', *Crosscurrents* 65/3 (2015), pp. 321–33.

Dunn, Tom Newton, '1 in 5 Brit Muslims' sympathy for jihadis', The Sun, 23 November 2015.

Esposito, John L. and Ibrahim Kalin, *Islamophobia: The Challenge of Pluralism in the 21st Century* (Oxford: Oxford University Press, 2011).

Francois, Myriam, 'Why is David Cameron using British Muslims as the scapegoat for his government failings?', *New Statesman*, 19 June 2015.

Gottschalk, Peter and Gabriel Greenberg, *Islamophobia: Making Muslims the Enemy* (Lanham, MD: Rowman and Littlefield, 2008).

Grenoble, Ryan, 'The *Daily Mail* anti-refugee cartoon is straight out of Nazi Germany', *Huffington Post*, 18 November 2015. Available at www.huffingtonpost.com/entry/daily-mail-nazi-refugee-rat-cartoon_us_564b526ee4b06037734ae115 (accessed 1 September 2017).

Guardian, 'Katie Hopkins reported to police after "final solution" Manchester attack tweet', *Guardian*, 23 May 2017.

Halliday, Fred, '"Islamophobia" reconsidered', *Ethnic and Racial Studies* 22/5 (1999), pp. 892–902.

Hattenstone, Simon, 'David Cameron accused of racial profiling in London mayoral letter', *Guardian*, 28 March 2016.

HOPE not hate, *Race, Faith, and Belonging in Today's England* (2017). Available at http://hopenothate.org.uk/research/fear-and-hope-2017/ (accessed 1 September 2017).

Hopkins, Steven, '"Deeply worrying" fears around Muslims and Islam revealed in damning report', *Huffington Post*, 30 August 2017. Available at www.huffingtonpost.co.uk/entry/fear-and-hope-report_uk_59a538b2e4b041393a205e00 (accessed 1 September 2017).

Houellebecq, Michel, *Submission: A Novel* (New York: Farrar, Straus and Giroux, 2015).

Human Rights Watch, 'France: Abuses under state of emergency', *Human Rights Watch*, 3 February 2016. Available at www.hrw.org/news/2016/02/03/france-abuses-under-state-emergency (accessed 21 September 2017).

Kavanagh, Trevor, 'Now Philip Hammond is finally Out he must shut the door behind him and take control over our laws, our trade and especially immigration', *The Sun*, 13 August 2017. Available at www.thesun.co.uk/news/4235655/now-philip-hammond-is-finally-out-he-must-shut-the-door-behind-him-and-take-control-over-our-laws-our-trade-and-especially-immigration/ (accessed 1 September 2017).

Kumar, Deepa, *Islamophobia and the Politics of Empire* (Chicago: Haymarket Books, 2012).

Lean, Nathan, *The Islamophobia Industry: How the Right Manufactures Fear of Muslims* (London: Pluto Press, 2012).

Lewis, Reina, *Muslim Fashion: Contemporary Style Cultures* (Durham, NC and London: Duke University Press, 2015).

Malik, Kenan, *From Fatwa to Jihad: The Rushdie Affair and its Legacy* (London: Atlantic Books, 2009).

Matharu, Hardeep, 'Slovakian Prime Minister says "Islam has no place in this country" – weeks before it takes over EU presidency', *Independent*, 22 May 2016. Available at www.independent.co.uk/news/world/europe/islam-has-no-place-in-this-country-says-slovakian-prime-minister-weeks-before-it-takes-over-eu-a7052506.html (accessed 20 September 2017).

McDuff, Phil, 'England is now more pro-immigrant – But it's more Islamophobic too', *Guardian*, 31 August 2017.

Meer, Nasar (ed.), *Racialization and Religion: Race, Culture and Difference in the Study of Antisemitism and Islamophobia* (London: Routledge, 2014).

Morey, Peter and Amina Yaqin, *Framing Muslims: Stereotyping and Representation After 9/11* (Cambridge, MA: Harvard University Press, 2011).

Nye, Catrin, 'Islamophobic tweets "peaked in July"', *BBC News*, 18 August 2016. Available at www.bbc.co.uk/news/world-europe-37098643 (accessed 3 March 2017).

O'Keefe, Ed, 'Jeb Bush: US assistance for refugees should focus on Christians', *Washington Post*, 15 November 2015.

Parfitt, Tom, 'More than 42 MILLION Muslims "support ISIS" – As experts warn the figure will grow', *Daily Express*, 1 July 2015.

Rappeport, Alan, 'Donald Trump says he would be open to closing US mosques to fight ISIS', *New York Times*, 22 October 2015.

Renton, James and Ben Gidley (eds), *Antisemitism and Islamophobia in Europe: A Shared Story?* (London: Palgrave Macmillan, 2017).

Sarsour, Linda, 'A Muslim woman was set on fire in New York. Now just going out requires courage', *Guardian*, 13 September 2016.

Sayyid, Salman, *A Fundamental Fear: Eurocentrism and the Emergence of Islamism*, 2nd edn (London and New York: Zed Books, 2003).

Sheehi, Stephen, *Islamophobia: The Ideological Campaign against Muslims* (Atlanta, GA: Clarity Press, 2011).

Siddiqui, Sabrina, 'Anti-Muslim rallies across US denounced by civil rights groups', *Guardian*, 10 June 2017.

Snowdon, Kathryn, 'Trevor Kavanagh's *The Sun* column slammed for failing to apologise for "The Muslim Problem" comment', *Huffington Post*, 17 August 2017. Available at www.huffingtonpost.co.uk/entry/trevor-kavanagh-the-sun-muslim-problem_uk_599567cde4b0acc593e55936 (accessed 1 September 2017).

Tarlo, Emma, 'Hijab online: The fashioning of cyber Islamic commerce', *Interventions* 12/2 (2010), pp. 209–25.

Toynbee, Polly, 'In defence of Islamophobia: Religion and the state', *Independent*, 23 October 1997.

Vakil, AbdoolKarim, 'Is the Islam in Islamophobia the same as the Islam in anti-Islam; or, When is it Islamophobia time?', in S. Sayyid and AbdoolKarim Vakil (eds), *Thinking through Islamophobia: Global Perspectives* (London: Hurst and Company, 2010), pp. 23–44.

Varadarajan, Tunku, 'Prophet of decline: An interview with Oriana Fallaci', *Wall Street Journal*, 23 June 2005.

Versi, Miqdaad, 'Like Sadiq Khan, Muslims in public life are being branded as extremists', *Independent*, 4 March 2016. Available at www.independent.co.uk/voices/like-sadiq-khan-in-public-life-are-being-branded-as-extremists-a6912056.html (accessed 3 March 2017).

Versi, Miqdaad, 'Why the British media is responsible for the rise in Islamophobia in Britain', *Independent*, 4 April 2016. Available at www.independent.co.uk/voices/why-the-british-media-is-responsible-for-the-rise-in-islamophobia-in-britain-a6967546.html (accessed 3 March 2017).

Warsi, Sayeeda, *The Enemy Within: A Tale of Muslim Britain* (London: Allen Lane, 2017).

Wike, Richard, Bruce Stokes and Katie Simmons, 'Negative views of minorities, refugees common in EU', *Pew Research Center*, 11 July 2016. Available at www.pewglobal.org/2016/07/11/negative-views-of-minorities-refugees-common-in-eu/ (accessed 20 September 2017).

Worley, Will, '*Sun* forced to admit "1 in 5 British Muslims" story was "significantly misleading"', *Independent*, 26 March 2016. Available at www.independent.co.uk/news/media/ipso-sun-british-muslims-story-headline-significantly-misleading-a6953771.html (accessed 3 March 2017).

Zapotosky, Matt, 'Hate crimes against Muslims hit highest mark since 2001', *Washington Post*, 14 November 2016.

Part One

Islamophobia, Politics and History

1

American Foreign Policy, Self-Fulfilling Prophecy and Muslims as Enemy Others

Nathan Lean

Introduction

Within the field of 'Islamophobia studies', insofar as such a thing exists, there is no shortage of scholarship that seeks to untangle the phenomenon of anti-Muslim prejudice and points to its root causes.[1] Indeed, as the plural 'causes' suggests, there is not simply one dynamic that has generated and sustained Islamophobia but rather myriad origins, triggers and bases. The issue of deciphering the germ of this pernicious form of prejudice, then, necessarily involves diverse approaches. Some scholarship situates Islamophobia within the lineage of other forms of prejudice that have reared their ugly heads (and continue to do so) in the so-called West, while others drill more deeply and link it to certain cognitive and psychological mappings that naturally cause one to fear, and subsequently loathe, that which is unfamiliar.[2] Understanding the ways in which humans develop and deploy stereotypes, often based on historical patterns, has called our attention to the reality that Islamophobia, like any other form of prejudice, is ultimately a product of the mind.[3] Thus, there is an ensuing sense of urgency to determine how it might be possible to shed such prejudices – a project that has tended to focus on the 'micro' levels of human interaction, engagement and relationships. These are critically important approaches, yet in recent years there has been a drift in the direction of 'macro' understandings of Islamophobia, which complicate the possibilities that exist for overcoming it more locally.[4] While I have aimed to hover between these two camps, I have resigned myself to the reality that it is the latter – those who see Islamophobia as a product of empire, and a prejudice that is tightly woven to the banner of 'Western' (European and American) power – that have touched on an uncomfortable, but inescapable, reality of our time. As much value as I see in interfaith engagement, the dissemination of reliable information, the importance of developing personal relationships and understanding the basic psychological impulses that generate and animate stereotypical views of the world, it is a hegemonic political structure, with ossified institutions, gargantuan budgets and an insatiable thirst for exerting cultural and economic influence in the world, that, in the end, has cultivated the climate of fear in which Islamophobia is manifested.

In this chapter, I examine this structure through an American lens that focuses on foreign policy, military engagements in Muslim-majority countries, the domestic ramifications of those engagements and the subcultures of Islamophobia that they spawn. I argue that this paradigm of 'macro-level' Islamophobia has produced a closed circle of sorts from which we cannot easily escape. It is tempting to understand the relationship between foreign policy and anti-Muslim prejudice in a unidirectional way: military campaigns in Muslim-majority countries trigger an emotional response among non-Muslims that results in sustained feelings of antipathy towards Islam and Muslims. This understanding, I will show, is premised on the notion that military ventures in places like Iraq and Afghanistan require little or no 'priming' of American and European populations. Surely, though, it is the case that propaganda is part and parcel of war, and that such endeavours necessitate narratives and images of the 'Other' that rally popular support, thus making Islamophobia not only a result of Western foreign policy in the Middle East, but a prerequisite for it. To show the degree to which Islamophobia is connected to this larger governmental system, I will first trace its contemporary origins and political expressions beginning in the 1970s. I will show that, unlike racism, anti-Semitism, homophobia and other similar prejudices, Islamophobia emerged along a different track – one that was significantly more in line with American imperial concerns, and thus more difficult to challenge. Importantly, I will also highlight the emergence of 'terrorism' as the primary focal point of foreign policy – a move that centres terrorism geographically outside of Western borders and locates it squarely within the territory to which Western powers turned their attention during the Arab Oil Crisis.[5] Finally, I will offer a few remarks about what I have called the 'foreign enemy, domestic threat phenomenon'. This theory suggests that increased fixation on threats posed to the United States and its allies abroad results in domestic policies that claim to protect the homeland from such threats. These policies, however, simultaneously reproduce the idea that threats exist to begin with, which consequently justifies an endless cycle of more foreign intervention and more domestic restrictions. This is somewhat akin to the 'military industrial complex', as Dwight Eisenhower described it in his 1961 farewell address, and for Muslims in the United States and in the Middle East, the effects of this system – Islamophobia and war, respectively – make it clear that any positive gains will require a systematic rethinking of the overarching power structures that govern our world today.

Rethinking Islamophobia's historical point of departure

In understanding Islamophobia as a phenomenon that is inseparable from the imperial ambitions of 'Western' powers and deeply rooted in American foreign policy structures, it is necessary to move beyond the now-clichéd argument that situates its contemporary origins and manifestations in or around the 1979 Iranian Revolution.[6] While this period undoubtedly gave rise to some of the first explicitly anti-Islamic narratives, memes and tropes, it is problematic to begin the conversation at the end of this decade because doing so assumes that Islamophobia is, in some way, nothing more than a reaction to the emergence of pronounced religious narratives on the part of world leaders like the Ayatollah Khomeini, and that it is entirely distinct from anti-Arab sentiment. The story, however, is more complex than that. While it is possible to trace the roots of politically inspired Islamophobia to a much earlier time in history, for the purposes of this chapter and its discussion of contemporary manifestations of Islamophobia it is worthwhile to step backwards some two decades in time. We should consider how discourses such as those that came to the fore in the late 1970s were actually the result of ongoing political conversations that zeroed in on the Middle East, its peoples and its cultures as a potentially worrisome region for American economic interests. It is within this setting that we can more clearly see the intricate and delicate relationship between politics and Islamophobia within Washington's halls of power.[7]

As Deepa Kumar has noted, the period from the late 1940s through the 1950s was a time of renewed American political interest in North Africa, the Middle East and Asia, and modernization theories coupled with prevailing Orientalist views during this time resulted in a post-war push for foreign policies that rested on the idea that the inhabitants of these areas exhibited a natural tendency for religious extremism.[8] President Harry Truman's Point Four Program for 'developing nations' was presented as a bulwark of sorts against the possibility of this, and it was clear that top US officials at that time, including the president, had low esteem for Arabs and Muslims. Under pressure from Saudi Arabia and its allies over America's recognition of the state of Israel, White House counsel Clark Clifford criticized the perception that the United States was 'trembling before the threats of a few nomadic tribes' and that the government should stop its 'shilly-shallying appeasement of the Arabs'.[9] George Kennan, the State Department's Soviet specialist and Chief of Policy Planning, said that during a visit to Iraq he had come to the conclusion that Arabs were a people prone to 'selfishness and stupidity' and that they were 'inclined to all manners of religious bigotry and fanaticism'.[10] Perhaps the most acerbic remark came from Robert McClintock, a Palestine desk officer, who stated that 'as for the emotion of the Arabs, I do not care a dried camel's hump'.[11] Institutionally, these views found resonance as well, with the Central Intelligence Agency's (CIA) 1949 psychological profile of the Middle East positing it as a land inhabited by people who were 'non-inventive and slow to put theories in practice', possessed an aversion to performing hard work and were capable of 'astonishing acts of treachery and dishonesty'.[12] Douglas Little had noted that in 1952, Adolf Berle, a Democratic Party insider and close associate of Truman, suggested that this profile applied to non-Arab Muslims – Iranians – too. 'Fanatic Mohammedan nationalism', he wrote, posed a threat to the Shah and would open the door to a 'Communist takeover' in Tehran.[13]

Thus, these traits – emotional, dishonest, fanatical, treacherous, selfish and stupid – were all thought to be reasons why those in Muslim-majority countries could not be left unchecked. 'Western' policies, the government believed, must therefore be put into place in order to ensure that Arabs did not veer into the path of the Soviet Union. As uncompromising as these stereotypes were, it was politics – not prejudice – that was ultimately driving them. As Dwight Eisenhower took over the presidency in January 1953, this sharpened into fuller relief. Eisenhower's views of Arabs and Muslims were shaped by his experiences in North Africa more than a decade earlier and were laid bare just three short years after his inauguration when, in July 1956, Egypt's president Gamal Abdel Nasser seized and nationalized the Suez Canal. 'If you go and live with these Arabs', Eisenhower told the National Security Council in 1959, 'you will find that they simply cannot understand our ideas of freedom or human dignity'.[14] This was an important period, for it cemented in the minds of many government officials the idea that the Middle East was a region of the world that could benefit from the exportation of Western political ideals, and that the United States would, as a result of exporting those ideals, protect its strategic interests abroad. Strategic interests, then, were conflated with national security, the latter of which justified a whole host of imageries that would be necessary to advance the former. If Nasser's seizing and nationalizing of the Suez Canal was a problem for Western interests, Iranian prime minister Mohammed Mossadegh's nationalization of Iran's oil market three years earlier – and his refusal to allow American companies access to the country – may have come as evidence that it was not just secular Arab nationalism that was a threat to American interests, but other cultural, perhaps religious, facets of Middle Eastern identity as well. This idea ebbed and flowed in Washington circles throughout the 1960s, with Arabs continually represented as ineffectual nomads with volatile temperaments who required a watchful Western eye. Their crushing defeat in the 1967 War not only underpinned their reputation in the eyes of the American government and public as feckless but also simultaneously bolstered the reputation of Israel and allowed for a move away from Nasser's pan-Arab nationalism. Anwar Sadat, Egypt's third president, appealed to religion, using the Muslim Brotherhood as a way to weaken secular nationalists.[15] Compounding this shift in strategy was the fact that, two years after Sadat's election, the Black September Organization, a Palestinian militant group, kidnapped and murdered eleven Israeli athletes and fatally shot a West German police officer during the 1972 Summer Olympics.[16] This, along with draconian proclamations from Libya's Mu'ammar Gaddafi about his intention to spread Islamic 'radicalism' and 'terrorism' worldwide, 'impacted U.S. official perceptions of Islamic revivalism long before the Iranian revolution', as Fawaz Gerges has noted.[17]

By 1979, the American political landscape was fertile for a shift towards increased focus on an ideological threat – especially a religious one. The stereotypical views of the Middle East, as expressed by high-ranking political officers and presidents, were indeed focused on 'Arabs', but not exclusively. The vernacular for these images at that time represented the reality of Arab nationalism as a threat to Western interests, but slowly morphed over the years into language that was less ethnic and eventually pointed to perceived cultural deficiencies that were thought to be religious. It is not surprising, then, that concerns about Islamophobia date back to this time, particularly during the height of the oil crisis of the early 1970s. Human Rights Watch reports that 'Arab and Muslim activists identified the 1973 Arab–Israeli war and oil embargo as a starting point for increased prejudice and hostility against their communities in the United States' and that hostilities towards Iranians and Arabs only intensified during the Iranian hostage crisis.[18] Importantly, during this time the term 'terrorism' crept into political discourse in a more obvious way, perhaps as a result of episodic attacks carried out by groups like Black September or statements by leaders like Gaddafi whose rhetoric rang out in a particular religious register. Also at play, however, was the reality that the Cold War was in its waning years, and while the American government had been battling the threat of communism on several fronts, including concerns that Middle Eastern states might become involved, there was an opportunity to cast terrorism – specifically 'Islamic terrorism' – as the next imminent ideological threat to the 'West'. The beady-eyed Ayatollah, with proclamations of 'Death to America' and the like, filled that space neatly, as did the hostage crisis, which came to be understood and described as an act of terrorism, perpetrated by the group Muslim Students of the Imam Khomeini Line, against Americans. Critically, the Iranian Revolution did not only mark the manifestation of a long-expected religious foe. It was also significant in that America's ally and guarantor of oil, the Shah, Mohammad Reza Pahlavi, was ousted and an energy crisis began. Thus, the Middle East was yet again represented as a volatile tinderbox that, without a stabilizing Western force, would burst into flames, only this time flames of an expressly religious hue. As one US official noted years later, 'The Iranian experience extremely conditioned the United States to think about the violent, anti-American nature of fundamentalist Islam'.[19] That may be so, but the term 'anti-American' did not only represent feelings of animosity and hatred towards the United States and its allies. Like Arab nationalism, it also signified a perceived threat to American strategic national interests and natural resources, and with the dawn of the 1980s, and continuing through the 2000s, national interests were again conflated with national security such that fighting terrorism, understood in a uniquely Islamic sense, became the new modus operandi for advancing imperial interests in the world. With that project, the catalogue of anti-Muslim prejudice grew, acquiring a significantly larger lexicon and manifesting itself in significantly uglier ways.

A forty-year marriage of war and stereotypes

The 1980s and the following three decades witnessed an American military presence in the Middle East that increased exponentially. With attention now paid to this part of the world, it became necessary in the minds of government officials to stabilize a region that was deeply unstable – a project that ineluctably involved ensuring that national interests like oil, strategic land access and the security of friendly regimes were protected. It is not surprising, then, that with this moment came the beginning of what is now a nearly four-decade-long entanglement with various countries there. As Andrew Bacevich of Columbia University noted in a 2014 op-ed in the *Washington Post*, since 1980 the United

States has invaded, bombed or occupied fourteen Muslim-majority countries. In some cases, states were subjected to multiple military skirmishes, and the tally does not include such things as drone strikes, the involvement in countries like Israel and Saudi Arabia (both of which include large Muslim populations, the latter almost entirely), nor does it include proxy wars where American interests were wrapped up in a conflict that played out between two other states.[20]

This time of inflamed political tensions was refracted in a media discourse that began to depict, almost exclusively, the military conflicts between the United States and Middle Eastern nations as civilizational in nature, with Muslim-majority states posing a palpable and existential threat to the Land of the Free. As Jack Shaheen has noted, the dehumanization of Arabs and Muslims in film during this time (which often included scenes of their slaughter) was supported with funding, equipment, personnel and technical assistance from agencies of the American government.[21] Roughly a third of the anti-Muslim films of the last century, he has shown, were made in the 1980s alone. As that decade bled into the beginning of the next, and the Gulf War became the prism through which discussions of the Middle East were refracted, these prejudiced representations became more entrenched not only in the media but also in political and military circles where the dehumanization of the Muslim enemy was seen as a necessary prerequisite for sustained conflict.

Accounts of key battle moments in the Gulf War show American pilots firebombing stranded Iraqi motorists, unable to reload their cluster bombs quickly enough to hit the innocent 'targets'.[22] It should go without saying that the slaughter of ordinary civilians attempting to flee the carnage was only possible as a result of conflating the guilty and the innocent, both of whom were offenders in the eyes of those dropping the bombs and both of whom, as a result of their shared Iraqi, Arab and Muslim identity, were likely seen as less than human. In the cockpits of some aeroplanes, as Erin Steuter and Deborah Wills have reported, American soldiers fired upon their Iraqi targets as the *William Tell Overture*, the theme song of *The Lone Ranger*, rang out.[23] In other instances, Iraqis were referred to as 'cockroaches' that scattered when the kitchen lights came on, only to be permanently squashed, while the air campaign, in another example, was likened to 'shooting fish in a barrel'.[24] This type of rhetoric, while not explicitly pronounced in official government circles, episodically characterized various moments of war that involved Middle Eastern targets throughout the 1990s and into the 2000s. It is reported that some soldiers aboard the USS John F. Kennedy watched pornography prior to launching missiles, allegorizing the cascading missiles that descended from American jets as the brutal male ejaculate being released on an effeminized Iraqi nation.[25] Importantly, it was the Gulf War, with its attending political and economic ambitions on the one hand and subsequent discourses about Arabs, Muslims and Iraqis on the other, that laid the groundwork for re-engagement with Iraq in 2003. While the Middle East as a region overall came to signify a 'stomping ground' for Western troops, it was Iraq that stood out as the central arena within this space and represented a shift away from Iran and the menacing Ayatollah to a more familiar, but equally loathsome, enemy: Saddam Hussein. It is in the person of Saddam that we can see, yet again, the nexus between American national interests and American national security. It is also in the person of Saddam, but more generally the Iraqi nation and its people overall, that the target of anti-Muslim narratives and tropes becomes more focused and in line with specific contexts of American wars. As Joan L. Conners has argued in her discussion of American political rhetoric and political cartoons, it was the George H. W. Bush administration's labelling of Saddam as an eminent threat that legitimized more popular (and prejudiced) rhetoric about Iraq; it was also the more popular rhetoric that, in circular fashion, legitimized for the Bush administration its attitude and policies towards the country.[26] Here we might recall the popular adage: 'One hand cannot clap on its own'. With Saddam marketed to the American public as an evil, that, according to George H. W. Bush, was worse than Hitler in some ways, a war fervour was nurtured that led to the largest outbreak of anti-Muslim prejudice in the United States since the time of the Iranian hostage crisis more than a decade earlier.[27] Saddam's gruesome atrocities (which were unquestionably a central part of the fear) along with his threats, images of Arabic-language backdrops and a steady stream of news reports that enumerated every instance of chaos contributed to a climate of anti-Iraqi sentiment, but more generally a pervasive feeling of loathing and detestation of Muslims and Islam – a sentiment that would undergird American foreign policy in Iraq and the greater Middle East well into the first two decades of the 2000s.[28]

Post-9/11 policies and institutionalization

Far too often, when talking about Islamophobia, focus is placed on its manifest presence, either in speech or in blatant acts. When discussing its relationship with government policies, there has also been much focus on those that are discernibly prejudiced in and of themselves. Yet since 9/11, anti-Muslim prejudice has been wedded to American foreign and domestic policies that are in some cases quite obvious and in other cases less so. It is equally important, therefore, to think about the ways in which particular views of minority groups (in this case Muslims) are reflected in policy choices and seemingly innocuous measures that are represented as safeguarding national security, protecting the homeland and exporting Western interests. It is also helpful to look more closely at policy makers, their advisers and the influencers whose voices and insights lead to these policies, for doing so gives us a fuller portrait of the ideological foundations on which government initiatives and programmes that contribute to anti-Muslim prejudice are pillared.

While 9/11 is frequently cast as a point of departure for anti-Muslim prejudice in the United States, the historical trajectory that we have seen thus far undermines that claim. It is unquestionable that Arabs and Muslims increasingly came under the spotlight in the years after that tragedy. The Federal Bureau of Investigation (FBI) reported, for example, that between 2000 and 2001, attacks targeting Muslim individuals in the United States jumped by 1,700 per cent.[29] The reality for many Muslims was that their daily lives became increasingly complicated. Going to work or school, a quotidian journey, became, in some cases, a risk. Where their religious identity was obvious, by their choice of clothing or some other signifier, the possibility of confrontation and backlash was palpable.

Apart from this reality, though, a look at systemic changes in the structure of the American government reveals a different level of Islamophobia that existed – one that was not recognizably pernicious in terms of daily activities and interactions, but that nonetheless makes plain the infrastructural enormity of its governmental workings. The case of the creation of the Department of Homeland Security (DHS) in November 2002 is a paradigmatic example. This move, in response to the attacks of 9/11, is evidence of what I have previously called the 'foreign enemy, domestic threat phenomenon', an idea which suggests that, in the wake of attacks carried out by certain enemies abroad, it is necessary to protect the homeland from the possibility of subsequent attacks.[30] This does not seem all that counterintuitive, though the important point is that in the aftermath of 9/11 the possibility of a Muslim terrorist group killing Americans on their own soil led to a range of responses that fed into (and grew) the narrative of an actual 'Muslim threat' through the implementation of domestic policies which made that threat apparent. In other words, the fear of Muslim terrorists spurred the creation of agencies, policies, projects and proposals that were designed to fight the possibility of an ever-present, ever-lurking Muslim terrorist: a self-fulfilling prophecy.

The creation of DHS was the largest realignment of the American federal government since the Second World War and, with a multibillion-dollar yearly budget, it quickly took stock of the post-9/11 landscape and set into motion a number of programmes and policies that swelled the perception of an impending terrorist attack and facilitated a range of pre-emptive measures that put Muslims under the microscope. Akin to the military industrial complex, some sixty-two agencies merged and enjoyed an operating budget of $62 billion for the purposes of 'securing borders' – the second largest governmental agency after the Department of Defense.[31] First and foremost among its projects was ramped-up surveillance of Arab and Muslim communities and neighbourhoods, which resulted in white papers and official briefs recounting the 'identification factors' of potential extremists, including mosque attendance or travelling to Muslim-majority countries.[32] Additionally, fingerprints and other identifying characteristics of American Muslims were compiled in government databases through a programme called 'Operation Frontline', which searched through the files of exchange students, among other things, to determine possible threats.

This rebranding of the government created more than 200,000 jobs, and not just in the corridors of Washington, D.C. Throughout the country, various pop-up outfits that claimed some affiliation with DHS emerged and drew on the supposed expertise of individuals who claimed to have special knowledge of Islam, Muslims, the Middle East, terrorism and foreign policy. (It should be noted here that the conjoining of these things – a world religion, wanton violence, a particular region of the world and government responses – has melded in the minds of many a particular relationship between them that does not necessarily exist.) Government contracts were awarded to think tanks that held especially conservative political views, or that put forth local and informally chosen speakers for public gatherings addressing issues related to counterterrorism. In some instances, legitimacy was a result of proximity. Thomas Cincotta, author of *Manufacturing the Muslim Menace: Private Firms, Public Servants, and the Threat to Rights and Security*, notes that 'the Department of Homeland Security, [the] Terrorist Screening Center, and [the] Federal Bureau of Investigation have implicitly sanctioned these un-vetted private offerings by participating in the very same conferences where problematic messages are delivered to public servants'.[33]

In this climate of hyperactivity, the White House also relied on speakers and authors whose views about the Middle East, Islam and Muslims evidenced a strong ideological bent. In the lead up to the controversial 2003 invasion of Iraq, for instance, it has been reported that the Bush administration relied on the advice and counsel of figures such as Bernard Lewis and Fouad Ajami, two men who have long advanced Orientalist notions of a troubled Arab and Muslim people whose cultural woes can only be reversed by American military intervention. Lewis and Ajami were regular visitors to the Oval Office, and so close was the former to the vice president, Dick Cheney, that the second-in-command held a private birthday party for him at the presidential mansion.[34] Ultimately, it was within this epistemological terrain that the Bush administration, reeling from 9/11 and with the advice of neoconservatives who had made careers from stereotyping Arabs, invaded Iraq in 2003, thrusting Saddam Hussein to the forefront of the American imagination for the second time. A foreign enemy, in the form of the 9/11 hijackers, led to a perceived domestic threat in the form of a bulky security establishment, which, in turn, led to the perception of another foreign enemy in the person of Saddam.

The inescapable terror of the 'War on Terror'

Nearly one year after the creation of DHS, the United States invaded Iraq on the premise that Saddam Hussein had weapons of mass destruction – a notion later proved abjectly false. Books could be, and have been, written on the numerous ways in which that decade-long war contributed to Islamophobia but, for the purposes of this discussion, it is worth highlighting three points to that end. The first is that the war birthed a government discourse on terrorism that, while long in the making, had not yet come to the fore in the prominent way that it did in the intervening years after the initial invasion of Baghdad. The so-called War on Terror transformed what had heretofore been a focus on specific targets (actors, states, groups, etc.) into a Cold War-esque focus on an ideology, and one that was presumably rampant among a certain group of people. In Washington, this led to a plethora of new expressions and phrases that eventually crept out into the media and mainstream and coloured the way in which the American public thought about, and subsequently talked about, Muslims and Islam. As Juan Cole has noted, this new foreign policy rhetoric gave rise to such constructions as 'Islamic fascism', 'political Islam', 'Islamic terrorism' and the like, which, while aiming to distinguish Islam writ large from a more specific focal point (Muslim terrorists), unfortunately resorted to framing the war in expressly religious language.[35] The rhetorical universe of the 'War on Terror', with its attendant expression of an overarching religious dynamic, nurtured similar expressions and views within military circles, too. In some instances, soldiers' fatigues featured various insignia with derogatory language about Muslims and reference to infidels, while in other instances key military officials in Iraq and Afghanistan referred to the wars in language that insinuated a cosmic battle between divine forces allied with American interests, and satanic forces of an Islamic character.[36]

Secondly, I would argue that it was precisely this subculture of Islamophobia, replete with language that rendered Islam a target – as opposed to violent actors who happened to be Muslim – that licensed a dehumanization of that religious group and its followers within very specific contexts overseas.[37] One of the uglier and more shocking scenes to come out of the Iraq War was the prisoner abuse scandal at the Abu Ghraib prison in the north-west province of Baghdad. Human rights violations towards captives held there – which included American soldiers posing with their nude and contorted bodies, hooded electrocutions, placing dog leashes around detainees' necks and routine beatings – were all based on, and fed into, the narrative that the Iraqis in the prison, on account of their ethnicity, nationality, religion and captivity, were inhuman and therefore subject to inhuman treatment. Two points are necessary here. Firstly, while it is possible that the toils of war lead soldiers to do unthinkable things in any context (the My Lai massacre of the Vietnam War comes to mind), the specific types of mistreatment that targeted Muslim prisoners in Abu Ghraib rests largely on certain stereotypical assumptions about the inherent sexual nature of Arabs and Muslims, the supposed proclivity of men to sexual taboos and an understanding of Islam's teachings regarding the impermissibility of homosexuality. Secondly, it is difficult to maintain that such dehumanizing treatment could have occurred without subtle occasions of anti-Muslim prejudice building up, in one way or another, over the years. In other words, these were not random acts but rather deeply contextualized within an arena where negative views of Arabs and Muslims had pervaded. This is, in part, why we have seen other similar instances of blatantly Islamophobic expressions within the military culture and especially during overseas wars. (The song 'Hadji Girl', written by US Marine Joshua Belile, which mocks a fictitious Iraqi family, and instances of military personnel urinating on copies of the Qur'an are but two examples.[38])

Thirdly, the inescapability of the 'War on Terror' reinforced domestic institutions that depended on its longevity. We might ask ourselves, if 'terrorists' are all defeated, what purpose do the organizations and outfits dedicated to fighting them serve? As we have seen, however, the very idea of a terrorist threat is based on the belief that it is not simply the terrorists themselves, but the ideology that drives them, that is the ultimate enemy. To that end, then, the 'foreign enemy, domestic threat phenomenon' relies as much on the latter part of that equation as it does on the former. Where perceived foreign enemies trigger feelings of a domestic threat, so too feelings of a domestic threat trigger the perception of foreign enemies. This is precisely what we have seen with the Iraq War. The perception of domestic threats, though, has also led to crackdowns on immigration, suspensions of visas, rejections of passport applications, deportations, unlawful searches and seizures, sting operations inside Muslim communities and mosques, and numerous other government-led programmes that have kept the possibility of an attack alive in the minds of many Americans. The Federal Bureau of Investigation, the Central Intelligence Agency, the Department of Homeland Security and other agencies have all worked in concert to target Muslim communities in the United States in one way or another. Even local groups, like the New York Police Department, have formalized government partnerships that resulted in extensive mapping and surveillance programmes within Arab or Muslim-majority neighbourhoods. In one bizarre case, the government paid an ex-convict, Craig Monteilh, to pose as a Muslim in a California mosque, sleep with Muslim women and report any suspicious activity that he found. In an ironic twist of fate, members of that mosque reported Monteilh to the FBI – the very group that sent him there. Regretting his involvement in the sting, he later declared, 'There is no real hunt. It's fixed.'[39]

Conclusion

With the emergence of ISIS in recent years, the chances of moving beyond anti-Muslim prejudice in the United States look quite dim. This is compounded by the reality that, under President Obama, overt war in Muslim-majority countries was replaced with covert drone warfare; rhetorical and optical changes were made but foreign and domestic policy measures remained largely the same. However, it is not the mere presence of bad actors like ISIS that will cause Islamophobia to remain. For, if this chapter has outlined anything, it is the constructed nature of this prejudice and its attachment to American and Western interests in the Middle East. Thus, until the United States casts its attention to another region of the world – until the alignment of natural resources and national interests are found elsewhere – the Middle East, a region predominantly populated by Muslims, will remain a place from which a whole host of negative images and stereotypes emerge. Bound as it is to foreign policy, and reinforced as it is by domestic policy, Islamophobia will remain prevalent and, depending on particular policy choices by American leaders in the future, may even get worse. Of course, the degree to which it was a central plank of the Republican Party's 2016 election strategy, and the degree to which it has characterized the rhetoric and policy proposals of President Donald Trump, can leave few to doubt that, at the very least, the religion of Islam will be politicized in an effort to advance a host of measures that are ostensibly geared towards protecting national security. Military initiatives that target ISIS with increased intensity, promises to ramp up surveillance of immigrant communities in the United States and the possibility of enacting a blanketed ban on Muslims coming to the country – all ideas that the Trump administration has seriously considered – continue to situate Muslims within a framework of security and thus underscore Orientalist notions of 'Self' and 'Other', Us and Them, that have long animated American approaches to governance. While micro-level corrections – interfaith engagement, the dissemination of good and reliable information, increased education and co-operation, public awareness campaigns and civil rights work – may alleviate the suffering caused by this prejudice at local levels, it is only through significant and lasting changes to the macro-level machinery that enables, and indeed demands, this prejudice that any meaningful change will ultimately come about. And when it does, the question we must all ask ourselves is, 'Who's next?'

Notes

1 In the past fifteen years, 'Islamophobia', or anti-Muslim prejudice as it is most commonly understood, has become situated within several established academic disciplines including, but not limited to, religious studies, international relations, history, political science and sociology.
2 See Nasar Meer and Tehseen Noorani, 'A sociological comparison of anti-Semitism and anti-Muslim sentiment in Britain', *Sociological Review* 56/2 (2008), pp. 195–219; Sabine Schiffer and Constantin Wagner, 'Anti-Semitism and Islamophobia: New enemies, old patterns', *Race & Class* 52 (2011), pp. 77–84; and Sherman Lee, Jeffrey Gibbons, John Thompson and Hussan Timani, 'The Islamophobia Scale: Instrument development and initial validation', *International Journal for the Psychology of Religion* 19/2 (2009), pp. 92–105.
3 It is necessary to mention here two key points regarding my use of the term 'Islamophobia'. Firstly, I define it as prejudice towards or discrimination against Muslims on the basis of their religious identity. Secondly, I believe there is value in using the term interchangeably with 'anti-Muslim prejudice', as it is this phrase that

is more commonly understood in public vernacular. 'Anti-Muslim prejudice' is also a succinct and accurate way to describe what Islamophobia is really all about.

4 See Deepa Kumar, *Islamophobia and the Politics of Empire* (Chicago, IL: Haymarket, 2012); and Arun Kundnani, *The Muslims Are Coming: Islamophobia, Extremism, and the Domestic War on Terror* (London: Verso, 2014).

5 For an excellent discussion on the Arab-Muslim nexus within the context of Islamophobia, see Peter Gottschalk and Gabriel Greenberg, *Islamophobia: Making Muslims the Enemy* (Lanham, MD: Rowman and Littlefield, 2008); Melanie McCalister, *Epic Encounters: Culture, Media and US Interests in the Middle East since 1945* (Berkeley, CA: University of California Press, 2001); and Jack Shaheen, *Reel Bad Arabs: How Hollywood Vilifies a People* (Northampton, MA: Olive Branch Press, 2001).

6 For instance, see John L. Esposito, 'Political Islam: Beyond the green menace', *Current History* 93 (1994), pp. 19–24.

7 My writing on the lineage of Islamophobia within American political discourses traces it back to the Barbary Wars and specifically examines the way in which gendered narratives about Muslim women during this early series of military skirmishes have persisted through time and continue today. See Nathan Lean, 'Gendered Islamophobia in Western war narratives: From the Barbary Coast to the graveyard of empires', in Douglas Pratt and Rachel Woodlock (eds), *Fear of Muslims: International Perspectives on Islamophobia* (New York: Springer, 2015), pp. 93–110.

8 Kumar, *Islamophobia*, p. 65.

9 See Douglas Little, *American Orientalism: The United States and the Middle East since 1945* (Chapel Hill, NC: University of North Carolina Press, 2008), p. 26.

10 Little, *American Orientalism*, p. 26.

11 Ibid.

12 Ibid.

13 Ibid., p. 27.

14 Ibid.

15 Kumar, *Islamophobia*, p. 68.

16 For a chilling eyewitness account of this event, see David Raab, *Terror in Black September: The First Eyewitness Account of the 1970 Hijackings* (New York: Palgrave, 2007).

17 Fawaz Gerges, *America and Political Islam: Clash of Cultures or Clash of Interests?* (Cambridge: Cambridge University Press, 1999), p. 42.

18 'We are not the enemy', *Human Rights Watch* 14/6 (2002).

19 Gerges, *America and Political Islam*, p. 42.

20 Andrew Bacevich, 'Even if we defeat the Islamic State, we'll still lose the bigger war', *The Washington Post*, 3 October 2014.

21 Shaheen, *Reel Bad Arabs*, p. 22.

22 Erin Steuter and Deborah Wills, *At War with Metaphor: Media, Propaganda, and Racism in the War on Terror* (Lanham, MD: Rowman and Littlefield, 2008), p. 55.

23 Steuter and Wills, *At War with Metaphor*, p. 56.
24 Ibid.
25 Jasmine Zine, 'Between orientalism and fundamentalism: Muslim women and feminist engagement', in Kim Rygiel and Krista Hunt (eds), *(En)Gendering the War on Terror: War Stories and Camouflaged Politics* (New York: Ashgate, 2008), p. 32.
26 J. L. Conners, 'Hussein as enemy: The Persian Gulf War in political cartoons', *Harvard International Journal of Press and Politics* 3/3 (1998), pp. 96–114.
27 Emran Qureshi and Michael Anthony Sells, *The New Crusades: Constructing the Muslim Enemy* (New York: Columbia University Press, 2003), p. 13.
28 Qureshi and Sells, *The New Crusades*, p. 13.
29 Curt Anderson, 'FBI reports jump in violence against Muslims', *Associated Press*, 25 November 2002.
30 Nathan Lean, 'The problems of Islamophobia', *Soundings: A Journal of Politics and Culture* 57 (2014), pp. 145–8.
31 Sabrina Alimahomed, 'Homeland Security Inc.: Public order, private profit', *Race & Class* 55/4 (2014), p. 84.
32 Alimahomed, 'Homeland Security Inc.', p. 84.
33 Thomas Cincotta, *Manufacturing the Muslim Menace: Private Firms, Public Servants, and the Threat to Rights and Security* (Somerville, MA: Political Research Associates, 2011).
34 Brian Whitaker, 'Bush's historian', *Guardian*, 2 May 2006. Available at www.theguardian.com/commentisfree/2006/may/02/thehistoryman (accessed 24 October 2016).
35 Juan Cole, 'Islamophobia and American foreign policy rhetoric', in John Esposito and Ibrahim Kalin (eds), *Islamophobia: The Challenge of Pluralism in the 21st Century* (Oxford: Oxford University Press, 2011), pp. 127–42; p. 129.
36 Tareq Y. Ismael and Andrew Rippin (eds), *Islam in the Eyes of the West: Images and Realities in an Age of Terror* (New York: Routledge, 2010), p. 48.
37 It should be noted here that some Iraqi militants and all of the 9/11 hijackers (and their mastermind Osama bin Laden) framed the violent conflict with the United States in terms of religion. However, the unfortunate consequence of that was the way in which the discourse of the American government, through the use of 'Islamic' as an adjective describing these people and groups, contributed to the perception among many that it was not just rogue actors that were to blame for terrorist attacks or the like, but everyone who would place themselves under the larger banner of Islam as a result of their Muslim identity.
38 It is necessary to mention that these acts do not characterize the beliefs of the American military and its personnel overall, but instead point to the way in which a history of anti-Muslim rhetoric and policies make these kinds of expressions easier.
39 Paul Harris, 'The ex-FBI informant with a change of heart: "There is no real hunt. It's fixed"', *Guardian*, 20 March 2012.

Works cited

Alimahomed, Sabrina, 'Homeland Security Inc.: Public order, private profit', *Race and Class* 55/4 (2014), pp. 82–99.
Anderson, Curt, 'FBI reports jump in violence against Muslims', *Associated Press*, 25 November 2002.
Bacevich, Andrew, 'Even if we defeat the Islamic State, we'll still lose the bigger war', *Washington Post*, 3 October 2014.
Cincotta, Thomas, *Manufacturing the Muslim Menace: Private Firms, Public Servants, and the Threat to Rights and Security* (Somerville, MA: Political Research Associates, 2011).
Cole, Juan, 'Islamophobia and American foreign policy rhetoric', in John Esposito and Ibrahim Kalin (eds), *Islamophobia: The Challenge of Pluralism in the 21st Century* (Oxford: Oxford University Press, 2011), pp. 127–42.
Conners, J. L., 'Hussein as enemy: The Persian Gulf War in political cartoons', *Harvard International Journal of Press and Politics* 3/3 (1998), pp. 96–114.
Esposito, John L., 'Political Islam: Beyond the green menace', *Current History* 93 (1994), pp. 19–24.
Gerges, Fawaz, *America and Political Islam: Clash of Cultures or Clash of Interests?* (Cambridge: Cambridge University Press, 1999).
Gottschalk, Peter and Gabriel Greenberg, *Islamophobia: Making Muslims the Enemy* (Lanham, MD: Rowman and Littlefield, 2008).
Harris, Paul, 'The ex-FBI informant with a change of heart: "There is no real hunt. It's fixed"', *Guardian*, 20 March 2012.
Human Rights Watch, 'We are not the enemy', *Human Rights Watch* 14/6 (2002).
Ismael, Tareq Y. and Andrew Rippin (eds), *Islam in the Eyes of the West: Images and Realities in an Age of Terror* (New York: Routledge, 2010).
Kumar, Deepa, *Islamophobia and the Politics of Empire* (Chicago, IL: Haymarket, 2012).
Kundnani, Arun, *The Muslims are Coming: Islamophobia, Extremism, and the Domestic War on Terror* (London: Verso, 2014).
Lean, Nathan, 'Gendered Islamophobia in Western war narratives: From the Barbary Coast to the graveyard of empires', in Douglas Pratt and Rachel Woodlock (eds), *Fear of Muslims: International Perspectives on Islamophobia* (New York: Springer, 2015), pp. 93–110.
Lean, Nathan, 'The Problems of Islamophobia', *Soundings: A Journal of Politics and Culture* 57 (2014), pp. 145–8.
Lee, Sherman, Jeffrey Gibbons, John Thompson and Hussan Timani, 'The Islamophobia Scale: Instrument development and initial validation', *International Journal for the Psychology of Religion* 19/2 (2009), pp. 92–105.
Little, Douglas, *American Orientalism: The United States and the Middle East since 1945* (Chapel Hill, NC: University of North Carolina Press, 2008).

McCalister, Melanie, *Epic Encounters: Culture, Media and US Interests in the Middle East since 1945* (Berkeley, CA: University of California Press, 2001).

Meer, Nasar and Tehseen Noorani, 'A sociological comparison of anti-Semitism and anti-Muslim sentiment in Britain', *Sociological Review* 56/2 (2008), pp. 195–219.

Qureshi, Emran and Michael Anthony Sells, *The New Crusades: Constructing the Muslim Enemy* (New York: Columbia University Press, 2003).

Raab, David, *Terror in Black September: The First Eyewitness Account of the 1970 Hijackings* (New York: Palgrave Macmillan, 2007).

Schiffer, Sabine and Constantin Wagner, 'Anti-Semitism and Islamophobia: New enemies, old patterns', *Race and Class* 52 (2011), pp. 77–84.

Shaheen, Jack, *Reel Bad Arabs: How Hollywood Vilifies a People* (Northampton, MA: Olive Branch Press, 2001).

Steuter, Erin and Deborah Wills, *At War with Metaphor: Media, Propaganda, and Racism in the War on Terror* (Lanham, MD: Rowman and Littlefield, 2008).

Whitaker, Brian, 'Bush's historian', *Guardian*, 2 May 2006. Available at www.theguardian.com/commentisfree/2006/may/02/thehistoryman (accessed 24 October 2016).

Zine, Jasmine, 'Between orientalism and fundamentalism: Muslim women and feminist engagement', in Kim Rygiel and Krista Hunt (eds), *(En)Gendering the War on Terror: War Stories and Camouflaged Politics* (New York: Ashgate, 2008), pp. 27–50.

2

Donald Trump at the Intersection of Nativism, Islamophobia and Anti-Muslim Sentiment: American Roots and Parallels

Peter Gottschalk

The surprise regarding Donald Trump's election victory in November 2016 may have only been surpassed by the astonishment of most professional commentators and many voters that his campaign could survive his provocative blend of racism and nativism (let alone claims of sexual assault and other seeming millstones). Along with the explicit statements, innuendo and dog whistles that he expertly wielded in regard to groups like Mexicans, blacks and Jews, his repeated claims about Muslims and Islam proved among the most popular with the electorate. Part of this success lay in the Republican candidate's ability to interweave Islamophobia and anti-Muslim sentiment into a seamless tapestry of threats that resonated with and amplified existing nativist sentiments. While many Americans may consider his electoral triumph an aberration, in fact, it reflects the concatenation of three divergent dynamics long evident in American history that have each been exploited and expanded upon by various Republican Party candidates over the previous decade: nativism, Islamophobia and anti-Muslim sentiment. Only by mapping the contours of these attitudes on the American cultural landscape and tracing their historical trajectory alongside parallel antipathies can we appreciate how Trump's victory represents not an aberration but a culmination of nativist energies.

Coming to terms

In a 2012 essay, the sociologist José Casanova compared instances of nativism in the United States and Germany. Although he noted the characterization by some Protestant nativists of the 'War on Terror' as a Christian 'crusade' against Islam, Casanova concluded the following: 'But those were relatively marginal voices that did not find much echo in American public opinion and did not feed public controversies about Islam in America or about Muslim immigrants' and that these 'are more the expression of anti-Obama politics than of an emerging anti-Muslim nativism'.[1] The pervasive use of anti-Muslim and Islamophobic sentiments by mainstream political candidates and the corresponding increase in negative poll results regarding public views of Muslims and Islam challenge Casanova's conclusions while also pointing to a need to define and distinguish from one another the terms of analysis.

The earliest use of the English term 'Islamophobia', according to the *Oxford English Dictionary*, appeared in a 1923 British review of a French book. The book's authors, E. Dinet and Sliman ben Ibrahim, used the term to identify and critique Western scholarship that, in the words of the reviewer, portrayed Muhammad as 'an epileptic, a charlatan, one suffering from hysteria, a socialist obsessed with the idea of an impending judgement'.[2] Few other English uses of 'Islamophobia' appeared until 1994, when Europeans increasingly recognized the rising discrimination among their societies against the growing number of migrants from Muslim-majority countries.

The milestone 1997 report by the Runnymede Trust entitled *Islamophobia: A Challenge for Us All* propelled the widespread use of the word in the United Kingdom, while in the United States the notion found expanding use following the 9/11 attacks and the resulting rise in antagonism towards Muslims and Islam in Europe and the United States. The authors of the Runnymede report duly noted that the term 'refers to unfounded hostility toward Islam' and 'refers also to the practical consequences of such hostility in unfair discrimination against Muslim individuals and communities, and to the exclusion of Muslims from mainstream political and social affairs'.[3] The report, therefore, views anti-Muslim antipathy as resulting from anti-Islamic antagonism. However, as we shall see, Westerners have often constructed racialist images of Muslims as Arabs and Turks, ascribing to them phenotypical characterizations like brown complexions and large, hawk-like noses as well as character traits such as conniving and simmering anger. This has prompted many scholars to seek a separate term that reflects such ethnic, racist and linguistic biases towards Muslims that do not appear to stem immediately from views of their religion.

Consequently, some scholars and other commentators objected to the focus on Islam implicit in the term 'Islamophobia'. For instance, Fred Halliday declared that the relevant negative attitudes reflect 'not so much hostility to Islam as a religion ... but hostility to Muslims'.[4] Some would strongly prefer that the focus on Muslims displace that on Islam inherent in Islamophobia. Others have gone so far as to redefine 'Islamophobia' as essentially a form of racism. However, these intellectual moves elide the fears of Islam generated by non-Muslim views of it as a competing religion, as a religion incompatible with secularism and as a transnational ideology challenging nation state ideologies. Nevertheless, Islamophobia increasingly proved too constrictive in application.

Among those developing definitions, Gabriel Greenberg and I in 2007 described the phenomenon as 'a *social* anxiety toward Islam and Muslim cultures that is largely unexamined by, yet deeply engrained in, Americans [among others]' (emphasis in original).[5] But the need to name antipathies towards Muslims that are less directly connected with Islam made this inadequate, so another term has increasingly been embraced: 'anti-Muslim sentiment'. This phrase emerged in the 1930s in regard to Hindu–Muslim tensions in India and has proved a capable term, focusing on imaginaries of and attitudes towards Muslim bodies, languages and cultures. 'Sentiment' proves to be a particularly versatile term given its allusion to feeling, sensation, belief and mental disposition. Reactions to the physical, social and cultural presence of a perceived 'Other' can emerge from one, some or all of these facets of sentiment. Together, Islamophobia and anti-Muslim sentiment operate as two different – yet not wholly distinct – sets of dynamics. Any particular example of prejudice or hostility towards Muslims may stem more from one dynamic than the other, or both. However, neither exists without some root in the other, however distant.

While Islamophobia and anti-Muslim sentiment – in tandem or separately – may be expressed in any number of situations, we particularly consider here contexts shaped by nativism. Nativism energizes these dynamics in specific ways that reorient their valences to align along strong nationalist polarities. As opposed to the chauvinism that new arrivals or seemingly unconventional residents may face in local communities, nativism defined by nationalist feelings, imaginaries and ideologies judges a certain group or groups as alien to the national community. Nationalists acting under nativist impulses seek to exclude even those whom they have never encountered and yet judge as not belonging to – and indeed even threatening – the nation at large as a corporate body of citizens. The historian Tyler Anbinder has defined nativism as 'a complex web of nationalism, xenophobia, ethnocentrism, and racism'.[6] Significantly, he reflects the historical variance of the term by acknowledging that nineteenth-century American nativists focused solely on immigration and so restricted their understanding of themselves as 'someone who fears and resents immigrants and their impact on the United States, and who wants to take some action against them, be it through violence, immigration restriction, or placing limits on the rights of newcomers already in the United States'.[7]

One American demonstrated many of these dynamics when he expressed his opposition to German settlement, querying why they should be allowed

> to swarm into our Settlements, and by herding together establish their Language and Manners to the Exclusion of ours? Why should Pennsylvania, founded by the English, become a Colony of *Aliens*, who will shortly be so numerous as to Germanize us instead of our Anglifying them, and will never adopt our Language or Customs, any more than they can acquire our Complexion?[8]

This was Benjamin Franklin in 1755, creating a perfect binary between English-heritage (natives) and German aliens as mapped against stark linguistic, behavioural and physical contrasts. Because of their failure to culturally acclimatize (with no reciprocal intercultural adjustment apparently desired or expected), a zero-sum game ensues in which sheer numbers will reward these immigrants. While parallels with similar alarmist and discriminatory dynamics today seem alluring, comparisons must begin with the recognition of historical differences.

Turning to the examples of anti-Catholicism and anti-Catholic sentiment in the early nineteenth century, anti-Judaism and anti-Semitism in the early twentieth century and Islamophobia and anti-Muslim sentiment in the early twenty-first century, we observe how these nativist eruptions diverged from one another in significant ways. Yet together they provide the opportunity to examine the dual construction of non-American 'Others' alienated by normative definitions of religion and race/ethnicity/culture.

Immigrants and natives

American antagonisms against Catholics, Jews and Muslims – and Catholicism, Judaism and Islam – long predated these specific moments, imported in some nascent form by the English, Spanish, French and Dutch who initially established both European colonies and sentiments on North American shores. Nevertheless, since American independence, latent sentiments among the Baptist, Episcopalian and Methodist majority seldom metastasized into explicit antagonism or violence. In each of the examples considered below, changes in immigration and declining economies coupled with period-specific social issues spurred rising religious and racial/ethnic/cultural stereotyping and marginalization.

This has certainly proved true in the current political climate in which attention to migration centres explicitly on economic and security concerns and implicitly on racial and cultural ones. While Trump has been the most acerbic, the matter of undocumented immigrants and Syrian refugees animated many of his fellow Republican primary candidates in 2015–16 who depicted Latinos, Arabs and Muslims as an economic and crime burden. Trump outmanoeuvred his competition using slippery language that at once stereotyped and offered plausible deniability of this. For instance, in June 2015 he declared, 'When Mexico sends its people, they're not sending their best. ... They're sending people that have lots of problems, and they're bringing those problems with us. They're bringing drugs. They're bringing crime. They're rapists. And some, I assume, are good people.' Within days of the predictable firestorm of outrage that followed, he bridled at the 'mainstream media's attempt to distort my comments regarding Mexico and its great people'.[9]

While Trump depicted Mexicans in the United States as menacing Americans through opportunistic small-scale crime, Muslims represented an endemic threat to national security because of an innate abhorrence of the United States. For this reason, on 7 December 2015 – timed to evoke the stealthy devastation of the Japanese surprise attack on Pearl Harbor seventy-four years earlier – he called 'for a total and complete shutdown of Muslims entering the United States until our country's representatives can figure out what is going on'. He stated,

> Without looking at the various polling data, it is obvious to anybody the hatred is beyond comprehension. Where this hatred comes from and why we will have to determine. Until we are able to determine and understand this problem and the dangerous threat it poses, our country cannot be the victims of horrendous attacks by people that believe only in Jihad, and have no sense of reason or respect for human life. If I win the election for President, we are going to Make America Great Again.[10]

After a vague and unlinked reference to well-regarded Pew Research polling, the statement cites and links to a poll from the Center for Security Policy. This organization, run by the professional Islamophobe Frank Gaffney, publishes polls and conclusions about Muslims that more highly esteemed research organizations largely contradict. The title of the Center's press release aptly communicates the gist of the supposed threat: 'Poll of U.S. Muslims reveals ominous levels of support for Islamic supremacists' doctrine of shariah, jihad.'[11]

Like his comment about the people 'Mexico sends', Trump's statement suggests that all Muslims are suspect for hating America and Americans while offering him enough room to manoeuvre towards nuance. After his spokeswoman stated that the travel ban would include Muslim American citizens currently abroad, Trump disagreed, and elsewhere spoke about having Muslim friends.[12]

On other occasions, Trump reasserted the supposed untrustworthiness of Muslim Americans. Following Omar Mateen's massacre of clubbers in Orlando, Florida, in June 2016, he declared, 'But the Muslims have to work with us. They have to work with us. They know what's going on. They know that he was bad. They knew the people in San Bernardino were bad. But you know what? They didn't turn them in. And you know what? We had death, and destruction.' He used the speech to pivot from a travel ban on all Muslims to one on those coming from 'areas of the world where there's a proven history of terrorism against the United States, Europe or our allies' and to differentiate those committed to 'radical Islam' from other Muslims.[13] Despite declarations by various law enforcement officials that Muslim Americans contribute significantly to the prevention of terrorism,[14] Trump describes a singular and uncooperative Muslim community that wilfully hid their supposed knowledge of these attackers' plans.

Occasional mollifying comments notwithstanding, Trump used his June speech to underline the 'Otherness' of Muslim Americans and 'their children' relative to 'our children'. He claimed,

> Altogether, under the Clinton plan, you'd be admitting hundreds of thousands of refugees from the Middle East with no system to vet them, or to prevent the radicalization of the children and their children. Not only their children, by the way, they're trying to take over our children and convince them how wonderful ISIS is and how wonderful Islam is and we don't know what's happening.

Using innuendo, the candidate reinforced Muslim non-Americanness with comments that elided Muslims as among other American victims of terrorist violence: 'I refuse to allow America to become a place where gay people, Christian people, Jewish people are targets of persecution and intimation by radical Islamic preachers of hate and violence.'[15] Throughout this and other speeches, Trump mentioned Muslims primarily as terrorists or enablers of violence, while he also ridiculed President Obama's claim that Muslim Americans include sport heroes. 'Obama said in his speech that Muslims are our sports heroes. What sport is he talking about, and who?', the candidate tweeted, despite having met Muhammad Ali.[16] Instead, he refused to retract his debunked claim that he saw New Jersey Muslims celebrating the carnage on 11 September 2001.

Overall, Trump – like other Republican presidential hopefuls such as Ben Carson and Ted Cruz – simultaneously projected Muslims as questionably American because of failures to assimilate and participate constructively in mainstream society. This leaves them with dangerous levels of hatred of the United States, which at the least lead to an unwillingness to break ranks and cooperate with law enforcement and at the worst create a Muslim collective in which terrorists prove indistinguishable from others. Yet, once again, this has a historical precedent.

Migration, non-assimilation and violence proved triple motivators of Protestant suspicions towards Catholics in New England and the mid-Atlantic states beginning in the 1820s and continuing for the following three decades. Anti-Catholic attitudes from Britain – cultivated during the era of 'Blood Mary' Tudor and Guy Fawkes's Gunpowder Plot against Parliament – pervaded many English colonies. During the Revolution Catholics found themselves suspected by patriots of being pro-English, because of an assumed preference for absolutism, and by loyalists as anti-English, because of a presumed affinity for Britain's Catholic French enemy. The support of so many for the rebellion won much good will, until the vast surge of immigration that began in the 1820s brought millions of newcomers, most of whom were Irish and German, and Catholic. Simultaneously, the opening of the American West created population shifts of long-standing Protestant families away from the East Coast, thus creating an economic downturn that threatened many of those remaining. In parts of New England, this emigration helped push the faltering previous Puritan order into a final decline, leaving many feeling disoriented and foundationless. In cities like Boston and Philadelphia, the Protestant majority conjured stereotypes of the Irish based on what they heard from English sources. These often described Catholic Ireland as filled by lazy drunks whose diminished mental and physical abilities doomed them to perpetual poverty. Suspicion of them deepened as a confident nationalism soared. Americanness became increasingly sharply defined, especially in contrast with the 'Old World' of Europe. Self-defined natives increasingly viewed European émigrés as a non-American, un-assimilable threat.

In Philadelphia, these tensions conspired to generate a riot that proved nothing less than devastating, even judged by the violent standards of this era before publicly appointed police forces. In 1842, the Catholic bishop of the city challenged its Protestant normativity when he petitioned the Board of Controllers to allow Catholic students an alternative to the King James Bible used in the public schools. When they denied the request, he won an allowance for Catholic students to leave the classroom during these lessons, including when teachers taught from textbooks with anti-Catholic messages. However, when a Catholic politician convinced one teacher to stop teaching the Bible entirely, many nativist Protestants reacted severely to the supposed Catholic effort to end all Bible education, which they viewed as leading to godlessness and a prime opportunity for the pope to assert himself in America. Protestants organized a rally in the predominantly Irish American Kensington neighbourhood in May 1844, which soon spiralled out of control with homes burning, churches attacked, snipers shooting and eventually two naval cannon from the local naval station brought to bear (though fortunately neither was fired).

For many of the Protestant nativists who viewed the United States as fundamentally Christian, Irish Catholics represented a corrupt Church, one that might not even count as Christian and, thus, American. Moreover, they seemed unwilling or unable to fit their new country's expectations of assimilation. In response to their displacement from Ireland and marginalization in the United States, many newly arrived Irish established exclusive organizations, militias, fire departments, hospitals, schools and pubs. Some Protestant Americans viewed this as an assertion of self-imposed difference among a community already suspect because of their association with an icon of undemocratic rule and superstition – the Pope.

Six decades later, another massive wave of immigration began to arrive on the East Coast, bearing large Jewish populations in particular. While Jews had lived in most of the English American colonies and smaller migrations of German and other Western European Jews preceded this period, the new immigrants increasingly hailed from Eastern Europe. The growth of America's Jewish population expanded from 200,000 in 1870 to a million by 1900.[17] Partly in reaction to these changing demographics, as well as from concerns about increasing Catholic and black American prominence in society, a second iteration of the Ku Klux Klan (KKK) emerged. In contrast with the mostly Southern range of its original version, which emerged following the Civil War in order to intimidate newly freed blacks, the new Klan found eager members nearly everywhere from New York to California. Propelled by fears of Bolsheviks and diminishing Protestant values, the KKK grew to as large as perhaps four million members by 1925 when 40,000 of them marched in full white-robed regalia along Pennsylvania Avenue in Washington, D.C. with the US Capitol Building as their backdrop.[18] They represented a new nativism.

Confronting the triple threat of blacks, Catholics and Jews, the Klan leadership set about publicizing their concerns through lectures, sermons and publications. Their successful membership drives ensured an influential collection of ministers, orators, authors and newspaper publishers. While attitudes towards Jews varied and allegations against them shifted, one potent theme emerged – especially after the First World War – of Jews as not truly American because they belonged to an international web of Jewish finance that had no patriotic impulse. However, the impoverished condition of many Jewish émigrés newly settled into crowded urban districts convinced other nativists of the degraded and inward-gazing quality of Jews. In either case, Jews were viewed as potentially un-assimilable and historically uninterested in helping develop the nation beyond their own narrow interests that led them towards 'money mongering'.

Another nativist voice worth noting is Henry Ford, the industrialist. Piqued by what he viewed as Jewish interference with a peace mission to the First World War stricken Europe, he committed himself and his resources to warning Americans about these 'world controllers' who operated through international finance. As a capitalist, Ford distinguished his financial ambitions from those of his stereotypical Jew by asserting his interest in benefiting the nation through, for instance, lower production costs, in which Jews supposedly demonstrated no interest. Instead, they acted as a 'super-nationality' that controlled a 'super-government' transcending – and not committed to – the borders of any one nation. Purchasing the *Dearborn Independent*, he publicized his views in nearly 100 essays to a rapidly expanding readership that appeared to value them, including the notion that anti-Semitism was 'instinctive' on the part of other races who sensed the innate threat Jews purportedly posed. He wrote, 'It is probably true that the commonest real cause of anti-Semitism is the action of the international Jew' and that this did not have to do with religion.[19] Ten million Americans bought copies of the book in which he assembled his collected essays, *The International Jew: The World's Foremost Problem*, which essentially recapitulated the arguments of the nefariously anti-Semitic 'Protocols of the Elders of Zion'.[20]

Given the decline in Jewish immigration to the United States since the last decades of the twentieth century, one would not suspect that anti-Semitic sentiment has much of a nativist inflection. Nevertheless, it remains notable that various Jewish organizations have alleged that Trump's campaign engaged in and/or enabled implicit and explicit anti-Semitic behaviour, which often projects an international financial conspiracy to work against American self-interests. The foremost Jewish American organization tracking anti-Semitism, the Anti-Defamation League, noted both that many of those harassing Jewish journalists were self-identified Trump supporters and that 'whether intentional or not, the images and rhetoric in [Trump's final campaign] ad touch on subjects that anti-Semites have used for ages'.[21] In this televised advertisement the candidate warned of 'global financial powers' and a 'global power structure', while images of three prominent Jewish financiers flashed by. In other instances, Trump warned of 'blood suckers' supporting international trade and one of his tweets depicted a Star of David atop a pile of cash.[22] In keeping with the dual themes Franklin espoused two centuries earlier, but relying on innuendo rather than explication, Trump's campaign depicted an alien, un-assimilable force threatening America.

Turning from this theme of aloofness and the inability to be assimilated to the reasons that nativists use to explain this, race emerges as a crucial factor. For instance, one recurring theme of modern anti-Semitism is the racial distinctiveness of Jews. This has been a double-edged sword. On the one hand, nativists have alleged that Jews hold themselves apart and resist genetic assimilation. On the other, some have promoted miscegenation rules to avoid diluting the 'pure stock' of true Americans. As the scholar Sherman Jackson has observed, 'There are ... – at least two – racially authentic Americans': whites and blacks. Whiteness serves as the norm, so that blackness reflects subordination, if not inferiority, to whiteness, yet is authentic Americanness nevertheless. Jackson notes that Jews' racial relationship with America has been mixed, having occasionally been granted 'honorary white' status.[23] The KKK's second imperial wizard for the twentieth century, Hiram W. Evans, reflected this ambivalence when he changed his earlier position that all Jews were Semites by distinguishing between 'Western Jews', who could contribute to the nation of their habitation (but should not for fear of diluting true Americans' 'Nordic stock'), and Ashkenazi or 'Eastern Jews', who were 'Judaized Mongols' and largely unable to assimilate.[24] For many non-Jewish white Americans, their Aryan racial identity contrasted absolutely with Jews' Semitism.

Jackson charges that, in contrast with Jews whose European experiences made them sensitive to and able to respond to racial profiling, Muslims whose families more recently landed in the United States (that is to say, they are not blacks descended from American slaves) arrive and live with an ideology of Islamic racial disinterest. In his autobiography, Malcolm X describes his own experience with this attitude during the hajj. Meanwhile, many Arab and South Asian heritage Muslims refuse a black racial identity, recognizing the stigma attached to it. Unsurprisingly, therefore, according to a Pew Research Center poll, 80 per cent of American Muslims of Middle Eastern and North African descent describe themselves as white, and 91 per cent of Pakistani heritage

Muslims describe themselves as Asian.[25] This makes most Muslims unable to engage constructively with the polarizations of American racism by embracing a black identity and at least garnering historically minded sympathies for white American injustice to black Americans. However, white Americans determine them as neither white nor black and, therefore, never authentically American (and hence forever suspect).[26]

Although 'race' had not yet coalesced into the genetically defined term used in the United States today, phenotypical stereotypes regarding Irish Catholics nevertheless proved prevalent. Early nineteenth-century political cartoons and verbal descriptions often portrayed them as ape-like: dishevelled, with hunched backs and protruding mouths. By the time biological racism matured mid-century, portrayals most often depicted Irish Catholics as having more in common with stereotypical Africans than northern Europeans. This paired somewhat with their depiction as dirty, lazy and superstitious.

Also prevalent in nativist discourse regarding the reasons for a group's inability or unwillingness to assimilate is the assertion that they hold values contrary to or incompatible with those of true Americans. It is here that the connections between anti-Muslim sentiments and Islamophobia, anti-Catholic attitudes and anti-Catholicism, and anti-Semitism and anti-Judaism become most apparent.

Immigrant and nativist religions

Recent scholarship has considered how states and societies work to shape particular forms of religious subjectivities among their citizens that hew to hegemonic norms.[27] However, nativist sentiment rejects the possibility that the differences that make a specific religious group appear constantly maladjusted and therefore foreign can ever be ameliorated. The prohibition by French legislation of Muslim women wearing head coverings in public schools provides one of the most telling examples of this social disciplining. Based on a concept of *laïcité* inflected with a Catholic normativity, the 2004 ban on 'ostentatious' religious symbols aimed to force Muslim women to eschew markers of religious difference from their bodies at a time when the growing Muslim population also began to assert public dissatisfaction with the economic and social marginalization many suffered. Significantly, law makers saw no need to discipline Christians in their self-decorative use of crosses. Unsurprisingly, the rising fortunes of the right-wing Republican and National Front parties threaten to further erode French commitments to multiculturalism. For instance, the 2017 Republican Party candidate François Fillon declared both that Islam represents a problem for the nation and that France must protect its identity, traditions and language.[28] Anthropologist Mayanthi Fernando has argued that religious communities in France have had to fashion their religious beliefs, practices and sentiments into a recognizable and acceptable 'religion' that coheres to a French norm of appropriateness.

In many countries, arguments about the acceptability of particular religions use the treatment of women as a litmus test. This is perhaps predictable in the United States, given patriarchal sensitivities that more often lead to criticizing marginalized 'Others' than to self-reflection among mainstream groups. Just such a situation unleashed the anti-Catholic and anti-Catholicism sentiment boiling in Boston during the 1830s. Tensions between recently arrived Irish and native Yankees regarding competing ethnic-specific taverns, schools and organizations erupted into violence when news spread in 1834 of a nun forced back into a girls' convent school in Charlestown from which she supposedly (but not actually) had escaped. Already primed by risqué bestselling publications about the secret degradations inflicted on nuns and female students by rapacious priests and bishops, this newsflash fuelled a conflagration. A mob burned the convent school, and the (Protestant) students and nuns escaped with their lives. Meanwhile, in the next century, the KKK promoted themselves as the protectors of 'pure womanhood'. Although most blacks and Jews were American-born, Klan nativists viewed their role as maintaining the racial purity of white American women, which was threatened by these inferior races, demonstrating a critical innovation from the previous century in protective patriarchal perspectives.

Returning to the twenty-first century, Republican presidential candidate Donald Trump gave voice to a prevalent Islamophobic trope regarding the supposed Islamic justification for the oppression of Muslim women when he suggested why Gold Star mother Ghazala Khan stood silently at the side of her husband at the Democratic National Convention as he spoke of losing their son, a soldier killed in combat in Iraq. 'If you look at his wife, she was standing there. She had nothing to say. She probably – maybe she wasn't allowed to have anything to say. You tell me,' he told an interviewer. (Khan then explained that she could not speak because of the pain she still felt.[29])

Trump and other Republican candidates have used the protection of women as a core reason to alert Americans to the 'sharia-ization' of the US judicial system. In part quoting the suspect research of Frank Gaffney, mentioned earlier, he claimed in 2015,

> [Muslims] want to change your religion, I don't think so. I don't think so. I don't think so. It's not going to happen. As part of the global jihad and 51 per cent of those polled, agreed that Muslims in America should have the choice of being governed according to Shariah. [more booing] You know what Shariah is? Fifty-one percent. Shariah authorizes such atrocities as murder against non-believers who won't convert, beheadings and more unthinkable acts that pose great harm to Americans, especially, especially women, I mean if you look, especially women. Tough stuff.[30]

In a few short minutes, Trump rolled fears of murder, misogyny, religious law and forced conversion into a singular bundle stamped 'Muslim' and inherently defined by 'Islam'. Simultaneously, his comment about proselytization projected a presumed religiosity onto his audience – '*They* want to change *your* religion' (my emphasis) – which excluded the possibility that any of that audience identified as American Muslims (or atheists or agnostics). In light of Trump's other comments, he clearly meant to affirm a Christian or Jewish norm for his audience while sowing a sense of threat. In doing this, Trump joined a number of current and earlier Republican presidential contenders in imagining a simultaneously secular and 'Judaeo-Christian' norm for America.

In this campaign cycle other candidates reiterated this double threat that Muslims purportedly represent. After stating that he would not support a Muslim president, erstwhile candidate Ben Carson was asked whether Islam is consistent with the Constitution. Carson replied, 'No, I don't – I do not'.[31] Later, he added that a 'shariah-adherent' Muslim would have to be 'schizophrenic' to be loyal to the Constitution in order to reconcile that with her or his innate loyalty to sharia law.[32] Meanwhile, Carson's wife, Candy, publicly disapproved of the overall tenor of Trump's campaign by stating, 'Our country was based on Judeo-Christian values, treating each other with respect and that sort of thing.'[33] These comments represent the latest in a trend in politics (or, at least, Republican politics) that, since 2008, has increasingly used defence against Muslims and Islam as a rallying point for candidates in ways that naturalize American secularism as inherently defined by 'Judaeo-Christian' values. In other words, Muslims and Islam have served as useful foils to negatively define the United States in a manner that ameliorates the seeming paradox of qualifying the United States as essentially 'Judaeo-Christian' *and* secular.

The anthropologist Talal Asad explains that, for many Westerners, 'the secular myth uses the element of violence to connect an optimistic project of universal empowerment with a pessimistic account of human motivation in which inertia and incorrigibility figure prominently'.[34] It is notable that Muslims have often represented such inertia and incorrigibility for many Europeans due to their Islamic resistance to religious conversion. The blood libels and other scandals historically committed by Christians against Jews demonstrate repeatedly that Jews have often found themselves, too, among incorrigibles in Christian European minds: a problem Nazis sought to overcome with their 'final solution'. All these stereotypical manifestations of the intractable Jew and prejudiced Muslim have long served as foils in fashioning and reaffirming a Western – and specifically American – 'civilization'.

Despite the historical marginalization of American Jews, since the Holocaust the public has increasingly embraced the notion that theirs is a 'Judaeo-Christian' civilization, defined in part by the shared heritage and values mentioned by Candy Carson. One senses that for the American majority this represents less an *expansion* of Christian hegemony to embrace Jewish values – such as keeping kosher or *Tikkun olam* ('repairing the world') – and more an inclusionary secular and civilizational *rhetoric* predicated on the long-standing Christian theological stance that Jews reflect the *roots* of the now-perfected Christian faith. However, for many conservative Christians, Judaism remains an eternal stumbling block to acceptance as well as salvation. In other words, American Christians could feel comfortable expanding their sense of American civilizational identity to include a hyphenated Jewish quality because of the unavoidably Jewish heritage of their religion. Undoubtedly wise to the Christocentric nature of this inclusivity, many Jews nevertheless have welcomed the Judaeo-Christian formulation of American civilization as a flawed yet helpful step towards mainstream acceptance.

Muslims, due to their commitment to Islam, are yet to see – or are they likely to see soon – a more expansive formulation of the United States as an 'Abrahamic civilization'. Whereas even Christians expressing the most belligerence towards Jews must admit the precedence of the 'Old Testament' and God's covenant with the Jews, no Christian theology relies upon acknowledging the authenticity of Islamic traditions. Moreover, as Asad remarks, formulations of European civilization – from which most American civilizational models still take their start – systematically elide mention of the historical presence of Muslims in Europe (such as in Moorish Spain and central Europe) and overlook their shared Hellenic intellectual roots. The resulting projection of Islam as a civilization in natural juxtaposition or even essential conflict with European civilization,[35] popular among nativists, finds no better expression than in the title of Samuel Huntington's famous book, *The Clash of Civilizations*. Meanwhile, another vein of thought argues that Islam does not represent a religion at all and warrants no treatment or protection as such. Lieutenant General Michael Flynn, a top Trump security advisor, said, 'I don't see Islam as a religion. I see it as a political ideology.' Many other Americans concur.[36]

The ubiquity of this perceived tension and the difference in fortunes between American Jews and Muslims is evident in recent polls. A 2015 Gallup poll asking which identities voters would accept or reject among presidential candidates found 93 per cent of respondents would vote for a Catholic candidate and 91 per cent for a Jewish one, but 60 per cent would vote for a candidate who was Muslim, that is, only two points above an atheist – an identity traditionally little trusted by the electorate yet one that has gained significantly in this regard over the past decade, while antipathy towards a Muslim candidate has remained steady.[37] Meanwhile, Pew polling over the past decade has demonstrated a decline in favourable views of Islam. Relative to other religions, Americans increasingly view Islam as more likely to encourage violence. These numbers are particularly high among Republicans. Underlining the yawning disparity between 'Islamic' and 'American' civilizations, a 2015 Public Religion Research Institute poll found that a majority of Americans viewed Islamic values as at odds with American values and way of life.[38] This appears to reflect the 'they hate us because we're free' mentality enunciated by George W. Bush in regard to militant Muslims, but viewed by many Americans as applicable to *all* Muslims.

The role of Muslims and Islam as long-standing foils to legitimate a Judaeo-Christian secular vision seems most convincing for explaining this and other asymmetries in perspective. For instance, although a 2006 poll found one-third of Americans thought that the Bible should have more influence on US laws than the will of the people,[39] such findings tend not to be reported by the news media, which often treats Judaism and Christianity as 'modernized' religious traditions that have adapted to secular environments. News outlets seldom treat Islam similarly. As a result of an organized campaign by law makers and professional Islamophobes like David Yerushalmi, at least thirty-two states have or are considering legislation that would prohibit the use of 'foreign laws' in courts, a cryptic reference to sharia. (Of course, the use of the term 'foreign' as a synonym for 'Islamic' is telling of the nativist dimension of Islamophobia.[40])

These Islamophobic fears of Muslims influencing or controlling American law courts and politics were presaged in previous centuries by fears of papal influence. Even in the colonial era, anti-Catholicism imported from England portrayed the pope as the grand schemer who used his Jesuit army to infiltrate and influence European courts. The advent of major migrations of Catholics exacerbated those fears in the nineteenth century. Roman Catholic schools and colleges sparked fears of foreign money helping to influence youngsters to convert and follow papal political diktats, as the burning of the Charlestown convent demonstrated all too readily. Although Catholics as individuals may have gradually met with more acceptance as the century wore on – and fiercely anti-Irish Boston became synonymous with Irish American pride – Catholicism remained suspect of Vatican subterfuge. After the Catholic identity of presidential candidate Al Smith in the 1920s contributed to the failure of his campaign, John F. Kennedy in 1960 felt compelled to make a public pledge before a meeting of Protestant ministers that 'the separation of church and state is absolute'. He remains the only Catholic US president in a nation in which the Roman Catholic Church is the largest and the population is 25 per cent Catholic.

However, Trump's personalized allegations against President Obama – a self-identified Christian – demonstrate that, despite some similarities, Islamophobia differs significantly from anti-Catholicism among nativists. These allegations include 'birther' claims that Obama is not American-born (as made by Trump and others at the start of the Obama presidency) and accusations that Obama is a covert Muslim schooled entirely in a madrasa. While popular assertions that the president isn't 'really black' because of his white mother are not connected with efforts to impugn Obama's Americanness, his relation to a Muslim grandfather is used to disqualify him. Obama, the fictive Muslim, represents the racial, civilizational and religious tensions within American secularity and evidences how secularism involves far more than simply public and state restrictions regarding religion, and the role of Islamophobia in affirming both American secularism and its supposed Judaeo-Christian quality.

Conclusion

Many Americans appeared nothing less than shell-shocked by the results of the 2016 presidential contest. Having what veterans have described as a 'thousand-yard stare' – their eyes fixed on no apparent point – these voters could not imagine that the religious bigotry, racial stereotyping and sexist language would not have repelled more of their fellow citizens than it obviously did. I would hazard to say that most Americans could not believe – or did not want to believe – that the nativist antagonisms and suspicions so prevalently aimed at Catholics and Jews (among others) in the past could have much currency today. Ennobled by a national progressivist teleology, these Americans acknowledge the sins of their predecessors and through that recognition they participate in a celebration of collective improvement. Despite the evident differences in nativist sentiments across the decades and centuries, some of their constitutive impulses have proved enduring. Among the shared dynamics of these various nativist moments, the different yet not distinct realms of antipathy towards specific religions and particular communities remain salient in this period of sustained Islamophobia and anti-Muslim sentiment.

Neither Islamophobia nor nativism is new to American history and, indeed, both can be traced at least as far back as the founding of the sovereign nation state, if not farther. Nativists in the nineteenth and early twentieth century commonly alleged that immigrant Jews and Catholics would promote the involvement of foreign powers in American politics. Although anti-Catholic and, particularly, anti-Semitic sentiments continue to exist, the expansion of a previously Protestant-defined cultural hegemony to include Jews and Catholics in a 'Judaeo-Christian' paradigm – even if only rhetorically – is significant. This would appear to be good news for Muslims too, at least according to the progressivist myth that immigrants are pushed up a ladder of escalating inclusion as more recently arrived groups take their place, facing the brunt of discrimination and persecution in society at large. Irish Catholics, Italian Catholics and Eastern European Jews are offered as evidence for the eventual acceptance of all groups.

However, no broadly accepted 'Abrahamic' paradigm has emerged that would allow the inclusion of Muslims, who are increasingly viewed unfavourably by other Americans, particularly many Republicans. I would argue that American Muslims face steeper challenges in overcoming existing nativism because of the particular form of secularity in the United States and the unusual position Muslims inhabit theologically and physically in the American landscape. In short, the condition of Muslims as racially and religiously suspect has not been mitigated, as it has been for Jews since the Second World War, owing to the Judaeo-Christian notion informing American secularity.

Notes

1. José Casanova, 'The politics of nativism: Islam in Europe, Catholicism in the United States', *Philosophy and Social Criticism* 38/4–5 (2012), pp. 485–95; p. 493.
2. Stanley A. Cook, 'History of religions', *Journal of Theological Studies* 25/97 (1923), pp. 101–9; p. 101.
3. Runnymede Trust, *Islamophobia: A Challenge for Us All* (London: Commission on British Muslims and Islamophobia, The Runnymede Trust, 1997), p. 4.
4. Fred Halliday, *Islam and the Myth of Confrontation: Religion and Politics in the Middle East* (New York: I.B. Tauris, 1996), p. 160.
5. Peter Gottschalk and Gabriel F. Greenberg, *Islamophobia: Making Muslims the Enemy*, (Lanham, MD: Rowman and Littlefield, 2008), p. 5.
6. Tyler Anbinder, *Nativism and Slavery: The Northern Know Nothings and The Politics of the 1850s* (New York: Oxford University Press, 1992), p. xiv.
7. Tyler Anbinder, 'Nativism and prejudice against immigrants', in Reed Ueda (ed.), *A Companion to American Immigration* (Malden, MA: Blackwell, 2006), p. 177.
8. Carol L. Schmid, *The Politics of Language: Conflict, Identity, and Cultural Pluralism in Comparative Perspective* (New York: Oxford University Press, 2001), p. 15.
9. Tal Kopan, 'What Donald Trump has said about Mexico and vice versa', *CNN*, 31 August 2016. Available at www.cnn.com/2016/08/31/politics/donald-trump-mexico-statements/ (accessed 20 December 2016).
10. 'Donald J. Trump statement on preventing Muslim immigration', *Donald J. Trump*, 7 December 2015. Previously available at www.donaldjtrump.com/press-releases/donald-j.-trump-statement-on-preventing-muslim-immigration (accessed 20 December 2016) [link no longer working]. For an account of the subsequent removal of this statement from Trump's campaign website, see Christine Wang, 'Trump website takes down Muslim ban statement after reporter grills Spicer in briefing', *CNBC*, 8 May 2017. Available at https://www.cnbc.com/2017/05/08/trump-website-takes-down-muslim-ban-statement-after-reporter-grills-spicer-in-briefing.html (accessed 2 July 2018).
11. 'Poll of U.S. Muslims reveals ominous levels of support for Islamic supremacists' doctrine of shariah, jihad', *Center for Security Policy*, 23 June 2015. Available at www.centerforsecuritypolicy.org/2015/06/23/nationwide-poll-of-us-muslims-shows-thousands-support-shariah-jihad/ (accessed 20 December 2016).
12. Ben Kamisar, 'Trump calls for "shutdown" of Muslims entering US', *The Hill*, 7 December 2015. Available at http://thehill.com/blogs/ballot-box/presidential-races/262348-trump-calls-for-shutdown-of-muslims-entering-us (accessed 20 December 2016).
13. Ryan Teague Beckwith, 'Read Donald Trump's speech on the Orlando shooting', *Time*, 13 June 2016. Available at http://time.com/4367120/orlando-shooting-donald-trump-transcript/ (accessed 20 December 2016).

14 Kristina Cooke and Joseph Ax, 'U.S. officials say American Muslims do report extremist threats', *Reuters*, 16 June 2016. Available at www.reuters.com/article/us-florida-shooting-cooperation-idUSKCN0Z213U (accessed 20 December 2016).
15 Beckwith, 'Read Donald Trump's speech'.
16 Meg Wagner, 'Donald Trump pays tribute to Muhammad Ali after declaring there are no Muslim American sports heroes', *New York Daily News*, 4 June 2016. Available at www.nydailynews.com/sports/more-sports/trump-mourns-muhammad-ali-denied-muslim-athletes-existence-article-1.2661074 (accessed 20 December 2016).
17 Eric L. Goldstein, *The Price of Whiteness: Jews, Race, and American Identity* (Princeton, NJ: Princeton University Press, 2006), pp. 19–21, 35, 126–7.
18 Thomas R. Pegram, *One Hundred Percent American: The Rebirth and Decline of the Ku Klux Klan in the 1920s* (Lanham, MD: Ivan R. Lee, 2011), p. 185.
19 Henry Ford, *The International Jew: The World's Foremost Problem* (Dearborn, MI: Dearborn Pub. Co., 1920), pp. 9, 10, 12, 21–4, 28, 30, 36–7, 47–9.
20 Robert Michael, *A Concise History of American Antisemitism* (Lanham, MD: Rowman and Littlefield, 2005), p. 139.
21 Jonathan Greenblatt, quoted in Anti-Defamation League, Twitter Post, 6 November 2016, 7.40 am. Available at https://twitter.com/adl_national/status/795289665809088512 (accessed 21 December 2016).
22 Elise Foley, 'Anti-hate group condemns Donald Trump's closing ad', *Huffington Post*, 6 November 2016. Available at www.huffingtonpost.com/entry/anti-defamation-league-donald-trump_us_581f6a6ce4b0aac624850cbf (accessed 21 December 2016).
23 Sherman Jackson, 'Muslims, Islam(s), race, and American Islamophobia', in John Esposito and Ibrahim Kalin (eds), *Islamophobia: The Challenge of Pluralism in the 21st Century* (New York: Oxford University Press, 2011), pp. 93–106; pp. 95–8.
24 H. W. Evans, 'The Klan's fight for Americanism', *North American Review* 223/830 (1926), pp. 33–63; pp. 40–1, 60.
25 'Muslim Americans: No signs of growth in alienation or support for extremism', *Pew Research Center*, 30 August 2011, p. 16. Available at www.people-press.org/2011/08/30/muslim-americans-no-signs-of-growth-in-alienation-or-support-for-extremism/ (accessed 1 May 2018).
26 Jackson, 'Muslims, Islam(s), race', pp. 100–2.
27 Saba Mahmood, *Politics of Piety: The Islamic Revival and the Feminist Subject* (Princeton, NJ: Princeton University Press, 2011); Sherine Hafez, *An Islam of Her Own: Reconsidering Religion and Secularism in Women's Islamic Movements* (New York: New York University Press, 2011).
28 Agence France-Presse in Paris, 'Marine Le Pen: No free education for children of "illegal immigrants"', *Guardian*, 8 December 2016. Available at www.theguardian.

com/world/2016/dec/08/marine-le-pen-says-no-free-education-for-children-of-illegal-immigrants (accessed 21 December 2016).

29 Steve Turnham, 'Donald Trump to father of fallen soldier: "I've made a lot of sacrifices"', *ABC News*, 30 July 2016. Available at http://abcnews.go.com/Politics/donald-trump-father-fallen-soldier-ive-made-lot/story?id=41015051 (accessed 21 December 2016).

30 F. Brinley Bruton, 'Donald Trump attacks Muslims: "Islam hates us"', *NBC News*, 10 March 2016. Available at www.nbcnews.com/politics/2016-election/donald-trump-attacks-muslims-islam-hates-us-n535656 (accessed 27 March 2016).

31 Eric Bradner, 'Ben Carson: U.S. shouldn't elect a Muslim president', *CNN*, 21 September 2015. Available at www.cnn.com/2015/09/20/politics/ben-carson-muslim-president-2016/ (accessed 21 March 2016).

32 Michael Kaplan, 'Ben Carson: Muslims who support American values and Islamic law are "schizophrenic"', *International Business Times*, 16 February 2016. Available at www.ibtimes.com/ben-carson-muslims-who-support-american-values-islamic-law-are-schizophrenic-2309566 (accessed 21 March 2016).

33 Todd Beamon, 'Candy Carson: Trump comments not "Judeo-Christian," respectful', *Newsmax*, 17 February 2016. Available at www.newsmax.com/Newsmax-Tv/candy-carson-donald-trump-comments-not/2016/02/17/id/714875/#ixzz43YQ2om1d (accessed 1 May 2018).

34 Talal Asad, *Formations of the Secular: Christianity, Islam, Modernity* (Stanford, CA: Stanford University Press, 2003), p. 60.

35 Asad, *Formations of the Secular*, pp. 168–9.

36 Matthew Rosenberg and Maggie Haberman, 'Michael Flynn, anti-Islamist ex-general, offered security post, Trump aide says', *The New York Times*, 17 November 2016. Available at www.nytimes.com/2016/11/18/us/politics/michael-flynn-national-security-adviser-donald-trump.html (accessed 21 December 2016).

37 Justin McCarthy, 'In U.S., socialist presidential candidates least appealing', *Gallup*, 22 June 2015. Available at www.gallup.com/poll/183713/socialist-presidential-candidates-least-appealing.aspx (accessed 21 December 2016).

38 Betsy Cooper, Daniel Cox, Rachel Lienesch and Robert P. Jones, *Anxiety, Nostalgia, and Mistrust: Findings from the 2015 American Values Survey* (Washington, DC: Public Religion Research Institute, 2015).

39 'Many Americans uneasy with mix of religion and politics', *Pew Research Center*, 24 August 2006, p. 5. Available at www.pewforum.org/2006/08/24/many-americans-uneasy-with-mix-of-religion-and-politics/ (accessed 1 May 2018).

40 Kimberly Railey, 'More states move to ban foreign law in courts', *USA Today*, 4 August 2013. Available at www.usatoday.com/story/news/nation/2013/08/04/states-ban-foreign-law/2602511/ (accessed 1 May 2018).

Works cited

Agence France-Presse in Paris, 'Marine Le Pen: no free education for children of "illegal immigrants"', *Guardian*, 8 December 2016. Available at www.theguardian.com/world/2016/dec/08/marine-le-pen-says-no-free-education-for-children-of-illegal-immigrants (accessed 21 December 2016).

Anbinder, Tyler, 'Nativism and prejudice against immigrants', in Reed Ueda (ed.), *A Companion to American Immigration* (Malden, MA: Blackwell, 2006), pp. 177–201.

Anbinder, Tyler, *Nativism and Slavery: The Northern Know Nothings and The Politics of the 1850s* (New York: Oxford University Press, 1992).

Anti-Defamation League, Twitter Post, 6 November 2016, 7.40 am. Available at https://twitter.com/adl_national/status/795289665809088512 (accessed 21 December 2016).

Asad, Talal, *Formations of the Secular: Christianity, Islam, Modernity* (Stanford, CA: Stanford University Press, 2003).

Beamon, Todd, 'Candy Carson: Trump comments not "Judeo-Christian," respectful', *Newsmax*, 17 February 2016. Available at www.newsmax.com/Newsmax-Tv/candy-carson-donald-trump-comments-not/2016/02/17/id/714875/#ixzz43YQ2om1d (accessed 1 May 2018).

Beckwith, Ryan Teague, 'Read Donald Trump's speech on the Orlando shooting', *Time*, 13 June 2016. Available at http://time.com/4367120/orlando-shooting-donald-trump-transcript/ (accessed 20 December 2016).

Bradner, Eric, 'Ben Carson: U.S. shouldn't elect a Muslim president', *CNN*, 21 September 2015. Available at www.cnn.com/2015/09/20/politics/ben-carson-muslim-president-2016/ (accessed 21 March 2016).

Bruton, F. Brinley, 'Donald Trump attacks Muslims: "Islam hates us"', *NBC News*, 10 March 2016. Available at www.nbcnews.com/politics/2016-election/donald-trump-attacks-muslims-islam-hates-us-n535656 (accessed 27 March 2016).

Casanova, José, 'The politics of nativism: Islam in Europe, Catholicism in the United States', *Philosophy and Social Criticism* 38/4–5 (2012), pp. 485–95.

Center for Security Policy, 'Poll of U.S. Muslims reveals ominous levels of support for Islamic supremacists' doctrine of shariah, jihad', *Center for Security Policy*, 23 June 2015. Available at www.centerforsecuritypolicy.org/2015/06/23/nationwide-poll-of-us-muslims-shows-thousands-support-shariah-jihad/ (accessed 20 December 2016).

Cook, Stanley A., 'History of religions', *Journal of Theological Studies* 25/97 (1923), pp. 101–9.

Cooke, Kristina and Joseph Ax, 'U.S. officials say American Muslims do report extremist threats', *Reuters*, 16 June 2016. Available at www.reuters.com/article/us-florida-shooting-cooperation-idUSKCN0Z213U (accessed 20 December 2016).

Cooper, Betsy, Daniel Cox, Rachel Lienesch and Robert P. Jones, *Anxiety, Nostalgia, and Mistrust: Findings from the 2015 American Values Survey* (Washington, DC: Public Religion Research Institute, 2015).

Evans, H.W., 'The Klan's fight for Americanism', *North American Review* 223/830 (1926), pp. 33–63.

Foley, Elise, 'Anti-hate group condemns Donald Trump's closing ad', *Huffington Post*, 6 November 2016. Available at www.huffingtonpost.com/entry/anti-defamation-league-donald-trump_us_581f6a6ce4b0aac624850cbf (accessed 21 December 2016).

Ford, Henry *The International Jew: The World's Foremost Problem* (Dearborn, MI: Dearborn Pub. Co., 1920).

Goldstein, Eric L., *The Price of Whiteness: Jews, Race, and American Identity* (Princeton, NJ: Princeton University Press, 2006).

Gottschalk, Peter and Gabriel F. Greenberg, *Islamophobia: Making Muslims the Enemy* (Lanham, MD: Rowman and Littlefield, 2008).

Hafez, Sherine, *An Islam of Her Own: Reconsidering Religion and Secularism in Women's Islamic Movements* (New York: New York University Press, 2011).

Halliday, Fred, *Islam and the Myth of Confrontation: Religion and Politics in the Middle East* (New York: I.B. Tauris, 1996).

Jackson, Sherman, 'Muslims, Islam(s), race, and American Islamophobia', in John Esposito and Ibrahim Kalin (eds), *Islamophobia: The Challenge of Pluralism in the 21st Century* (New York: Oxford University Press, 2011), pp. 93–106.

Kamisar, Ben, 'Trump calls for "shutdown" of Muslims entering US', *The Hill*, 7 December 2015. Available at http://thehill.com/blogs/ballot-box/presidential-races/262348-trump-calls-for-shutdown-of-muslims-entering-us (accessed 20 December 2016).

Kaplan, Michael, 'Ben Carson: Muslims who support American values and Islamic law are "schizophrenic"', *International Business Times*, 16 February 2016. Available at www.ibtimes.com/ben-carson-muslims-who-support-american-values-islamic-law-are-schizophrenic-2309566 (accessed 21 March 2016).

Kopan, Tal, 'What Donald Trump has said about Mexico and vice versa', *CNN*, 31 August 2016. Available at www.cnn.com/2016/08/31/politics/donald-trump-mexico-statements/ (accessed 20 December 2016).

Mahmood, Saba, *Politics of Piety: The Islamic Revival and the Feminist Subject* (Princeton, NJ: Princeton University Press, 2011).

McCarthy, Justin, 'In U.S., socialist presidential candidates least appealing', *Gallup*, 22 June 2015. Available at www.gallup.com/poll/183713/socialist-presidential-candidates-least-appealing.aspx (accessed 21 December 2016).

Michael, Robert, *A Concise History of American Antisemitism* (Lanham, MD: Rowman and Littlefield, 2005).

Pegram, Thomas R., *One Hundred Percent American: The Rebirth and Decline of the Ku Klux Klan in the 1920s* (Lanham, MD: Ivan R. Lee, 2011).

Pew Research Center, 'Many Americans uneasy with mix of religion and politics', *Pew Research Center*, 24 August 2006, p. 5. Available at www.pewforum.org/2006/08/24/many-americans-uneasy-with-mix-of-religion-and-politics/ (accessed 1 May 2018).

Pew Research Center, 'Muslim Americans: No signs of growth in alienation or support for extremism', *Pew Research Center*, 30 August 2011, p. 16. Available at www.people-press.org/2011/08/30/muslim-americans-no-signs-of-growth-in-alienation-or-support-for-extremism/ (accessed 1 May 2018).

Railey, Kimberly, 'More states move to ban foreign law in courts', *USA Today*, 4 August 2013. Available at www.usatoday.com/story/news/nation/2013/08/04/states-ban-foreign-law/2602511/ (accessed 1 May 2018).

Rosenberg, Matthew and Maggie Haberman, 'Michael Flynn, anti-Islamist ex-general, offered security post, Trump aide says', *The New York Times*, 17 November 2016. Available at www.nytimes.com/2016/11/18/us/politics/michael-flynn-national-security-adviser-donald-trump.html (accessed 21 December 2016).

Runnymede Trust, *Islamophobia: A Challenge for Us All* (London: Commission on British Muslims and Islamophobia, The Runnymede Trust, 1997).

Schmid, Carol L., *The Politics of Language: Conflict, Identity, and Cultural Pluralism in Comparative Perspective* (New York: Oxford University Press, 2001).

Trump, Donald J., 'Donald J. Trump statement on preventing Muslim immigration', *Donald J. Trump*, 7 December 2015. Previously available at www.donaldjtrump.com/press-releases/donald-j.-trump-statement-on-preventing-muslim-immigration (accessed 20 December 2016) [link no longer working].

Turnham, Steve, 'Donald Trump to father of fallen soldier: "I've made a lot of sacrifices"', *ABC News*, 30 July 2016. Available at http://abcnews.go.com/Politics/donald-trump-father-fallen-soldier-ive-made-lot/story?id=41015051 (accessed 21 December 2016).

Wagner, Meg, 'Donald Trump pays tribute to Muhammad Ali after declaring there are no Muslim American sports heroes', *New York Daily News*, 4 June 2016. Available at www.nydailynews.com/sports/more-sports/trump-mourns-muhammad-ali-denied-muslim-athletes-existence-article-1.2661074 (accessed 20 December 2016).

Wang, Christine, 'Trump website takes down Muslim ban statement after reporter grills Spicer in briefing', *CNBC*, 8 May 2017. Available at https://www.cnbc.com/2017/05/08/trump-website-takes-down-muslim-ban-statement-after-reporter-grills-spicer-in-briefing.html (accessed 2 July 2018).

3

Islamophobia: The Muslim Problem? A Discussion between Dibyesh Anand, Myriam Francois and Jim Wolfreys

Chaired by Peter Morey

This discussion took place at the Bradford Literature Festival on 2 July 2017. Panellists Dibyesh Anand (DA), Myriam Francois (MF) and Jim Wolfreys (JW) considered the so-called Muslim Problem, setting Islamophobia in its various historical and national perspectives and arguing for its utility to governments otherwise unable to create consent for inequitable neoliberal politics. They analysed international differences and similarities in Islamophobia, the inconsistencies of liberalism's attitude to it, the rise of populist politicians and the role of the media in propagating Islamophobia, as well as what might be done to contest it.

* * *

PM: Why would you say Islamophobia seems to be on the increase? Is there a 'Muslim Problem' as such?

MF: I first off want to make a reference to the title, if that's ok. I want to ask the audience if they think that in another room, somewhere else in the Bradford Literary Festival, there might be a talk entitled 'The Jewish Problem' or 'The Christian Problem'. Just the title in itself speaks to a climate in which you can regard Muslims as a problem. You can discuss Muslims in all their variety, in all their socio-economic, ethnic and cultural diversity as one lump problem. And I think that is indicative of the level of Islamophobia we have reached in our society. The idea that we can talk about Muslims as a bulk, homogeneous, as if we all believe the same thing, we all subscribe to the exact same ideals and beliefs, and as if we all behave the same way.

Why is it on the increase? Well, obviously there are multiple reasons that are coming to a head at this time in history. One I think is to do with the changing nature of society. Post-mass immigration there is the idea of a more visible, a more vocal, confident minority, not just Muslims, who aren't necessarily feeling like they have to 'be invisible', that they have to bow to the norms of society because this *is* their society. They are also allowed to engage in conversation in terms of what national identity is or what British values are. I think there is an inherent reticence from the majority in accepting any concessions to that and there is a fightback, which we see within populist movements, but also in much of the mainstream press, which uses a form of supposedly more legitimate nationalism to assert that the voices of certain minorities are less acceptable as part of that conversation. So 'British values' have to be dictated by the government to Muslims as if Muslims aren't British and can't be part of that conversation.

And the second thing, obviously, is the broader political climate. The obvious one would be the post-9/11 world in which there is the reality of terrorism by people who claim to be acting as Muslims. As Muslims we grapple with that reality day-to-day: that there are people claiming to speak in our name and acting in ways that are inherently at odds with the ways in which the vast majority of us understand our faith. It is unrecognizable to most of us. And then there is also just the reality of international wars or foreign invasions that have led to the necessary normalization of the dehumanization of Muslims in order to justify violence against them abroad. And that discourse is important and normalized on our home territory as well.

DA: The way I see it, Islamophobia or Muslim-phobia – because it's largely a fear of Muslims rather than a fear of religion as such – in a sense is connected to various forms of prejudice that exist in societies around identity. It's quite casual. People say things like, 'Oh, the Muslims do this.' Sometimes Muslim-identifying individuals will use the same kind of internalized racism in language about themselves: 'This is what we do as Muslims.' It's quite common. I don't think people would come up with the 'Jewish Problem' or 'Christian Problem' in the same way, but this particular prejudice is rampant in various societies. There are various forms of identity-based prejudices and bigotry that occur. At the same time there is something peculiar about it. What's particularly dangerous is that it's quite convenient. Unlike other forms of prejudice and bigotry, it has become quite easy for the state to securitize on the basis of anti-Muslim prejudice.

So I would say this is the reason why it has become so prominent. It's not even the acts of a few people using faith for what they do, but more about why the military–security industry in various countries benefits from it. It is a very convenient tool for them. For instance, anti-Muslim racism has been used to strengthen not only the police and the surveillance industry but also to justify wars as well. I was thinking of the example of India. In the Indian context it's the other way round in a way; Muslims are 140 million people, that is 14 per cent of the population, but they have become less visible than ever. They are 'invisibilizing' themselves. They are not assertive and yet you have a rise in Hindu fascism scapegoating them. So we can't even say that it's the visibility of Muslims that is leading to it. I am sure there are different reasons in different parts of the world, but the commonality I find is that it is easy to securitize Muslims and demonize them. Conversely, at the same time there's also the tendency in some quarters to glorify them, as in Saudi Arabia. So it resolves itself into a good Muslim/bad Muslim paradigm, but there is an entire industry that benefits. Security and bureaucratic interests in different countries benefit from Muslim-phobia.

JW: There's a frequent refrain when politicians talk about responding to people's concerns, as if they're responding to something that just exists at large in society. I think that one of the features of Islamophobia is that it's been constructed from above quite consciously at the intersection of a number of different trajectories. One is the international situation, the 'War on Terror' that creates the notion of an enemy within, so society has to be vigilant because there are people who could become terrorists in the same way that 'reds under the bed' climate of suspicion functioned during the Cold War. That dovetails with problems that mainstream parties have in winning positive affiliation to their political agendas and that means there is an increased reliance on other solutions, especially authoritarianism. There is a greater reliance on the legal framework of the state rather than the representative framework, a greater reliance on policing and security.

So, for example, France, since the autumn of 2015, has been under a permanent state of emergency, boosting the multi-trillion dollar international security industry, but I think there's something else going on as well, which is that all this is happening at a time of rising inequality. So why is Islamophobia on the rise in France? On the one hand, politicians have created an environment where latent prejudices that people might hold that they don't feel able to express are given the green light by national, cross-party campaigns: 'The hijab is such a problem in schools, it's conflicting with our national values.' The niqab, halal meat, praying in the street, suddenly these things which are not particularly visible become very visible because everybody is talking about them all the time. So you construct a problem that gives the green light to street-level prejudice and it appears as though you're simply reflecting something that is happening in society at large. In the case of France, in a country where there are profound inequalities, huge disparities of wealth and income, that's a very convenient distraction. It's a way of blaming the people who are suffering the consequences of inequality for their own situation. 'It's because of your separatist values, it's because you want to hide yourselves away in the *banlieues*, in impoverished housing estates on the outskirts of town and eat your halal meat that you're in that situation.' It's turning things on their head, blaming the victim and appearing to respond to a concern in society at large that has instead been constructed from above.

PM: But there must be something that's changed in the centre of gravity of politics too. Previously, most politicians, barring a few – such as Enoch Powell in Britain, for example, or Jean-Marie Le Pen in France – were distancing themselves from racist rhetoric and views in the name of some liberal consensus, loosely speaking. Nowadays people with extreme views are much more often to be found in the mainstream. So what's happened to make that kind of racism respectable in that way. Something has shifted in the language of politics, hasn't it?

MF: I think something has shifted in the nature of liberalism certainly. The liberalism you refer to was a tool for the articulation of difference, whereas what we have now is so-called muscular liberalism, which is an imposition of an acceptance of things that are going to necessarily and inherently run contrary to the beliefs of certain communities including some religious communities, and one of the most visible instances of that will be Muslims.

I can give a very concrete example of the way in which I think liberalism is now an all-pervasive ideology. The former Liberal Party leader Tim Farron is an interesting example. Think, for a second, if tomorrow Sadiq Khan said he felt he had to resign as Mayor of London because his views as a Muslim might be in conflict with his work as a politician. Just think about how that information would be assessed and mediated, how that information might then make you feel about his beliefs as a Muslim. And now think about Tim Farron's decision to resign allegedly because of his Christian beliefs being in conflict with his position as leader of the Liberals. There's a double standard whereby certain views in the public sphere, socially conservative views, are seen as a form of dangerous extremism if you're a Muslim, but just a form of narrow-mindedness if you are from another community – which is why Tim Farron resigned without much controversy, whereas if he had been a Muslim you know the coverage would have been very different.

To come back to why Islamophobia is coming up as a more contentious issue now, one of the reasons is how multiculturalism as a solution to issues of difference was based on the idea that if we just respect each other's views we can all get along. What we've seen developing recently is a hardening critique of multiculturalism. Allegedly multiculturalism has failed – I'm not convinced – and what we 'need', in the official discourse, is a form of 'muscular liberalism', which is essentially the imposition of a set of views, defined primarily by government, onto all communities as an acceptable form of Britishness and that inherently creates an Othering, particularly for certain religious communities. When you tie that with other issues that we've discussed, it just aggravates matters.

JW: I don't think there ever was a golden era of multiculturalism. A particular form of society never just drops from the sky. It comes about as a result of conflict and struggle. And it took a long time in Britain, for example, to get to the stage that people are at now. It took the Brixton riots, the Tottenham riots, Stephen Lawrence: it took a whole series of very significant struggles for a lot of prejudice to be overcome. So I think when we talk of Islamophobia, there are commonalities between different countries in terms of the framework that they exist within but then there are specifics as well. Specific flashpoints, specific moral panics are created. One of the tendencies that takes a different form in different countries is the construction of Islamophobia as a progressive form of racism. So it can be presented as something where 'we need to be firm on this question because of our commitment to women's liberation or because of our commitment to gay rights'. This results in subjecting Muslims to a set of criteria that wouldn't apply to other people. To give an example, all the candidates in the presidential race in France agreed to participate in a debate with Marine Le Pen, who holds a number of bigoted views on a whole series of issues. But some of those people would also refuse to share a platform with Tariq Ramadan, the Oxford Professor of Islamic Studies, because of his views on x, y, z, subjects. They are sensationalized and put across in the media and people are asked, 'Do you agree with what Tariq Ramadan or his brother or his grandfather might have said about this?' Whereas Marine Le Pen, whose father is a man who carried out torture during the Algerian war of independence and was openly anti-Semitic, racist and homophobic as leader of the Front National, is not held to the same set of criteria. So part of the dynamic of Islamophobia is that people can hold Islamophobic views but present them as somehow liberal and progressive, which is a difference from other forms of racism.

PM: As well as a change in the nature of liberalism, might we point to the eclipse of other alternative visions of social and economic organization playing a role in all this? For example, in India perhaps the decline of that model of Nehruvian secularism, which was more of a socialist programme, might be a factor in the rise of Islamophobia there?

DA: It would be. In terms of the Indian context, yes. Broadly speaking the state is officially secular. The secular version of India was one which differentiated itself from this Western notion of the separation between the Church and the State, and emphasized that India was a *multi-religious* society. If the state, or state leader, has a priest, then they will get also an imam, they will also get a Christian priest, they will try to get everyone. So it was outwardly a multi-religious society, though the subtext and the subconscious of the state remained largely Hindu. But there has been a decline in that. There has been a decline in socialism and there has been a rise in Hindu right-wing nationalism or Hindu fascism, as I would call it, which now of course people call populism. So there has been a shift that Muslims in India have had no influence over. They have become a sort of a scapegoat within that. It's largely around how Hindu society has transformed itself, broadly speaking, from one that believed in some form of liberal secularism, at least officially, to one where they don't even believe in it officially. Nowadays they end up justifying all forms of Islamophobia, all forms of anti-Christian prejudice, all forms of anti-minoritarianism by saying, 'Oh, but we had Muslim presidents in the past, so we allow it. Look at the West, they don't even allow it.' That kind of thing.

But going back to what's specific and what's new, I was thinking of the ways in which maybe Islamophobia brings together different kinds of prejudices. So, for instance, what I hear from my Muslim-identified friends is that when they're stopped by the police in London they're not stopped because they look Muslim only, but they also look brown or black. So, in a sense, it brings together racism, along with anti-faith prejudice in secular societies, and a specific anti-Muslim and also anti-immigrant prejudice. These three things – anti-immigrantism, racism and Islamophobia – come together to constitute Muslims as *the* problem for the society. I wasn't in Britain in the 1960s and 1970s, but from what I've read society wasn't that great then in terms of very open prejudice against people with different skin colour. The kind of rhetoric that the British and the French Empires used of the civilizing mission – the notion that we have to save brown women from uncivilized brown men, that kind of thing – that was there. So I would see Islamophobia as a continuity. I would see it as a coming together of these pre-existing things, but what makes it more dangerous is it is connected to empire building, which is not that easy anymore.

PM: What about the kinds of political personality that have come to the fore to lead this front of Islamophobia at a national level? I'm thinking here of the supposed 'strong' leaders, these macho men with their swagger and their swank – the Modis, the Trumps and the Putins – and there are various others around the world (and some of them are Muslim, of course). Why have those kinds of figures emerged now? Why do these national 'hero' figures – with their cults of personality – arise?

DA: If we take Erdoğan in Turkey and Modi in India we can see some big similarities. First, they both use religion as a weapon. Second, they trade on a *majoritarian* form of religion. On top of that is the whole idea of them personally being strong men whose masculinity is constantly emphasized. They're very much selling a notion of masculinity that's devoted to the nation. And they always talk in national terms. It's a strange throwback in a way, when you think that nationalism is the ideology that's killed the most people in the last two hundred years at least. No ideology has killed as many people as nation statism. So what they are doing – Erdoğan, Trump, but also Putin, Modi and others – is combining certain forms of nationalism with certain dominant forms of identity, in this case the dominant religious identity.

Now, why are societies open to it? Well, in the Indian context, as some of you may know, in recent times there have been lynchings, mostly of Muslim men, but also occasionally of non-Muslims: dalits. Dalits are those who have been seen as untouchable from time immemorial and who are the targets of what we might call 'casteism'. Now this is something that is particular to India, Pakistan and other places, where 90 per cent of Muslims belong to these marginalized castes. So the discrimination against some of them is a double whammy. They are discriminated against because they are Muslims and they are also discriminated against by upper-caste Muslims because they are lower caste. It's a combination of both. In India Modi sold the dream that he is a strong Hindu nationalist, but that he's also going to bring growth and development of the top-down kind. So the economists and the mainstream media and the businesses, who would usually be uncomfortable with very open anti-minoritarianism, started praising him for being the leader who would liberate the economy. They started saying, 'Oh maybe his Hindu nationalism is secondary, he's going to be the modernizer, a reformer.' Well, we know that 'reformer', 'modernizer', these are neoliberal dominant terms. But what he has done of course is that he has played to these constituencies and he has made acceptable the kind of prejudices that were not acceptable in the past (at least in public).

Now Muslims are not politically organized in India because there's always the scar of Partition. It's Muslims who created Pakistan and, therefore, they have to be forever guilty for that. (In fact, of course, the

Muslims of India never created Pakistan, they're the ones who stayed in India.) Yet they face a covert combination of big business and the mainstream media, who essentially carry the same message. About Modi they tend to say something like 'he has allowed for the lynching of hundreds of Muslims, but that's fine; incremental genocide is ok as long as he's opened up the economy'.

PM: That relationship between nationalism and liberalism is an interesting one. Jim, did you have any thoughts on that and the hero figure?

JW: Yes, I think it comes back to the question of the crisis of politics that fuses with a crisis also of national identity. So, again, to take the example of France, I think the key figure in the twenty-first century in making racism respectable was Nicolas Sarkozy. There was a very interesting study conducted in a working-class area on the outskirts of Paris, one of the so-called *banlieues*, where resentment about immigrants coming and moving into the neighbourhood was discussed in terms of people's sense of social relegation or social decline being reflected back at them by the presence of immigrants. The study told the story of one of the area's residents who couldn't identify with Jean-Marie Le Pen because that would also reflect a sense of social relegation back at him: 'I've been reduced to this, I've been reduced to identifying with this marginal, openly racist organization with fascist roots.' But when Sarkozy said the same things as Le Pen, that made them more respectable. The same individual could feel comfortable with expressing his views in that way.

A bill was introduced in 2005 which initially contained a measure instructing schools to teach the benefits of French colonialism. The clash of civilizations isn't something new, it was very much alive in 1950s France and Algeria. And so the spectacle of a hyper-individualized, political elite that puts more and more emphasis on figures like Sarkozy or even Macron – where we see a cult of personality developing around an individual who barely has a party apparatus to back him up – is symptomatic of a crisis of representative democracy. The crisis of the state and democracy is also expressed via the rise of so-called populist figures using demagogic and xenophobic arguments. The state is no longer confident enough to deal with society as it really exists. It has to isolate sections of society in order to shore up its own power and does so often in terms that are almost at the point of caricature. For instance, one of Sarkozy's bugbears was that some municipal swimming pools were devoting separate timetables to women-only aquagym classes. And in some places this was blamed on Muslim women who were apparently attacking republican universalism by having separate swimming pool times. And so he would make speeches saying, 'On the territory of the Republic there will be no separate swimming pool timetables for women!' In his attempt to become the mainstream right presidential candidate in 2017 he talked about alternative menus in schools. Some schools serve pork without providing an alternative. Sarkozy made a speech saying, 'If people want an alternative to ham and chips, they will have to have a double portion of chips.' He said, 'That's the Republic!' If it has been reduced to that then Sarkozy is saying much more than the actual words he's speaking. This says more about the problems of political parties and political actors, and their inability to marshal support or positive affiliation to their ideas, than it does about the individuals and groups within society at large that are being targeted in this way. Nothing symbolizes the identity crisis of the republican state, its inferiority complex, better than Sarkozy walking the world stage in his two-inch stacked heels.

PM: What also seems to come through strongly here is some sort of crisis of masculinity. Is that fair to say?

MF: I wanted to complement something that Jim just said. Interestingly the women-only sessions that have been organized by the municipalities began with a group of 'heavy' older women who didn't feel comfortable swimming during regular swimming times and requested them for that reason. This, I would suggest, says a lot about sexism in France: that somehow if your body type doesn't conform to what a woman 'should look like', you should go and separate yourself off so that men don't have to be confronted with your possible rolls of fat. They can put theirs out, but you need to go and have yours hidden away! And I just thought that was an interesting sideline, which was obviously never brought out. The whole question was framed as if it was only Muslim women who might want to have women-only sessions. In this country you will also find that women say, 'I prefer to attend them. I want to go swimming, but I don't want to wonder if people are looking at me. I just want to go and do my swimming.' And I think, to come back slightly to multiculturalism, there was an era when people were just like 'fair enough'. Fair enough, you want a women-only section, whereas today everything is politicized through the lens of this 'Muslim Problem'.

Again, to come back to Sarkozy and the issue of France, in what world is Sarkozy's response of not wanting vegetarian options acceptable? There are now municipalities in France and mayors that have prohibited the schools that they control from serving vegetarian options. So the suggestion that children should eat a second portion of fries … I mean, the kids were delighted, by the way, the kids were happy with that, but should parents be happy with that, regardless of your faith? Are you happy that today, with all we know about diet, nutrition, health, concentration, that children are being fed a double portion of fries? And your objection is that Muslims get a vegetarian option? I mean, sometimes I look at the discussions and I really despair because I sort of think it really isn't up to Muslims to stand up at this point … it's really up to everyone else to point out the 'BS', because that's really what it is. I mean there's a certain point where it's just so absurd that it doesn't warrant Muslims saying, 'But we should be entitled to have an alternative option.' Enough! Just call it what it is.

But, to come back to the broader issue of Islamophobia, I wanted to bring in something about the crumbling post-empires because this applies really well, I think, to France, which has been grappling with its identity as a former colonial power. We have a glorified version of Empire in this country too. France is like here on acid, but you have it here too. You have it here when they sell tea as some sort of quaint colonial product. We even have it with holidays sold with messages like 'come along and see our beautiful colonial architecture'. I mean, if you were living under Empire that's not necessarily a selling point. But obviously it's going to make some people buy into it and that should raise questions about how we think about colonialism and Empire still as a society today. And then think about the dynamics of what happens when the descendants of our former colonial subjects are now part of 'us' and want to speak on equal terms. As a society we haven't really come to terms with our imperial past. The centres of empire haven't deconstructed the impact of thinking of ourselves as superior to the rest of the world for a very long time.

So it really isn't a surprise to me that there continues to be a level of arrogance vis-à-vis other cultures, which is then particularly acute when it comes to issues of religion, because Europe tends to pride itself – and France is sort of the prime example of this – as the heart of the Enlightenment. Secularism is then supposed to be the answer to all of the world's woes. Incidentally there are countries where there are ways to manage diversity other than secularism. I know this is a grand idea, but there are other ways of doing things than the way we do things. And I think that we continue to persist in what I regard as a form of cultural arrogance: that our way is the only way, and by our way I mean a way of looking at the world that is still rooted in a very white, secular, liberal (in an increasingly restricted sense) way. And that means that minorities are increasingly struggling to speak at an equal level with the rest of society. There might be a few concessions because broader society prides itself on being tolerant. And we could talk about what tolerant means as well because I think tolerance is also grounded in a form of arrogance: 'I'm up here but I will tolerate you down there.' How about you just regard me as an equal and we talk as equals. I'll tolerate you, you tolerate me!

PM: So many of the attitudes and incidents we have been discussing here come to us courtesy of the press and media. Do we need greater accountability for some of the things that are published? Is it a matter of tighter press regulation, better journalistic practices, press ownership or something else?

MF: Those of you that followed the Leveson enquiry into unethical press practices might know that there was a significant amount of public money spent, which, owing to government reluctance to legislate, essentially culminated in an unsatisfactory fudge. Basically, the Press Complaints Commission – which was a largely toothless organization that you could go to if you were maligned in the press – was replaced by another organization, the Independent Press Standards Office, that's more or less identical but just has a different name. So nothing has really changed at that level. But the main point that I would raise with regard to press regulation is that it is reactive. What happens is, if a false article goes out that says, for example, that one in five British Muslims support jihadis – as happened a while ago – the offending newspaper will be required to issue an apology. But these apologies tend to be issued in very small print on like page number six in a corner so people don't pick up on it in the way they pick up on the headline. And because it's reactive and inadequate it means that you can get away with having this headline out there for weeks and weeks with all the impact that it has in this current climate. Because of that climate there seems to be a massive resistance to providing proper redress for Muslims in particular, but not only Muslims. I mean you see these stories where immigrants and refugees are described like cockroaches, people who are on benefits are 'scroungers'. Poor people in general are talked about as a useless burden draining our society, which is so far removed from the reality of the fact that they are, by and large, the hardworking cogs that keep the wheels of society spinning.

But one issue I find in the media that impedes any discussion on how we could better regulate any conversation with Muslims is the fact that actually Islamophobia itself is a contested term. I have to regularly speak to people who say, 'Oh, I mean, it's not real, is it? It's just some legitimate criticism of Islam that Muslims don't want to hear and you just want to shut down debate by using the word Islamophobia.' And I actually think a lot of people would subscribe to this view and would be more or less willing to say it openly. The only thing I can say to that is Islamophobia is very real to people experiencing it and just because you haven't experienced it doesn't mean that it isn't real. And frankly the idea that Islamophobia is about shutting down discussion about Islam is probably the most egregious argument within that narrative, not least because I struggle to think about anything that we discuss more in the media. I mean, there's hardly a day when there isn't a headline, some sort of phantasmagorical line about Muslims wanting to eat your babies! There's just always something. So the idea that somehow this is used as a shield to stop people talking about Islam is outrageous.

There's a kind of doublespeak about it, as when, after the recent London and Manchester terror attacks, there was the right-wing terrorist attack on Finsbury Park mosque. A guy drove his van into people praying outside Finsbury Park, and it was described by several papers as a 'retaliatory attack'. How is it retaliatory? These are just regular people, your neighbours, your friends, your colleagues out praying. How is it retaliatory? But how many people picked that up? How many people bothered to write to the papers to complain about that? Language is important and it feeds then into a sense of Muslims feeling increasingly embattled, alone, scared: scared of acid attacks, scared of mosques being attacked, scared about their children being pulled aside in schools under the Prevent strategy for having said something that doesn't conform to the political narrative, whether they have strong views about the Palestinian situation or they want to start wearing a headscarf. There is a climate of fear and Muslims are living it day in and day out. There needs to be a point where that doesn't become just a struggle for Muslims, it needs to transcend that.

PM: Some people would say that that's the price we pay for a free press, though.

DA: I remember when the Finsbury Park thing happened, there was a Russian radio station that wanted to interview me and they kept asking, 'Do you think the government should exercise more control over the internet?' I thought, what is the connection there? They also asked me what impact it would have on Brexit negotiations. They emphasized, once again, more control, more surveillance, more regulation. I must say I'm very sceptical of that kind of argument because look at the history of the way surveillance has taken place. You have 9/11 and after that all these anti-globalization protests, of which many of us were part, got closed down. Society is now fixated on certain kinds of spectacular acts of violence. They think that is the main threat but all the while rights are being eroded, the public sector is being removed, neoliberalism – which is the most violent form of ideology that exists today – is becoming stronger. So my anxiety with this kind of rhetoric you hear – 'Let's be more secularist' – is that we have to trust the state or regulatory body to actually be interested in tackling the hate crime. Yes, I do think regulations are crucial, but a lot of regulations already exist. It's more about sensitizing people and, as you pointed out, getting the media or the people writing this stuff to take their responsibilities more seriously.

You also need to keep in mind the way these governments can be quite selective when it comes to dealing with minorities, and Muslims have been victims of this. I remember when I came to this country in the late 1990s, I'd keep hearing the term 'community leaders'. Now I don't like communities and I don't like leaders, so you can imagine my approach to community leaders. There would never be a 'community leader' for the 'white community'. Community leaders are also a way for the Hindus, the Muslims, the Jewish people and the LGBT community to be more easily managed. That partly reflects the old imperial divide and rule policy: positing different identities as irreconcilable and the British establishment as being the one that hold the balance.

So those are the problems we face. Better regulation might help, but it is largely also about contesting prejudice. It is important for everyone to say, 'Not in my name'. I know some critics suggest that 'Not in my name' implies 'You can do it so long as it's not in my name'. Not at all! As we know with the anti-war marches, 'Not in my name' also means challenging the state every time to say, 'Look, you can't do this. This is not acceptable.'

There's an entire amalgam of prejudices that are coming together. I know when we talk of fascism people say, 'Oh it's not really fascist, we still have opposition.' I'm sure in the early 1930s people in Germany thought that they could manage Hitler, and the elite thought: this is an uncouth person, but a useful idiot for us. And then we know what happened. So I do see that the kind of changes we have been witnessing in India and Turkey, even possibly in America with Trump, in the Philippines – you never know what may happen – but they do seem to have all the qualities of fascism. But it's a fascism that becomes respectable so long as it targets a visible minority. But targeting a visible minority goes hand-in-hand with actually clamping down on the majority also.

JW: There was a story in France a few years ago of a woman who said she'd been violently attacked by a group of anti-Semitic North African men that created a big sensation, was all over the press, and then it turned out she'd made the whole story up. One newspaper editor who had run the story admitted that he hadn't questioned anything because 'it rang true'. This kind of scapegoating is not new. I remember the Irish jokes I heard as a kid and the stories about the Irish being stupid and unreliable and dangerous. The process of scapegoating hasn't been invented in the last decade, but I think the process has intensified because of increased competition and the privatization of the media. The drive for readership at a time of crisis for a lot of newspapers has meant that things have escalated. On the question of regulation, you have Theresa May after this year's London

Bridge attacks saying, 'Perhaps we've been too tolerant or perhaps there's too much tolerance': the subtext being, 'Muslims are sheltering people that are carrying out these attacks or being too tolerant of them.' Then after the Finsbury Park mosque attack she was saying, 'I think Islamophobia should be considered a form of extremism.' Now I work in a university where if we have events – and this has happened on several occasions – where there have been Muslim speakers, they are subjected to a process of scrutiny and regulation that doesn't apply to other speakers. They gather the speakers together, who are told by the university security, 'This is our safe space.' Obviously this doesn't happen at other events. So there's something about creating a legal framework that legitimizes additional scrutiny, additional monitoring, additional suspicion, that means that people, however well-meaning, by complying with this, boost and legitimize those processes and the narratives they serve.

Part Two

Islamophobia and Representation

4

Islamophobia and the War of Representations: Martin Amis's 'The Last Days of Muhammad Atta'

Nath Aldalala'a and Geoffrey Nash

Literary fiction and the War on Terror

Since 9/11, in the words of Daniel Pipes, 'all Muslims, unfortunately, are suspect'.[1] Muslim communities in the West (which should be stretched to include the Russian Caucasus and former Soviet republics in Central Asia) have been the target of a discourse in which they are branded a permanent threat. Muslims are no longer defined according to their racial, social or economic markers relative to mainstream society, and yet they are not defined on purely religious grounds either. Their faith is understood as a site of violence and cultural deficit. In the decade following 9/11, literature has become a vehicle to convey over-determined images of oppositional constructions perpetuated by the rhetoric of the dominating War on Terror. Although highly visible as the signifiers of threat, paradoxically Muslims are silenced by the very discourse that projects their ominous and ubiquitous presence. Chris Allen states that 'the first decade of Islamophobia' began in 1997 with what he calls 'the landmark publication of the highly influential report entitled, *Islamophobia: A Challenge for us all: a report of the Runnymede Trust Commission on British Muslims and Islamophobia*'. However, the appearance of this document was, Allen adds, 'of course ... not when the phenomenon of Islamophobia began: it was only the year in which the first major report was published'. He goes on to instance a number of key 'debates' at the opening of the twenty-first century that helped define Islamophobia, in the Netherlands, France and Switzerland, over what the West more generally considers such typical manifestations of Islam as the niqab, the erection of mosques and minarets and the prospect of 'the overthrow of Christian Europe'.² The OIC Observatory report on Islamophobia for 2010–11 spoke of 'the tendency on the part of the media and motivated individuals and groups of inflicting ["collective guilt" on] the psyche of over 1.5 billion Muslims'. It went on to arraign them for 'playing on the devious logic of "guilt by association"' and for joining justification and accusation together to present a 'self-fulfilling prophecy [on] the utter failure of multiculturalism' with its necessary corollary: 'The incapacity of Europe to harmoniously absorb and live alongside Muslims.' Overall, the report opined that 'radical views against Islam were allowed to be expressed, render[ing] intolerance against Muslims socially acceptable and morally and intellectually justifiable'.³ Blustering and fantastical though such formulations were, and accumulative in their momentum, few then might have predicted the sway Islamophobia has since gained: how, for instance, Donald Trump successfully ran on an explicitly Islamophobic platform in the 2016 US presidential election campaign.

One of the least debated aspects connected to the prevalence of Islamophobia in Western societies is the degree to which intellectuals and writers, across the political spectrum and not merely of the right, have either made common cause with governments, politicians and the media in occupying a platform against Islam and sometimes Muslim communities in their midst, or have set up their own independent campaigns. The phenomenon of the anti-Muslim intellectual whose credentials are libertarian rather than racist has probably been most noted in Holland, in figures like Pym Fortuyn and Theo van Gogh, or in Denmark, in author and journalist Flemming Rose. However a similar mindset could be attributed to anglophone writers and intellectuals such as Christopher Hitchens, Gisèle Littman and Martin Amis. Distinguishing between 'us' and 'them', Amis coined the term 'Horrorism', and Littman (who writes under the pen name Bat Ye'or) introduced concepts such as 'Eurabia' and 'dhimmitude' to denote an attitude of surrender towards Islam, while Christopher Hitchens and others highlighted the menace of 'Islamofascism'. Masquerading as a profound debate about Muslims, these over-determined conceptualizations, by attempting to define terrorism and yoking fascism with Islam, gesture towards the latter's totality of significance; this frame of reference forces fascism beyond its historically situated associations with twentieth-century horrors to become an autonomous representation of Islam. Terrorism is no longer associated with singular actions, but with the totality of a discourse whereby the 'War on Terror' informs and sustains a cultural conflict. In an attempt at qualification, Amis announces his respect for Islam even while he castigates it:

> We are not hearing from moderate Islam. Whereas Islamism, as a mover and shaper of world events, is pretty well all there is. ... We respect Islam ... But Islamism? No, we can hardly be asked to respect a creedal wave that calls for our own elimination. More, we regard the Great Leap Backwards as a tragic development in Islam's story, and now in ours.

The prospect of 'our' elimination sits at the heart of this thesis of Horrorism, and in Anglo-American writing is inflected through the portrayal of Muslims. Terrorism slips into the background in a world in which Islamophobia governs the West's relationship to Islam. Horrorism operates within a religio-cultural discourse. Amis confesses that 'all religions, unsurprisingly, have their terrorists, Christian, Jewish, Hindu, even Buddhist. But we are not hearing from those religions. We are hearing from Islam'.[4]

By joining a debate over the fear and threat of Islamism in this way, Amis provided another instance of a writer becoming involved in what is primarily a political conflict and translating it in the process into a cultural context. To be more specific, literary fiction, for which Amis is of course better known, has been informed over the last few decades in various ways by this politico-cultural conflict. Since 9/11, British and American literature has been one vehicle among others for conveying negative clichés about Islam and Muslims. This, in turn, built on a period emerging out of the Rushdie Affair in Britain during which anti-Muslim discourse became almost standard and hegemonic among intellectuals. One of the main starting points of this chapter is therefore the assumption that the contribution made by writers and intellectuals to Islamophobic discourse can by no means be considered negligible.

Though there is still no internationally accepted definition of terrorism, literary writing on the subject of the September 2001 attacks on America has been assigned to the genre of 'terrorist' or more specifically 'post-9/11' fiction.[5] For over a century and a quarter, the amorphous, protean space of terrorism has attracted the attention of imaginative writers and hack novelists, politicians, newspaper columnists and latterly television anchors, with the general public in the role of consumers. The public dimension to terror is fixed when a generalized threat becomes embodied in a dangerous individual or group. The persona of the terrorist has been assigned to figures purportedly proclaiming a variety of political causes: anarchists, nationalists, communists, ethnic extremists, Palestinians or anyone the CIA cares to designate. In the immediate aftermath of the end of communism in the 1990s, the 'red terrorist' was replaced by religiously inspired perpetrators of violence from extremist Islamist groups. In spite of the problems surrounding agreement on a definition of terrorism, terror is regularly invoked and the image of the terrorist incites ubiquitous and constant vigilance. Since 9/11 the 'Muslim terrorist' has become public enemy number one. The equation between religion and terror has helped fuel Islamophobia, and each terror outrage is either by default assumed to be the work of Muslims – *vide* the initial response to the July 2011 massacres committed by the Norwegian neo-Nazi Anders Behring Breivik – or, when perpetrators are discovered to belong to specific terror organizations (previously Al Qaeda and latterly so-called Islamic State), blame has spread collectively to Muslims as a whole.

Versluys notes, 'In the immediate aftermath of [the 9/11 attacks …] the opinions of American novelists were eagerly solicited by newspapers and magazines.'[6] The same was true of their British counterparts. In this chapter we examine how a British creative writer constructs an image of the Muslim-as-terrorist such that it becomes the generic symbol of an entire faith. Through an analysis of Martin Amis's short story 'The Last Days of Muhammad Atta' we will demonstrate how Amis's 'Othering' of Atta carries a polemical force and purpose that firmly locates it in the category of the war of representations, which is a subset of Islamophobic discourse.[7] The main argument proposed is that Amis's condemnation of Atta and his fellow conspirators is founded not just on their involvement in a single set of events, the terrorist attacks. The (re)presentation of Atta and other Islamists is produced through the conflictive nature of defining 'Otherness'. Islamists, both in fiction and journalism, are virtually never portrayed in terms of their faith or even the religiously informed cultural codes to which they adhere. They conform only to the constructs necessary for their role as the 'Other'. The timing of Amis's story's publication is critical; with the world engaged upon what Bush and his cabinet declared a 'War on Terror', their place is within a totality of discourse that informs and sustains the War on Terror's military and propagandist conflict with the Islamic world.[8] Amis's articles and stories were his contribution to the accompanying war of representations, for it is to this category of discourse – what we are tempted to term a form of creative propaganda – that the journalistic and fictional work of Amis after 9/11 properly belongs. The war of representations feeds off and functions as an adjunct to the meta- or master-narrative that is the War on Terror.

Defining the terrorist in (dead) time

In the period between the 9/11 attacks and the publication of *The Second Plane* in 2008 Martin Amis conducted what amounted to a vociferous personal campaign in the press against an undifferentiated Muslim community. Denying he was an Islamophobe, he asserted that it was not Islam that must be feared and contested but Islamism. His claim to respect Islam but declare war on Islamism is underwritten by the presumption that the West's fight with the latter is a deadly battle for survival, which the bulk of Muslims have failed to assuage by not staging a collective condemnation of Islamism. Yet for all his accumulation of material from ideology streams and earlier events – the neo-Orientalist rehash of Islamic history and biographies of the founders of Islamic militancy like Sayyid Qutb that pepper *The Second Plane* – to assemble a back story that nominally produced Atta, Amis cannot stretch to consider the real terrorist's religio-political mindset. Instead he creates a fictive character who departs significantly from the figure who emerges from information in the public domain assembled by journalists and the *9/11 Commission Report* (hereafter cited as *9/11CR*). Amis's Atta is an individual creation, more typical of his own idiosyncrasies than the popular image of the fanatic who is prepared to commit mass murder on behalf of an avenging deity. Indeed, the most striking thing about this object-embodiment of an evil Islamist terrorist is that underneath the Muslim posture he is turned into an unbelieving nihilist. Amis's narrative both utilizes and overturns factual material from the *9/11CR*. Nowhere in the latter is there any suggestion of the atheism, the hidden apostasy he attributes to Atta in his short story, though material from the report – such as Atta's direction not to have a woman view his dead body – is lifted from his last will and testament and incorporated into the narrative.[9] In the story Amis weighs neither Atta's particular brand of the corruption that is terrorist Islamism nor the Islam 'we respect'; he is almost totally uninterested in his metaphysical orientations. Rather it is his death drive and how this emerges on the last day of his life out of a mundane world of meaningless boredom that is Amis's major concern in 'The Last Days of Muhammad Atta'.

The mundane and the apocalyptic are brought together in Amis's tale. The soon-to-be terrorist wakes up in a cheap hotel in Maine at four o'clock in the morning and goes for a shower. While in the shower he spends 'an unbelievably long time trying to remove a hair from the bar of soap'.[10] This process appears to normalize Atta, while at the same time suggesting some obsessive qualities. Beginning his day thus, he could be anybody. His everyday ablutions anchor the concept of terrorism by lifting it out of the realm of abstraction. Humdrum activities and minutiae form a counterpoint to the enormity of what is planned. This sense of banality extends to the airport where Atta attempts to check in for his flight. At the counter he participates in a dialogue with the clerk that serves to mark what Amis describes as 'the net increase in world boredom'.[11]

> 'Did you pack these bags yourself?'
> Muhammad Atta's hand crept towards his brow. 'Yes,' he said.
> 'Have they been with you at all times?'
> 'Yes.'
> 'Did anyone ask you to carry anything for them?'
> 'No. Is the flight on time?'
> 'You should make your connection.'
> 'And the bags will go straight through.'
> 'No, sir. You'll need to recheck them at Logan.'
> 'You mean I have to go through all this *again*?'[12]

The slightly schizophrenic quality intrudes again. The exchange is banal, but Atta's weary nervousness indicates concerns of which we, with the benefit of hindsight, are aware, but the check-in clerk is not. Boredom laced with impending apocalypse gives a peculiarly sharpened quality to the mundane that otherwise serves to normalize Atta's day. Stagnant time is equated with death when the narrative voice muses on

> the misery of recurrence, like the hotel elevator doing its ancient kneebend on every floor, like the alien hair on the soap changing its shape through a succession of different alphabets, like the (necessarily) monotonous gonging inside his head. It had occurred to him before that his condition, if you could call it that, was merely the condition of boredom, unbounded boredom, where all time was dead time.[13]

At the same time, however, as Atta reiterates the perfunctory questions of the airport staff, they take on the form of an indictment of the emptiness of America:

> 'Did you pack these bags yourself?'
> '*What* bags? As I took the trouble to explain ...'
> 'Sir, your bags will be on our next flight. I still need to ask the security questions, sir.'
> Americans – the way they called you sir. They might as well be calling you 'Mac'.
> 'Did you pack these bags yourself?'
> '*What* bags?'[14]

The interchange defines Atta's terrorism in such a way as to elevate him for a moment above dead time, giving him the right to reinterpret ironically the procedures of American officialdom. This ability to stand outside, at an oblique angle, to the justificatory procedures of an imperial power recalls his earlier meeting with the dying imam, who encourages Atta in his mission: '"Remember we are in the lands of unbelief," [he] said ... and went on to list the crimes of the Americans.'15 Yet even here the exchange has something of the already-heard for Atta. The tone and its familiar litany are well known:

> America was responsible for this or that many million deaths. ... Certain weapons systems claimed to be precise; power was not precise. Power was always a monster. And there had never been a monster the size of America. Every time it turned over in its sleep it entrained disasters that would have to roll through villages. There were blunderings and perversities and calculated cruelties; and there was no self-knowledge – none.16

In keeping with Amis's view that terror is a close neighbour of boredom, Atta is hollowed out in terms of motive, moved more by nihilism than by any religious or political commitment. This presents certain challenges as Amis seeks to combine a mimetic representation of a three-dimensional person with thoughts and behaviour patterns that might constitute a paradigmatic Muslim terrorist, even while, at the same time, downplaying Atta's religious beliefs. Though adopting an adherence to the outer rind of rituals of Islam ('Like the others, he was attending to his prayers, disbursing his alms, washing often'), Atta is presented as without possession of an interior faith.17 It is clear that his outer Muslimness is being deployed as shorthand for a ready propensity to violence. It is enough to say that Atta is a Muslim – outwardly adhering to aspects of the faith's formal requirements – and is intent on murderous violence. The association of 'Muslim' and 'violence' can be left to do its work.

For a writer to co-opt the mind of a terrorist implies that he has been able to penetrate that individual's psyche and hence laid bare his terrorist motives. Atta's obsessive traits displayed in the hours and minutes prior to his death have the effect of suggesting a form of pathology (strong insight into character psychology being a reputed strength of Amis's fiction). Like countless other Amis characters, Atta is driven more by the torments of the flesh – specifically his urge to avoid temptations of any kind, to *not* do certain things – and such drives are infinitely more powerful than any religious or cultural overlay. Amis may succeed in giving the impression of recreating Atta's mind, because for him his motive is clear: the terrorist's sole aim is to kill, to annihilate. What Amis does is to fictionalize the

'Muslim' as a death-machine: he has abstracted an image of what a 'Muslim' killer could be and projected it as the mind of the historical personage who was Muhammad Atta.

The story of Atta's last hours is first and foremost part of a conflictive debate. Produced in the days and months immediately after 9/11, it attempts to characterize what was immediately taken to be a new form of terrorism and a new type of terrorist. Atta however is not so much an individual as an aura; beyond the physical descriptions the text provides, he is constructed as an idea. His personality, thinking and behaviour become a template for our recognition of a specific form of terror:

> Purify your heart and cleanse it of stains. Forget and be oblivious to the thing which is called 'World'. Muhammad Atta was not religious; he was not even especially political. He had allied himself with militants because jihad was, by many magnitudes, the most charismatic idea of his generation. *To unite ferocity and rectitude in a single word*: nothing could compete with that. He played along with it, and did the things that impressed his peers; he collected quotations, citations, charities, pilgrimages, conspiracy theories, and so on, as other people collect autographs or beer mats. And it suited his character. If you took away all the rubbish about faith, then fundamentalism suited his character, and *with an almost sinister precision*.[18]

In subsuming himself within a set of received ideas taken to justify mass murder, Atta the actual hijacker thus loses individuality and becomes the composite 'deadly Muslim terrorist'. Amis's much-vaunted insights into male psychology come up short in his attempts to render Atta. Amis – like most other Anglo-American fiction writers who have attempted to render Islamist terrorists – is unable to penetrate his protagonist's mind; he remains outside of and distant from his subject. Martin Randall opines, 'Amis's Atta ... owes a great deal to other fictional men in the author's oeuvre ... the "core reason" [for his death/killer instinct] [is] located in the failings of his body, his violent misogyny and his intense dislike of laughter, music and sex.'[19] True, features such as atheism, self-loathing, boredom, obsession with bodily conditions like headaches and constipation, manliness and hang-ups about sex are typically seen not only in Amis's writings about Islamists (notably Sayyid Qutb) but also in characters of his earlier fiction. This, however, may not be the whole story. Amis himself, in a moment of flippancy, told the Australian television journalist Tony Jones,

> I read everything I could find about Mohammad Atta, but I took an enormous liberty in that I made him an apostate, rather than a religious maniac, which

is probably what he was – almost certainly what he was. I did that for purely utilitarian reasons, in that it would have bored me blind to look into the mind of someone who was fanatically religious. I make him a cynic who is there just for the killing, and I wanted to emphasise that, that it's a secret no longer well-kept, that killing people is tremendously empowering and exciting.[20]

What, we might wonder, were the 'purely utilitarian reasons' that led Amis to portray Atta as an apostate rather than a religious maniac? Terry Eagleton perhaps gives us a clue in the introduction to his book *Ideology: An Introduction* where he castigates Amis:

In an essay entitled 'The Age of Horrorism' published in September 2006, the novelist Martin Amis advocated a deliberate programme of harassing the Muslim community in Britain. 'The Muslim community', he wrote, 'will have to suffer until it gets its house in order. What sort of suffering? Not letting them travel. Deportation – further down the road. Curtailing of freedoms. Strip-searching people who look like they're from the Middle East or from Pakistan … Discriminatory stuff, until it hurts the whole community and they start getting tough with their children ….' Amis was not recommending these tactics for criminals or suspects only. He was proposing them as punitive measures against all Muslims, guilty or innocent. The idea was that by hounding and humiliating them as a whole, they would return home and teach their children to be obedient to the White Man's law. There seems something mildly defective about this logic.[21]

Eagleton's juicy concluding understatement, drawing attention to the limitations in this and other, more toned-down statements in *The Second Plane*, nonetheless points up the unabashed bullying of a vulnerable ethnic minority that Amis is recommending. For Amis, one feels, it is almost a point of honour *not* to attempt the presentation of a three-dimensional personality in his Atta. Atta's religious personality, however fanatical it might have been, is hollowed out because Amis has no interest in it. It is merely a more violent manifestation of that 'dependent mind' Amis castigates elsewhere in *The Second Plane*. He is only interesting as a death-machine. The portrayal of Atta is a means to realize Amis's real end, which is to 'Other' all Muslims in a wider project that takes the form of a reassertion, in fictional form, of the superiority of Western secularism, rationality and right thinking. Martin Randall asks, '[If] Amis' Atta is so forcibly shown to be different from his fellow hijackers, is the fiction revealing its lack of interest in or its inability to represent the reality of the attacks?'[22] Since, for the hard-core secularist, it might be a matter of pride not to be able to enter the totally corrupted, dependent mind of the religious terrorist, we think the former diagnosis is likely to be closer to the truth.

Amis's victory: Imagined retribution as eternal recurrence

The narrative ends where it begins, coming round full circle to the morning of September 11. Another key feature in Amis's representation of Muhammad Atta is that he is not so much interested in the terrorist-hijacker as in the mythical persona that comes after, what we might term the 'post-terrorist'. A post-terrorist exists at the stage of death, when death itself represents and signifies the consummation of terrorism. It is in this guise that the figure of Atta is brought back in order to punish him. His death and the deaths of the others who participated in the attacks provide the grounds for fictionalizing them and theorizing about them; for Atta, 'all the putting to death' is the validation, the 'core reason' for terror.[23] As media bogeymen, their continuing existence after death is double-edged: their very readiness for death remains unnerving because it is incomprehensible to the American and Western mind. However, though lacking clear definitions for terror and terrorism, the public is able to intuit these terms as cohering around the categories of death and revenge. It would be preferable if Atta were still alive in order for him to be punished and the effect – also the affect – of his actions to be repudiated. But Atta is not alive: the subsequent restoration of the dead terrorist through an imagined belief-system projected onto him is the very systematization of the process of defining terror. In 'Terror and Boredom: The Dependent Mind', Amis quotes Sam Harris, 'Islamism is not merely the latest flavour of totalitarian nihilism. There is a difference between nihilism and a desire for supernatural reward. Islamists could smash the world to atoms and still not be guilty of nihilism, because everything in their world has been transfigured by the light of paradise.'[24] Strangely, though, for Atta in the story this turns out not to be the case.

Both the hijackers and their American enemies are hostage to their polarized notions of death to such an extent that it becomes a matter of defining death rather than defining terror. Yet, because Amis does not construct Atta as a religious fanatic but as a nihilist, there appears an inconsistency in the application of Harris's words to him. ('He didn't expect paradise. What he expected was oblivion. And, strange to say, he would find neither.'[25])

Idiosyncratic though the fictional personality Amis creates for Atta is, it is produced out of a frustration on the author's part. In effect, given that death was Atta's ultimate goal, his wish had been granted, in the process inflicting death on as many others as possible. This act was accomplished in such a way as to render him immune to the retribution of this world. Such a heinous escape from justice could only be offset by bringing him back to be punished and re-punished in a process that bypasses the actual meaning of paradise in Islam. For the believer the light of paradise is a practical reality; it is the reward for faith; in its simplest terms, it is the proper conclusion to being a good Muslim. In the work of Amis and most other post-9/11 writers, there is no representation of such 'faithful' Muslims since the promise of paradise is anathema to the secular artist, and because reward must be negated by an imposed fictional justice that takes account of terrorist actions and their consequences in the world itself.

As if to underline the trajectory of wish-fulfilment as revenge, the story ends with an attempt to invoke instant death, emphasizing corporeal dissolution and vaporization. One feels here an effort forcibly to reconnect Atta, in the last moment of his consciousness, with the consequences of his action – the reality of 'all the putting to death' that will roll down the years as a result. Atta is made to experience his final moments in slow motion, less as a consummation than as 'a defeat, a self-cancellation':

> And then the argument assembled all by itself. The joy of killing was proportional to the value of what was destroyed. But that value was something a killer could never see and never gauge. And where was the joy he thought he had felt – where *was* that joy, that itch, that paltry tingle? Yes, how gravely he had underestimated it. How very gravely he had underestimated life. His own he had hated, and had wished away; but see how long it was taking to absent itself – and with what helpless grief was he watching it go, imperturbable in its beauty and its power.[26]

A forced humanist reckoning for all Atta's repression of spontaneity, life and pleasure occurs, courtesy of the author. For Atta there is to be neither paradise nor oblivion, only the misery of eternal recurrence: his last few hours played out over and over again in some kind of posthumous Groundhog Day. The text at the end returns us to its opening lines: 'On September 11, 2001, he opened his eyes at 4 a.m., in Portland, Maine; and Muhammad Atta's last day began.' The same events will take place again, always and forever. Here the afterlife has been re-tooled to provide an imaginative justice the author sees as fitting. Muslim and atheist, both the possible appellations suggested for Atta are trumped by a pseudo-Buddhist cycle of eternal recurrence concocted to allow the author and his presumed readership to 'get even'.

Conclusion

In this chapter we have seen how, in the wake of the 9/11 attacks, the figure of the terrorist is put to ideological use by Martin Amis and made to fit the War on Terror agenda. Amis's version of Muhammad Atta's story serves to elevate the terrorist leader to the level of an embodiment of all Islamist terrorism, at the same time conflating Islam and Islamism and inflecting the narrative with a secular bias. Amis is simply not interested in the religious aspect of Atta's personality. The second dimension of the story is that it projects an environment of punishment, torture and horror – for the terrorist as much as for the terrorized. This is a psycho-environment where the readers are invited to live out their vengeance against Atta both as individual and as terrorist. The third area of significance concerns Amis's employment of 'Otherness' and how this feeds Islamophobia. Building on our discussion of Islamophobia in the introduction, we have seen how Amis has inscribed Atta as a suitable object of loathing, eliding religious and cultural dimensions to his character in order to make him a monomaniac in love with killing. In the process a myth of the terrorist has been employed, in which Muslims collectively constitute a potential threat to society and are textually punished by being set up as the discursive 'Other'. At each of these levels the worlds of reality, media commentary and creative fiction are made to feed off one another.

In the debate between Amis and Eagleton, the former was accused of racism, anti-Semitism, misogyny, being anti-gay and of pandering to Islamophobia. Eagleton's arraignment of Amis, some might argue, amounted to no more than a *littérateur*–academic spat that cut no ice outside of the columns of the quality British press. Yet this is to underestimate the extent to which the pronouncements of high-profile intelligentsia figures can lend respectability to insidious and pervasive prejudices, all the more so when articulated via the powerful instrument of the media. Muslims in Amis's interventions are homogenized and placed beyond the boundaries of a Western definition of self and society which prides itself on the supposed practice of equality, democracy, freedom of speech and support for human rights. He makes no concession to the aspirations of

Muslims to coexist and prosper alongside the non-Muslim majority in Western nations. While paying lip service to the distinction between Islam as a religious faith and Islamism as a political ideology, he knowingly takes the terrorists' creed at face value. Though he knows Atta's extremism is not endorsed by the majority of Muslims, rather than separate out Islamist terrorism as the work of a tiny minority that is only a peripheral subset of the vastly larger Muslim community, he projects its spokespersons and actors' performances of horror with such accentuation that these thereby acquire the reality of some kind of inexorable contemporary norm, enveloping all Muslims within the scope of its blame. Amis the serious writer, by constructing Atta as a generic hate-figure and inciting the desire for punishment and revenge, has, we consider, intentionally added fuel to the flames of Islamophobia.[27]

Notes

1 Daniel Pipes, *Militant Islam Reaches America* (New York: W.W. Norton, 2002), p. 140.
2 Chris Allen, *Islamophobia* (Farnham: Ashgate, 2010), pp. 3–4. A succinct elucidation of the term can be found in Salman Sayyid's short introductory article in Sayyid and Vakil, *Thinking through Islamophobia*. See also Yahya Birt's essay ('Governing Muslims after 9/11') in the same volume.
3 *Fourth OIC Observatory Report on Islamophobia (Intolerance and Discrimination against Muslims): May 2010 to April 2011*, presented at Astana, Republic of Kazakhstan 28–30 June 2011, pp. 1–3. Available at http://ww1.oic-oci.org/uploads/file/Islamphobia/2011/en/islamphobia_rep_May_2010_to_April_2011_en.pdf (accessed 18 June 2017).
4 Martin Amis, *The Second Plane, September 11: 2001–2007* (London: Jonathan Cape, 2008), pp. 49–50; Nath Aldalala'a and Geoffrey Nash, 'Coming out for Islam? Critical Muslim responses to postcolonialism in theory and writing', in Esra Mirze Santesso and James E. McClung (eds), *Islam and Postcolonial Discourse* (Abingdon, Oxon.: Routledge, 2017), pp. 231–2.
5 See, for example, Alex Houen, *Terrorism and Modern Literature: From Joseph Conrad to Ciaran Carson* (Oxford: Oxford University Press, 2002), p. 7; Richard Gray, *After the Fall: American Literature since 9/11* (Chichester: Wiley-Blackwell, 2011); Martin Randall, *9/11 and the Literature of Terror* (Edinburgh: Edinburgh University Press, 2011); Kristiaan Versluys, *Out of the Blue* (New York: Columbia University Press, 2009).
6 Versluys, *Out of the Blue*, p. 150.

7 'The Last Days of Muhammad Atta' is a short story that first appeared in the *New Yorker* on 24 April 2006, and was subsequently included in *The Second Plane* (London: Jonathan Cape, 2008; all quotations from this edition).
8 On Bush's employment of the phrase 'War on Terror', Mona Baker argues,

> The choice of *terror* rather than *terrorism* is significant here and offers a good example of the discursive work required for successful circulation and adoption of narratives. *Terrorism* refers to one or more incidents that involve violence, with localized and containable impact. Terror, by contrast, is a state of mind, one that can rapidly spread across boundaries and encompass all in its grip. To qualify as a meta or master narrative, a narrative must have this type of temporal and physical breadth, as well as a sense of inevitability or inescapability. *Terror* indexes such features much better than *terrorism*.

'Translation and activism', in Maria Tymoczko (ed.), *Translation, Resistance and Activism* (Amherst, MA: University of Massachusetts Press, 2010), pp. 23–41; pp. 26–7; italics in text.
9 For a detailed analysis of the broader truth claims of the US government's narrative of 9/11 see Michel Chossudovsky, *War and Globalisation: The Truth Behind September 11* (Shanty Bay, Ont.: Global Outlook, 2002); *America's 'War on Terrorism'*, 2nd edn (Montreal: Global Research Publishers, 2005). For an overview of the discrepancies between Amis's Atta and the picture presented in investigative journalism and the *9/11 Commission Report* see Oana Gheorghiu, '"Extreme Otherness": Representations of 9/11 in two Anglo-American writers', *Journal of Intercultural Inquiry* 2 (2016), pp. 4–21.
10 Amis, *Second Plane*, p. 96.
11 Ibid., p. 108.
12 Ibid., pp. 107–8.
13 Ibid., p. 113.
14 Ibid.
15 Ibid., p. 110.
16 Ibid., pp. 110–11.
17 Ibid., p. 96.
18 Ibid., p. 101 (emphasis added).
19 Randall, *9/11 and the Literature of Terror*, pp. 46, 49.
20 Lateline, 'Tony Jones speaks to Martin Amis', *ABC*, 1 November 2006. Available at www.abc.net.au/lateline/content/2006/s1779157.htm (accessed 3 August 2017).
21 'Terry Eagleton on Martin Amis', *Verso UK's Blog*, 24 February 2010. Available at https://versouk.wordpress.com/2010/02/24/terry-eagleton-on-martin-amis/ (accessed 3 August 2017).
22 Randall, *9/11 and the Literature of Terror*, p. 52.

23 Amis, *Second Plane*, p. 122.
24 Ibid., p. 80.
25 Ibid., p. 102.
26 Ibid., p. 124.
27 See Ronan Bennett, 'Shame on us', *Guardian*, 19 November 2007. For further discussion that situates Amis in the context of Islamophobia see Nasar Meer and Tariq Modood, 'The racialisation of Muslims', in Sayyid and Vakil, *Thinking through Islamophobia*, pp. 67–83.

Works cited

Aldalala'a, Nath and Geoffrey Nash, 'Coming out for Islam? Critical Muslim responses to postcolonialism in theory and writing', in Esra Mirze Santesso and James E. McClung (eds), *Islam and Postcolonial Discourse* (Abingdon, Oxon.: Routledge, 2017), pp. 228–44.

Allen, Chris, *Islamophobia* (Farnham: Ashgate, 2010).

Amis, Martin, *The Second Plane, September 11: 2001–2007* (London: Jonathan Cape, 2008).

Baker, Mona, 'Translation and activism', in Maria Tymoczko (ed.), *Translation, Resistance and Activism* (Amherst, MA: University of Massachusetts Press, 2010), pp. 23–41.

Bennett, Ronan, 'Shame on us', *Guardian*, 19 November 2007.

Chossudovsky, Michel, *America's 'War on Terrorism'*, 2nd edn (Montreal: Global Research Publishers, 2005).

Chossudovsky, Michel, *War and Globalisation: The Truth behind September 11* (Shanty Bay, ON: Global Outlook, 2002).

Gheorghiu, Oana '"Extreme Otherness": Representations of 9/11 in two Anglo-American Writers', *Journal of Intercultural Inquiry* 2 (2016), pp. 4–21.

Gray, Richard, *After the Fall: American Literature since 9/11* (Chichester: Wiley-Blackwell, 2011).

Houen, Alex, *Terrorism and Modern Literature: From Joseph Conrad to Ciaran Carson* (Oxford: Oxford University Press, 2002).

Lateline, 'Tony Jones speaks to Martin Amis', *ABC*, 1 November 2006. Available at www.abc.net.au/lateline/content/2006/s1779157.htm (accessed 3 August 2017)

Meer, Nasar and Tariq Modood, 'The racialisation of Muslims', in S. Sayyid and AbdoolKarim Vakil (eds), *Thinking through Islamophobia* (London: Hurst & Co., 2010), pp. 67–83.

Organization of the Islamic Conference, *Fourth OIC Observatory Report on Islamophobia (Intolerance and Discrimination against Muslims): May 2010 to April 2011*, presented at Astana, Republic of Kazakhstan 28–30 June 2011, pp. 1–3.

Available at http://ww1.oic-oci.org/uploads/file/Islamphobia/2011/en/islamphobia_rep_May_2010_to_April_2011_en.pdf (accessed 18 June 2017).
Pipes, Daniel, *Militant Islam Reaches America* (New York: W.W. Norton, 2002).
Randall, Martin, *9/11 and the Literature of Terror* (Edinburgh: Edinburgh University Press, 2011).
Sayyid, S. and AbdoolKarim Vakil (eds), *Thinking through Islamophobia* (London: Hurst & Co., 2010).
Versluys, Kristiaan, *Out of the Blue* (New York: Columbia University Press, 2009).
Verso UK, 'Terry Eagleton on Martin Amis', *Verso UK's Blog*, 24 February 2010. Available at https://versouk.wordpress.com/2010/02/24/terry-eagleton-on-martin-amis/ (accessed 3 August 2017).

5

'A Sly and Stubborn People': *Game of Thrones*, Orientalism and Islamophobia

Roberta Garrett

Introduction

George R. R. Martin's *A Song of Ice and Fire* saga comprises five bestselling novels with more planned to complete the series. The novels have also spawned a successful game franchise and D. B. Weiss and David Benioff's award-winning and highly popular HBO *Game of Thrones* television adaptation. Following the commercial success of Peter Jackson's film adaptation of J. R. R. Tolkien's *Lord of the Rings* trilogy in the late 1990s, Martin's *A Song of Ice and Fire* novels and HBO's adaptation offer many of the familiar tropes and motifs associated with high fantasy. These include a fully realized secondary world (complete with maps and a range of languages), the unapologetic use of magic, multiple quest narratives, total war and a looming 'end of days' scenario involving both human power struggles and supernatural evil. Much of the success of the series, particularly among female and young adult viewers and readers, has been attributed to Martin's gritty and 'authentic' version of the high fantasy genre. However, this chapter will suggest another way of understanding the relationship between Martin's take on history and the contemporary moment. It will examine the series in relation to long-standing Orientalist tropes, the recent history of Western military intervention in the Middle East, and the associated rise in state and media-led Islamophobia from the early 1990s onwards. It argues that, while Martin's work challenges many of the androcentric, class-biased tropes and motifs of mid-century high fantasy, it nonetheless reproduces a familiar cluster of Eurocentric, Orientalist and Islamophobic attitudes. Past and present Western prejudices and assumptions about the Muslim world are conflated in the depiction of both Daenerys Targaryen's conquest of what are presented as backward, non-democratic Middle Eastern states and through the saga's increasing preoccupation with the threat of religious fundamentalism in the West. Indeed, as this chapter demonstrates, Martin's endorsement of the female heroine Daenerys Targaryen as a Western liberator of brown women, children and oppressed men is inseparable from the saga's perpetuation of Orientalist and Islamophobic perspectives.

Westeros and Essos

In accordance with his stated desire to challenge the 'Disney Middle Ages'[1] mode of high fantasy, Martin introduced complex female characters, grinding poverty, violence, torture and dismemberment, lingering and painful death scenes and scenes of explicit sexual behaviour (both consensual and non-consensual) to provide a more accurate picture of life in medieval Europe. He has frequently emphasized his extensive knowledge of the culture and politics of this period and his conscious inclusion of references to key historical events, such as the Wars of the Roses. By drawing on such events and depicting their devastating effects on the lives of the poor rather than just the high-born, Martin claims that the saga is closer to historical fiction than the sanitized view of the past offered by prior high fantasy writers.[2] Alongside his 'blood, mud, sex and violence' approach to medieval grittiness,[3] Martin rejects the androcentric, homosocial world of chivalry and high ideals imagined by mid-twentieth-century writers, such as Tolkien, in favour of a wide assortment of damaged, frustrated and pragmatic male and female characters. He displays a particular fondness for disempowered men (such as the dwarf Tyrion or the bastard Lord's son Jon Snow) and women who kick against patriarchal gender roles, allotting them key roles as chapter focalizers and allowing them to survive into the later novels.

As critics less interested in the historical accuracy of mock-medieval fantasy and more drawn towards its potential allegorical meanings have pointed out, these differences in tone and characterization reflect broader cultural shifts. Tolkien's work was written in the mid-1950s. The notable absence of female characters reproduces the revisionist sexual politics of the immediate post-Second World War era while the treatment of the military threat to Middle Earth evokes and explores the rise of fascism in the 1930s from the vantage point of peace, rising prosperity, hope and social consensus.[4] In contrast, Martin's work begins in the mid-1990s, amid a neoconservative backlash against the gains of various progressive social movements, particularly feminism. This is also a moment in which the sociopolitical consensus that underpinned social democracy in the United States and Western Europe began to collapse under the weight of neoliberal economic policies and post-Cold War Eastern Europe descended into a series of bitter ethnic struggles. *A Song of Ice and Fire*'s depiction of failed states, reawakened ethnic conflicts and the brutal treatment of women and the poor have therefore been interpreted as a neoliberal nightmare or, as John Wilkinson puts it, a fantasy which reflects a new geopolitical reality in which 'the filiated project of western civilisation is over, succeeded by a financialisation of the world when rapacious interests have broken cover from "civilisation", naked and happy to jettison the benefits and ideals concomitant with the enlightenment and post-war welfarism'.[5]

Wilkinson's reading of *A Song of Ice and Fire* as an allegory of the neoliberal assault on cherished Western notions of human rights and social democracy indirectly raises the question of how non-Western societies are imagined in Martin's series. The numerous plotlines situated in mock-medieval Europe ('Westeros') are accompanied by a smaller but significant narrative strand set in the warmer easterly regions known collectively as 'Essos'. This is another key difference between the work of 'Oxford fantasists', such as Tolkien and C. S. Lewis, and contemporary gritty medievalism, as the former rarely acknowledges a world beyond a thinly disguised representation of medieval Europe. As Helen Young has argued, this inclusion of an imagined East might initially appear to signal a more balanced reworking of the high fantasy map, but it is also the point at which Martin's desire to present a more nuanced and inclusive picture of the past becomes embroiled in an Orientalist, racialized vision of the world which lies to the east of Westeros. Discussing 'gritty' high fantasy more generally, Young argues that 'texts, authors and audiences draw directly on the habits of Whiteness established largely through the kind of Fantasy it claims to have rejected. Not only does Gritty Fantasy invoke Eurocentric fantasy conventions, it also reflects and reproduces race theory of the eighteenth and nineteenth centuries.'[6]

This is evident in the *Game of Thrones* series in a number of ways. Firstly, the Westeros plotlines depict a range of distinct cultures that are loosely based on the late medieval to Renaissance cultures of Britain and of mainland northern Europe, southern Europe and Scandinavia. In contrast, vast swathes of Essos are distinguished only by the difference between the (north-eastern) savage, nomadic Dothraki tribal culture and the somewhat more advanced but despotic and cruel culture of a number of warm, dry, dusty and barely distinguishable states in the southerly area of Slaver's Bay. As the name given to this region makes clear, one of the essential, plot-driving differences between Westeros and Essos is that, despite the brutal treatment of the peasantry by the nobility, slavery has been outlawed in all regions of the western continent for a thousand years before the origins of the 'war of seven kingdoms' plotline of *A Song of Ice and Fire*.

Slaver's Bay contains some evidence of prior civilizations, through the presence of ancient pyramids and statues, and the slave-owning class wear fine clothes and jewellery. Yet the cultures of this region are predominantly depicted as backward and despotic. They have only limited art and culture and appear isolated from the more civilized parts of Martin's world. They are hierarchical, patriarchal and display no desire to modernize or evolve. The near and Middle Eastern states of Essos, which are inhabited largely by darker-skinned people, are therefore primarily marked by this difference in levels of social progress. Before the outbreak of civil war, Westeros has been ruled by a hierarchical but multi-tiered structure at the head of which is the King, his second-in-command, a privy council and numerous regional lords and bannermen along with a number of high-ranking church officials. The relative power awarded to these institutions and roles and the competition between them is a key source of dramatic interest and plot development in the Westeros narrative. In contrast, readers are given little information about the socio-economic or political structure or history of the Slaver's Bay countries of Astapor, Yunkai and Meereen, other than that they are rigidly divided cultures that are ruled exclusively by the slave-owning classes. These are referred to ironically as the 'good', 'great' or 'wise' masters and appear interchangeable in terms of their cruelty.

The period in which the novels were published (1996–2011) is, of course, also one that has been marked by a series of Western military interventions in the Middle East. As numerous critics have observed, from the 1991 Gulf War through to the 2003 invasion of Iraq and beyond, the pursuit of US neo-imperialist campaigns in this region was justified by a longer term narrative of Western superiority to the Muslim-majority nations of the region. As Deepa Kumar argues, the 'clash of civilizations' thesis popularized by right-wing thinkers, such as Bernard Lewis and Samuel Huntington, draws on a number of pre-existing Orientalist myths regarding the inferior nature of such cultures and their inability to evolve without Western intervention.[7] In the following section I will begin to examine how these myths surface readily in Martin's series, wrapped in an alluring and progressive female revenge/empowerment plotline.

Daenerys Targaryen: The making of a white saviour

The quasi-Middle Eastern (Essos) sections of *A Song of Ice and Fire*'s main plotline contain the tale of Daenerys Targaryen's conquest and 'liberation' of Slaver's Bay. Significantly, this storyline begins in Martin's 2000 volume *A Storm of Swords*. The third instalment of the series was therefore published before 9/11 and the 'War on Terror', but during a period in which US neoconservative rhetoric was laying the groundwork for public acceptance of military invention in the Middle East, justified on the grounds of a humanitarian need for regime change. To fully understand the Daenerys storyline and its allegorical significance, it is useful to consider Martin's initial cultivation of Daenerys Targaryen as a key character and her evolution into a 'white saviour' figure with whom modern audiences will sympathize and identify. In the first novel in the series, *Game of Thrones* (1996), the reader is given the backstory to the thirteen-year-old Daenerys's Eastern exile. She and her cruel and arrogant brother are the sole survivors of the deposed Westeros Targaryen line. Her story begins when her brother sells her to the leader of a nomadic tribe (the Dothraki) in order to further his attempts to regain power.

The dominant Westeros narrative is concentrated in the late medieval and Renaissance periods but Martin plays fast and loose with the history and culture of the Essos sections. Like the later sections in Slaver's Bay, Dothraki culture is more sketchily drawn than the detailed accounts of the different cultures and practices of Westeros. The depiction of the Dothraki and their warrior leader, the 'Khal', clearly refers to Genghis Khan's domination of Mongolia in the early thirteenth century: a good hundred years or so before events take off in mock-medieval Westeros. The chief function of this section of the narrative is to establish sympathy for Daenerys, who is the sole character focalizer for Essos plotlines until the arrival of other key Westeros characters later in the series. The Genghis Khan reference not only allows the reader/viewer to revel in a savagery that far exceeds anything in Westeros but also provides the ideal context to situate Daenerys as a vulnerable young white girl in the midst of a violent, hyper-masculine foreign culture. Daenerys learns to rely on the advice and support of another white, Westeros exile: an older, disgraced knight, Sir Jorah Mormont, who helps her to understand the Dothraki's strange and savage customs.

Although initially terrified, Daenerys increasingly comes to respect the Dothraki's brutal but guileless culture and the fearless Khal. In this sense, the portrayal of Daenerys echoes Matthew W. Hughey's depiction of the white saviour in a number of recent 'post-racial' American films. Analysing the behaviour of this figure across a wide range of forms and genres, Hughey observes that

> not long after the protagonist enters the foreign land, he or she learns that the original reason for the journey was wrong and slowly becomes uncomfortable with his or her role. The saviour then comes to admire the noble savagery and lack of pretence in the indigenous or local culture. And slowly the saviour comes to learn about the native techniques for defending themselves from the few bad white people of whom the savior was formerly a part.[8]

In a similar manner, Daenerys gradually comes to question her brutal and mercenary brother's authority and doubt whether he has the noble spirit to direct armies and recapture the Iron Throne of Westeros: he has already threatened to sell her to the highest bidder to secure his own power. As an alternative, she immerses herself in Dothraki culture, becoming a proficient horsewoman, adopting their dress code and showing tolerance towards their savage customs. Her greater empathy with, and respect for, other cultures leads to acceptance among the tribe and augments her ability to challenge her brother's authority along with his overtly Eurocentric and racist attitudes.

The north-eastern plotline thus serves two important narrative functions in terms of encouraging the reader to accept Daenerys as white saviour and, later, as conqueror of Slaver's Bay, while not appearing overtly tyrannical or imperialist. Firstly, it demonstrates that, although she is high-born, white and from a more sophisticated culture, unlike her brother she is not an ignorant bigot. Secondly, it shows that she has had to overcome unfair treatment on the grounds of her gender, a backstory that justifies her drive to reform the misogynistic cultures she encounters in the Middle Eastern states. As suggested above, despite featuring high levels of sexual violence and misogyny, *A Song of Ice and Fire* has proved far more popular with female readers and viewers than earlier forms of fantasy fiction. This is largely attributed to Martin's creation of a range of interesting, likeable and complex female characters and the emphasis placed on gender power dynamics in different regions of the saga's secondary world. Daenerys's character development follows the individualistic journey of the empowered 'victim-survivor' and thus chimes well with a particular version of popular feminism in neoliberal cultures. This era has also seen a repudiation of feminism among some women who see individualism as yielding greater rewards than solidarity in pursuit of social justice – the overriding priority in earlier forms of feminism – to the extent that some young women reject the label 'feminist' entirely. As Christina Scharff,[9] Nancy Fraser[10] and Lila Abu-Lughod[11] have pointed out, in the last two decades a particular view of feminism has become absorbed into popular culture that tends to be associated with the success of certain high-profile, white Western women who are able to advance within patriarchal culture. This media-friendly version of feminism jettisons the movement's long-standing association with wealth redistribution, pacifism, anti-racism and opposition to neo-imperialism. Within this narrative, non-Western women in general and Muslim women in particular are understood as downtrodden and in need of assistance from their more empowered white, Western sisters. As we shall see, in Martin's work the promotion of Daenerys Targaryen as a strong 'feminist' heroine relies on the belittlement and marginalization of brown women and the uncontested idea that she, and she alone, can oppose the power of tyrannical Middle Eastern men.

'Breaker of Chains': Slaver's Bay and benevolent conquest

Far from consciously promoting a neoconservative agenda, Martin has made no secret of his liberal attitudes and credentials. He is widely known to have been a conscientious objector during the Vietnam War, is clearly sympathetic to women's issues and has described the Republican Party as 'oligarchs and racists clad in the skins of dead elephants'.[12] It is therefore unlikely that the plotline in Martin's 2000 volume *A Storm of Swords* in which Daenerys Targaryen travels to the East and conquers the three slave states of Astapor, Yunkai and Meereen, was intended to endorse the rising tide of media Islamophobia or to browbeat the American public into accepting the necessity of military intervention. Indeed, despite Martin's stated intention to avoid allegorical plotlines, his 2011 addition to the series, *A Dance with Dragons: Blood and Dust*, depicts the long-term failure of misconceived and ill-planned conquests of foreign cultures in terms that clearly reference the US occupation of and retreat from Iraq and Afghanistan. Nevertheless, the persistent use of blatantly Orientalist and Eurocentric images and motifs in the Essos plotlines of *A Storm of Swords* and *A Dance with Dragons* – alongside their depiction on screen – fed into a political and social climate in which Muslim nations were increasingly presented as misogynist, brutal and backward.

As Deepa Kumar argues, the Islamophobia of the past two decades draws much from the longer history of Orientalist tropes, ideas and motifs. Martin's description of Daenerys Targaryen's conquest of Slaver's Bay emphasizes the cultural difference between East and West by reproducing a number of familiar Orientalist fantasies. Although Western attitudes towards Islamic cultures underwent a series of changes from the Middle Ages onwards – ranging from overt hostility and paranoia through to indifference and appreciation – the most well-documented phase of scholarly and artistic Orientalism is that associated with the eighteenth and nineteenth centuries. Martin's depiction of the homogenized culture of Slaver's Bay draws on this familiar Western view of the Orient. There are three key elements of this fantasy that recur in Martin's work: despotism, the degrading treatment of women and the presence of castrated, lower-class men. Historically, this cluster of Orientalist themes emerged as the Ottoman Empire lost military ground to the West in the mid-eighteenth century. It was accompanied by a growing sense of Western sociopolitical superiority, which persisted throughout the eighteenth and nineteenth centuries and resurfaced in the post-Second World War period.

Although such cultures had previously been respected for their accumulation of wisdom or feared for their military acumen, from the mid-seventeenth century the notion that hotter climates produced a lazy, servile population and that Muslim nations were therefore doomed to suffer under despotic rulers was widely propagated by respected Enlightenment thinkers such as Montesquieu and reinforced by the most prominent philosophers of the Age of Reason.[13] Alongside the fantasy of cruel or servile men was the growing interest in the role of Muslim women. According to Mohja Kahf, in medieval and early modern Western discourse the Muslim woman was frequently presented as powerful and authoritative: a figure to be feared rather than pitied.[14] This also changed in the seventeenth century as Western philosophers and writers became fascinated by the symbolism of the veil and the culture of the harem. As Kahf points out, it is no coincidence that the Western preoccupation with the veil and the harem slave coincided with the rise of the Western ideology of femininity purity and domestication: 'Harem discourse rationalises for men and women the gentler suppressions of patriarchy at home. It releases a whole series of soothing rationalizations from the point of view of patriarchal authority, at least our women are "free", at least our women are autonomous individuals with souls, not animals, at least we have a single sexual standard.'[15] This discursive 'Othering' increased until 'Muslim women were wholly defined by helplessness and subdued speech'.[16] Closely aligned to the figure of the enervated and oppressed Muslim woman was a male figure who personified the supposed servile and effeminate character of Muslim men: the eunuch. Again, the Enlightenment fascination with this figure drew life from European domestic concerns. Following events such as the Glorious Revolution in England in 1688, and the later fall of the aristocracy in France after 1789, the idea of the subservient and effeminate man came to be associated with grovelling male courtiers and the despised and outdated culture of absolutism.

Moreover, the continued existence of slavery looms large over the Essos plotline. Astapor is the first of the three countries that Daenerys conquers in Slaver's Bay. Her initial reason for stopping there en route to Westeros is to purchase a group of highly trained eunuch slave warriors known as 'the Unsullied'. At this point in the story, the exiled white princess is no longer under the control of her vicious brother or savage husband. By giving birth to dragons, rather than the dying Khal's son, and assuming power over the Dothraki tribe, she has also unquestionably established her right to the Iron Throne and Seven Kingdoms of Westeros. It is therefore all the more significant that Martin swiftly diverts the storyline from the exiled princess's self-serving quest to purchase eastern slave labour into a humanitarian crusade on behalf of women, children and a slave army of eunuchs. In one of the most powerful scenes in the Essos section, Daenerys 'liberates' the Unsullied by tricking their brutal master, Kraznys, into believing that she will offer him the largest and most powerful of her dragons in payment for the Unsullied. Daenerys, who is proficient in many languages, has been pretending to use the cruel master's young female child scribe, Missandei, to translate his comments but is really fluent in 'high Valyrian' and thus understands all the demeaning and misogynist remarks that Missandei has tactfully edited from his speech. Kraznys concludes his charm offensive by slicing off one of the Unsullied's nipples to illustrate their inability to respond to any cruelty inflicted upon them by the superior class. The reader/viewer is thus prompted to cheer wholeheartedly when Daenerys exchanges the dragon for the phallic staff that controls the Unsullied and promptly instructs them to kill all the masters while also directing her dragon to immolate the cruel and misogynist Kraznys. Despite her former motivations for stopping in Slaver's Bay, her second act is to offer the Unsullied a freedom which they decline in favour of willingly following her.

In this and many subsequent scenes, Daenerys, as empowered, weaponized, white, Western woman, inflicts a vengeful punishment on the misogynist males of Essos on behalf of those they oppress within their own cultures. Such scenes reanimate Orientalist stereotypes of the despotic or craven Middle Eastern male for modern audiences. As Jack G. Shaheen's comprehensive analysis of Hollywood depictions of the Arab world has established, the Western fantasy of the cruel, licentious Arab male was enthusiastically taken up by early cinema.

Over a century later it is still evident in recent Hollywood products such as *The Mummy* series (1999, 2001, 2008) and the Abu Dhabi-based *Sex and The City 2* (2010). The lavish HBO adaptation of *Game of Thrones* visualizes the avaricious and misogynist Kraznys very much in terms associated with the long-standing Hollywood 'bad Arab' stereotype described by Shaheen; Kraznys is hook-nosed, bearded, robed and bejewelled. Appearing within a lengthy saga in which characterization is rarely black and white, Kraznys's only plot function is to provide a suitable target for Daenerys's righteous feminist rage. Shaheen points out that a crucial element of the bad Arab stereotype is the idea that Arab men 'kill one another and drool over the Western heroine, ignoring their own women'.[17] This dynamic is reproduced in *A Song of Ice and Fire* as little is seen of the indigenous women of Essos while dark-skinned, Middle Eastern men are obsessed by the pale-skinned and platinum-haired Western Princess.

The scene between Daenerys, Missandei, Kraznys and the Unsullied in Astapor sets the tone for all Daenerys's future encounters with the men of this region. They are either powerful, arrogant, cruel and shockingly misogynistic or grateful, childlike and adoring, like the Unsullied. Hughey's analysis of white saviour narratives observes that 'the key people of color to be saved from their darker communities (generally the few with a speaking role, or the folks who say more than a few stereotypical and racialized lines in a diction associated with their group) are exceptions to the rule'.[18]

Hughey's analysis of recent US film narratives is highly relevant to Martin's treatment of ethnicity here. Of the many freed slaves of Astrapor, Daenerys only acquires two new members of her intimate circle: the child scribe Missandei and the childlike Grey Worm, the latter being the only member of thousands of the Unsullied to be drawn as an individual character. Both are of a darker hue and are more than willing to submit to the superior wisdom offered by Daenerys and her two high-born, white, male Western advisors. In more general terms, all the cultures of Slaver's Bay appear almost comically patriarchal and violent. Although we are told that, unlike in Astapor, 'Yunkai is known for training bed slaves, not warriors', indigenous women appear to have even less status than in Dothraki tribal culture, leaving Daenerys to assert the dignity of her sex against what appears to be an entirely male-dominated culture. As Hughey also states, in white saviour narratives, 'For the white saviour to materialize, he or she must do so not for the reason of saving a sole person of colour. Rather, the chosen person … must be contextualized within an overall culture of non-white poverty, dysfunction, and pathology from which there is no self-salvation.'[19]

Martin's gritty medievalism depicts much cruelty, violence and poor treatment of women in Westeros. Hanging and dismemberment are common punishments; knights die screaming after jousting contests; peasants' armies are slaughtered at the behest of lords who care nothing for them; and numerous villages are razed to the ground in the war of the five kings. Yet there are also strong codes of civility and honour. The worst butchery disrupts the social order and is therefore treated with distaste. Women are regarded as inferior to men in terms of inheritance and the ability to hold high office, but they are also a strong presence within the Westeros narrative and are able to wield power at court through the influence of their sons, brothers and fathers. In comparison to prior high fantasy forms, the story also includes a high number of likeable and intelligent fighting women, such as Arya Stark and the female knight Brienne of Tarth. One of the key Westeros characters is also a eunuch, Lord Varys, who began life as a slave in Essos but is able to rise to high office in Westeros. The depiction of such obvious differences in the potential for social mobility and levels of tolerance and equality is linked to the suggested visual and cultural association between the hot, dusty and underdeveloped Middle Eastern states of Slaver's Bay and more recent Western images of Muslim-majority nations. For example, the popular HBO series repeatedly presents scenes in which the indigenous population of Slaver's Bay are visible only at mass gatherings. While the handful of white Western characters in Essos are shown engaging in reasoned discussions in the few shady and palatial buildings in the city, the local population is depicted as a dirty and hysterical street mob. By reproducing such images of Middle Eastern societies in Essos, Martin's secondary world covertly reinforces the idea that Muslim-majority areas of the globe are 'unchanging, barbaric, misogynist and uncivilized'.[20]

In contrast, all the key character focalizers in Westeros are gifted with a 'modern' consciousness and the power of self-reflection. This allows them to see through the backward customs and beliefs of their age. They are thoughtful, pragmatic, self-aware characters turned loose in a pre-modern fantasy world. This is particularly evident in the case of Daenerys Targaryen. Despite possessing some fairly unique inborn talents, such as being able to walk through fire unburnt and give birth to a trio of terrifying dragons, Daenerys is also a cultured and intelligent woman. She has never set foot on Westeros but exhibits the most advanced enlightened thinking of the more sophisticated Westeros characters. Following her conquest of Astapor, Daenerys attempts to rescue and re-educate this barbaric culture by leaving it in the hands of a coalition of more civilized men, led by a healer, a scholar and a priest: *'Wise men all, she thought, and just'*.[21]

She begins her campaign to invade the desert city of Yunkai by recruiting another army of disempowered men, a group of mercenaries known as 'the second sons', and bombarding the city walls with the chains of her freed slaves. When the slaves of the walled city are persuaded to kill their masters and accept her rule, they open their gates to her, and she is passed among them while they chant 'Mhysa, Mhysa' ('Mother') in unison. Martin describes the scene in the following manner:

> 'Mhysa!' a brown skinned-man shouted out at her. He had a child on his shoulder and she screamed the same word in a thin voice. 'Mhysa, Mhysa!'
> Dany looked at Missandei, 'What are they shouting?'
> It is Ghiscari, the old pure tongue. It means 'Mother'.
> Dany felt a lightness in her chest. I will never bear a living child, she remembered. Her hand trembled as she raised it. Perhaps she smiled. She must have because the man grinned and shouted again, and the others took up the cry. 'Mhysa! MHYSA!' They were all smiling at her, reaching for her, kneeling before her.
> Ser Jorah urged her to go, but Dany remembered a dream she had dreamed in the house of the Undying. 'They will not hurt me', she told him. 'They are my children, Jorah.'[22]

The imperialist white saviour overtones of this event were heightened when depicted on screen as the 'little scribe' Missandei (a child in the novels) is made older to become a friend and mixed-race 'sidechick' for Daenerys. By recasting Missandei as an adoring follower rather than an intelligent child, the series emphasizes Daenerys's authority over Missandei through race and culture, rather than age. Missandei looks on in wonder as the pale-skinned, blonde Daenerys crowd-surfs over a vast sea of brown faces and bodies. Much of the crowd is female and wearing headscarves, thus specifically evoking images of those veiled Muslim women supposedly to be set free by the interventions of others.

Given the gender and racial power dynamics of such scenes, it is not difficult to see how Martin's early twenty-first-century white saviour narrative, twinned with the themes of Middle Eastern despotism and misogyny, carries echoes of the Western media's consistent portrayal of Muslim-majority cultures as backward and women-hating during this period. As Lila Abu-Lughod reminds us, in the period prior to and during the so-called War on Terror, the wives of Western leaders, such as Laura Bush and Cherie Blair, were enlisted to speak out on behalf of oppressed Muslim women.[23] In the United States, in particular, national news outlets repeatedly ran stories on the brutal treatment of Afghan women by fathers, brothers, husbands and in-laws in Taliban-controlled areas. Abu-Lughod argues that such stories raised Western fears as to the fate of women in Muslim countries without Western intervention or support. Daenerys's crowd-pleasing conquest of Astapor and Yunkai, and, in particular, her repeated attempts to rescue the oppressed men, women and children of Slaver's Bay, offers a high fantasy justification for real world neo-imperialist invasions. It evokes an older, post-war notion of 'benevolent supremacy', in which conquest is justified when it leads to the establishment of modern democratic states, and echoes the more recent neoconservative strategy of justifying intervention through a more direct human rights agenda. For all its feminist trappings, in the series the Western mission to 'rescue' Muslim women from the men in their own communities is played out once more.

Religion, radicalization and resistance in West and East

I want finally to consider the more ambivalent aspects of Martin's treatment of the East–West divide in *A Song of Ice and Fire*: his treatment of religion and the development of the Essos plotline in the context of the aftermath of the Iraq invasion and the intensification of fears of radicalization among Muslims in Western countries. As we have seen, *A Song of Ice and Fire* displays a consistent interest in gender inequality and class exploitation and a scepticism towards traditional forms of male heroism that bear all the traces of Martin's youthful engagement with the countercultural politics of the 1960s and 1970s. The instinctive anti-authoritarianism associated with that era of American youth politics is also evident in his treatment of organized religion. Indeed, although Martin's recurring use of Eurocentric perspectives and Orientalist motifs dovetails with the intensification of state and media Islamophobia in the last two decades, religion is not a prominent part of Martin's negative depiction of the Eastern states. His mistrust of organized religion is very much in evidence in all other aspects of the narrative. *A Song of Ice and Fire* features a number of different religions but there are four which are given particular attention: the 'Old' northern pagan gods; the quasi-Viking religion of the 'Drowned God'; the 'Faith of the Seven' (the most powerful religion in Westeros) and the upstart 'new' religion of R'hllor, 'Lord of the Light'. Of these four, only the first is portrayed as relatively harmless. The Old Gods are associated with the 'House of Stark': a dour clan of no-nonsense northerners and the only noble house that provides the series with more than a couple of good-hearted characters. As Peter O' Leary observes, the wise and just father of the Stark clan, Eddard Stark, 'belongs to an old faith whose primordiality is ascertained from legendary implications: children of the forest, a heroic ancestor, the dawn of time'.[24]

The faith of the Old Gods is presented as the most venerable and authentic of the faiths. It is also the religion that chimes most easily with contemporary eco-politics and Martin's countercultural roots, as it encourages harmony with nature, has no clerical hierarchy and imposes few constraints on human pleasure. The religion of the Drowned God is crude and warlike but limited in influence whereas the two more powerful religions in the series – the established Faith of the Seven, roughly based on Renaissance Christianity, and the rising, eastern religion of R'hllor – are depicted as bigoted, oppressive and cruel. The uncompromising religion of R'hllor combines aspects of Zoroastrianism and Islam: the former through the importance of fire rituals and its followers' belief in the coming of a hero called Azor Ahai, and the latter, more overtly, through its challenge to the 'Faith of the Seven'. Echoing the Christian belief in the Holy Trinity and the Catholic cult of Mary, the established Church of Westeros believes in the existence of multiple divine figures of both sexes. The eastern religion of R'hllor has no female godheads and its principle challenge to the established Church of Westeros is based on the superiority of monotheism and 'the one true god'. However, its eastern roots are not emphasized in the series. Instead, its destructive influence is felt in Westeros largely through the actions of a 'red priestess' who delights in burning those who oppose her faith. More pertinently, Martin, a lapsed Catholic himself, is equally critical of the corrupt and misogynistic quasi-Christian Faith of the Seven.

The later novels focus extensively on the challenge to the wealthy and corrupt Westeros Septons by an ascetic and punitive sect known as the 'Faith Militant' and led by a charismatic, manipulative character known as the 'High Sparrow'. The saga moves more towards historical than fantasy fiction at this point as it parallels the Protestant challenge to the power of Rome in sixteenth-century Europe in fairly direct terms. In this sense, Martin is even-handed in his evident suspicion of all organized religion. The Faith Militant plotline could be seen as undermining the Orientalist view that religious fanaticism is a specifically Eastern phenomenon and reminding readers and viewers that the modern European states emerged through a series of bitter religious struggles. However, in the context of a rising tide of Islamophobic propaganda, in which a particular community's levels of religiosity are viewed as an index of their capacity for hatred and violence, *A Song of Ice and Fire*'s fictitious reworking of the Reformation is double-edged in terms of its potential associations. The Faith Militant are opposed to all forms of pleasure. They are ascetic, homophobic, misogynist and either weak and gullible or bitter and vindictive. Female converts wear long robes with only their faces uncovered. They delight in torturing and humiliating women who have transgressed sexually, with one key scene depicting a high-born female character, Cercei Lannister, forced to strip naked and walk through the streets of the capital city, followed by two women ringing a bell and shouting the word 'shame'. Male converts patrol the city in gangs and are easily persuaded to commit acts of terrorism. They are also portrayed as troubled young men who seek affirmation through group recognition and acceptance. Despite being an offshoot of what is broadly representative of early Protestantism, Martin's critique of the cult of the High Sparrow and its appeal to disaffected members of society thus veer dangerously close to reproducing the media cliché of gendered patterns of radicalization and Islamic fanaticism.

Fear of radicalization and insurgency also surface in the Essos plotline during the same timeframe. This is linked to Daenerys Targaryen's inability to establish fully a more complex and egalitarian system of government in Slaver's Bay. As we have seen, in her role as white saviour Daenerys swiftly conquers the Middle Eastern states through a combination of dragon-led 'shock and awe' and a well-developed sense of moral and ethical superiority. Although there are many scenes that encourage the reader to cheer her on, Astapor and Yunkai are left in chaos owing to her rapid departure and inability to lay the groundwork for an alternative economic system. This results in civil war and the renewed dominance of the slave-owning class. In Meereen, Daenerys's rule is undermined by the rise of a group of masked, armed guerrillas known as 'The Sons of the Harpy'. Again, this suggests a conscious reference to the growth of Islamic insurgency groups in the 'Sunni Triangle' area around Baghdad, Fallujah and Tikrit in the aftermath of the US withdrawal. After several terrorist incidents – including an attack on a brothel – Daenerys attempts to retain control and quell rebellion by marrying a member of the former slave class and reopening the banned fighting pits. Her reluctant compromises do little to deter the insurgents, and Daenerys becomes increasingly hostile to and dismissive of the indigenous population.

In Weiss and Benioff's adaptation (which takes the story beyond Martin's published novels) this culminates in a public massacre by the insurgents and Daenerys's literal flight from the region. Martin's choice to publish his account of the rapid and hubristic conquest of large regions of Essos followed by armed insurrection, sectarian violence and retreat during the period in which the US invasion of Iraq and Afghanistan followed the same course is unlikely to be coincidental. The gap in time between the 2000's volume *A Storm of Swords*, which anticipates the invasion, and 2011's two-volume *A Dance with Dragons*, which depicts organized insurgency and the eventual retreat of the occupying power, is of particular significance. Yet the allegorical critique of the conflict is only partially based on a suspicion of neo-imperial motives. Daenerys is swept away on a tide of ego-boosting adulation and makes poor decisions. Echoing the chaos that followed the occupation of Iraq and Afghanistan, she fails to provide any alternative plan after dismantling the economy and the infrastructure of Yunkai and Astapor subsequently collapses, leading to civil war. She also deals too harshly with her enemies and underestimates the power of organized resistance to her rule, but these failings are set alongside what is presented as a more fundamental problem with the backward culture and mindset of the people in the mock-Middle Eastern regions of Slaver's Bay.

The secondary world reimagining of the invasion and occupation of Iraq and Afghanistan in *A Song of Ice and Fire* emphasizes the region's inability to embrace freedom and individualism rather than the Western desire to dominate and conquer. The inner thoughts of Daenerys, as key character focalizer in this section, are the reader's sole guide to the character and behaviour of the inhabitants of Essos and Slaver's Bay. As Daenerys is depicted as one of the few fair-minded and moral characters in the saga, we are encouraged to accept her reflections on the intrinsic cowardice and ignorance of the inhabitants of the region through comments such as, '*I gave them their city, and most of them were too frightened to take it*'.[25] We are also informed that the people of Meereen '*were a sly and stubborn people that resisted her at every turn*'.[26] Daenerys's attitude towards them becomes increasingly condescending and dismissive in the later books, with observations such as, '*To rule the Meereense, I must win the Meereense, however much I may despise them*'[27] and finally, '*Perhaps I cannot make my people good, she told herself, but I should at least try to make them a little less bad*'.[28] Daenerys's prejudiced comments thus compromise Martin's allegorical critique of US foreign policy. They also work to reinforce current forms of Islamophobia through the visual and cultural association of Essos with contemporary Western attitudes towards the indigenous populations of Muslim-majority nations.

Conclusion

As the multi-volume saga reaches its denouement, the ideological inconsistencies within the Essos plotline become increasingly evident. In series five of the HBO adaptation – based on Martin's long-awaited and as yet unpublished *The Winds of*

Winter – two of the most sophisticated and politically astute Westeros characters finally arrive in Essos. Westeros spymaster, Lord Varys, and the pragmatic and intelligent Lord Tyrion Lannister plan to swear allegiance to the queen but find the 'liberated' states in chaos. They immediately put in place effective counter-insurgency strategies and implement some much-needed negotiating skills to broker a more gradual transition towards primitive democracy. The Western characters then set sail to retake the Iron Throne with Daenerys as their figurehead. The conclusion of the Essos strand of the narrative – planned originally as a minor plotline but later extended by Martin – therefore provides something approaching an upbeat resolution but at the price of the series' liberal and feminist credentials. As we have seen, Daenerys's role as liberator is justified by a popular feminist ideology of female empowerment and individualism, linked to a broader mission to rescue women, children and disempowered men in the slave states. This fails, in part, due to Martin's later decision to rework the Essos storyline as an allegory of the US's failed attempts to 'liberate' Iraq and Afghanistan. After leaving Astapor and Yunkai in chaos and with a growing insurgency movement in Meereen, her disastrous attempts at regime change are redeemed by Daenerys's newly arrived Westeros supporters. This tangled knot of feminist and anti-imperialist storylines thus concludes in a manner that undermines one of the more progressive aspects of the series, as Daenerys's role as liberator and moral authority is supplanted by two elder statesmen. More significantly, Tyrion and Varys's ability swiftly to restore peace and stability to the region presents a fantasy resolution of the catastrophic destabilization of the Middle East that has continued in the wake of the real-world invasion and occupation.

Despite his liberal credentials and evident sympathy for the (Western) underdog, Martin's expanded vision of a global secondary world thus succeeds only in reanimating a number of well-worn Orientalist tropes, motifs and stereotypes. The Essos/Slaver's Bay strand of the novels and highly popular HBO adaptation of Martin's *A Song of Ice and Fire* invests much readerly/audience pleasure in Daenerys Targaryen's role in what Hughey, in other contexts, defines as a 'white saviour' narrative. Many pivotal scenes in Slaver's Bay draw emotional force from the conflict between Daenerys, as a liberated woman and a liberator of oppressed men, women and children, and what are presented as backward Middle Eastern cultures. Such cultures are symbolized by the figure of the cruel, licentious Arab male that Shaheen identifies as ubiquitous in over a century of Middle Eastern-based popular US films. Martin's work therefore connects with a number of pre-existing ethnic stereotypes and racist plotlines. Specifically, by harnessing the white saviour plot and the familiar 'bad Arab' stereotype to his allegorical treatment of recent US military campaigns in the Middle East, Martin indirectly contributes to the store of anti-Muslim imagery that has escalated during the period in which his series has achieved both widespread popularity and critical acclaim. *A Song of Ice and Fire*'s clumsy recycling of Orientalist clichés in a highly popular fantasy world thus not only displays an acute lack of racial and cultural sensitivity but risks reinforcing the worst aspects of hardline state and media Islamophobia in the context of escalating real-world discrimination against Muslims.

Notes

1 George R. R. Martin quoted in Helen Young, *Race and Fantasy Fiction: Habits of Whiteness* (Oxford: Routledge, 2015), p. 63.
2 Martin in Young, *Race and Fantasy Fiction*, p. 67.
3 Ibid., p. 64.
4 Edward James, 'Tolkien, Lewis and the explosion of genre fantasy', in Edward James and Farah Mendlesohn (eds), *The Cambridge Companion to Fantasy Fiction* (Cambridge: Cambridge University Press, 2012).
5 John Wilkinson, 'Editorial introduction', *Game of Thrones* special issue, *Critical Quarterly*, 57/1 (2015), p. 1.
6 Young, *Race and Fantasy Fiction*, p. 64.
7 Kumar, *Islamophobia*, pp. 39–40.
8 Matthew W. Hughey, *The White Savior Film: Contents, Critics, and Consumption* (Philadelphia, PA: Tempress, 2015), p. 28.
9 Christina Scharff, 'Disarticulating feminism: Individualization, neoliberalism and the Othering of Muslim women', *European Journal of Women's Studies* 18/2 (2011), pp. 119–34.
10 Nancy Fraser, 'Feminism, capitalism and the cunning of history', *New Left Review* 56 (2009) pp. 97–117.
11 Lila Abu-Lughod, *Do Muslim Women Need Saving?* (Cambridge, MA and London: Harvard University Press, 2013), pp. 81–112.
12 George R. R. Martin, '"Game of Thrones" Author Slams Republicans for "Voter Suppression"', *Huffington Post*, 13 August 2012. Available at www.huffingtonpost.com/2012/08/13/game-of-thrones-author-republicans_n_1773283.html (accessed 15 September 2017).
13 Deepa Kumar, *Islamophobia and the Politics of Empire* (Chicago, IL: Haymarket Books, 2012), p. 22.
14 Mohja Kahf, *Western Representations of the Muslim Woman: From Termagant to Odalisque* (Austin, TX: University of Texas Press, 1999).

15 Kahf, *Western Representations of the Muslim Woman*, p. 135.
16 Ibid., p. 122.
17 Jack G. Shaheen, *Reel Bad Arabs: How Hollywood Vilifies a People* (Northampton, MA: Olive Branch Press, 2003), p. 8.
18 Hughey, *White Savior*, p. 168.
19 Ibid., p. 168.
20 Kumar, *Islamophobia*, p. 33.
21 George R. R. Martin, *A Storm of Swords, Vol. 2: Blood and Gold* (London: Harper Voyager, 2011), p. 3. Italics in original.
22 Martin, *A Storm of Swords*, p. 19.
23 Abu-Lughod, *Do Muslim Women*, p. 31.
24 Peter O'Leary, 'Sacred Fantasy in *Game of Thrones*', *Game of Thrones* special issue, *Critical Quarterly*, 57/1 (2015), p. 7.
25 Martin, *A Storm of Swords*, p. 3.
26 George R. R. Martin, *A Dance with Dragons, Vol. 2: After the Feast* (London: Harper Voyager, 2012), p. 40.
27 Martin, *A Dance with Dragons*, p. 41.
28 Ibid., p. 183.

Works cited

Abu-Lughod, Lila, *Do Muslim Women Need Saving?* (Cambridge, MA and London: Harvard University Press, 2013).

Fraser, Nancy, 'Feminism, capitalism and the cunning of history', *New Left Review* 56 (2009), pp. 97–117.

Huffington Post, 'George R. R. Martin, "Game of Thrones" Author Slams Republicans for "Voter Suppression"', *Huffington Post*, 13 August 2012. Available at www.huffingtonpost.com/2012/08/13/game-of-thrones-author-republicans_n_1773283.html (accessed 15 September 2017).

Hughey, Matthew W., *The White Savior Film: Contents, Critics, and Consumption* (Philadelphia, PA: Tempress, 2015).

James, Edward, 'Tolkien, Lewis and the explosion of genre fantasy', in Edward James and Farah Mendlesohn (eds), *The Cambridge Companion to Fantasy Fiction* (Cambridge: Cambridge University Press, 2012).

Kahf, Mohja, *Western Representations of the Muslim Woman: From Termagant to Odalisque* (Austin, TX: Texas University Press, 1999).

Kumar, Deepa, *Islamophobia and the Politics of Empire* (Chicago, IL: Haymarket Books, 2012).

Martin, George R.R., *A Dance with Dragons, Vol. 2: After the Feast* (London: Harper Voyager, 2012).

Martin, George R.R., *A Storm of Swords, Vol. 2: Blood and Gold* (London: Harper Voyager, 2011).

O'Leary, Peter, 'Sacred Fantasy in *Game of Thrones*', *Game of Thrones* special issue', *Critical Quarterly* 57/1 (2015).

Scharff, Christina, 'Disarticulating feminism: Individualization, neoliberalism and the Othering of Muslim women', *European Journal of Women's Studies* 18/2 (2011), pp. 119–34.

Shaheen, Jack G., *Reel Bad Arabs: How Hollywood Vilifies a People* (Northampton, MA: Olive Branch Press, 2003).

Wilkinson, John, '"Editorial introduction", *Game of Thrones* special issue', *Critical Quarterly* 57/1 (2015).

Young, Helen, *Race and Fantasy Fiction: Habits of Whiteness* (Oxford: Routledge, 2015).

6

Islamic Feminism in a Time of Islamophobia: The Muslim Heroines of Leila Aboulela's *Minaret* and Elif Shafak's *Forty Rules of Love*

Amina Yaqin

Introduction

Traditionally, ethnographies and Orientalist narratives have played a major part in translating the veil and Muslim women for the West, but more recently creative writing by Muslim women in particular has captured public attention for its seemingly authentic confessional style promising to lift the veil on women's subjugation.[1] From the polemical feminist position of a well-known Egyptian writer such as Nawal el-Sadawi to the psychological 'feminine' writing of the British Sudanese writer Leila Aboulela, we can see varied interpretations grappling with specific historical moments in Muslim women's identification with pious forms of dress. In literature, the veil has been one of the 'myths of the Orient' that has fascinated European travellers and contributed to fantastical representations of the mystic East in which women figure as sexual slaves or as queens.[2] Therefore, Muslim women writers undertaking the task of writing about the veil are not just responding to contemporary Islamophobia, but are also in conversation with those earlier representations that objectify women. In their attempt to reclaim women's individual subjectivities within Islam, stories by Muslim women writers have traversed transnational and global geographies from Iran to South Asia, from North Africa to the United States and the nations of Europe. These narratives often illustrate complementary and competing ideological positions and shifting perspectives representing Muslim women for a global audience.

In this chapter, I wish to consider how Muslim women's writing engages with the veil, women's rights and Islamic feminism, and whether it challenges or reinforces Islamophobic ideas of the veiled woman as a passive victim of a patriarchal religion. In particular, I will interrogate the work of two women authors, Leila Aboulela and Elif Shafak, who have made significant contributions to the field of English literature with distinctive stories about historical and contemporary global Muslim cultures in the West. I analyse their writing through the lens of Islamic feminism in an attempt to interrogate how gender, culture and identity are dealt with in their fiction, as well as reflecting on their broader attempts to contest Islamophobia through introspective stories that explode popular myths about Muslim women as victims of sharia. In my reading of Leila Aboulela's *Minaret*, I consider the protagonist Najwa as a flawed character. The psychological and moral growth of her character, represented in the form of the traditional *Bildungsroman*, does not lead to a happy ending. Instead, she is cast adrift, unable to find peace through either her romantic involvements or her religious affiliations, and retreats into a nostalgic yearning for the past. Her female experience is marked by loss and a mourning for her mother, pulling against her romantic relationships and desire to form bonds, based in Islam, that will play out genuine male–female complementarity in her life. By contrast, *The Forty Rules of Love* by Elif Shafak goes beyond the veil to tell the story of a disillusioned suburban North American housewife, Ella, and her attraction to a wandering Sufi traveller, Aziz.[3] Shafak uses the literary device of *mise en abîme* to embed within the framing twenty-first-century narrative the historical story of Rumi and his companion Shams in thirteenth-century Turkey. This ancient tale is refracted through her contemporary characters who come together in the pursuit of an eternal love. In the process of reiterating Sufism as a softer side of Islam, Shafak arguably reproduces an Orientalist sensibility, but her innovation lies in the critique of the stereotypical identification of women as passive victims. My purpose in contrasting these two very different novelists is to consider their depiction of male–female relationships and to trace possible affinities to a vision of complementarity between men and women, emerging from recent Islamic feminist translations of Sura Al-Nisa in the Qur'an that emphasize gender equality instead of patriarchal supremacy. Writing at a time of heightened Islamophobia, both Aboulela and Shafak are responding to the limited trajectories available to women in stereotypical representations of Islam. To change the narrative of a patriarchal and oppressive Islam, they connect with traditional and modern, conservative and liberal Islamic filters to articulate female subjectivities that affirm the centrality of women's roles beyond passive stereotypes. In doing so, they contribute to a global Islamic feminism that, according to miriam cooke, offers 'multiple critiques', traversing transnational networks and forging 'strategic alliances' to put forward an alternative representation of female agency that challenges the normative understanding of women as second-class citizens in Islamic discourse.⁴

Both Aboulela and Shafak offer alternative visions of Islam that demand a deeper engagement from their readers beyond the cliché of the veil as a signifier of Muslim Otherness. Their stories contribute to the diverse landscape of global Islamicate cultures, revealing intricate narratives of morality and ethics that are shaped by tradition but which also connect with other perspectives. Aboulela's writing carries the trademark of visible Muslim identification. Her storylines seek to translate the lives of pious Muslim women living as migrants in a non-Muslim society. She attempts to depict what might be called an 'Islamic consciousness' in her novels. That her fiction is responding to Islamophobia is especially evident in her second novel, *Minaret*, published in 2005 and long-listed for the Orange Prize for Fiction and the IMPAC prize. Lindsey Moore has described the novel as a spiritual *Bildungsroman* with its characterization and 'personal transformation' of a diasporic Sudanese female protagonist, Najwa. Moore argues that the novel challenges 'reader perceptions of feminist discourse and practice' with a heroine who reflects 'feminine' rather than 'feminist values'.⁵ In contrast to this first-person story of a Sudanese girl is the epic bestselling Sufi romance *The Forty Rules of Love* by the celebrated and award-winning Turkish novelist and public intellectual Elif Shafak. A recipient of many international prizes, Shafak is a frequent commentator in the English news media, known for her fictional rewriting of the Ottoman period with contemporary twists and her cosmopolitan outlook. She describes writing a novel as a 'secular act of faith. ... I don't want religions to hijack faith. I want the concept of faith back.'⁶ *The Forty Rules of Love* is a book that is shaped by the desire to familiarize its readers with Islam's heterodox traditions. Telling the story of a Western housewife who follows a Sufi path, having been introduced to the moral disputes of Rumi and his companion Shams, the novel suggests a way in which women can be beneficiaries of progressive Islamic values.

The visibility of Muslim women, sharia and Islamic feminism

In both novels, the veil is a literal and metaphoric presence in the representation of characters and storylines. Mohja Kahf has shown how depictions of Muslim women have changed through the centuries from a medieval fascination with the symbolic figure of the powerful Eastern queen to post-eighteenth-century Romantic notions of the passive Oriental female, cooped up in the harem or behind the veil, waiting to be rescued by the Western male hero. Kahf points out how this shifting view of the Muslim woman coincides with changes in European models of femininity, which themselves came to emphasize the chaste middle-class woman inhabiting domestic space.[7] In the current landscape, the literary and cultural sphere has contributed to a reimagining of Muslim women by a wider spectrum of individuals and grass-roots groups that challenge such normative ideals.[8] Some of these suggest a link between femininity – even a certain mode of indigenous feminism – and piety.[9]

In Islamic societies, the debate is often about the visibility of women in the public sphere, sharia and women's rights. Leila Ahmed's pioneering study on *Women and Gender in Islam: Historical Roots of a Modern Debate* offered a nuanced understanding of gender relations in Islam by interrogating the notion of an embedded patriarchy in the religion. She contested the naturalized view of women's oppression by looking at the specificity of historical and regional contexts in Islamic societies, and provided, among other things, an alternative way of reading the veil.[10] Since then there have been many contributions to the field, and new directions have emerged from post-secular approaches. For instance, *The Politics of Piety*, Saba Mahmood's ethnographic study of the mosque movement – a women's revivalist Islamic grass-roots (*da'wa*) piety movement in the mosques of Cairo – provides an insight into the debate that has taken place among its members over how female modesty (*al ihtisham al-haya*) 'should be lived' and the necessity of wearing the veil to prove one's 'virtue'. Mahmood observes that

> while wearing the veil serves at first as a means to tutor oneself in the attribute of shyness, it is also simultaneously integral to the practices of shyness: one cannot simply discard the veil once a modest deportment has been acquired, because the veil itself is part of what defines that deportment. This is a crucial aspect of the disciplinary program pursued by the participants of the mosque movement, the significance of which is elided when the veil is understood solely in terms of its symbolic value as a marker of women's subordination or Islamic identity.[11]

Emphasizing the point about the performativity of the veil as a marker of piety and the inner transformation of the soul, she offers a reading that explains how, within the movement, sharia is absorbed as a moral and ethical duty.

For the believing woman, the outward performative journey to piety leads to a deeper inward belief. Mahmood's hermeneutic analysis incorporates critical strategies deployed by Talal Asad and Judith Butler, to advance a post-secular feminist interpretation of Muslim women's agency in the mosque movement, in opposition to that of liberal feminism which emphasizes material agency *in the world*. She argues that, while certain aspects of the movement challenge secular beliefs, such as the distinction between public and private, there are also other qualities that are similar to secular concepts, such as the understanding of teleology, cause and effect and so on.[12]

The re-visioning of the veil is thus inevitably linked to discussions about 'Islamic feminism', a contested term among critics and activists. The feminist historian Margot Badran is of the view that Islamic feminism should not be seen as a derivative phenomenon borrowed from the West. She argues that it remains 'grounded in Qur'anic interpretation or *tafsir*' with the aim of explaining and establishing gender rights and justice in Islam.[13] Islamic feminists, in her view, build their case for equality by focusing on the Qur'anic concepts of *khilafa* ('trusteeship') and *tawhid* ('oneness of God') as qualities that cannot be diminished by biological gender. An area that is often seen as troubling to their vision of gender equality in Islam is the institution of marriage, which, in conventional patriarchal interpretations, understands women to be subordinate to men. One of the ways Islamic feminists have addressed this is by reinterpreting the controversial Sura Al-Nisa ('Women') 4:34, which is usually read as providing proof of the elevation of men over women. The key phrase that Islamic feminists have re-appropriated is the much-debated Qur'anic term '*qawwamuna 'ala*' from the Sura, which has been interpreted in a variety of ways, generally so as to support established gender hierarchies. The verse that has caused disagreement has been translated by various scholars. Below, I juxtapose two translations of this verse by two Islamic scholars: the first is from the classic translation of the Qur'an published in 1930 by Mohammed Marmaduke Pickthall and the second a feminist 'interpretive' translation by Amina Wadud in 1992.

> Men are in charge of women, because Allah hath made the one of them to excel the other, and because they spend of their property (for the support of women). So good women are the obedient, guarding in secret that which Allah hath guarded. (4.34)[14]

> Men are [*qawwamuna 'ala*] women, [on the basis of] what Allah has [preferred] (*faddala*) some of them over others, and [on the basis] of what they spend of their property (for the support of women). So good women are [*qanitat*],

guarding in secret that which Allah has guarded. As for those from whom you fear [nushuz], admonish them, banish them to beds apart, and scourge them. Then, if they obey you, seek not a way against them. (4.34)[15]

If we contrast the two translations, then, in the second feminist rendition by Wadud we can see that some key words from the Arabic language have been retained and not translated, such as *qawwamuna 'ala* (meaning 'complementary to'), to avoid the pitfalls of gender-specific associations of the older translation. The significance of this can be understood in particular when we consider Pickthall's translation of the line 'men are in charge'. The feminist interpretation is aimed at re-visioning this patriarchal division of power by emphasizing a mutual relationship or complementarity between women and men that they take to be implied in the original. This allows for a correlation between the two genders instead of a construction of hierarchically divided separate spheres. In order to emphasize complementarity, Wadud applies a hermeneutic approach to the translations to highlight the equal rights of married women by interpreting the mother's role as equivalent to that of the male breadwinner. Her work is in conversation with other Islamic feminists who have also critiqued the idea of equal rights.[16] Linguistic knowledge, translation and a hermeneutic approach are thus key to the reconsideration of Qur'anic verse by Islamic feminists. The general consensus, as summarized by Badran, is that Islamic feminism continues to evolve with the changing nature of the family in modern Islamic societies and diasporas.[17]

The Forty Rules of Love

This concern with Islamic feminism and women's rights is also something that preoccupies Elif Shafak in her novel. In particular, the novel's engagement with Sura Al-Nisa emphasizes her feminist position on the question of women's subservience in Islam. *The Forty Rules of Love* narrates the story of a middle-aged Jewish American housewife, Ella, and her affair with a wandering traveller, the Sufi convert Aziz Zahara. Ella is unhappily married to a dentist, and when she is not looking after her grown children spends her time cooking or going to farmers' markets. In order to bring some novelty to her life she starts working part-time for a literary agency. Here she is given a book manuscript entitled *Sweet Blasphemy* written by Aziz. Deploying the literary device of a story within a story, Shafak transports her readers, through Aziz's manuscript, to the thirteenth-century tale of the Persian Sufi mystic Jalaluddin Rumi and his companion Shams. Ella finds herself drawn to Rumi's story and what follows is an epistolary romance between Ella and Aziz. As they gravitate towards each other, she grows apart from her family and their relationship ends up replicating the intense companionship of Rumi and Shams. The plot alternates between the characters of Rumi and Shams and Ella and Aziz, as the American housewife experiences a rekindling of the desire for love. She is shown to be in a moral vacuum because her life is governed by material needs and not shaped by a spiritual quest, but she is saved from falling into the depths of depression by her discovery of Sufism. Shafak's Sufi narrative reflects an ideologically liberal vision of Islam emphasizing coexistence and harmony, encapsulated in the overarching relationship between Shams and Rumi. The narrator depicts Shams as Rumi's saviour who helps him to reject the strictures of orthodox theology in order to develop a syncretic Sufi philosophy of tolerance and love. Under Shams's tutelage and influence, Rumi withdraws from his family with whom he has had a close relationship, in particular his Christian wife, Kerra, and his adopted daughter, Kimya.

These thirteenth-century figures, Kerra and Kimya, along with another woman, Desert Rose the Harlot, are key to the narrator's re-visioning of women's position in Islam. Their fragmented narratives, although minor, are significant to the plot as they translate some of the controversial positions on women's secondary status in Islam and return us to the context of Sura Al-Nisa. In fact, the omniscient narrator makes a direct reference to Sura Al-Nisa in an attempt to reinterpret it through an androgynous Sufi filter that harmonizes 'womanhood' and 'manhood' as one. Her translation of Al-Nisa echoes the approach taken by Amina Wadud and, more recently, Kecia Ali, who has modified classic translations of the Sura that prioritize the status of men over women by explaining the complexity of linguistic gender construction in the Qur'an, and by applying the principles of complementarity in her interpretation.[18] In the novel, we encounter the Sura halfway into the book, in the story-within-the-story, when Kimya, Rumi's adopted daughter, is confused by the teachings of Al-Nisa. Her questions are answered by Rumi's companion Shams. As her guide, he presents her with two translations of the troubling section: one in which women are shown to be secondary and subordinate to men and the other in which they are shown as the support of men and their other halves. Explaining his position to Kimya, he tells her that there are three ways of reading the Qur'an: literal, deep and esoteric. He sees her confusion about women's status as a result of a surface reading of the Qur'anic text and tells her, 'If you read the Nisa with your inner eye open, you'll see that the verse is not about womanhood and manhood. And each and every one of us, including you and me, has both femininity and masculinity in us, in varying degrees and shades. Only when we learn to embrace both can we attain harmonious Oneness.'[19]

Through the voice of Shams, the novel gives its reader an image of androgyny and a lesson in the feminist principle of complementarity in Islam. Yet, this philosophical moment is immediately followed by a shift that destroys complementarity by reintroducing the gender split quite starkly. This takes the form of an erotic encounter between Kimya and Shams. Kimya, who secretly desires Shams, finds that she is distracted by his body and 'manliness':

> I felt my youth in all its fullness, and yet somewhere inside me a maternal instinct sprawled, exuding the thick, milky scent of motherhood. I wanted to protect him. ... Shams put his hand on my shoulder, his face so close to mine that I could feel the warmth of his breath. ... He held me captive with his touch, caressing my cheeks, his fingertips as warm as a flame against my skin. ... Now his finger moved down, reaching my bottom lip. ... But no sooner had he touched my lips than Shams drew his hand back.[20]

I would suggest that this encounter, coming immediately after the philosophical endorsement of androgyny and complementarity, works against the central Sufi message by reinstating a heterosexual charge, required by the novel's romance features, and expected by the Western reader. It arguably distracts from the elucidation of an Islamic feminist position by shifting the mood from the ethical to the erotic. The arousal that both student and teacher feel is interpreted by Kimya as something that should end in sexual cohabitation through marriage. To that end she willingly agrees to marry Shams only to find out that he practises sexual abstinence. Kimya's romantic feelings and desire for sexual intimacy in marriage are within the philosophic spirit of complementarity, but it is not lived out in her experience. Here the narrator is caught between two moves: the scriptural translation of Al-Nisa through Kimya and the Sufi tradition of unrequited love via Shams. Kimya's position shifts from being the harbinger of gender equality and complementarity to symbolizing the 'lower nafs', the base feminine instinct in Sufi thinking that has to be suppressed in order for Shams to attain his spirituality. In the development of plot, Kimya's character becomes an obstacle in the path to Sufi realization for Shams, who understands Kimya less as a corporeal desiring subject than as a celestial being and an ideal of the 'feminine' who should help him to achieve his union with God. (As this example shows, the link between the generic features of the popular romance and scriptural Sufism is not always seamless in Shafak's novel, and they tend to interrupt and contradict one another.)

Female characters such as Kimya are caught between the stereotypical role of the prostitute and the familial ones of mother, wife and daughter. Within the narrative, spiritual attainment for women is only available to those who have undergone the rites of passage of sexuality, family and/or the brothel. Jamal Elias has observed that historically 'asceticism and celibacy were more prevalent among female than male mystics'.[21] In Shafak's story, this type of asceticism and celibacy is represented through the character of Desert Rose the Harlot, in the thirteenth-century parts of the story. She breaks the rules of society by entering the mosque disguised as a man and is discovered and saved from the wrath of the crowd by Shams, who calls into question the baser instincts of the men chasing her and persuades them to leave her alone. This marks a change in Desert Rose's life as she gives up prostitution and becomes an ascetic under the protection of Rumi. But Desert Rose is a minor character and her celibacy is always at risk from previous clients who disregard her transformation. The individuals who are highlighted as the true pinnacles of asceticism in the novel are the men, Rumi, Shams and Aziz, who seem to practise a more successful form of celibacy than the women who aspire to be mystics, such as Ella, Kerra, Kimya and Desert Rose. Women, it seems, are trapped within their bodies and cannot reach spiritual attainment.

Through her modern-day protagonist Ella, Shafak articulates her particular brand of feminism to show how an engagement with Islam's heterodox traditions can bring a positive change to a lacklustre life in the West. Aziz becomes Ella's fixation and her unattainable beloved, all the while softening her view of Islamic culture. Ella gives up her family for Aziz but their union is short-lived as he dies of cancer soon after. Earlier in the novel, when she learns of his fatal illness, she tells him emphatically that she is not a Sufi. At that point in the story he has been asking her to follow him to Konya where he wishes to die following in the footsteps of Rumi and Shams. He tells her, 'I know you're not a Sufi. ... Just be Rumi.'[22] Thus, Ella's subjectivity is manipulated by Aziz, whose needs take precedence and come to shape the pliant woman's character once again. By the end of the novel she seems to have become less an autonomous woman than a vessel through which the author can communicate Rumi's eternal message of love: '*A life without love is of no account. Don't ask yourself what kind of love you should seek, spiritual or material, divine or mundane, Eastern or Western. ... Divisions only lead to more divisions*'.[23]

While Shafak does give her heroine the agency to choose a Sufi route over family life, she channels this character's destiny along the paths of a romanticized notion of Sufism that appeals to a Western perception of Islamic mysticism.

In this framework Ella is merely a receptacle of individual enlightenment, liberating herself from societal restrictions in the twenty-first century in the same way as any discontented modern woman who might seek the frisson of self-discovery offered by another culture, rather than dedicating herself to any more wide-ranging or meaningful social transformation.[24] Thus Shafak's novel offers an instrumentalist reinterpretation of Islam as positive, relying on Orientalist tropes about Sufism to convey a vision that appeals to an American literary market. Elena Furnaletto in her reading of the novel sees it as an example of the 'Rumi phenomenon' in the United States that builds on Orientalist staples, 'privileging the aesthetics and the interests of the American reader' who already has a 'contemporary understanding' of Rumi based on Coleman Barks's popular translation *The Essential Rumi*. The Rumi phenomenon refers to the bestselling status of Rumi's poetry in the United States set off by Barks's translations in 1995. Furnaletto connects this comparatively recent popularity of Rumi with an older fascination in American literature with Sufi poetry and a nostalgic return to the West's colonial encounter with the mystic East, as well as the marketing phenomenon of the exotic in the publishing field in the 1990s.[25]

In *The Forty Rules of Love*, Elif Shafak attempts to rewrite the stereotype of the veiled female body, referring to Qur'anic and Sufi injunctions to contest negative perceptions of the treatment of women in Islam, allowing space for a feminist interpretation that is in keeping with the findings of recent feminist scholars. However, while using her novel to articulate feminist perspectives on complementarity, as a writer with an essentially secular worldview she tends to restrict the development of her main protagonist, Ella, in such a way that she becomes simply an embodiment of liberal Sufi doctrine, rather than an active, fulfilled agent in the world. She illustrates another possible way of understanding gender roles and relations, but, in the end, it is almost as if her efforts are weighed down by the expectations attendant on Sufism as the acceptable face of Islam for the West today.

Minaret

Leila Aboulela's novel, by contrast, is about a heroine who turns to piety as a means to inner transformation but who is thwarted by societal constraints and a somewhat literalist understanding of sharia that restrains her from developing relationships of complementarity with men. Najwa, the central character of *Minaret*, is the daughter of a Sudanese politician who is removed from office in a coup and hanged for corruption. She flees to England with her mother and brother to live in exile, although her mother soon succumbs to cancer. Najwa's twin brother, the wild child of the family, is caught drug dealing and jailed. While living in London, she runs into an old boyfriend, Anwar, whose Marxist principles had brought him into conflict with her father. Ironically, now Anwar is the victim of regime change himself and seeking refuge in London. They become romantically involved, and she ends up financially supporting him by paying for his degree and helping him improve his English to assist his journalistic career. However, she is uneasy about the sexual nature of their relationship, and once it is clear that Anwar will not marry her, she leaves him and reinvents herself as a modest Muslim woman: wearing a hijab and attending Qur'an and *Tajweed* classes and community functions at the mosque. To make ends meet, she works as a maid with a rich London family of expatriates where she falls in love with her employer's younger brother, Tamer, who is a devout practising Muslim. She sees the relationship as offering her another chance at a married life but his family intervene. Tamer's more secular mother convinces Najwa to leave her son by giving her money to go on hajj, in return agreeing to let Tamer change his college degree from Business to Islamic Studies.

In an interview with Claire Chambers, Aboulela has said that she 'wanted to write about faith itself and how spiritual development is a need which is as valid and as urgent as love and career. I wanted to write about the average, devout Muslim and the dilemmas and challenges he or she faces.'[26] Her representation of the pious Muslim woman's spiritual journey as a rite of passage towards self-realization has led to strong criticism from some who see her writing as dismissive of secular values. Sadia Abbas has criticized Aboulela for effectively contaminating the world of the secular novel with a religious narrative that she sees as an apologetics for radical Islamism. She argues that the novel shuts off other perspectives that could be critical of religion, such as that of the Marxist Anwar, while 'the female heroine's desire for peace presented as properly, devoutly womanly, and the ostensible ability of religion to deliver this peace, is cast explicitly as an antidote to a world in social flux'.[27] Paradoxically, although religion becomes the main focus of the novel and the answer to Najwa's needs, this is achieved by turning it into a wholly private affair; Najwa is uncomfortable whenever mention is made of actually existing Islamic politics as it blights various countries around the world. This critical attack is also pursued by Waïl Hassan, who reads Aboulela through the lens of migrant fiction, comparing her writing with earlier trends in Arab fiction set by writers such as Tayeb Salih, who is seen to be representative of more desirable 'Arab secular ideologies of modernity'.

According to Hassan, Aboulela's Muslim immigrant fiction presents a departure from that earlier model of Arab fiction and is at odds with the progressivism towards 'gender and political agency' that was a defining quality of Salih's work.[28] He understands Aboulela as a writer who is offering a translation of Islamic theology for those who live in secular or non-Muslim societies. Yet the Islamic principles outlined in Aboulela's writing for him involve 'a complete disavowal of personal liberty as incompatible with Islam, of feminism as a secular and godless ideology, of individual agency in favour of an all-encompassing notion of predetermination and of political agency as well'.[29] He sees a total rejection of feminism in her work and perceives her ideological position as one that advocates Islamism and 'regressive' thinking. Hassan concludes that her fiction bears all the hallmarks of 'fundamentalism' in its espousal of traditional values and only stops short of categorizing it as 'radical fundamentalism' because of its 'apolitical nature', which causes the novel and its protagonist to turn away from the world affairs that are nonetheless shaping the story.[30]

So, can *Minaret* be read as an example of Islamic feminism or is it, as Abbas implies, an Islamist text that seeks to domesticate Muslim women? The answer is by no means straightforward. The uncertainty of the protagonist, Najwa, is captured right at the start when, returning home in the early morning after a party in Khartoum, she hears the sound of the *azan* and thinks of 'the words and the way the words went inside me, ... through the fun I had had at the disco ... to a place I didn't know existed. A hollow place. A darkness that would suck me in and finish me'.[31] Earlier she mentions feeling 'self-conscious' in her clothes, 'my too short skirts and too tight blouses', when she sees 'provincial girls' who dress modestly in their *tobes*: 'pure white cotton covering their arms and hair'.[32] However, she is at pains to tell us that she has a happy life with her parents, who are loving and generous: 'There was nothing that I didn't have, couldn't have. No dreams corroded in rust, no buried desires. And yet, sometimes, I would remember pain like a wound that had healed, sadness like a forgotten dream.'[33] It is this void that is constantly present in Najwa's life. She tries to find structure through her relationships but it keeps eluding her and, in the end, she is propelled towards metaphysical love instead. Will this be the answer to Najwa's problems? We never find out. The action of giving up Tamer is consistent with Najwa's other vacillations. Indeed, the only time she gains a sense of structure is in the *Tajweed* class, where she finds relief in focusing on the incantatory quality of Qur'anic language. By contrast whenever she is called upon to participate in broader discussions she 'becomes fragmented and deflated ... agreeing with whoever is speaking or with the one I like best'.[34]

It can be argued that Najwa strives for an Islamic-style complementarity by reaching out first to Anwar and then to Tamer as her potential life partners. But she is limited in her approach because of her lack of confidence and neediness; both times she is unsuccessful in maintaining her romantic relationships with them. Anwar is someone to whom she is sexually attracted but who also holds a nostalgic attachment for her because of their time together in Khartoum. He, on the other hand, objectifies her by talking about her 'tight skirts', her prettiness and her knowledge of the English language. Although she falls into a sexual relationship with him, she never feels respected by him as an equal. For her, an equality between them can only be brought about through marriage. Anwar rejects her idea of getting 'officially engaged'.[35] This is the breaking point of their affair for Najwa, who feels that she is prostituting herself for Anwar. She reflects, 'It was becoming clear that I had come down in the world. I had skidded and plunged after my father's execution and through my mother's illness, when I dropped out of college, then after Omar's arrest and through my relationship with Anwar.'[36] To get away from Anwar she seeks moral renewal through the women's community at the mosque, embodied especially by Wafaa, 'the woman who had shrouded my mother'.[37] Instead of sexual pleasure she turns to spiritual solace, seeking redemption and a nostalgic return to her parents: 'I yearned to see my parents again, be with them again like in my dreams.'[38] The constant presence of parental figures in her consciousness locates her moral centre in a dutiful relationship towards family that is deeply connected to her later adherence to the rules of sharia, particularly those that emphasize obedience towards parental authority. It is at this point that she takes up the veil and a conservative way of dressing that also returns her to an older generational style of modest dressing previously observed by her mother.

Najwa might be described as an agnostic Muslim during her early life in Sudan. The cultural norms of the elite society to which she belongs marginalize women through an objectification of their bodies, and this occasionally troubles her. In the migrant space of London, struggling to find herself after her mother's death and her break-up with Anwar, Najwa turns to her faith as an alternative home. The only reminder left of life in Khartoum is her brother in jail whom she visits from time to time. Harbouring ambivalent feelings of rage and despair towards him, she feels safe and protected in the mosque and is able to cope with the adjustments that are needed to live in a secular society with the help of her faith community. Her attraction to the pious Tamer, the brother of her employer Lamya, promises to bring her spiritual life to completion, as he, unlike Anwar, is respectful of her modest lifestyle and expresses his desire to marry her. That he shares her moral universe is a point brought home to the reader when he expresses outrage at one of the guests at his sister's party who mocks Najwa's pious dress by turning up in a 'beige headscarf, a floor-length skirt and a short coat that doesn't reach the knees', following it up with a striptease to reveal a skimpy black sleeveless dress underneath.[39]

Tamer offers Najwa emotional protection from such perceived attacks, and it is this bonding over religion that triggers their first moment of intimacy.[40] At last, Najwa seems to have found her complement, her life partner. But Najwa is unable to pursue this relationship, instead allowing herself to be led away from Tamer by his mother because of that same understanding of the pre-eminent importance of loyalty to family and duty to parents. In the end, she does not want to come between Tamer and his mother. The narrator offers a somewhat abbreviated and enigmatic reading of Sura Al-Araf ('The Heights') from the Qur'an to explain Najwa's moral reasons for abandoning Tamer and giving in to his mother's demands. She thinks that otherwise she will be consigning Tamer to hell because to be with her he will have to break his mother's heart.

So Najwa takes the moral high ground by leaving Tamer. She is not able to persuade his mother to think about their relationship positively and sees her as an obstacle to his spiritual growth. Yet, despite this, because she is an obedient child who has always done what she has been told by her own parents, she gives in. She also sees flashes of her brother Omar in Tamer and has a maternal desire to save him, something that she could not do for her brother. She remembers how her mother 'cursed Omar' when he demanded money from her: '"I hope he is never ever successful. I hope he is never very happy." ... This is how a mother can curse her son.'[41] She feels that her mother's curse has poisoned Omar's life, and she does not want the same fate to befall Tamer. Here Najwa's emotions are jumbled between her feelings for Omar and the maternal responsibility she feels towards him. Her maternal instincts lead her to translate her brother's failed relationship with her mother as a life lesson of the punishment that can ensue from parental disobedience. Tamer becomes an extension of Omar in her mind. This comparison is in her subconscious from the start of their relationship when, on first hearing Tamer quarrelling with his mother, she is reminded of her mother's disagreements with Tamer and thinks, 'But Omar and Tamer are miles apart, miles apart'[42]: a comment that comes to carry ironic overtones as the story plays out. Her decision in the end to remove herself from the picture as Tamer's potential bride is one that is born out of her piety. She is fatalistic in her approach towards Islam and doesn't feel that Tamer can step outside the bounds of duty without ruining his life. In her mind he is unable to exercise self-control when it comes to his duty towards his parents whereas her sense of self is determined by righteousness and filial duty.

In its final pages the novel takes a decisive step away from depicting Najwa as an independent woman. She is shown in a confused, feverish state, imagining herself back in her parents' bed in Khartoum: 'I roll over, luxurious, sure that they love me. Around us, beyond the bed, the room is dark and cluttered, all the possessions that distinguish us in ruins. ... the ceiling has caved in, the floor is gutted and the crumbling walls are smeared with guilt.'[43] This enigmatic ending suggests that Najwa has not been able to come to terms with growing up and has returned to an earlier childlike state, albeit scarred by the subsequent family failures. Every time she has taken a step forward, she has had a set-back. Before her separation from Tamer, when she confesses her feelings for him to her friend Shahinaz, she is made to feel ashamed by her reaction. Shahinaz tells her, 'When I think of a man I admire, he would have to know more than me, be older than me. Otherwise I wouldn't be able to look up to him.'[44] Najwa, unable to defend her feelings for a younger man, retreats into an Orientalist fantasy of security: 'I stare down at my hands, my warped self and distorted desires. I would like to be his family's concubine, like something out of the Arabian nights, with life-long security and a sense of belonging. But I must settle for freedom in this modern time.'[45] This fantasy of regression is typical of Najwa, and it is significant that what she craves is less the sexual intimacy of the concubine role than its guarantee of a place within the family. A few paragraphs later she recognizes this characteristic in herself: 'I circle back, I regress; the past doesn't let go. It might as well be a malfunction, a scene repeating itself, a scratched vinyl record, a stutter.'[46] In the end, Aboulela does not give us a self-confident heroine who is able to negotiate human relationships successfully or find complementarity in romantic relationships. Instead, she leaves us with Najwa in mental turmoil and a state of Freudian psychosis. While the veil and the mosque have contributed to her identity formation as a migrant Muslim they have not necessarily restored her self-confidence. Her emotional growth is stunted by her experience of male–female relationships that draw on internalized, established hierarchies and leave her feeling powerless. For this perpetual outsider, performing an Islamic life through participating in mosque culture has not helped to resolve her inner moral dilemmas. Her only option seems to be a fantasy return to childhood to escape her perennial existential condition.

Conclusion

In a global environment in which the burqa and female veiling continue to be framed as one of the main sources of intercultural controversy today, a novel such as *The Forty Rules of Love* appears to offer an alternative, with its representation of the heterodox tradition of a softer Sufi Islam. The popularity of this brand of Islam among liberal audiences is evident from the novel's bestselling status. At the other end of the spectrum, the psychologically dense story of *Minaret* reinforces a conservative view of Islam that carries a certain appeal both to a niche Muslim readership who wants to see an account of the spiritual life in print and – for totally different reasons – to a hostile Islamophobic readership looking for more examples of women's oppression in Islam. The clash of perspectives between Aboulela and Shafak is to be found in the respective fates of their representative heroines, delivered through the popular genres of romance and historical fiction for a global English readership. While they both contest Islamophobia as they map efforts towards female agency through Islamicate models, they also reiterate certain myths about Islam, from heterodox mysticism to pious renewal through the veil.

The Islamic feminist ideal of complementarity is played out in Shafak's novel through the characterization of the heroine Ella, who is projected as a modern woman getting in touch with her Sufi soul. She fulfils the feminist ideal of a woman capable of surviving modern life on her own without a man and her family to protect her. Yet, however appealing we may find this character, Ella's resilience is ultimately recuperated within a narrative arc that validates an apolitical Sufi Islam as the soft option: the preferred Muslim affiliation that is least threatening to the West. Aboulela's novel is more unsettling, with its adherence to controversial Islamic practices such as veiling, its lack of a strong and developing central subject and its effective rejection of communal solidarities in favour of withdrawal and despair. Najwa is hesitant about taking charge of her own life and, although she strives for complementarity between genders, she remains finally subservient to family duty. Both novels reiterate the significance of male–female relationships and attempt to inject different strands of Islamic feminism into their narratives. In their very different ways they offer distinctive transnational perspectives on how ideals of complementarity might be understood and lived out in the world, dramatized through their protagonists' respective attempts to follow a path of faith. While, as I have argued, in neither case are these attempts wholly successful, they do reveal alternative modes of female Muslim identification, thereby gesturing to contemporary female experiences that cannot be contained by simple stereotypes. In that sense, these two popular texts contest Islamophobia by suggesting that there are many ways to be a Muslim woman in the modern world.

Notes

1 See, for example, Azar Nafisi, *Reading* Lolita *in Tehran: A Story of Love, Books and Revolution* (London: I.B. Tauris, 2003); Leila Aboulela, *Minaret* (London, Berlin, New York, Sydney: Bloomsbury, 2005); Fawzia Afzal-Khan, *From Lahore with Love: Growing Up with Girlfriends Pakistani Style* (Syracuse, NY: Syracuse University Press, 2010); Shelina Zahra Janmohamed, *Love in a Headscarf* (London: Aurum Press, 2014).
2 Rana Kabbani, *Europe's Myths of the Orient: Devise and Rule* (London: Pandora Press, 1986).
3 Elif Shafak, *The Forty Rules of Love* (London: Penguin, 2010).
4 miriam cooke, 'Women, religion and the postcolonial Arab world', *Cultural Critique* 45 (Spring 2000), pp. 150–84; p. 177. Available at www.jstor.org/stable/1354370 (accessed 3 October 2017).
5 Lindsey Moore, 'Voyages out and in: Two (British) Arab Muslim women's Bildungsromane', in Rehana Ahmed, Peter Morey and Amina Yaqin (eds), *Culture, Diaspora and Modernity in Muslim Writing* (London: Routledge, 2012), pp. 68–86.
6 Elif Shafak, 'When women are divided it is the male status quo that benefits', *Guardian*, 5 February 2017. Available at www.theguardian.com/books/2017/feb/05/elif-shafak-turkey-three-daughters-of-eve-interview (accessed 3 October 2017).
7 Kahf, *Western Representations of the Muslim Woman*.
8 Autobiographical books such as Malala Yousafzai's *I Am Malala: The Girl Who Stood Up for Education and Was Shot by the Taliban* (with Christina Lamb) (London: Weidenfeld and Nicolson, 2013) and Mukhtar Mai, *In the Name of Honor: A Memoir* (New York: Washington Square Press, 2006) present grass-roots Muslim women at the heart of changing conventional attitudes towards Muslim women's education and honour crimes that target women. This turnaround in representation can also be seen in popular publications such as the US-based *Ms Marvel* comic book series, which introduced the Muslim supergirl heroine, Kamala Khan, by writer G. Willow Wilson, as the leader of their new series in 2014.
9 See Lila Abu-Lughod, *Do Muslim Women Need Saving?* (Cambridge, MA: Harvard University Press, 2015). Also see the award-winning (and Emmy-nominated) Pakistani animated series *Burka Avenger*, first aired in 2013 (available at www.burkaavenger.com). Described as 'conservative Pakistan's new animated liberal

superheroine' (http://world.time.com/2013/08/01/burka-avenger-conservative-pakistans-new-animated-liberal-superheroine/), the series has gained popularity across India, Pakistan and Afghanistan and in 2017 was picked up by the United Nations in the fight back against extremism.

10 Leila Ahmed, *Women and Gender in Islam: Historical Roots of a Modern Debate* (New Haven, CT: Yale University Press, 1993).
11 Mahmood, *Politics of Piety*, 2005, p. 158.
12 Ibid., p. xv.
13 Margot Badran, *Feminism beyond East and West: New Gender Talk and Practice in Global Islam* (New Delhi: Global Media Publications, 2007), p. 36.
14 *The Meaning of the Glorious Koran*, trans. Mohammed Marmaduke Pickthall (New York and Scarborough, Ontario: Mentor, n.d.), Surah IV, Verse 34.
15 Quoted in Amina Wadud, *Qur'an and Woman: Revealing the Sacred Text from a Women's Perspective* (Kuala Lumpur: Penerbit Fajar Bakti Sdn. Bhd., 1992), p. 70.
16 See Fatima Mernissi, *The Veil and the Male Elite: A Feminist Interpretation of Women's Rights in Islam*, trans. Mary Jo Lakeland (New York: Addison-Wesley Publishing, 1992). Also see cooke, 'Women, religion and the postcolonial Arab world'.
17 An important intervention is also made by miriam cooke who reviews Islamic feminist contexts emerging from complex colonial relationships of power in the Arab world leading to new transnational allegiances and a critique of the 'West'. See cooke, 'Women, religion and the postcolonial Arab world', pp. 176–7.
18 In a more recent response to the debate on *qawwamun*, Kecia Ali has argued that because of the connotations of 'contested' meanings associated with the Arabic terms, she has chosen not to translate them and keeps to the original Arabic, expecting a degree of literacy in Arabic from her readership. Kecia Ali, *Sexual Ethics and Islam: Feminist Reflections on Qur'an, Hadith and Jurisprudence*, revised edn (London: Oneworld, 2016). See '"If you have touched women": Female bodies and male agency in the Qur'an', pp. 146–72.
19 Shafak, *The Forty Rules of Love*, p. 195.
20 Ibid, p. 199.
21 Jamal Elias, 'Female and feminine in Islamic mysticism', *Muslim World* 78/3–4 (1988), pp. 209–24; p. 211.
22 Shafak, *The Forty Rules of Love*, p. 326.
23 Ibid., p. 350.
24 There are many examples of this sort of modern consumerist exotic narrative of discovery. Perhaps the most famous is Elizabeth Gilbert's *Eat, Pray, Love*, from 2006, which was later turned into a successful Hollywood film. Maureen Callahan of the *New York Post* dismissed this kind of book, with its inevitable fetishization of non-Western cultures, as 'narcissistic New Age reading'. See Maureen Callahan,

'Eat, pray, loathe: Latest self-help best seller proves faith is blind', *New York Post*, 23 December 2007.
25 Elena Furnaletto, 'The "Rumi phenomenon" between Orientalism and cosmopolitanism: The case of Elif Shafak's *The Forty Rules of Love*', *European Journal of English Studies* 17/2 (2013), pp. 201–13. Available at http://dx.doi.org/10.1080/13 825577.2013.797210 (accessed 25 March 2017); Coleman Barks, *The Essential Rumi* (New York: HarperCollins, 1995).
26 Claire Chambers, 'Leila Aboulela', in *British Muslim Fictions: Interviews with Contemporary Writers* (Houndmills, Basingstoke: Palgrave Macmillan, 2011), pp. 95–112; p. 112.
27 Sadia Abbas, 'Leila Aboulela, religion and the challenge of the novel', *Contemporary Literature* 52/3 (Fall 2011), pp. 430–61. Available at www.jstor.org/stable/41472503 (accessed 3 October 2017).
28 Waïl S. Hassan, 'Leila Aboulela and the ideology of Muslim immigrant fiction', *Novel* 41/2–3 (2008), pp. 298–318; pp. 298–9.
29 Hassan, 'Leila Aboulela and the ideology', p. 313.
30 Ibid., pp. 316–7.
31 Aboulela, *Minaret*, p. 31.
32 Ibid., p. 14.
33 Ibid., p. 15.
34 Ibid., p. 79.
35 Ibid., p. 233.
36 Ibid., p. 239.
37 Ibid., p. 240.
38 Ibid., p. 242.
39 Ibid., p. 222.
40 Ibid., pp. 222–4.
41 Ibid., p. 264.
42 Ibid., p. 207.
43 Ibid., p. 276.
44 Ibid., p. 215.
45 Ibid.
46 Ibid., p. 216.

Works cited

Abbas, Sadia, 'Leila Aboulela, religion and the challenge of the novel', *Contemporary Literature* 52/3 (Fall 2011), pp. 430–61. Available at www.jstor.org/stable/41472503 (accessed 3 October 2017).

Aboulela, Leila, *Minaret* (London: Bloomsbury, 2005).
Abu-Lughod, Lila, *Do Muslim Women Need Saving?* (Cambridge, MA: Harvard University Press, 2015).
Afzal-Khan, Fawzia, F*rom Lahore with Love: Growing Up with Girlfriends Pakistani Style* (Syracuse, NY: Syracuse University Press, 2010).
Ahmed, Leila, *Women and Gender in Islam: Historical Roots of a Modern Debate* (New Haven, CT: Yale University Press, 1993).
Ali, Kecia, *Sexual Ethics and Islam: Feminist Reflections on Qur'an, Hadith and Jurisprudence*, revised edn (London: Oneworld, 2016).
Badran, Margot, *Feminism Beyond East and West: New Gender Talk and Practice in Global Islam* (New Delhi: Global Media Publications, 2007).
Barks, Coleman, *The Essential Rumi* (New York: HarperCollins, 1995).
Callahan, Maureen, 'Eat, pray, loathe: Latest self-help best seller proves faith is blind', *New York Post*, 23 December 2007.
Chambers, Claire, 'Leila Aboulela', in *British Muslim Fictions: Interviews with Contemporary Writers* (Houndmills, Basingstoke: Palgrave Macmillan, 2011), pp. 95–112.
cooke, miriam, 'Women, religion, and the postcolonial Arab world', *Cultural Critique* 45 (Spring 2000), pp. 150–84. Available at www.jstor.org/stable/1354370 (accessed 3 October 2017).
Elias, Jamal, 'Female and feminine in Islamic mysticism', *Muslim World* 78/3–4 (1988), pp. 209–24.
Furnaletto, Elena, 'The "Rumi phenomenon" between Orientalism and cosmopolitanism: The case of Elif Shafak's *The Forty Rules of Love*', *European Journal of English Studies* 17/2 (2013), pp. 201–13. Available at http://dx.doi.org/10.1080/138 25577.2013.797210 (accessed 25 March 2017).
Hassan, Waïl S., 'Leila Aboulela and the ideology of Muslim immigrant fiction', *Novel* 41/2–3 (2008).
Janmohamed, Shelina Zahra, *Love in a Headscarf* (London: Aurum Press, 2014).
Kabbani, Rana, *Europe's Myths of the Orient: Devise and Rule* (London: Pandora Press, 1986).
Kahf, Mohja, *Western Representations of the Muslim Woman: From Termagant to Odalisque* (Austin, TX: University of Texas Press, 1999).
Mahmood, Saba, *Politics of Piety: The Islamic Revival and the Feminist Subject* (Princeton, NJ: Princeton University Press, 2005).
Mai, Mukhtar, *In the Name of Honor: A Memoir* (New York: Washington Square Press, 2006).
Mernissi, Fatima, *The Veil and the Male Elite: A Feminist Interpretation of Women's Rights in Islam*, trans. Mary Jo Lakeland (New York: Addison-Wesley Publishing, 1992).
Moore, Lindsey, 'Voyages out and in: Two (British) Arab Muslim women's Bildungsromane', in Rehana Ahmed, Peter Morey and Amina Yaqin (eds), *Culture, Diaspora and Modernity in Muslim Writing* (London: Routledge, 2012), pp. 68–86.

Nafisi, Azar, *Reading* Lolita *in Tehran: A Story of Love, Books and Revolution* (London: I.B. Tauris, 2003).
Pickthall, Mohammed Marmaduke (trans.), *The Meaning of the Glorious Koran* (New York and Scarborough, ON: Mentor, n.d.).
Shafak, Elif, *The Forty Rules of Love* (London: Penguin, 2010).
Shafak, Elif, 'When women are divided it is the male status quo that benefits', *Guardian*, 5 February 2017. Available at www.theguardian.com/books/2017/feb/05/elif-shafak-turkey-three-daughters-of-eve-interview (accessed 3 October 2017).
Wadud, Amina, *Qur'an and Women* (Kuala Lumpur: Penerbit Fajar Bakti Sdn. Bhd., 1992).
Yousafzai, Malala (with Christina Lamb), *I Am Malala: The Girl Who Stood Up for Education and Was Shot by the Taliban* (London: Weidenfeld and Nicolson, 2013).

Part Three

Youth Contesting Islamophobia

7

Countering Islamophobia in the Classroom

Sarah Soyei

I hate racism, I don't know how anyone could be racist, racists should be locked up. But, Muslims ... they should wear our clothes and eat our food. If they don't like it they should get out of our country.

Year 9 student, Bexley

This chapter will explore issues of Islamophobia within British schools and suggest practical methods to counter them in the classroom. Firstly, it will look at the issues that prevent schools from effectively engaging with Islamophobia, then give examples of some strategies to support schools in effectively working with young people to challenge Islamophobia, with the aim of increasing understanding and fostering good relations between Muslim and non-Muslim pupils. The chapter will finish with an exploration of how schools can better recognize British Muslim identities and take a holistic approach to promoting equality and inclusion of Muslim pupils and staff.

Young people are not immune from the Islamophobia that pervades society, with the consequence that Islamophobic attitudes and behaviours are seeping into classrooms. A poll of 1,000 young people, conducted by BBC Radio 1 *Newsbeat* in 2013, found that 44 per cent believed that Muslims did not share the same values as the rest of the population, while 28 per cent said that Britain would be better off with fewer Muslims.[1] Schools and teaching unions have reported that incidents of Islamophobia have been rising over recent years, spiking after terrorist incidents. The charity ChildLine has also reported that Islamophobia is a particular issue in schools, with young Muslims, and those perceived to be Muslim, reporting that they are being called 'terrorists' and 'bombers' by classmates.[2]

Experiencing Islamophobia can have a very negative impact on the lives of young Muslims who are in the process of building their personalities and identities. When young people are constantly exposed to Islamophobic acts and attitudes it can lead to a lack of self-esteem and low confidence and impact upon their sense of belonging.[3] Islamophobia needs to be challenged among young people as it is during these formative years that they are developing their value systems and thus it is at this time too that Islamophobia can be most easily challenged and prevented.[4] The education system cannot be expected to eliminate Islamophobia alone, as it pervades social and political structures. However, schools are uniquely placed to influence young people's understanding of Islamophobia and to counter misinformation and stereotypes.[5]

Despite this, many young people have never had the opportunity to discuss issues of racism or Islamophobia in a formal setting. In a packed curriculum, issues of equality can be seen as peripheral, particularly when there is a lack of emphasis on work in this area from central government. Seventy-eight per cent of teachers surveyed by EqualiTeach cited lack of time as the biggest barrier to promoting equality and tackling discrimination.[6] Teachers can feel that trepidation, apprehension, a lack of knowledge and insufficient confidence prevent them from broaching these subjects. Conducting reflective conversations with young people requires careful guidance and skilled teaching, and in research conducted in 2011 only 61 per cent of all teachers and only 35 per cent of teachers who had graduated in the last ten years had received any training at all in tackling prejudice and promoting equality; of those who had, most felt that the training was cursory and had not equipped them to deal with the issues in the classroom.[7]

Teachers may be genuinely ignorant of the prejudicial attitudes within their classroom because children as young as four become aware that they should not express such views in front of adults, and this awareness increases as they get older.[8] Pupils on the receiving end are often wary of reporting their experiences, with worries about being dismissed or making their situation worse. In addition, there can be an idea that if there are few or no Muslim children in the school then Islamophobia is not an issue that the school needs to deal with, effectively laying the blame at the feet of Muslim children themselves. However, in schools where there are few Muslim children, young people are more in danger of picking up received misinformation and of it going unchallenged.[9] Engaging with school-linking can be an excellent way to provide pupils with opportunities to learn and socialize with those from different faith and cultural backgrounds. Traditionally, schools have linked up with others from around the world, but it is not necessary to travel that far. The value of connecting a small rural primary school with a large urban school 20 miles up the road should not be underestimated: providing young people with the opportunity to develop conversations and relationships with young people from different backgrounds, thereby promoting understanding and community cohesion.[10]

Some teachers are concerned that it is not acceptable to express their thoughts on issues as they need to demonstrate impartiality. The Education Act 1996 prohibits teachers from promoting partisan political views; however, it is perfectly acceptable for teachers to stress the values outlined in the Universal Declaration of Human Rights or the Equality Act, and to provide young people with support and guidance to reject misinformation and stereotypes.[11] Values are highly personal and core to our understanding of the world. Therefore, values cannot be imposed externally. Teaching about values requires a participatory approach in partnership with the learner, which involves the questioning of evidence in order for the learner to come to their own, evidence-based conclusions. The right to freedom of speech is often cited as a reason to leave comments and harmful opinions unchallenged. It is true that freedom of speech and expression is recognized under the European Convention of Human Rights. However, this is not an absolute right and ends where speech impacts on someone else's rights. The Racial and Religious Hatred Act of 2006 created an offence of inciting religious hatred. Young people need to be supported to recognize that with freedom of speech comes responsibility and that all opinions are not equally valid; they need to be able to back up their ideas with research and facts.

Finally, there is a widespread belief that simply talking about issues and raising awareness might somehow create problems out of nowhere; that by ignoring the issues they will simply disappear, and if left alone young people will just be naturally immune to prejudice. However, young people do not exist in a bubble and are aware of local and global issues in the news. They pick up prejudices and misinformation from a variety of sources: from friends and family, social media, newspaper headlines and hearsay. A study of 352 articles in a week during 2007 found that 91 per cent of articles about Muslims were negative and a Channel 4-commissioned survey of 974 articles from 2000 to 2008 found that two-thirds portrayed British Muslims as a 'threat' and a 'problem'; references to 'radical Muslims' outnumbering references to 'moderates' by 17 to 1.[12]

The media portrays Islam and Muslims as inferior, violent, irrational, oppressive and undemocratic, contrasted with the West as superior, reasonable, enlightened and democratic.[13] The use of counter-narratives is vital to break down the mainstream Islamophobic picture, which prevails in the minds of many young people. However, Muslims' own narratives and condemnation of terrorist acts are often not disseminated, and, if they are, they are often not believed.[14] Many young people do not buy newspapers, but they will see the papers that their parents or carers bring home, read the headlines in the shop or receive the information via word of mouth or social media. EqualiTeach delivers over 500 workshops a year to young people. During these workshops, facilitators hear these stories repeated by young people who feel ownership of the information and are absolutely certain that they are true.[15]

This plethora of misinformation with which young people are bombarded has the potential to create fear and mistrust between communities. Young people who have not had the opportunity to have their misinformation, fear and prejudice addressed may not even recognize their opinions as prejudicial, such as the young man from Bexley quoted at the top of the chapter. When told of a hate crime committed against a young Asian man, another boy replied, 'Well that's kind of bad, but kind of OK because the Asian boy might have been a terrorist or something and just no-one had found out yet.' It is not possible to be continually at the side of every young person to shield them from misinformation and provide an alternative view. It is therefore absolutely vital that young people are encouraged to think critically about the information that they receive, so that they are able to differentiate between fact, opinion and fiction. Young people are interested in political and controversial issues and need to be provided with opportunities to develop political skills that will allow them to effect change in a peaceful and responsible manner.[16]

Effective social justice education is based on human rights, encouraging the participation of young people and empowering them to become active citizens.[17] Schools have a statutory duty to promote pupil voice: listening to and involving pupils in matters that affect them.[18] Unless young people are provided with opportunities to ask questions and express their concerns, it will not be possible for teachers to ascertain what prejudice and misinformation they may be carrying or what identity-based bullying or discrimination they may be experiencing. There are many different ways to provide pupils with a platform to raise questions and concerns, such as utilizing online questionnaires, providing a box into which young people can post questions or post-it notes completed anonymously at the start of a lesson. Below are a couple of comments from Year 9 pupils in Buckinghamshire in an online questionnaire that EqualiTeach uses in order to tailor our workshops:

> People take the p**s out of my hijab. Some call my friends black and ugly. They treat Muslims as if we're animals and call us names like P*ki, freshy. I don't know what to do! Well what can I do? I can't do nothing! Sometimes I feel like not coming to school.
>
> Every single day someone comments rudely about me and where I come from. Some people make fun of girls' headscarves, I don't wear one but it's still offensive because it's from my religion and my friends and family wear it. What's the point of coming to school? Sometimes I feel like crying. It's 2016, grow up and learn respect. Please come in and talk about it.

Collecting young people's thoughts and questions in this way affords them the opportunity to have their voices heard, allows schools to use this information in order to develop a body of work which is pitched at the right level and helps young people to feel engaged in the programme of work from the beginning. This information can also provide a baseline assessment and pupils can be consulted again after the work has taken place in order to measure the impact of interventions.[19]

If openness is to be encouraged during a workshop or discussion, it is important that young people are not worried that they will be laughed at or penalized for expressing their opinion on an issue and that the debate is not dominated by one or two students. In addition, if young people feel attacked or shouted down, they may feel unable to contribute, and it could lead to a breakdown in relationships within the classroom. It is therefore vital to create a safe space at the start of the session within which all pupils feel respected and able to take part. This can be done through the collaborative creation of ground rules. EqualiTeach outlined some suggested ground rules in the educational guide *Universal Values*, and these are reproduced below:

> *Be open and honest:* We don't want anyone to feel that they can't ask their question or express their opinion. Therefore, we will not laugh at others' opinions, or shout each other down.
>
> *Respect the feelings of others:* We will think about the impact of our words and body language on others and try to express our opinions in a respectful fashion. We will listen to the opinions of others, even if they are different to our own.
>
> *Direct challenges to the front of the room, not at each other:* It is fine to disagree and challenge each other's ideas. However, if we do disagree with something that someone else says we will direct our challenge to the front of the room, so

that person does not feel attacked and the whole class remains involved in the conversation.

Depersonalise comments: It is fine to talk about your experiences with other people, but ensure that you do not name those involved or disclose details that could identify those involved.

It can be a good idea to create a space where pupils can choose to go for some time out if they become upset or uncomfortable during the session. If this information is shared with pupils before the discussion begins they can take the decision as to whether they need this space, rather than the teacher needing to decide upon a course of action once an issue has arisen.

A useful way to begin working with young people on issues of Islamophobia is to explore the impact of stereotypes with them. One method that EqualiTeach employs to open up these discussions with teenagers is to conduct an activity entitled 'Who Do We Really Know?' In groups of five or six, young people are given a piece of flip-chart paper with the descriptor of a person in the middle, for example, a Muslim, a hoodie-wearing teenager or an immigrant, together with a selection of felt-tip pens. Then they write down as many words that they associate, or that they have heard associated, with someone who belongs to this group. The sheets are swapped throughout the session so that everyone has the opportunity to contribute and then stuck up on the wall, leading to a whole group discussion where young people can challenge each other's perceptions and facts can be provided to counter pervasive stereotypes (Figure 7.1).

A hoodie-wearing teenager inevitably draws out ideas of gangs, drugs, violence and criminality, even though nearly every young person in the group fits the original description. Despite it often being completely contradictory to their lived experience, young people frequently estimate that over three-quarters of teenagers are involved in crime and that teenagers are more likely to be involved in crime than the rest of the population. In reality, only 1.8 per cent of young people were arrested in 2014–15, accounting for only 6 per cent of the total number of people sentenced.[20] Facilitators ask the young people why they think they had such an incorrect and negative view of a group to which they themselves belong. Students consider the impact of the media on their perceptions and why newspapers might choose to focus on negative stories and inflammatory headlines rather than positive news, such as the fact that teenagers are far more likely to be involved in volunteering than other sectors of the population.[21]

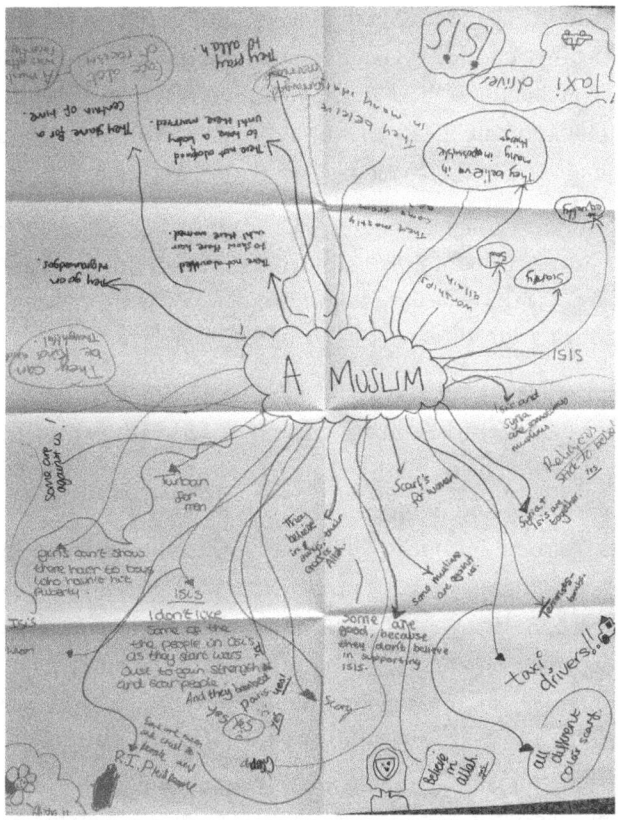

Figure 7.1 The Spread of False Information. Image courtesy of Equaliteach.

Regardless of the area of the country, or the diversity of the group, when asked who they think an immigrant is, the answer is inevitably someone who sneaks into the country. Hardly surprising, when a recent study by the Migration Observatory has found that 'illegal' is the most common descriptor for immigrants in the UK press.[22] Young people are often confused about the current situation with regard to refugees; the media's persistent use of the words 'swarm', 'flood' and 'invasion' has caused many to believe that the UK is currently experiencing extremely high numbers of refugees entering the country. Students ask, 'Why they are all coming to this country?', 'Why can't they go to other countries?', even 'Why they can't be contained away from the native population?' They are often astonished to find out that Britain is host to less than 1 per cent of the world's refugee population.[23]

The discussions about Muslims are predictably dominated by terrorism, although they often also encompass ideas of religiosity, ethnicity, culture, sharia law and halal food. The young people have the floor to share their thoughts, challenge each other, consider the opinions of others and develop their own ideas. The workshop facilitator is there to challenge, add facts and present alternative views but not to dominate the discussion.[24] Below is a comment written by a Year 9 pupil who took part in these discussions:

> I really liked the first activity because, for example, one girl wrote 'dark skin' on the Muslim poster, but I then explained and shared with the class that being Muslim is about what you believe, not where you come from or your skin colour. (Year 9 pupil, Enfield)

In discussions with Year 9 pupils in Buckinghamshire a girl stated, 'I know that not all Muslims are terrorists, but all terrorists are Muslims', to which several other pupils agreed. Other pupils challenged this by bringing forward their knowledge of the IRA and of far-right terrorists. The facilitator was able to add in the figures from the European Union Terrorism and Situation Trend Report 2015 to show that there were 201 terrorist attacks in the European Union in 2014, of which only two were carried out by Islamic extremists, and to open up discussions about different types of terrorism and why we hear more about some than others. The young people worked in groups to discuss what the word 'terrorism' means and to try to come up with a definition and agreed on 'using violence to frighten people to try to achieve a political goal'. Then they looked at the 2016 murder of the Labour MP Jo Cox. The man convicted of her murder stated that his name was 'death to traitors, freedom for Britain' when asked for it in court. The class agreed that his actions fitted the definition of terrorism that they had come up with, and questioned why the newspapers had not used the word 'terrorism' when reporting on this incident.

In another school in Brent, a Year 8 pupil stated that 'Muslim women have no freedom, like they can't even drive in Saudi Arabia'. Other pupils questioned if this was a fair thing to say, as Muslim women can drive in the UK and many other countries. The discussion went back and forth with pupils bringing in incidents of oppression and honour killings that they had heard of and others countering with examples where Muslim women experienced freedom and where women who were not Muslim experienced violence and oppression. Eventually it was agreed that there are some countries in the world where people's freedoms are more limited than others, but that this could be separated from religion and that cultural and political ideas were also at play.

Once discussions have concluded the young people are able to look back at what they wrote on the flip-charts at the beginning and conclude that many of the comments are stereotypes and to explore the harm that believing in stereotypes can cause. A pupil from Brent stated,

> Stereotypes are harmful, because people look at me in my hijab and assume that I've been forced to wear it and that I don't have my own opinions and ideas. They sometimes talk to me like I'm stupid. They think that they know who I am before they've even spoken to me.

Another wrote, 'The first activity really made me think, it's easy just to get scared because of all the things that you hear on the news, but not everyone is the same.'

Having an ability to recognize stereotypes and assumptions lays the foundations for pupils to be reflective about their own beliefs, their perspective on life and their interest in and respect for people whom they perceive as being different from them. Once young people are aware that they are picking up damaging stereotypes based on prejudice and misinformation, it is important that they consider where they are getting their information from and how reliable this is, introducing ideas of bias, propaganda and persuasion; even simple activities such as 'whisper down the line' can illustrate how easily information can be exaggerated and changed as it passes from person to person.

Encouraging young people to look for the truth behind newspaper headlines is an extremely rewarding activity, and this doesn't have to fall to the English or PSHE teacher. After some teacher training that I delivered a couple of years ago, a secondary school chemistry teacher reported back that he had taken to bringing in a newspaper every few days and discussing it with his form group, and this had provided a brilliant platform for discussion as well as livening up form periods. EqualiTeach sets pupils in Key Stage 3 the task of finding an article on their social media feed or other news source that they think might not be true. They are then required to research the truth behind the article that they have found. This could include checking the source for bias, checking the accuracy of the information by comparing it to other articles on the same story, investigating the author's reasons for writing it and the harm that could arise from someone believing in the false information. Young people then present their findings as a poster, speech, piece of writing or PowerPoint presentation (Figures 7.2 and 7.3).

Building upon this by providing young people with opportunities to debate topical issues, pertinent to their lives, within a safe and welcoming environment, is an important tool in challenging Islamophobic ideas. For young people to get the most out of this activity, time should be taken to allow students to develop in-depth knowledge of all sides of an issue, as having access to

Figure 7.2 'Facts' versus Research. Image courtesy of Equaliteach.

accurate information is a necessary pre-condition for making sense of complex, controversial issues.[25] In order for young people to be able to successfully structure a debate, the sub-issues within the main topic must be considered. If, for example, pupils are debating whether the niqab should be allowed in UK schools, pupils could consider different rules for pupils and teachers, different age restrictions and how the niqab is viewed within, between and outside of Muslim communities.

EqualiTeach's resource *Universal Values* contains an activity that explores the nature of individual liberty and asks young people to compare how liberated different groups of people are and how this perception changes with different viewpoints. For example, a person wearing a hijab is sometimes perceived to be without liberty as it is believed that they are obliged to wear one by society or religion, whereas others perceive it as a symbol of choice, of freedom to express religion and culture and to dress in a manner of your own choosing. This can be compared to women wearing bikinis – an exercise of their liberty to show their bodies and enjoy their free time on the beach or constraint by societal expectations of how a woman should dress, how their bodies should look and how they should be attractive to the opposite sex. This activity, along with others

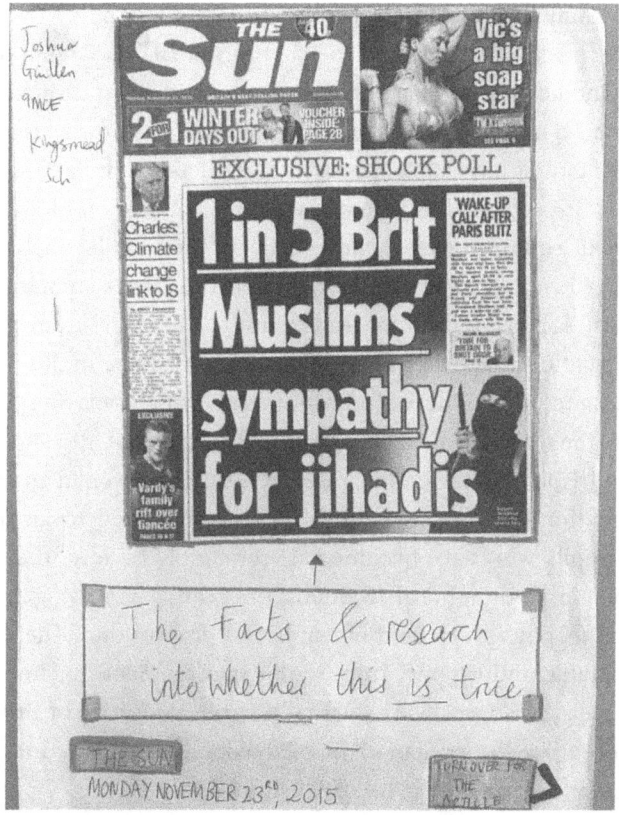

Figure 7.3 Muslim Flip-chart. Image courtesy of Equaliteach.

in the resource, provides a good starting point in helping young people to understand that many issues do not have simple right and wrong answers but are influenced by value judgements based on societal and cultural influences and to appreciate that other people can have a different perspective on an issue. Debates and discussions should be structured carefully, in line with a 'discussion or debate charter' created between teachers and students to give guidance on how to make points effectively and counter ideas. In order to be effective, care should be taken to avoid the teacher being the main focus of the discussion and pupil input being limited to one or two pupils. Rather, there should be simultaneous active participants, and the discussion should be carried and developed by the pupils, with a large number of pupils involved in the discussion, and the teacher just providing facts, reasoning and enquiry questions to guide the discussion and to help pupils think critically about their ideas. This provides students with ownership of the discussion and tests their knowledge as they respond to new ideas quickly. Activities such as these provide a foundation upon which further work can take place, breaking down perceptions of Islam as a monolith 'Other' of the West, and helping young people to recognize the vast diversity that exists among Islam's 1.6 billion followers across the world and how Muslim and non-Muslim communities have a long history of interdependence and shared values.

However, it is not just young people who need education on these issues. If educators are ill-equipped to respond effectively, they will be unable to support young people when they approach them to report that an Islamophobic incident has occurred. Teachers and senior leaders are not immune from the prejudice and misinformation that exists about Islam and Muslims. In 2015 the Prevent duty became statutory in schools. This duty states that schools must demonstrate 'due regard to the need to prevent people from being drawn into terrorism'.[26] This duty covers all aspects of terrorism and extremism; however, in an environment of misinformation and fear, the duty has sometimes led to an unfair focus on Muslim pupils who have become suspect simply because they are openly displaying religiosity or political awareness or because something that they have said has been misinterpreted and blown out of proportion.[27] Therefore, school staff need training and support from senior management to allow them to be able to provide a broad, inclusive curriculum, be supportive of British Muslim identities, recognize the human right of freedom of religion and ensure that their classrooms are truly inclusive of Muslim pupils.

The senior leadership team and governors are responsible for ensuring that schools meet their duties under the Equality Act 2010 and creating an environment where all pupils and staff feel included. Often when schools are asked where they promote equality, the answer will be 'we do it everywhere', which may sometimes equally be translated as 'we do it nowhere'. Research has shown that schools where bullying and Islamophobic incidents are low have a clear set of inclusive values that run through their policies and practice and which staff and pupils are able to articulate. There is respect for individual differences and pupils develop empathy, understand the effect that bullying can have on people and take responsibility for trying to prevent it.[28] The way in which these schools have planned and delivered the curriculum has helped to bring about these positive attitudes by giving pupils a wide range of opportunities to develop their knowledge and understanding of diversity and an assortment of strategies to protect themselves from bullying.

Effective schools have strategies for engaging with parents and the wider community. The importance of parental involvement for raising the achievement of all pupils is widely recognized, but Muslim parents are often described as 'hard to reach' when really the school hasn't opened the door to them. Schools can develop relationships with the local mosque or Islamic community centre and utilize this relationship to open lines of communication and develop joint projects. They can also arrange meetings and develop Muslim parent support groups, arranging interpreters where necessary.[29]

Schools need clear procedures for recognizing and responding to Islamophobic incidents. The working definition of an Islamophobic incident is 'any incident which is perceived to be Islamophobic by the victim or any other person'. This was first recommended as a working definition for racist incidents by *The Stephen Lawrence Inquiry* and has since been extended to cover all prejudice-related incidents.[30] Utilizing this definition ensures that the incident is investigated. Importantly, it ensures that people are listened to. Pupils and staff are more likely to speak up about Islamophobia if they know that they will be taken seriously. Historically targets have been dismissed or ignored, which can be devastating for them, preventing others from speaking up and allowing incidents to escalate. It is important to note that there is no mention of intention in this definition; the fact that someone didn't intend to offend doesn't change the impact of the action. Intention is important when considering what action needs to be taken with the perpetrator, but a lack of intent does not prevent it from being an Islamophobic incident. The definition empowers everyone to act. The onus is not just on the target to speak up. The inclusion of the phrase 'or any other person' means that anyone who perceives an Islamophobic incident to have occurred can instigate an investigation. This also ensures that incidents where there is no direct target, such as graffiti or casual use of Islamophobic language, are also picked up.[31]

It is important that schools have a robust, centralized system in place to record Islamophobic incidents, which is overseen by a designated member of the senior management team. All staff should receive training that outlines why the school is recording this information, the procedures that they need to follow and why it is important to record every Islamophobic incident that they or their pupils experience or witness. Incidents should be recorded within an agreed timescale, for example, two working days. Pupils may be reluctant to report incidents. Schools can take steps to overcome this by promoting pupil voice, creating a positive ethos where pupils are encouraged to speak up and know that the school will deal with issues effectively. Schools can also put in place systems of peer support, so that others can report incidents to staff rather than the target always having to be the one that comes forward. It is also useful to create opportunities for young people to report incidents anonymously, by creating systems where they can submit notes about their experiences and including questions about prejudice-related bullying in student surveys.[32]

Effectively tackling Islamophobia will improve the school environment for everyone, increasing attainment and well-being for pupils and staff. Only when there is a whole school and societal approach to tackling Islamophobia and promoting equality will we be truly ensuring that our schools provide spaces where all of our young people feel safe and able to achieve.

Notes

1. Sima Kotecha, 'Quarter of young British people "do not trust Muslims"', *BBC Newsbeat*, 25 September 2013. Available at www.bbc.co.uk/newsbeat/article/24204742/quarter-of-young-british-people-do-not-trust-muslims (accessed 25 August 2016).
2. National Society for the Prevention of Cruelty to Children (NSPCC), *Can I Tell You Something? ChildLine Review of 2012/13* (London: NSPCC, 2014). Available at https://www.nspcc.org.uk/globalassets/documents/research-reports/childline-review-2012-2013.pdf (accessed 23 August 2016).
3. Ingrid Ramberg, *Islamophobia and its Consequences on Young People* (Strasbourg: Directorate of Democratic Citizenship and Participation of the Council of Europe, 2004).
4. Alistair Ross, 'Institutional racism: The experience of teachers in schools'. Paper presented at the British Educational Research Association Conference, Exeter, 2002.
5. Robin Richardson and Berenice Miles, *Racist Incidents and Bullying in Schools* (Stoke-on-Trent: Trentham Books, 2008).
6. EqualiTeach, *Universal Values* (2016). Available at www.equaliteach.co.uk/universal-values/ (accessed 19 July 2018).
7. Sarah Soyei, *The Barriers to Tackling Racism in England's Schools* (Newcastle upon Tyne: Show Racism the Red Card, 2011).
8. Jane Lane, *Young Children and Racial Justice* (London: National Children's Bureau, 2008).
9. Chris Gaine, *We're All White Thanks* (Stoke-on-Trent: Trentham Books, 2005).
10. Keith Ajegbo, *Diversity and Citizenship Curriculum Review* (Annesley: Department for Education and Skills, 2007). Available at www.educationengland.org.uk/documents/pdfs/2007-ajegbo-report-citizenship.pdf (accessed 30 August 2016).
11. Robin Richardson, 'Principles for classroom discussion', Sensitive and Controversial Issues in Schools, Walsall 2011. Available at www.insted.co.uk/principles-for-discussions.pdf (accessed 31 August 2016).

12. Kerry Moore, Paul Mason and Justin Lewis, *Images of Islam in the UK: The Representation of British Muslims in the National Print News 2000–2008* (2008). Available at www.channel4.com/news/media/pdfs/Cardiff%20Final%20Report.pdf (accessed 17 August 2016).
13. Runnymede Trust, *Islamophobia: A Challenge for Us All* (London: Commission on British Muslims and Islamophobia, The Runnymede Trust, 1997).
14. Anna Mansson McGinty, 'The "mainstream Muslim" opposing Islamophobia: Self-representations of American Muslims', *Environment and Planning A: Economy and Space* 44/12 (2012), pp. 2957–73.
15. EqualiTeach, *Universal Values*.
16. Citizenship Advisory Group, *Education for Citizenship and the Teaching of Democracy in Schools* (London: Qualifications and Curriculum Authority, 1998). Available at http://dera.ioe.ac.uk/4385/1/crickreport1998.pdf (accessed 31 August 2016).
17. Shirin Housee, 'What's the point? Anti-racism and students' voices against Islamophobia', *Race, Ethnicity and Education* 15/1 (2012), pp. 101–20.
18. Department for Education, *Listening to and Involving Young People* (2014). Available at www.gov.uk/government/uploads/system/uploads/attachment_data/file/437241/Listening_to_and_involving_children_and_young_people.pdf (accessed 31 August 2016).
19. EqualiTeach, *Universal Values*.
20. Ministry of Justice, *Youth Justice Statistics 2014/2015: England and Wales* (2016). Available at www.gov.uk/government/uploads/system/uploads/attachment_data/file/495708/youth-justice-statistics-2014-to-2015.pdf (accessed 31 August 2016).
21. Jonathan Birdwell, *Introducing Generation Citizen* (London: Demos, 2014). Available at www.demos.co.uk/project/introducing-generation-citizen/ (accessed 1 November 2016).
22. William Allen and Scott Blinder, *Migration in the News: Portrayals of Immigrants, Migrants, Asylum Seekers and Refugees in National British Newspapers, 2010–2012* (Oxford: Migration Observatory, COMPAS, University of Oxford, 2013). Available at www.migrationobservatory.ox.ac.uk/wp-content/uploads/2016/04/Report-Migration_News.pdf (accessed 17 August 2016).
23. Kate Lyons, 'Six wealthiest countries host less than 9% of the world's refugees', *Guardian*, 18 July 2016. Available at www.theguardian.com/world/2016/jul/18/refugees-us-china-japan-germany-france-uk-host-9-per-cent (accessed 6 November 2016).
24. Hilary Claire and Cathie Holden, *The Challenge of Teaching Controversial Issues* (London: Institute of Education Press, 2007).
25. Anne Slwika, 'Should the hijab be allowed in school? A structured approach to tackling controversial issues with older students', in Claire and Holden, *The Challenge of Teaching Controversial Issues*.

26 Home Office, *Revised Prevent Duty Guidance: For England and Wales* (2015). Available at www.gov.uk/government/uploads/system/uploads/attachment_data/file/445977/3799_Revised_Prevent_Duty_Guidance__England_Wales_V2-Interactive.pdf (accessed 18 August 2016).
27 Muslim Council of Britain, *Meeting between David Anderson QC and the MCB: Concerns on Prevent* (London: Muslim Council of Britain, 2015). Available at www.mcb.org.uk/wp-content/uploads/2015/10/20150803-Case-studies-about-Prevent.pdf (accessed 24 August 2016).
28 Ofsted, *No Place for Bullying* (Manchester: Ofsted, 2012). Available at www.gov.uk/government/uploads/system/uploads/attachment_data/file/413234/No_place_for_bullying.pdf (accessed 30 August 2016).
29 Muslim Council of Britain, *Meeting the Needs of Muslim Pupils in State Schools* (London: Muslim Council of Britain, 2007). Available at www.religionlaw.co.uk/MCBschoolsreport07.pdf (accessed 25 August 2016).
30 United Kingdom Parliament, *The Stephen Lawrence Inquiry: Report of an Inquiry by Sir William MacPherson of Cluny*, Cm 4262-I (1999). Available at www.gov.uk/government/uploads/system/uploads/attachment_data/file/277111/4262.pdf (accessed 22 August 2016).
31 EqualiTeach, *Equally Safe* (2015). Available at http://www.equaliteach.co.uk/wp-content/uploads/2017/08/EQUALLY-SAFE-2015.pdf (accessed 19 July 2018).
32 EqualiTeach, *Equally Safe*.

Works cited

Ajegbo, Keith, *Diversity and Citizenship Curriculum Review* (Annesley: Department for Education and Skills, 2007). Available at www.educationengland.org.uk/documents/pdfs/2007-ajegbo-report-citizenship.pdf (accessed 30 August 2016).

Allen, William and Scott Blinder, *Migration in the News: Portrayals of Immigrants, Migrants, Asylum Seekers and Refugees in National British Newspapers, 2010–2012* (Oxford: Migration Observatory, COMPAS, University of Oxford, 2013). Available at www.migrationobservatory.ox.ac.uk/wp-content/uploads/2016/04/Report-Migration_News.pdf (accessed 17 August 2016).

Birdwell, Jonathan, *Introducing Generation Citizen* (London: Demos, 2014). Available at www.demos.co.uk/project/introducing-generation-citizen/ (accessed 1 November 2016).

Citizenship Advisory Group, *Education for Citizenship and the Teaching of Democracy in Schools* (London: Qualifications and Curriculum Authority, 1998). Available at http://dera.ioe.ac.uk/4385/1/crickreport1998.pdf (accessed 31 August 2016).

Claire, Hilary and Cathie Holden, *The Challenge of Teaching Controversial Issues* (London: Institute of Education Press, 2007).

Department for Education, *Listening to and Involving Young People* (2014). Available at www.gov.uk/government/uploads/system/uploads/attachment_data/file/437241/Listening_to_and_involving_children_and_young_people.pdf (accessed 31 August 2016).

EqualiTeach, *Equally Safe* (2015). Available at http://www.equaliteach.co.uk/wp-content/uploads/2017/08/EQUALLY-SAFE-2015.pdf (accessed 19 July 2018).

EqualiTeach, *Universal Values: A Teacher's Resource* (2016). Available at http://www.equaliteach.co.uk/universal-values/ (accessed 19 July 2018).

Gaine, Chris, *We're All White Thanks* (Stoke-on-Trent: Trentham Books, 2005).

Home Office, *Revised Prevent Duty Guidance: For England and Wales* (2015). Available at www.gov.uk/government/uploads/system/uploads/attachment_data/file/445977/3799_Revised_Prevent_Duty_Guidance__England_Wales_V2-Interactive.pdf (accessed 18 August 2016).

Housee, Shirin, 'What's the point? Anti-racism and students' voices against Islamophobia', *Race, Ethnicity and Education* 15/1 (2012), pp. 101–20.

Kotecha, Sima, 'Quarter of young British people "do not trust Muslims"', *BBC Newsbeat*, 25 September 2013. Available at www.bbc.co.uk/newsbeat/article/24204742/quarter-of-young-british-people-do-not-trust-muslims (accessed 25 August 2016).

Lane, Jane, *Young Children and Racial Justice* (London: National Children's Bureau, 2008).

Lyons, Kate, 'Six wealthiest countries host less than 9% of the world's refugees', *Guardian*, 18 July 2016. Available at www.theguardian.com/world/2016/jul/18/refugees-us-china-japan-germany-france-uk-host-9-per-cent (accessed 6 November 2016).

McGinty, Anna Mansson, 'The "mainstream Muslim" opposing Islamophobia: Self-representations of American Muslims', *Environment and Planning A: Economy and Space* 44/12 (2012), pp. 2957–73.

Ministry of Justice, *Youth Justice Statistics 2014/2015: England and Wales* (2016). Available at www.gov.uk/government/uploads/system/uploads/attachment_data/file/495708/youth-justice-statistics-2014-to-2015.pdf (accessed 31 August 2016).

Moore, Kerry, Paul Mason and Justin Lewis, *Images of Islam in the UK: The Representation of British Muslims in the National Print News 2000–2008* (2008). Available at www.channel4.com/news/media/pdfs/Cardiff%20Final%20Report.pdf (accessed 17 August 2016).

Muslim Council of Britain, *Meeting between David Anderson QC and the MCB: Concerns on Prevent* (London: Muslim Council of Britain, 2015). Available at www.mcb.org.uk/wp-content/uploads/2015/10/20150803-Case-studies-about-Prevent.pdf (accessed 24 August 2016).

Muslim Council of Britain, *Meeting the Needs of Muslim Pupils in State Schools* (London: Muslim Council of Britain, 2007). Available at www.religionlaw.co.uk/MCBschoolsreport07.pdf (accessed 25 August 2016).

National Society for the Prevention of Cruelty to Children (NSPCC), *Can I Tell You Something? ChildLine Review of 2012/13* (London: NSPCC, 2014). Available at https://www.nspcc.org.uk/globalassets/documents/research-reports/childline-review-2012-2013.pdf (accessed 23 August 2016).

Ofsted, *No Place for Bullying* (Manchester: Ofsted, 2012). Available at www.gov.uk/government/uploads/system/uploads/attachment_data/file/413234/No_place_for_bullying.pdf (accessed 30 August 2016).

Ramberg, Ingrid, *Islamophobia and its Consequences on Young People* (Strasbourg: Directorate of Democratic Citizenship and Participation of the Council of Europe, 2004).

Richardson, Robin, 'Principles for classroom discussion', Sensitive and Controversial Issues in Schools, Walsall 2011. Available at www.insted.co.uk/principles-for-discussions.pdf (accessed 31 August 2016).

Richardson, Robin and Berenice Miles, *Racist Incidents and Bullying in Schools* (Stoke-on-Trent: Trentham Books, 2008).

Ross, Alistair, 'Institutional racism: The experience of teachers in schools'. Paper presented at the British Educational Research Association Conference, Exeter, 2002.

Runnymede Trust, *Islamophobia: A Challenge for Us All* (London: Commission on British Muslims and Islamophobia, The Runnymede Trust, 1997).

Slwika, Anne, 'Should the hijab be allowed in school? A structured approach to tackling controversial issues with older students', in Hilary Claire and Cathie Holden (eds), *The Challenge of Teaching Controversial Issues* (London: Institute of Education Press, 2007).

Soyei, Sarah, *The Barriers to Tackling Racism in England's Schools* (Newcastle upon Tyne: Show Racism the Red Card, 2011).

United Kingdom Parliament, *The Stephen Lawrence Inquiry: Report of an Inquiry by Sir William MacPherson of Cluny*, Cm 4262–I (1999). Available at www.gov.uk/government/uploads/system/uploads/attachment_data/file/277111/4262.pdf (accessed 22 August 2016).

8

Resisting Islamophobia: Muslim Youth Activism in the UK

Tania Saeed

The Muslim community in Britain has increasingly been subjected to a form of 'securitization',[1] becoming prime suspects in the aftermath of terrorist attacks committed by Muslims with allegiance to Daesh/ISIS (or previously Al Qaeda and its affiliates). This securitization has made Muslims more vulnerable to Islamophobia, whether in schools, universities or the workplace, on the internet or in their day-to-day lives, particularly those who stand out because of their religious appearance and observance.[2] These Islamophobic encounters include not only verbal or physical abuse but also more indirect abuse, especially in education through institutionalized mechanisms that may be directed towards Islamic student societies (ISocs) or Muslim student behaviour deemed 'suspicious' or problematic.[3] In educational institutions, the so-called 'Prevent duty' element of the Counter-Terrorism and Security Act 2015 imposes a statutory responsibility on educators to report on any student (predominantly Muslim) perceived to be vulnerable to radicalization, resulting in more and more innocent students being singled out.[4] With tragedies such as the London Bridge, Westminster and Manchester attacks of 2017,[5] law-abiding Muslim citizens are increasingly becoming easy targets, held responsible for the terror unleashed by a fellow member of their religion.[6] However, as Islamophobia has been on the rise, responses, reactions and resistance to it have also increased. This is especially evident among young Muslims who are engaged in a process of changing mindsets, through their educational institutions or through the internet.

    This chapter not only explores these challenges in the context of young Muslims' engagement in universities in the UK and on the internet but also examines the limitations of such acts. Drawing on Judith Butler's conception of the subject and agency, the chapter recognizes that in approaching 'what to change and how to change', one is 'already within the confines of a language, a discourse, and an institutional apparatus that will orchestrate ... what will or will not be deemed possible'.[7] Therefore, while it is important to recognize acts of contestation against Islamophobia, it is also crucial to highlight how such actions are located in a context where the struggle to redefine the narrative on Muslims unfairly places the Muslim community against a discourse that continuously categorizes them as dangerous and suspicious.[8] In this context Muslims are *subjected to* and *subjected by* tools and a vocabulary that are externally defined, often by a larger non-Muslim community. However, hope lies less in the *act* of contestation than in the *process* of contestation that is evoked: the realization and sense of responsibility taken on by young Muslims who believe in their right as British citizens to challenge the wider narrative, irrespective of whether their vocabulary is located or informed by the dominant discourse.

This chapter draws on research conducted between 2010 and 2012, studying forty young British and Pakistani Muslim women in universities across England who shared their experiences of and responses to Islamophobia in their daily lives. These women were contacted through university student societies. All of them were either current students or alumni.[9] The chapter further engages with the online activism of young Muslims, through campaigns such as #NotInMyName, and student activism through 'Students not Suspects'.[10] Exploring these narratives and campaigns, the chapter highlights the importance of recognizing such voices and the need for the state to engage with young people, while acknowledging the limitations of such contestations in a context where Islamophobia has increasingly become part of the social 'psyche' of Britain.[11]

The Muslim 'subject': Framing moderates and extremists

Acts of contestation against Islamophobia in Britain need to be understood within the context of the wider discourse on Muslims in Britain. In contextualizing these narratives, the work of Judith Butler on 'subject' and 'agency' is central. It is especially important in exposing the positionality of young Muslims who are contesting a discourse about their identity that is informed through a sociohistorical narrative about Islam in the West. Liz Fekete, Jonathan Lyons, Chris Allen, Nasar Meer, Peter Morey and Amina Yaqin, among others,[12] have discussed this phenomenon in their work, with Islamophobia described as evoking Orientalist tropes about Islam, with roots located as far back as the Crusades, Europe's and in particular Britain's colonial ventures and the movement of the 'coloured' colonial subject to the heart of the Empire in the 1950s and 1960s.[13] The Muslim subject therefore is perceived as an outsider, and a foreigner belonging to a religion that in Europe was historically associated with barbarism. Within this context, representations of Muslims today in media and political rhetoric invoke 'a kind of moral index, confirming non-Muslim viewers of these images in their sense of superiority and cementing the threatening strangeness of the Muslim Other'.[14] Furthermore, in the British social structure the 'coloured' immigrants who came in the 1950s were predominantly to become members of the working class, which structurally placed them in greater positions of vulnerability. Their arrival also sparked racism, as witnessed in the race riots of the 1950s and the subsequent decades.[15]

In her book *Frames of War*, Butler discusses the framing of the 'subject', arguing that the 'normative conditions for the production of the subject produce an historically contingent ontology, such that our very capacity to discern and name the "being" of the subject is dependent on norms that facilitate that recognition'. These norms 'emerge and fade depending on broader operations of power'. It is the 'recognition' of the subject that 'becomes part of the very practice of ordering and regulating subjects according to pre-established norms'. As Butler argues, 'We are given genders or social categories, against our will, and these categories confer intelligibility or recognizability, which means that they also communicate what the social risks of unintelligibility or partial intelligibility might be.' However, for Butler it is important to recognize that these norms and the normative framework are not static but an 'iterative' process acting 'productively to establish (or disestablish) certain kinds of subjects, not only in the past but also in a way that is reiterated through time'.[16] The iterative process takes the shape of a 'performative': 'One of the powerful and insidious ways in which subjects are called into social being from diffuse social quarters, inaugurated into sociality by a variety of diffuse and powerful interpellations.'[17] It is through the 'breakage' in the iterative process, through a 'performative politics', that contestation is possible, where 'the social performative' becomes 'a crucial part' of both 'subject formation' and 'the ongoing political contestation and reformulation of the subject as well'.[18]

The language and means of contestation employed by young Muslims in this chapter highlight such ruptures and breakages within the dominant discourse. Their responses against Islamophobia are often constructed in reaction to a securitized discourse on Muslim identity, where images, associations and identifiers are predominantly about violence and intimidation. Morey and Yaqin, in their analysis of political and media representations of Muslims, highlight how such 'limited framing narratives' have resulted in a 'Muslim issues matrix', based on an ideological agenda where Muslims are continuously 'framed' as threatening, which further 'creates a cognitive relationship between the "representation" of the world and how people come to perceive it in their minds'.[19] The perception of Muslims as evident in media representations is clear: the 'veiled' Muslim woman is perceived to be both vulnerable to cultural and religious savagery and also a threat hidden in plain sight[20]; the bearded Muslim man through his very presence interrupts the civilized landscape of modern-day Britain[21]; the minaret in places like Switzerland is perceived as a symbol of 'Islamic power' taking over the enlightened European landscape,[22] while sharia law is perceived as 'creeping' over the rights and liberties of Americans in the United States.[23] An attack by a terrorist who claims loyalty to Daesh evokes yet again the threatening nature of Islam and the Muslim community, and the fear of a terrorist hidden among *us*.

The creation of acceptable categories of Muslimness, through the use of terms such as 'moderate', or by engaging with Muslim organizations and institutions (such as the Quilliam Foundation) that meet the government's criteria of the acceptable Muslim, implies that others following a different political position or expressing a different degree of religiosity are placed beyond the socially acceptable. Morey and Yaqin argue that these terms of engagement are 'subject to the vicissitudes of government agendas', which are reinforced through the media, allowing certain 'authentic voices' to be heard while others are silenced or ignored.[24] Those outside this 'authentic' category oscillate between the murky terrain of moderate and extremist, where their level of religiosity (often determined by physical appearance) places them on a sliding scale of potential suspicion at the end of which is the '*at risk*' category of extremist.[25] Under the UK government's Counter-Extremism Strategy 2015, extremism is defined as 'the vocal or active opposition to our fundamental values, including democracy, the rule of law, individual liberty and the mutual respect and tolerance of different faiths and beliefs'.[26] The Counter-Extremism Strategy aims to uphold what the government calls 'British values'. However, a 2016 survey of 250 ethnic minority school pupils in one of England's most diverse cities, Peterborough, found the term 'British values' problematic.[27] The students were often unclear about the term; more than 'half were silent, or answered "don't know what you mean" to the survey question asking for their ideas about British Values', while 'the remainder offered popular icons such as "fish and chips", "drinking tea" and "celebrating the Queen's birthday"'.[28] There is clearly a disconnect between state policies and the language that is used to communicate these policies and their understanding at the community level. The survey also found an increase in 'racial abuse' experienced especially among Muslim students. Qureshi argues that in upholding these so-called fundamental values, the 'narrative' on Muslims and extremism 'has moved well beyond the threat of violence that is posed to the UK population, but rather, is more about whether individuals have "extreme" opinions, and the extent to which that "extremism" can be curbed'.[29]

This was further reiterated in David Cameron's speech in 2015 where he described a process of 'radicalization' that may be triggered through exposure to 'non-violent extremists' and that 'may begin with hearing about the so-called Jewish conspiracy and then develop into hostility to the West and fundamental liberal values, before finally becoming a cultish attachment to death'.[30] Despite lack of evidence to prove such a process or causation of radicalization, the UK government has nonetheless pursued a policy that aims to 'Prevent' such radicalization, as evident in Counter-Terrorism and Security Act 2015. After the Finsbury Park mosque attack, the prime minister Theresa May recognized the need to challenge all forms of extremism, including Islamophobia, yet the answer to this challenge, far from engaging with the Muslim community, was to reiterate her promise to set up a 'new Commission for Countering Extremism'.[31]

While, at the time of writing, the powers of this 'new Commission' are yet to be unveiled, the existing Act, in reinforcing efforts to challenge extremism, has instead curbed religious freedom and political speech. The place of the Muslim subject continues to be confined and curtailed by these policies, which may aim to challenge extremism but in the process are defining what is considered a socially acceptable (read: moderate) Muslim. Tyrer, in his discussion of moderates and extremists, argues that, far from existing as binaries, these categories are located within what Gilles Deleuze and Félix Guattari describe as 'degrees of alterity' where the level of acceptability of the Muslim is determined by a largely non-Muslim host community.[32] This is especially evident in cases where Muslim students have been reported by educational institutions under the terms of the UK government's counterterrorism policy. In 2015, a total of 3,955 referrals of 'vulnerable individuals' were made to the UK government's counterterrorism programme, Channel.[33] In the West Midlands, a total of 788 referrals were made, out of which 248 were children below the age of 14, and 235 were within the age bracket of 15 to 19.[34]

The majority of the referrals were of Muslims, though according to a report by the National Police Chiefs' Council (NPCC), 'religion is not a mandatory field and is not always completed'.[35] However, the Open Society Justice Initiative's evaluation of the Prevent agenda found that it 'creates a serious risk of human rights violations'.[36] The report further goes on to argue that, in a post-Brexit UK with heightened anti-immigration sentiments, 'the statutory Prevent duty to identify and report to Channel individuals at risk of being drawn into terrorism (including violent and non-violent extremism) gives legal backing to potentially discriminatory determinations of "extremism" by frontline professionals'.

Teachers have also complained about lack of clarity in determining signs of radicalization and vulnerability under this strategy, and expressed dissatisfaction with their training under Prevent.[37] The kind of confusion that arises from such a statutory duty is evident in the case of a four-year-old toddler who drew a picture of his father cutting cucumbers, which was mistaken by the nursery staff to be that of his 'father making a "cooker bomb"'.[38] The child eventually was not reported to the authorities after the nursery staff discussed the problem with the child's mother, only to realize their error.[39] However, in other cases children have been referred to the authorities. In one case, a teenager who was campaigning for the Boycott, Divest and Sanction Israel movement, one that has been supported by left-wing activists and politicians, was reprimanded by his school authorities and reported for having radical tendencies. The child was harassed to the point that he changed schools and was eventually visited by government personnel at his home to determine if he was radical or supported terrorist groups such as Daesh. In another case, a teenager was taken to an 'inclusion centre' in his school after he used the term 'eco-terrorism' in a classroom debate about eco-activism.[40] Universities have also committed errors in referring students, including the case of Mohammed Umar Farooq, reported for reading a coursebook on terrorism in his university library.[41] The extent to which those reported to the authorities are actually vulnerable to radicalization is still unclear. Conversely, there has been the case of a fifteen-year-old – the 'UK's youngest convicted terrorist' – who was reported to the Channel programme in 2013, but was released and continued to incite 'terrorism overseas'.[42] Thus, the extent to which such counter-extremism programmes are successful, especially when they involve reporting by educational institutions, is yet to be proved. What is clear though is that these programmes are creating a sense of insecurity both among the Muslim community and about the Muslim community within and beyond educational institutions. Despite these limitations Muslim students have not been silenced, as illustrated in the next section.

Unframing Muslims: Student activism, universities and the internet

> My committee, the student affairs committee deals with politics. We have a campaigns committee as well which deals with Islamophobia. Their focus is about mainstream Islamophobia in societies. Our focus really, I suppose the way we counter, is to ensure Muslim students' safety. We take it from that angle. Combating Islamophobia comes in many levels. Some of it can be loud campaigning, anti-Islamophobia campaigning, holding conferences and so on. That is not our focus, our focus is to talk to Muslim students, empowering them to know their issues, be aware of where they are being wronged, and be aware of reasons to engage. It is only when you engage on campus, run for student positions, have representation there, which means that you are the first to know about any issues, people trust you, come to you first.
>
> FOSIS representative, 2011[43]

The study undertaken in universities across England between 2010 and 2012 asked young Muslim women not only about their experiences of Islamophobia but also about what they thought were mechanisms to challenge such discrimination. Students' responses varied, often depending on how politically driven they were, but one way of challenging Islamophobia was addressing its root cause, which for students was ignorance and misunderstanding. As Faiza (not her real name), a twenty-two-year-old humanities undergraduate from Yorkshire, observes,

> Again I think Islamophobia is more an attitude that people that don't even know what Islam around them is, they don't even know what they believe themselves, they just want to pick at straws, just trying to pinpoint things ... because they are too scared to control what is going on in their own minds or in their own societies.

The fact that the only exposure the non-Muslim public has to Islam is through media, and political rhetoric was perceived to be a problem that would naturally result in a negative perception about Muslim identity and religion. The solution was felt to be simple: engage in a dialogue, become more visible rather than invisible in situations beyond ISocs, visible in activities and activism that one is passionate about, which may not always be linked to one's religion. That visibility, at a time where the only space given to the Muslim subject is within the confines of the moderate–extremist spectrum, is a way to contest the overarching Islamophobic discourse. Butler points to 'that moment in which a speech act without prior authorization nevertheless assumes authorization in the course of its performance [that] may anticipate and instate altered contexts for its future reception'.[44] The direction that speech acts take cannot be pre-empted, but it is the attempt at engaging in that conversation, at taking back the narrative even as an individual, that presents a challenge against Islamophobia. The participants in the research were young women, who are most likely to be perceived as 'victims' of religion or culture and who are positioned at the periphery in any discussion or debate about their identities. Yet these are just the young women who refuse to be *subjected* and limited by such an overarching discourse.

Narratives of young women like Nadia, a law undergraduate from West Yorkshire, who is the head sister of the ISoc at her university, also offer examples. She believes that the attempt to have a conversation with young people who do not know about Islam is important, which is why even if at first she fails to convince someone she keeps inviting them to have a discussion, to show them that despite wearing a hijab and jilbab she is not a 'monster' but someone who has similar views and is equally a British citizen.

> But yeah like for me it is good to have that challenge. … if I smile and I go out of my way to help people then maybe they will kind of realize that and if I might be that Muslim who will kind of change their way of looking at things.

The ISocs have also been engaged in raising awareness about Islam through week-long student society events that educate students and the general public about their religion. Nadia, for instance, organized a 'hijab awareness' workshop where Muslim and non-Muslim students were provided with information about the hijab and an opportunity to ask questions. Students, especially members of ISocs, have encountered Islamophobia within and outside their universities and have had to defend constantly their right to invite Muslim speakers. Nadia believed that it was her university's middle management that continued to obstruct ISoc events by cancelling venue bookings for speakers at the last minute even when the university had given them permission to invite those speakers.[45] Romeena, a welfare officer at her university and a member of the university ISoc's Executive Committee, highlighted similar problems at her university in south-east England. She shared an anecdote about an ISoc speaker event where 'security guards' were called in by the university at the last minute to check students who were attending the event. The ISocs were not informed about the presence of security personnel before, which she believed 'was an alienating experience'.[46] Yet, despite these obstacles ISocs are resisting and persisting by engaging with the university and other students, while challenging unfair policies within the university.

Young students are also involved in internet campaigns such as #NotInMyName. Owing to the ease of access it provides to forums and material, the internet has been implicated in the counter-extremism strategy as one of the spaces that can radicalize youth, with counter-extremism efforts dedicated to 'contesting the online space'.[47] Daesh has used the internet to promote its narrative and agenda, recording and showing videos of terror, including the infamous beheadings of British citizens by a fellow citizen named 'Jihadi John' who was recruited by Daesh. Rogers has argued that these videos belong 'to a particular genre of propaganda, produced for a specific body of consumer-spectators, coded "the West"'.[48] They serve as 'an advertisement campaign for apocalyptic war ... that draws from horror films, video-game-style "immersive media", and models of public diplomacy's "soft power" arsenal'.[49] While nearly '800 Britons' are thought to have joined Daesh and affiliated groups,[50] out of a population of more than 2.7 million Muslims in Britain, the target population of young Muslims in the 'West' are using the same medium to answer back through the #NotInMyName campaign, with young Muslims uploading videos to the internet of them responding against Daesh and showing their fellow citizens that such terrorist groups do not represent Islam.

While these campaigns are important to recognize as spaces utilized by Muslims to speak up against terrorism and also to educate the public about Islam thereby challenging Islamophobia, the reason for initiating such campaigns also needs to be investigated. In contesting Islamophobia by engaging with a general public that has 'misunderstood' Islam, or is 'ignorant' about Islam, the responsibility falls on innocent Muslims whose only common denominator with the terrorist is a religion followed by 1.8 billion people.[51] Dilly Hussain is critical of such initiatives precisely because of the apologetic and guilt-ridden sentiment that drives these campaigns.[52] As he argues, 'If white Christian Americans/Britons/Europeans are willing to condemn and apologise for centuries of colonialism, the actions of G. W. Bush, Tony Blair over Iraq and Afghanistan; Abu Ghraib, Bagram and Guantanamo Bay prisons; extra judicial murder and illegal renditions ... then maybe Muslims will comfortably come forward to say "not in my name, not in my religion".[53] In response to this unfair burden to take responsibility for the actions of terrorists that are equally a threat to Muslims, a counter internet campaign, #MuslimApologies, was launched. Through humour and satire, Muslims attempted to show the absurdity of this expectation, apologizing for anything and everything, with one tweet asking if 'the Christians' were going to be asked 'to apologize for Hitler?'[54] These contestations highlight how, in responding to the overarching discourse about their identities, the Muslim subject is constrained by the tools and vocabulary at his/her disposal. The responsibility taken on by young Muslims is no doubt a result of the unequal power relations that inform their identity, as evident in criticism levelled against such acts of contestation, which challenge the frame by which such exchanges are supposed to be governed. One needs to be cognizant of these tensions, but they do not undermine the efforts of young people in attempting to create a counter-narrative. These points of contestation and re-contestation further allude to Butler's proposition that 'speech acts', through their performative action, produce effects that cannot be fully controlled and comprehended; there may be unintended consequences, and there will always be limitations. Yet, 'the possibility for the speech act to take on a non-ordinary meaning, to function in contexts where it has not belonged, is precisely the political promise of the performative, one that positions the performative at the center of a politics of hegemony, one that offers an unanticipated political future for deconstructive thinking'.[55] Placing the onus on Muslims or Muslim students to produce a counter-narrative to the prevailing discourse is no doubt a problem and one that should also be contested; yet one cannot deny the importance of recognizing acts of contestation that young Muslims have willingly engaged in or have initiated, in the belief that they have the power to change mindsets of one person or institution at a time.

This counter-narrative is further evident in the 'Students not Suspects' campaign organized by different student groups with the National Union of Students in opposition to Prevent. The importance of students joining forces, especially the NUS becoming an active force in supporting the rights of Muslim students, becomes even more significant in light of the history of the NUS and ISocs. Both the Federation of Student Islamic Students (FOSIS) representative and a racism and welfare officer for a university in London highlighted how the NUS has become an important ally today because of the active efforts of Muslim students. Historically, the NUS and ISocs have had an antagonistic relationship.[56] The success of Muslim students is evident in the appointment of the first Muslim female president of the NUS, Malia Bouattia, though her appointment was a source of contention.[57] As the FOSIS representative highlights, 'We are also campaigning to make sure issues are made public, so we are working continuously. Alhumdulillah we have a situation that if something happens we have the NUS and other organizations who are there to support Muslim students.'[58]

In a context where students and organizations opposing the Prevent agenda are being reprimanded by the government, the Students Not Suspects campaign should be recognized as a space where students are fighting for their religious and political rights. The NUS in collaboration with 'the Black Students' Campaign' organized a 'Students not Suspects tour' around campuses in the UK, and held workshops and training sessions about students' rights, institutional obligations and ways of resisting Prevent.[59] A student handbook on countering the Prevent agenda on campus was also created by members of the NUS. The handbook provides a comprehensive review of Prevent and its impact on Muslim students, as well as guidance for students in 'Preventing PREVENT'. The guidance provides information to student unions about their rights, suggesting ways to circumvent Prevent, advising student unions to refuse any funds that may lead to 'extra monitoring of certain clubs and societies and changes to ... unions' external speaker approval system, as well as resisting the threat of investigation by the Charity Commission'.[60] The rationale given is that universities and the NUS have an existing 'no platform' policy for any type of hate speech, whereas implementing Prevent in the guise of 'preventing extremism' promotes an agenda of 'top-down' surveillance of Muslim students, deemed unnecessary. The main aim of 'Preventing PREVENT' is to 'Educate, Educate, Educate' – 'Educating the student and academic body about the PREVENT agenda, their rights, and how they can counter-campaign against it' to 'Organise, Organise, Organise' – 'Challenge and counter the changes' that institutions are implementing in compliance with the Prevent duty and ultimately 'to try and make PREVENT "unworkable"'.[61] While 'Preventing PREVENT' has thus far not succeeded in limiting state powers, the presence of an opposing voice, especially of students, both Muslim and non-Muslim, is important in a context where opposition is increasingly being viewed with greater suspicion and hostility, rather than celebrated as part of a democracy.

Muslim students engaging in dialogue and spreading awareness about Islam; FOSIS encouraging students to get involved in activism beyond their ISocs and the NUS and other student groups engaged in standing up against Islamophobic policies such as Prevent – these interventions represent an attempt to claw back the debate, or at least the power of self-definition within it. In the mainstream, such contestations are often overlooked or silenced within the prevailing discourse about Muslims and their identity as a problem. As Butler observes, 'If one is "framed," then a "frame" is constructed around one's deed such that one's guilty status becomes the viewer's inevitable conclusion. Some way of organizing and presenting a deed leads to an interpretive conclusion about the deed itself.'[62] Such a contestatory counter-narrative would work against the 'frame' or the 'Muslim issues matrix' that Morey and Yaqin have highlighted, which is why such voices are often absent from mainstream media or political discourse.

While acknowledging the limitations of campaigns and initiatives that place an expectation on Muslim students and the Muslim community to defend their religion in the event of a terrorist attack, one nonetheless needs to recognize the efforts of young people in creating an alternative narrative. As Farzana, a twenty-year-old medical student from south-west England, observes,

> I can't stop a negative but I can make a positive. I can't stop my friend from reading the *Daily Mirror* which is like a Muslim person sneezed, it caused I don't know influenza you know ridiculous stories like that. … I can at least counter it with a bit of positive. [With my friend] she talks to her family now and tells them. She gets it. … I told her so she knows. … She hadn't been to a mosque before. I said let's go to a mosque. … Stuff like that helps. Literally if I didn't speak to her she would have grown up like that and would have told her kids the same things.[63]

Beyond the frame: Contestations and resistance

This chapter has illustrated the various ways in which young Muslims and students are contesting Islamophobia in Britain today. Challenging Islamophobia in a context where innocent civilians have been attacked by terrorists with allegiance to ISIS/Daesh has become increasingly difficult. The resultant Islamophobic attacks on Muslims, who become scapegoats for such atrocities, have increased. In turn, Islamophobia further serves as propaganda for groups such as ISIS/Daesh, reinforcing the notion that Muslims and the West are antithetical and a violent clash is imminent. However, young Muslims through such contestations also challenge the ideology of terrorist groups, demonstrating their democratic rights as British citizens by taking a stand against Islamophobia and Islamophobic legislation in their country.

The extent to which such contestation will be successful remains to be seen, but what is important is recognizing the efforts of young Muslims. Butler has argued that 'the agency of the subject is not a property of the subject … but an effect of power, it is constrained but not determined in advance'.[64] However, 'the point is not to eradicate the conditions of one's own production but only to assume responsibility for living a life that contests the determining power of that production; in other words, that makes good use of the iterability of the productive norms and, hence, of their fragility and transformability'.[65] These narratives of contestation against Islamophobia are proof of this 'responsibility', taken on by students and young Muslims, to change the discourse that informs their daily lives and identities as Muslims in Britain.

Notes

1 See Stuart Croft, *Securitizing Islam: Identity and the Search for Security* (Cambridge: Cambridge University Press, 2012).
2 'Manchester attack: Islamophobic hate crime reports increase by 500%', *BBC News*, 22 June 2017. Available at www.bbc.com/news/uk-england-manchester-40368668 (accessed 23 June 2017). Mark Easton, 'Muslim women most disadvantaged, say MPs', *BBC News*, 11 August 2016. Available at www.bbc.co.uk/news/uk-37041301 (accessed 25 May 2017). See also Tania Saeed, *Islamophobia and Securitization: Religion, Ethnicity and the Female Voice* (London: Palgrave Macmillan, 2016).
3 NUS Black Students, *Preventing PREVENT: A Student Handbook on Countering the PREVENT Agenda on Campus* (London: NUS, 2015). Available at www.nusconnect.org.uk/resources/preventing-prevent-handbook (accessed 3 June 2017); Tania Saeed and David Johnson, 'Intelligence, global terrorism and higher education: Neutralising threats or alienating allies?', *British Journal of Educational Studies* 64/1 (2016), pp. 37–51.
4 United Kingdom Parliament, *Counter-Terrorism and Security Act 2015* (UK, 2015); NUS Black Students, *Preventing PREVENT*; Aislinn O'Donnell, 'Securitisation, counterterrorism and the silencing of dissent: The educational implications of Prevent', *British Journal of Educational Studies* 64/1 (2016), pp. 53–76.
5 'Eight people were killed in central London when three attackers drove a van into pedestrians on London Bridge and launched a knife attack in Borough Market' – see 'London attack: What we know so far', *BBC News*, 12 June 2017. Available at www.bbc.com/news/uk-england-london-40147164 (accessed 16 June 2017). In Westminster 'Six people died, including the attacker, and at least 50 people were injured after a terror attack near the Houses of Parliament on 22 March' – see 'London attack: What we know so far', *BBC News*, 7 April 2017. Available at www.bbc.com/news/uk-39355108 (accessed 16 June 2017). In the Manchester attack 'Twenty-two people were killed and 116 injured in a suicide bombing at Manchester Arena' – see 'Manchester attack: What we know so far', *BBC News*, 12 June 2017. Available at www.bbc.com/news/uk-england-manchester-40008389 (accessed 16 June 2017).
6 This is further evident in so-called revenge terrorist attacks on the Muslim community by right-wing extremists. 'One person died and 11 were injured' in June 2017 'after a van was driven into a crowd of Muslim worshippers in Finsbury Park, in north London' – see Vikram Dodd and Jamie Grierson, 'Finsbury Park attack suspect was probably "self-radicalised"', *Guardian*, 21 June 2017. Available at www.theguardian.com/uk-news/2017/jun/21/finsbury-park-mosque-attack-two-victims-in-critical-care (accessed 23 June 2017).

7   Sara Salih with Judith Butler, *The Judith Butler Reader* (Oxford and Malden, MA: Blackwell Publishing, 2004), p. 334.
8   See Chris Allen, *Islamophobia* (Farnham and Burlington, VT: Ashgate Publishing Ltd., 2010); Nasar Meer, 'Complicating "radicalism" – Counter-terrorism and Muslim identity in Britain', *Arches Quarterly: Terrorism and Counter Terrorism: Spotlight on Strategies and Approaches* 5/9 (2012), pp. 10–19; Liz Fekete, *A Suitable Enemy: Racism, Migration and Islamophobia in Europe* (London: Pluto Press, 2009).
9   The participants were studying in universities located in north- and south-west England, north- and south-east England, the West Midlands, West Yorkshire and London. These participants were primarily contacted through the Islamic student societies and the Pakistan student societies in these universities. They were aged between eighteen and twenty-eight. At the time of this research, they were either enrolled in undergraduate and graduate courses ranging from the social sciences to medicine or had recently graduated. The participants further expressed different levels of religiosity from wearing the niqab (the face veil), the hijab (headscarf), the jilbab (a long gown often worn with a headscarf or a face veil) and the cultural shalwar kameez (tunic with loose pants, often worn with a scarf). The author followed the ethics protocols for research defined by the University of Oxford, ensuring that participants had sufficient time to learn about the study, could opt out of the study and had the right to refuse to answer any question. Pseudonyms have been used to ensure the anonymity of the participants.
10 Active Change Foundation, #NotInMyName (n.d.). Available at http://isisnotinmyname.com (accessed 19 June 2017). National Union of Students (NUS), the NUS Black Students' Campaign, Federation of Student Islamic Students (FOSIS), the University and College Union (UCU) and Defend the Right to Protest (DtRtP), *Students Not Suspects* (n.d.). Available at https://studentsnotsuspects.com/about-2/ (accessed 30 May 2017).
11 See Saeed, *Islamophobia and Securitization*.
12 Fekete, *A Suitable Enemy*; Jonathan Lyons, *Islam through Western Eyes* (New York: Columbia University Press, 2012); Allen, *Islamophobia*; Meer, 'Complicating "radicalism"'; Peter Morey and Amina Yaqin, *Framing Muslims: Stereotyping and Representation after 9/11* (Cambridge, MA: Harvard University Press, 2011).
13 Tariq Modood, *Multicultural Politics: Racism, Ethnicity, and Muslims in Britain* (Minneapolis, MN: University of Minnesota Press, 2005); Judith M. Brown, *Global South Asians: Introducing the Modern Diaspora* (Cambridge: Cambridge University Press, 2006).
14 Morey and Yaqin, *Framing Muslims*, p. 3.
15 Ian R. G. Spencer, *British Immigration Policy since 1939: The Making of Multi-Racial Britain* (New York: Routledge, 1997).
16 Judith Butler, *Frames of War: When is Life Grievable?* (London: Verso, 2009), pp. 4, 141, 167.

17 Judith Butler, *Excitable Speech: A Politics of the Performative* (New York: Routledge, 1997), p. 160.
18 Butler, *Excitable Speech*, p. 160.
19 Morey and Yaqin, *Framing Muslims*, p. 63.
20 Gholam Khiabany and Milly Williamson, 'Veiled bodies – Naked racism: Culture, politics and race in the Sun', *Race & Class* 50/2 (2008), pp. 69–88.
21 Katherine E. Brown, 'Gender, prevent and British Muslims', *Public Spirit*, 16 December 2013. Available at www.publicspirit.org.uk/gender-prevent-and-british-muslims-2/ (accessed 19 June 2017); Saeed, *Islamophobia and Securitization*.
22 'Swiss voters back ban on minarets', *BBC News*, 29 November 2009. Available at http://news.bbc.co.uk/2/hi/europe/8385069.stm (accessed 16 June 2017).
23 Safia Samee Ali, Ali Gostanian and Daniella Silva, 'ACT for America stages marches against "Sharia Law" nationwide, arrests made', *NBC News*, 10 June 2017. Available at www.nbcnews.com/news/us-news/anti-muslim-act-america-stage-marches-against-sharia-law-nationwide-n767386 (accessed 20 June 2017).
24 Morey and Yaqin, *Framing Muslims*, p. 15.
25 David Tyrer, 'Flooding the embankments: Race, bio-politics and sovereignty', in S. Sayyid and AbdoolKarim Vakil (eds), *Thinking through Islamophobia: Global Perspectives*, (London: Hurst & Co., 2010), pp. 93–110.
26 United Kingdom Parliament, *Counter-Extremism Strategy*, Cm 9148 (2015), p. 9.
27 'Pupils left puzzled by the term "British values"', *Open University*, 14 September 2016. Available at https://www3.open.ac.uk/media/fullstory.aspx?id=30560 (accessed 18 June 2017).
28 Open University, 'Pupils left puzzled'.
29 Asim Qureshi, 'PREVENT: Creating "radicals" to strengthen anti-Muslim narratives', *Critical Studies on Terrorism* 8/1 (2015), pp. 181–91; p. 183.
30 David Cameron, 'Extremism: PM speech', 20 July 2015. Available at www.gov.uk/government/speeches/extremism-pm-speech (accessed 10 June 2017).
31 Theresa May, 'PM statement following terror attack in Finsbury Park', 19 June 2017. Available at www.gov.uk/government/speeches/pm-statement-following-terror-attack-in-finsbury-park-19-june-2017 (accessed 20 June 2017).
32 Tyrer, 'Flooding the embankments'.
33 National Police Chiefs' Council Freedom of Information Request Reference Number: 000026/16 (7 March 2016). Available at www.npcc.police.uk/Publication/NPCC%20FOI/CT/02616ChannelReferrals.pdf (accessed 19 June 2017).
34 Ibid.
35 Ibid.
36 Open Society Justice Initiative, *Eroding Trust: The UK's PREVENT Counter-Extremism Strategy in Health and Education* (New York: Open Society Foundations, 2016), p. 15.
37 Open Society Justice Initiative, *Eroding Trust*, pp. 35, 42–3.

38 Ben Quinn, 'Nursery "raised fears of radicalisation over boy's cucumber drawing"', *Guardian* (11 March 2016). Available at www.theguardian.com/uk-news/2016/mar/11/nursery-radicalisation-fears-boys-drawing-cooker-bomb (accessed 10 June 2017).
39 Quinn, 'Nursery "raised fears of radicalisation over boy's cucumber drawing"'.
40 Simon Hooper, 'Stifling freedom of expression in UK schools', *Al Jazeera*, 23 July 2015. Available at www.aljazeera.com/indepth/features/2015/07/stifling-freedom-expression-uk-schools-150721080612049.html (accessed 15 June 2017). Vikram Dodd, 'School questioned Muslim pupil about Isis after discussion on eco-activism', *Guardian*, 22 September 2015. Available at www.theguardian.com/education/2015/sep/22/school-questioned-muslim-pupil-about-isis-after-discussion-on-eco-activism (accessed 15 June 2017).
41 Randeep Ramesh and Josh Halliday, 'Student accused of being a terrorist for reading book on terrorism', *Guardian*, 24 September 2015. Available at www.theguardian.com/education/2015/sep/24/student-accused-being-terrorist-reading-book-terrorism (accessed 15 June 2017).
42 Jessica Elgot, 'UK schoolboy given life sentence for Australia terror plot', *Guardian*, 2 October 2015. Available at www.theguardian.com/world/2015/oct/02/uk-schoolboy-life-sentence-australia-terror-plot (accessed 15 June 2017).
43 Federations of Student Islamic Societies – an umbrella organization representing ISocs in universities across the UK.
44 Butler, *Excitable Speech*, p. 160.
45 Saeed and Johnson, 'Intelligence, global terrorism and higher education', p. 45.
46 Ibid., p. 42.
47 United Kingdom Parliament, *Counter-Extremism Strategy*, p. 24.
48 Amanda Rogers, 'The strategic success of ISIS propaganda (video lecture)', *The Postcolonialist*, 4 November 2014. Available at http://postcolonialist.com/arts/strategic-success-isis-propaganda-video-lecture/ (accessed 19 June 2017).
49 Rogers, 'The strategic success of ISIS propaganda (video lecture)'.
50 Samuel Osborne, 'Young British Muslims think Isis fighters returning from Syria should be reintegrated into society, research finds', *Independent*, 17 April 2017. Available at www.independent.co.uk/news/uk/young-british-muslims-uk-isis-fighters-syria-return-reintegrate-society-research-a7682836.html (accessed 19 June 2017).
51 Figure for 2015 – see Michael Lipka and Conrad Hackett, 'Why Muslims are the world's fastest-growing religious group', *Pew Research Center*, 6 April 2017. Available at www.pewresearch.org/fact-tank/2017/04/06/why-muslims-are-the-worlds-fastest-growing-religious-group/ (accessed 20 June 2017).
52 Dilly Hussain, 'The Muslim blame game – "Not in my name"', *HuffPost United Kingdom*, 17 October 2014. Available at www.huffingtonpost.co.uk/dilly-hussain/the-muslim-blame-game_b_5682830.html (accessed 18 June 2017).

53 Hussain, 'The Muslim blame game – "Not in my name"'.
54 '#BBCtrending: "Sorry for algebra" and more #MuslimApologies', *BBC News*, 25 September 2014. Available at www.bbc.com/news/blogs-trending-29362370 (accessed 20 June 2017).
55 Butler, *Excitable Speech*, p. 161.
56 David Tyrer, 'Institutionalized Islamophobia in British universities' (PhD thesis, University of Salford, Institute of Social Research, 2003).
57 Jessica Elgot, 'Malia Bouattia's election as NUS president proves deeply divisive', *Guardian*, 22 April 2016. Available at www.theguardian.com/education/2016/apr/22/malia-bouattia-election-nus-president-deeply-divisive-jewish-student-groups (accessed 20 June 2017).
58 Saeed, *Islamophobia and Securitization*, p. 155.
59 National Union of Students (NUS), 'The NUS Black Students' Campaign, Federation of Student Islamic Students (FOSIS), the University and College Union (UCU) and Defend the Right to Protest (DtRtP)', *Students Not Suspects* (n.d.). Available at https://studentsnotsuspects.com/about-2/ (accessed 30 May 2017).
60 NUS Black Students, *Preventing PREVENT*, p. 48.
61 Ibid., p. 51.
62 Butler, *Frames of War*, p. 8.
63 Katherine E. Brown and Tania Saeed, 'Radicalization and counter-radicalization at British universities: Muslim encounters and alternatives', *Ethnic and Racial Studies* 38/11 (2015), pp. 1952–68; p. 1962.
64 Butler, *Excitable Speech*, p. 139.
65 Butler, *Frames of War*, pp. 170–1.

Works cited

Active Change Foundation, #NotInMyName (n.d.). Available at http://isisnotinmyname.com (accessed 19 June 2017).
Ali, Safia Samee, Ali Gostanian and Daniella Silva, 'ACT for America stages marches against "Sharia Law" nationwide, arrests made', *NBC News*, 10 June 2017. Available at www.nbcnews.com/news/us-news/anti-muslim-act-america-stage-marches-against-sharia-law-nationwide-n767386 (accessed 20 June 2017).
Allen, Chris, *Islamophobia* (Farnham and Burlington, VT: Ashgate, 2010).
BBC News, 'London attack: What we know so far', *BBC News*, 7 April 2017. Available at www.bbc.com/news/uk-39355108 (accessed 16 June 2017).
BBC News, 'London attack: What we know so far', *BBC News*, 30 May 2017. Available at www.bbc.com/news/uk-england-london-40147164 (accessed 16 June 2017).

BBC News, 'Manchester attack: Islamophobic hate crime reports increase by 500%', *BBC News*, 22 June 2017. Available at www.bbc.com/news/uk-england-manchester-40368668 (accessed 23 June 2017).

BBC News, 'Manchester attack: What we know so far', *BBC News*, 12 June 2017. Available at www.bbc.com/news/uk-england-manchester-40008389 (accessed 16 June 2017).

BBC News, 'Swiss voters back ban on minarets', *BBC News*, 29 November 2009. Available at http://news.bbc.co.uk/2/hi/europe/8385069.stm (accessed 16 June 2017).

BBC Trending, '#BBCtrending: "Sorry for algebra" and more #MuslimApologies', *BBC News*, 25 September 2014. Available at www.bbc.com/news/blogs-trending-29362370 (accessed 20 June 2017).

Brown, Judith M., *Global South Asians: Introducing the Modern Diaspora* (Cambridge: Cambridge University Press, 2006).

Brown, Katherine E., 'Gender, prevent and British Muslims', *Public Spirit*, 16 December 2013. Available at www.publicspirit.org.uk/gender-prevent-and-british-muslims-2/ (accessed 19 June 2017).

Brown, Katherine E. and Tania Saeed, 'Radicalization and counter-radicalization at British universities: Muslim encounters and alternatives', *Ethnic and Racial Studies* 38/11 (2015), pp. 1952–68.

Butler, Judith, *Excitable Speech: A Politics of the Performative* (New York: Routledge, 1997).

Butler, Judith, *Frames of War: When is Life Grievable?* (London: Verso, 2009).

Cameron, David, 'Extremism: PM speech', 20 July 2015. Available at www.gov.uk/government/speeches/extremism-pm-speech (accessed 10 June 2017).

Croft, Stuart, *Securitizing Islam: Identity and the Search for Security* (Cambridge: Cambridge University Press, 2012).

Dodd, Vikram, 'School questioned Muslim pupil about Isis after discussion on eco-activism', *Guardian*, 22 September 2015. Available at www.theguardian.com/education/2015/sep/22/school-questioned-muslim-pupil-about-isis-after-discussion-on-eco-activism (accessed 15 June 2017).

Dodd, Vikram and Jamie Grierson, 'Finsbury Park attack suspect was probably "self-radicalised"', *Guardian*, 21 June 2017. Available at www.theguardian.com/uk-news/2017/jun/21/finsbury-park-mosque-attack-two-victims-in-critical-care (accessed 23 June 2017).

Easton, Mark, 'Muslim women most disadvantaged, say MPs', *BBC News*, 11 August 2016. Available at www.bbc.co.uk/news/uk-37041301 (accessed 25 May 2017).

Elgot, Jessica, 'Malia Bouattia's election as NUS president proves deeply divisive', *Guardian*, 22 April 2016. Available at www.theguardian.com/education/2016/apr/22/malia-bouattia-election-nus-president-deeply-divisive-jewish-student-groups (accessed 20 June 2017).

Elgot, Jessica, 'UK schoolboy given life sentence for Australia terror plot', *Guardian*, 2 October 2015. Available at www.theguardian.com/world/2015/oct/02/uk-schoolboy-life-sentence-australia-terror-plot (accessed 15 June 2017).

Fekete, Liz, *A Suitable Enemy: Racism, Migration and Islamophobia in Europe* (London: Pluto Press, 2009).

Hooper, Simon, 'Stifling freedom of expression in UK schools', *Al Jazeera*, 23 July 2015. Available at www.aljazeera.com/indepth/features/2015/07/stifling-freedom-expression-uk-schools-150721080612049.html (accessed 15 June 2017).

Hussain, Dilly, 'The Muslim blame game – "Not in my name"', *HuffPost United Kingdom*, 17 October 2014. Available at www.huffingtonpost.co.uk/dilly-hussain/the-muslim-blame-game_b_5682830.html (accessed 18 June 2017).

Khiabany, Gholam and Milly Williamson, 'Veiled bodies—Naked racism: Culture, politics and race in the Sun', *Race & Class* 50/2 (2008), pp. 69–88.

Lipka, Michael and Conrad Hackett, 'Why Muslims are the world's fastest-growing religious group', *Pew Research Center*, 6 April 2017. Available at www.pewresearch.org/fact-tank/2017/04/06/why-muslims-are-the-worlds-fastest-growing-religious-group/ (accessed on 20 June 2017).

Lyons, Jonathan, *Islam through Western Eyes* (New York: Columbia University Press, 2012).

May, Theresa, 'PM statement following terror attack in Finsbury Park', 19 June 2017. Available at www.gov.uk/government/speeches/pm-statement-following-terror-attack-in-finsbury-park-19-june-2017 (accessed 20 June 2017).

Meer, Nasar, 'Complicating "radicalism" – Counter-terrorism and Muslim identity in Britain', *Arches Quarterly: Terrorism and Counter-Terrorism – Spotlight on Strategies and Approaches* 5/9 (2012), pp. 10–19.

Modood, Tariq, *Multicultural Politics: Racism, Ethnicity, and Muslims in Britain* (Minneapolis, MN: University of Minnesota Press, 2005).

Morey, Peter and Amina Yaqin, *Framing Muslims: Stereotyping and Representation after 9/11* (Cambridge, MA: Harvard University Press, 2011).

National Police Chiefs' Council Freedom of Information Request Reference Number: 000026/16 (7 March 2016). Available at www.npcc.police.uk/Publication/NPCC%20FOI/CT/02616ChannelReferrals.pdf (accessed 19 June 2017).

National Union of Students (NUS), 'The NUS Black Students' Campaign, Federation of Student Islamic Students (FOSIS), the University and College Union (UCU) and Defend the Right to Protest (DtRtP)', *Students Not Suspects* (n.d.). Available at https://studentsnotsuspects.com/about-2/ (accessed 30 May 2017).

NUS Black Students, *Preventing PREVENT: A Student Handbook on Countering the PREVENT Agenda on Campus* (London: NUS, 2015). Available at www.nusconnect.org.uk/resources/preventing-prevent-handbook (accessed 3 June 2017).

O'Donnell, Aislinn, 'Securitisation, counterterrorism and the silencing of dissent: The educational implications of Prevent', *British Journal of Educational Studies* 64/1 (2016), pp. 53–76.

Open Society Justice Initiative, *Eroding Trust: The UK's PREVENT Counter-Extremism Strategy in Health and Education* (New York: Open Society Foundations, 2016).

Open University, 'Pupils left puzzled by the term "British values"', *Open University*, 14 September 2016. Available at https://www3.open.ac.uk/media/fullstory.aspx?id=30560 (accessed 18 June 2017).

Osborne, Samuel, 'Young British Muslims think Isis fighters returning from Syria should be reintegrated into society, research finds', *Independent*, 17 April 2017. Available at www.independent.co.uk/news/uk/young-british-muslims-uk-isis-fighters-syria-return-reintegrate-society-research-a7682836.html (accessed 19 June 2017).

Quinn, Ben, 'Nursery "raised fears of radicalisation over boy's cucumber drawing"', *Guardian*,11 March 2016. Available at www.theguardian.com/uk-news/2016/mar/11/nursery-radicalisation-fears-boys-cucumber-drawing-cooker-bomb (accessed 10 June 2017).

Qureshi, Asim, 'PREVENT: Creating "radicals" to strengthen anti-Muslim narratives', *Critical Studies on Terrorism* 8/1 (2015), pp. 181–91.

Ramesh, Randeep and Josh Halliday, 'Student accused of being a terrorist for reading book on terrorism', *Guardian*, 24 September 2015. Available at www.theguardian.com/education/2015/sep/24/student-accused-being-terrorist-reading-book-terrorism (accessed 15 June 2017).

Rogers, Amanda, 'The strategic success of ISIS propaganda (video lecture)', *The Postcolonialist*, 4 November 2014. Available at http://postcolonialist.com/arts/strategic-success-isis-propaganda-video-lecture/ (accessed 19 June 2017).

Saeed, Tania, *Islamophobia and Securitization: Religion, Ethnicity and the Female Voice* (Basingstoke: Palgrave Macmillan, 2016).

Saeed, Tania and David Johnson, 'Intelligence, global terrorism and higher education: Neutralising threats or alienating allies?', *British Journal of Educational Studies* 64/1 (2016), pp. 37–51.

Salih, Sara with Judith Butler, *The Judith Butler Reader* (Oxford and Malden, MA: Blackwell Publishing, 2004).

Spencer, Ian R.G., *British Immigration Policy since 1939: The Making of Multi-Racial Britain* (New York: Routledge, 1997).

Tyrer, David, 'Flooding the embankments: Race, bio-politics and sovereignty', in S. Sayyid and AbdoolKarim Vakil (eds), *Thinking through Islamophobia: Global Perspectives* (London: Hurst & Co., 2010), pp. 93–110.

Tyrer, David, 'Institutionalized Islamophobia in British universities', PhD thesis, University of Salford, Institute of Social Research, 2003.

United Kingdom Parliament, Counter-Extremism Strategy, Cm 9148 (2015).

United Kingdom Parliament, Counter-Terrorism and Security Act (2015).

Young Muslims in Germany and Their Use of New Media to Counter Islamophobia

Asmaa Soliman

Introduction

In the aftermath of the refugee crisis in Europe and the increase in ISIS attacks, questions about Muslims' place in Europe have become central again. Heated discussions about the compatibility of Muslim and European culture take place every day. In the context of increasing securitization and immigration controls, young Muslims form an important group contributing to debates on Muslim cultures. Second- and third-generation Muslims show stronger public engagement than their forebears. These young Muslims have created their own identities, often with the help of new media, and are challenging mainstream discourses. In this chapter I will draw on the Habermasian idea of a public sphere, along with Michael Warner's and Nancy Fraser's representation of alternative identities through the idea of counterpublics. Scholars have noted the utility of the internet as a platform that enhances counterpublics. I discuss this trend with the aid of two examples from Germany, namely Kübra Gümüşay's blog *Ein Fremdwörterbuch* ('A Dictionary of Foreign Words') and Nuri Senay's online video platform *muslime.tv*.[1] I will examine how their counterpublics offer a public anti-Islamophobic engagement and a representation of Muslim issues and identities from the perspective of young Muslims in Germany.

There are three main characteristics of counterpublics visible in the case studies offered here: that minorities feel excluded, restricted and misrepresented by mainstream representations; that individuals are reclaiming the ability to define themselves publicly in their own ways; and that these individuals shape and circulate counter-discourses that are critical of the mainstream public and its views. The two examples are part of my broader research project, in which

I qualitatively examined several case studies of second-generation Muslims in Germany and their different modes of public engagement. The material results from two years of ethnographic research and in-depth interviews that took place between 2012 and 2014 across various cities in Germany. My research participants identify as German Muslims and are actively involved in various spaces of the public sphere including media, the arts and civic society.

Theoretically, there are two concepts that are relevant to this topic: the concept of the public sphere and the notion of counterpublics. The term 'public sphere' was originally introduced by Jürgen Habermas. He used it primarily to describe an emerging space of political discussion within eighteenth-century European bourgeois society from which he developed a more general theory.[2] Habermas argues that in liberal democratic societies the public sphere is characterized by discursive equality and inclusion of all citizens. He stresses that consensus should be arrived at freely under fair conditions and that it should not be pre-structured. According to him, all human expressions raise validity claims whose normative accuracy and veracity need to be examined. Habermas favours the view that argumentation and communicative rationality should be used to redeem problematic validity claims.[3] Reason is seen as the guiding light that will lead to the legitimization of public opinion. Although Habermas argues that religion is relevant and should have a place in the public sphere, he maintains that religious language has to be neutrally translated into secular language, without interfering in or challenging it.[4] In arguing that religion must adapt itself to the authority of those sciences that claim a monopoly on world knowledge and that religious citizens have to respect the precedence of secular reasoning, Habermas's secular bias comes to the fore.[5]

In reaction to the Habermasian public sphere and the silencing of disadvantaged minorities, scholars such as Fraser and Warner have introduced the concept of counterpublics, particularly in relation to minority groups such as women and queer culture.[6] They criticize the Habermasian public sphere for promulgating informal mechanisms of exclusion and ignoring power relations between the dominant culture and subordinated groups. According to them, the mainstream public has an ideological bias that prefers some expressions over others. They accuse it of being predefined and of ignoring the plurality of actual citizens. Despite Habermas's rhetoric of an accessible, inclusive and liberal public sphere, Fraser and Warner accuse his work of subjecting minorities to assimilative pressures. This prompts them to develop their own counterpublics, which offer minorities a space to define themselves and circulate discourses that are ignored by the mainstream public. Counterpublics use these spaces to expand their life-world and self-image, thereby overcoming the denial of their public existence, circulating alternative discourses, formulating oppositional interpretations of their identities and contesting specific assumptions that were previously exempt from criticism. Fraser stresses that through counterpublics minorities are able to speak with their own voice and construct their own cultural identity, offering alternatives to ascribed identities. As Warner puts it, minorities involved in counterpublics demand majority culture to recognize their identities as normal. He describes a counterpublic's relation to the dominant public as follows:

> A counterpublic enables a horizon of opinion and exchange; its exchange remains distinct from authority and can have a critical relation to power ... counterpublics are, by definition, formed by their conflict with the norms and contexts of their cultural environment.[7]

While Fraser and Warner have looked at different ethnic minority groups, the concept of 'counterpublics' has also been used of religious minorities. Scholars like Nilüfer Göle, Stine Eckert and Kalyani Chadha have looked at different examples of European Muslim counterpublics.[8] In my case studies below I bring together these methodological approaches to reflect on critical interventions made by young Muslim counterpublics in the German media sphere.

The German public sphere

The mainstream public sphere includes discourses, political debates, public opinion and media that deal with Muslims in Germany. It is not an exaggeration to say that the mainstream public sphere is often negative and Islamophobic. Islam is usually associated with danger, violence and Otherness, and since 9/11 Muslims in Germany have frequently been associated with terrorism.[9] Discourses and political debates are thus often critical of Islam; the idea that Muslims are an integral part of the wider society is still often questioned.[10] Public rhetoric reflects a polarized relationship between Islam and Germany, seen in the regular appearance of headlines such as 'Fear of Islam', 'The headscarf and Quran: Has Germany capitulated?' or 'How much Islam can the state bear?'[11] Suspicious attitudes towards Muslims are not only limited to Islamist extremist groups but also affect the wider Muslim community. Werner Schiffauer argues that there is a 'moral panic' underlying discourses and representations of Muslims, characterized by exaggerated claims about threats and an atmosphere of suspicion.[12]

This 'moral panic' can be exemplified by the recent German public reaction to the refugee crisis following the breakdown of order in Iraq, Syria and Libya and the rise of so-called Islamic State or ISIS. Although the country's response to the refugee crisis was the most welcoming in Europe, the substantial intake of refugees was heavily contested. It was criticized not only by right-wing parties like the Alternative für Deutschland but also by politicians from the chancellor Angela Merkel's own circle. An example is the politician and former interior minister Hans-Peter Friedrich from the Christian Social Union (CSU), the sister party to Merkel's Christian Democratic Union of Germany (CDU), who denounced Merkel's refugee policy as a mistake.[13] Politicians have associated Syrian refugees' presence with the fear of ISIS fighters entering the country, and it has been seen as a danger to Germany's culture. The CSU politician Markus Söder, for example, warns that 'if more people migrate to Germany this year than are born here, that will affect the cultural statistics of a society'.[14] This concern has been repeatedly raised by various politicians, most notably in the context of the *Leitkultur* ('leading culture') debate, institutionalized when the interior minister Thomas de Maizière presented his plan on a German *Leitkultur* in April 2017.[15] The term has been highly contested since its first political use in 2000 by politician Friedrich Merz, who acted as chair of the CDU/CSU coalition and who demanded that immigrants adapt to a German leading culture. Critics argue that the term implies the superiority of one (majority) culture over others.[16]

A 2015 study by the John Stuart Mill Institut für Freiheitsforschung in Heidelberg found that the majority of Germans are of the opinion that Islam does not belong in Germany.[17] Another study published in 2015 by Bertelsmann Stiftung shows similar results.[18] It notes the spread of Islamophobia, arguing that it has become more common. The research illustrates German society's attitude towards Muslims in the second decade of the twenty-first century. The study's first leading statement 'Islam is threatening' was embraced by 57 per cent in 2014. The second statement 'Islam does not fit into the Western world' was supported by 61 per cent. The third statement reads as follows: 'Muslims make me feel like a foreigner in my own country.' It was embraced by 40 per cent. The last statement, which was supported by 24 per cent of German society, says 'Muslim immigration should be prohibited'.

It is worth mentioning here that there has been a critique of the term 'Islamophobia', put forward by several scholars in Germany. Iman Attia, for example, argues that it is not necessarily only about fear of Islam as a religion, but rather about anti-Muslim racism.[19] This is important, as it turns our attention to the element of racialization that is integral to Islamophobia. Furthermore, by explaining that the process of racialization involves the singling out of those who are visibly Muslim, it becomes clear that Islamophobia is not solely about fearing Islam as a faith system, but about prejudice against individuals in a religious group who are perceived to be homogenous.

The two case studies examined here are Nuri Senay's online video platform *muslime.tv*[20] and Kübra Gümüşay's blog *Ein Fremdwörterbuch*.[21] Senay was born in Bremerhaven in Germany, of Turkish ethnic origin. He lives in Cologne where he teaches English and Turkish. Senay is the founder of *muslime.tv*, an online video platform that presents stories about Muslims from Germany in a documentary style, which he started in June 2010. Gümüşay is also of Turkish origin but was born and raised in Hamburg. She studied political science and works in the media sector. In 2008 she founded her blog *Ein Fremdwörterbuch*. The themes of Islam and Muslims in Germany play an essential role in her blog, which was nominated for the Grimme Online Award in 2011 and has up to 13,000 visitors per month.[22] A closer look at both online platforms reveals typical features of counterpublics, such as the perception of an exclusive mainstream public, the circulation of alternative self-definitions and counter-discourses, as well as criticism of mainstream representations.

Frustration with the mainstream public

Both Senay and Gümüşay express feelings of frustration towards Germany's mainstream public and its representation of Muslims. They criticize it for associating Muslims with negative characteristics, such as violence, oppression and backwardness. According to them, the mainstream public is exclusionary and restrictive. It does not offer free spaces of expression for Muslims. This is true not only at the political level but also in public discourses and mainstream media where Muslims are often being talked about, rather than being given a voice to talk themselves. As for the few instances when Muslims are invited to participate in mainstream discourses, these are perceived as one-sided and biased against them. Senay expresses his frustration with the mainstream media's depiction of Muslims:

> My wife and I were sitting in front of the TV watching a programme titled 'Veil and Sharia – Does Islam fit in Germany?' We see that the topic is already defined and that it goes in a particular direction, that the guests are selected, that a Muslim woman in a hijab is sitting there on her own. We see that she is verbally torn to pieces. And this is broadcast on ZDF at a time where everyone

is watching TV. Then, of course, I get disappointed and change the channel. I tell my wife it is always the same, one gets sick of it. But then I realise that even if I change the channel millions of other people watch this programme and are shaped by contents like this.[23]

This passage brings to the fore Senay's disappointment and frustration with the way in which mainstream discourses about Muslims are framed on television and with the real-world pressure that Muslims are thereby subjected to. It should be mentioned that ZDF, which stands for Zweites Deutsches Fernsehen ('Second German Television'), is one of the biggest public service broadcasters in Europe and is the most watched television station in Germany.[24] Senay's insistence that mainstream television programmes about Muslims like those aired by ZDF are 'already defined' and 'go in a particular direction' reflects the perception of a pre-structured and biased mainstream public sphere. The description that Senay gives of how the woman is 'torn to pieces' conveys that sense of hostility she faces as the object of discourse on the show, rather than a speaking subject able to articulate her own perspective. Senay argues that since 9/11 the media has become more hostile to Muslims and that Islamophobic statements have become more common and, thereby, legitimized. According to him, German mainstream media is both inaccurate and destructive in its coverage of Muslims. He accuses it of showing only negative opinions, images and reports about Muslims and of playing on people's fears. Again and again extremist Muslims are portrayed in the media, although they constitute a very small minority of all Muslims in Germany.

In a similar manner, Gümüşay reports her personal experience of participating in mainstream talk shows. She feels that there is a clear attempt to create an image of an enemy and to stir up fear of Muslims. She has repeatedly had to confront Islamophobic statements and attitudes during these television appearances. She argues that Muslims often feel forced into an imposed negative narrative, which they then have to fight against:

I don't think I follow the script in those talk shows. I was always trying to avoid it. When they ask those questions I know what they meant but I wanted to give my opinion. I tried to look at it as a game. They wanted to make me look a certain way and I didn't want to look that way. ... In these TV shows it was never for me about religion. They didn't want to have a theological debate. It's more about racism. It's about fear, creating the enemy, the image of the enemy. And I saw my task being to understand the game and destroy it. Basically, that was my whole strategy... not giving those answers, not falling into those traps. When there are questions they give you a frame. So, every time they asked a question I always thought, okay, how is this question limiting my answer, and tried to look for ways to escape this frame they were giving me. So, I have to avoid the script they have written.[25]

Gümüşay's statements convey how challenging the media frame is. The way in which she describes her experiences indicates a very strained arena where one has to develop strategies to cope with the different forces at play. Using terms like 'game' and 'trap' to describe how television shows work and arguing that they want to make her 'look in a certain way' expose how television structures work to target Muslims in specific ways and through specific agendas. Moreover, emphasizing the need to 'destroy the game' and not to fall into 'traps' illustrates the particular burdens that she faces as a Muslim.

In one of her blog posts, titled 'When the cameras are switched off', Gümüşay offers a detailed account of the blogger's personal experience of appearing on a talk show and meeting guests who speak differently about Muslims in front of the camera than they do behind the camera. The show was titled 'Headscarf and curry sausage', which, according to Gümüşay, is a typical title used for Islam-related topics. It contrasts the stereotypical Islamic headscarf with a typical German food: 'A pinch of Islam here, a pinch of something typically German there.'[26] Looking at the list of guests Gümüşay realized that there was one guest who was an experienced talk-show guest given to stirring up controversy. Knowing that he could cause trouble, Gümüşay decided to meet him prior to the show, hoping that this would contribute towards a more constructive on-air discussion. She describes a cordial meeting during which they discussed issues in the Muslim community and problem-solving approaches. They also talked about the problem of Islamophobia, and Gümüşay was reassured by her impression that the man was a pleasant interlocutor. However, once they were sitting in the studio in front of a rolling camera, Gümüşay remarks that his words completely changed. Suddenly, he was ridiculing and dismissing the issue of Islamophobia. He argued that the word sounded like an illness and asked Gümüşay, in an attempt at provocation, whether she was insinuating that all Germans were ill. Gümüşay recalls how she was left completely speechless by his statements and asks, 'How is one to respond?' The moderator did not intervene when she was attacked by other guests or heckled by the audience. After the show she asked the guest why he compared Islamophobia to an illness. Admitting that the comparison was merely polemical and destructive, he responded that 'yes, maybe it was a mistake'. She stresses the irresponsibility of such behaviour, wondering how people can 'be consciously provocative and say something deliberately wrong when it comes to sensitive topics?'[27]

The blog entry 'When the cameras are switched off' offers a stringent criticism of the German mainstream media's way of talking about Muslims. It is also sceptical of the way in which Muslims themselves are co-opted into the media sphere. Gümüşay suggests this is part of a much broader and more pervasive condemnation of, and attack on, Muslims in public. It reflects an obvious bias in the media, providing one of the main vehicles by which Muslims may be targeted. This example does not only show how words are changed on air, it also illustrates the way in which Muslims are 'framed' before they even enter that arena.[28] By asking Gümüşay whether she is implying that all Germans are ill, the guest turns the tables and Gümüşay's attitude to Germany and Germans is suddenly questioned. Indeed, her own German identity is likewise brought into doubt.

Examples such as those of Senay and Gümüşay reveal the media – one of the most important sites of the public sphere – to be strongly biased in both attitudes and structures, perennially placing Muslims at a disadvantage and portraying them in a negative light. The Habermasian idea of a neutral and unprestructured liberal democratic public clearly does not find resonance here. Instead we see majority culture silencing or restricting minority expression. As Iris Young stresses, participatory norms of dominant publics are 'powerful silencers or evaluators of speech in many actual speaking situations where culturally differentiated and socially unequal groups live together'.[29] The research participants' statements accentuate feelings of being pushed into using a specific language that expects only particular responses to guiding questions, constructing the discourse in a particular way. Their experience illustrates how the mainstream public exerts assimilative pressures on minority cultures, allowing for only one narrative to be articulated. This inequitable phenomenon has also been noted by other critics of the Habermasian public sphere, such as Judith Butler.[30]

In contrast to the dominant mainstream public, young Muslims perceive the counterpublics they create as free spaces where they can express themselves as they like. Gümüşay, for example, says that she appreciates her blog's freedom of expression:

> Obviously, you are your own editor-in-chief when you have your own blog. No one censors you except for yourself. No one edits you except for yourself. So you are basically your own boss. You decide what you want to do, you decide the context you are in. So, it is basically all in your hands. ... There is more in your control than in a TV show where the script is already written.[31]

The ability to speak in one's own voice, as Fraser puts it, plays a major role for Gümüşay.[32] The relevance of free spaces that offer individuals the possibility to be their own authors, to choose their own ways in which themes are addressed and to represent themselves as they wish is crucial in the appeal of counterpublics. Overall, one can say that the perception of a restrictive and Islamophobic mainstream public has played an important role in the formation of Senay's and Gümüşay's counterpublics. Indeed, personal Islamophobic experiences have also influenced their decisions to found their online platforms.

Self-definitions and alternative identity representations

The second main feature of counterpublics, the circulation of self-defined, alternative identity representations, can be found in both online platforms. Senay emphasizes that *muslime.tv* aims to deliver a factual, informative picture of Muslims in Germany. Gümüşay expresses a similar intention. When asked why she founded her blog, she says she wanted to 'create a space of encounters for people who have never met a Muslim woman before and to give an insight into a Muslim woman's life in Germany'.[33] By offering a first-person insight into Muslim life and stripping away the negative connotations, their counterpublics challenge Islamophobia. Both argue that their online platforms are meant to break down prejudices and to improve relations between Muslims and wider German society. A main motivation is to show Muslim life from an insider perspective, countering the mainstream image of Muslims in a manner that recalls Fraser's idea of a counterpublic that enables minorities to circulate their self-image.[34]

Diverse topics are featured in *muslime.tv* and *Ein Fremdwörterbuch*. There are two notable themes in relation to identity. The first deals specifically with Muslim identity and the relevance of Islam in the lives of Gümüşay and the Muslims presented on *muslime.tv*. Matters that concern practising Muslims, like Islamic prayer, spirituality, charity, Islamic marriage, pilgrimage and fasting, come to the fore. The second aspect is the relationship of Muslim identity to Germany. German Muslim lifestyles are conveyed and the perception that Muslims do not belong to Germany is challenged. Several videos on *muslime.tv* express the compatibility of Islamic values and German culture. An example is a video showing an interview with Melih Kesmen, the founder of Styleislam, an online shop selling modern Islamic clothes and other products. Kesmen elaborates on the philosophy of Styleislam, saying that it represents a mixture of Eastern and Western fashion. It is meant to cater for the wishes of practising German Muslims who are looking for Western fashions that take into account Islamic dress codes. Furthermore, German Muslim identity is associated with positive features. Muslim women's involvement in voluntary work, as well as their support for education, reveals a picture of participative, active and educated German Muslim women. Ali Özgür Özdil, a German Muslim scholar who comes from an academic background, and Muslim students who offer counselling also contribute to the idea that Muslims greatly value education.

There is an implicit call for the normalization of German Muslim identity embedded in the project. Senay's interview with Kesmen, in which the stylist holds forth about broader issues, such as his favourite musician or his latest holiday trip, offers an instance of *muslime.tv*'s attempt to move beyond the usual 'Muslim issues'. It projects a lifestyle that is not dissimilar to that considered mainstream. In a similar vein, Gümüşay addresses a broad array of issues in her blog, such as travel, arts, music, movies and recipes. She emphasizes that her primary goal is to show the routine of a Muslim woman's life as distinct from the prevalent negative, Islamophobic image. The blogger stresses that, by showing this multifaceted identity, her aim is to educate German society so that it recognizes the normality of German Muslim identity. She reflects that 'I didn't want to talk necessarily about Islam and Muslims. It was important for me to say I am a Muslim and it plays a huge role in my life because it does play a huge role in my life, but you know there are so many other things that also play a role in my life and you know I am normal.'[35] Her statement illustrates Warner's argument that minorities engaged in counterpublics demand the recognition of their identity's normality.[36]

The variety of depictions of Muslims on both platforms offers an alternative, multifaceted picture that differs from the one portrayed in the mainstream public. The involvement of Muslims in fields such as music, sports, arts, charity work, education and fashion counters Islamophobic representations that associate them solely with violence, oppression and terrorism. This communicates not only the compatibility of Islam and Germany and the normality of German Muslim identity but also the idea that Muslims participate fully in German society.

Circulation of counter-discourses and criticism of the mainstream public

Senay's and Gümüşay's counterpublics not only offer them a space to challenge Islamophobia but also allow them to criticize the lack of serious attention to anti-Muslim prejudice in the mainstream. Their platforms serve as alternative media reporting on Islamophobic incidents that are largely ignored elsewhere.

Muslims have repeatedly complained about the mainstream public's failure to talk about Islamophobic attacks, arguing that there is a lack of awareness about the presence of this form of prejudice in Germany.[37] This shortcoming is also reflected in Germany's judiciary. In contrast to several other European countries, German police and public prosecutors do not register instances of racism as they are not incorporated in the German Criminal Code.[38] They record cases of hate speech and hate crime that are politically motivated, which can sometimes overlap with the phenomenon of racism, depending on the definition that is used. However, Islamophobic incidents are not captured separately in Germany, either within police criminality statistics or within reports about Politically Motivated Criminality (PMC).[39] Racist attacks come under the general category of hate crime and are defined as 'PMC', although homophobia and anti-Semitism, for example, are separate categories within PMC.[40] This makes it very difficult to find any solid statistics about Islamophobic attacks.

An example of how counterpublics function as alternative media can be seen in the reporting of the Islamophobic murder of Marwa El-Sherbini, which has repeatedly been addressed in Gümüşay's blog. Marwa El-Sherbini was a young Muslim woman who was murdered on 1 July 2009 during an appeal hearing at a law court in Dresden.[41] She was ironically stabbed to death in the courtroom at the very moment when she was charging her murderer with Islamophobic abuse. The murderer plunged a knife into her eighteen times, while the victim was in the dock telling the judge about his previous racist attack. Security personnel and policemen arrived too late, allowing the killing to happen. Gümüşay criticizes the mainstream media's silence about this tragic incident, arguing that it was not publicly recognized as an Islamophobic attack. She stresses that the Muslim blogosphere played a crucial role in raising awareness about El-Sherbini's murder:

> There were a few incidents where we [Muslim bloggers] sort of felt that we have power ... and there was one incident when Marwa El-Sherbini was murdered in Dresden because we all knew about it and were blogging about [it] but no national newspaper was writing about this topic. ... There were newspapers writing about it saying there was a woman murdered in a court room but nobody actually said this was the first Islamophobic murder we had in Germany. It is a historical tragedy and it should be put in that context and not just say, 'it's about security problems we had in Dresden'. No it's a societal problem, it lies much deeper than just security issues with court rooms. ... There were many bloggers blogging about it at that time and from my memory it was the first time that respected journalists from German newspapers would approach us as bloggers and ask about our opinion, and it was the first time that the Muslim blogosphere became more public and interacted with traditional media.[42]

As critics of the Habermasian public sphere argue, counterpublics can provide crucial complementary spaces, allowing subordinated groups to engage in communicative processes that are not under the majority culture's supervision.[43] Rather than conceiving her blog as a weak counterpublic that does not reach out to the wider German society, Gümüşay thus aims to engage with the dominant public on important issues. It becomes clear that minorities involved in counterpublics interact with the mainstream public in order to make their 'private' matters public. As Fraser and Warner argue, rules about what counts as a public matter and what should be kept in the private realm are inevitably constructed by the mainstream public's majority culture.[44] Therefore, opportunities for minorities to put their concerns on the agenda are limited. By creating counterpublics, minorities have the opportunity to talk about their concerns, challenging the dominant public's line between public and private matters.

Conclusion

To conclude, it can be said that new media offer Muslims an important platform to develop counterpublics and to challenge Islamophobia in different ways. As has become clear, the mainstream public's discourse about Muslims is often negative and saturated with Islamophobic statements. This is true not only of political discourses but also of media representations and debates. Three main features of counterpublics can be found in both platforms. Firstly, the exclusion and pressure that Muslims are subjected to by the mainstream public, as well as negative representations of Muslims, have prompted both the online activists discussed here to create their own public. An obvious frustration with the mainstream public comes to the fore. Habermas's rhetoric of an accessible, inclusive public that is not pre-structured is not borne out by the evidence here. Secondly, the circulation of Muslim self-representation and of alternative identities challenging mainstream representations plays a crucial role. Thirdly, both platforms offer counter-discourses that criticize the mainstream public. Islamophobic discourses come in for strong criticism, while the absence of public awareness of anti-Muslim hate crimes – coupled with a lack of redress within the German legal system – receives an airing. It is important to bear in mind that the two examples cited in this chapter are by no means exceptional. There are many cases of young Muslims across Europe who develop their own publics, often using the resources afforded by new and social media forms. In the light of increasing Islamophobia, which has become more visible since the refugee crisis in Europe, these counterpublics gain even more relevance. Although their accessibility and influence is much less than that of the mainstream public, their role should not be underestimated in understanding the complexity and diversity of Muslim youth cultures in Germany.

Notes

1 Jeffrey Wimmer, 'Gegenöffentlichkeit 2.00: Formen, Nutzung und Wirkung kritischer Öffentlichkeiten im Social Web', in Ansgar Zerfaß, Martin Welker and Jan Schmidt (eds), *Kommunikation, Partizipation und Wirkungen im Social Web: Strategien und Anwendungen: Perspektiven für Wirtschaft, Politik, Publizistik* (Köln: Herbert von Halem, 2008), pp. 210–30; Dimitra Milioni, 'Probing the online counter public sphere: The case of Indymedia Athens', *Media, Culture & Society* 31/3 (2009), pp. 409–31.
2 Jürgen Habermas, *The Structural Transformation of the Public Sphere: An Inquiry into a Category of Bourgeois Society* (Cambridge, MA: MIT Press, 1989).
3 Lincoln Dahlberg, 'The Habermasian public sphere: A specification of the idealized conditions of democratic communication', *Studies in Social and Political Thought* 10 (2004), pp. 2–18.
4 Jürgen Habermas, 'What is meant by a "post-secular society"? A discussion on Islam in Europe', in *Europe: The Faltering Project* (Malden, MA: Polity Press, 2009), pp. 59–77.
5 Jürgen Habermas, '*Faith and Knowledge*: Peace Prize of the German Book Trade 2001, Acceptance Speech' (2001). Available at https://www.friedenspreis-des-deutschen-buchhandels.de/sixcms/media.php/1290/2001%20Acceptance%20 Speech%20Juergen%20Habermas.pdf (accessed 6 July 2018). Jürgen Habermas, *Zwischen Naturalismus und Religion: Philosophische Aufsätze* (Frankfurt am Main: Suhrkamp, 2009), p. 145.
6 Nancy Fraser, 'Rethinking the public sphere: A contribution to the critique of actually existing democracy', *Social Text* 25/26 (1990), pp. 56–80; Michael Warner, *Publics and Counterpublics* (Cambridge: Zone Books, 2002).
7 Warner, *Publics and Counterpublics*, pp. 56, 63.
8 Nilüfer Göle, 'Die Sichtbare Präsenz des Islam und die Grenzen der Öffentlichkeit', in Nilüfer Göle and Ludwig Ammann (eds), *Islam in Sicht: Der Auftritt von Muslimen im Öffentlichen Raum* (Bielefeld: Transcript Verlag, 2004), pp. 11–44; Stine Eckert and Kalyani Chadha, 'Muslim bloggers in Germany: An emerging counterpublic', *Media, Culture & Society* 35/8 (2013), pp. 926–42.
9 Daniel Bosse and Eduardo Vior, *Politische Partizipation von Migranten mit muslimischem Hintergrund in Deutschland: Entwicklung und Probleme* (Magdeburg: Institut für Politikwissenschaften, 2005).

10 Almut S. Bruckstein Çoruh, 'Wo Muslime fremd sind, sind wir es auch: Plädoyer für ein Atelier der kosmopolitischen Wissenschaftler und Künste in Berlin', *Islam.Kultur.Politik: Dossier zur Politik und Kultur* 1 (2011), pp. 274–8; Nina Mühe, *Muslims in the EU: Cities Report. Germany* (n.p.: Open Society Institute, EU Monitoring and Advocacy Program, 2007). Available at www.opensocietyfoundations.org/sites/default/files/museucitiesger_20080101_0.pdf (accessed 28 June 2016).
11 Çoruh, 'Wo Muslime fremd sind', p. 274.
12 Werner Schiffauer, 'Enemies within the gates', in Tariq Modood, Anna Triandafyllidou and Ricard Zapata-Barrero (eds), *Multiculturalism, Muslims and Citizenship: A European Approach* (London: Routledge, 2006), pp. 74–116.
13 'CSU denounces Merkel's refugee policy as a "mistake"', *Deutsche Welle*, 11 September 2015. Available at www.dw.com/en/csu-denounces-merkels-refugee-policy-as-a-mistake/a-18708181 (accessed 23 April 2017).
14 Söder cited in *Deutsche Welle*, 'CSU denounces Merkel's refugee policy as a "mistake"'.
15 Lukas Wallraff, 'Die Wiederkehr der Leitkultur-Debatte: Ein Kampfbegriff', *Deutschlandfunk* (2017). Available at www.deutschlandfunk.de/die-wiederkehr-der-leitkultur-debatte-ein-kampfbegriff.720.de.html?dram:article_id=385548 (accessed 2 May 2017) [link no longer working].
16 Pascal Beucker, 'Die Konjunktur der Leitkultur', *Goethe Institut*, March 2017. Available at www.goethe.de/de/kul/ges/20721837.html (accessed 1 May 2017).
17 Stefan von Borstel, 'Für die meisten gehört der Islam nicht zu Deutschland', *Die Welt*, 6 October 2015. Available at www.welt.de/politik/deutschland/article147280667/Fuer-die-meisten-gehoert-der-Islam-nicht-zu-Deutschland.html (accessed 26 April 2016).
18 'Religionsmonitor verstehen was verbindet: Sonderauswertung Islam 2015-Die wichtigsten Ergebnisse im Überblick', *Bertelsmann Stiftung* (2015). Available at https://www.bertelsmann-stiftung.de/fileadmin/files/Projekte/51_Religionsmonitor/Zusammenfassung_der_Sonderauswertung.pdf (accessed 6 July 2018).
19 Iman Attia, personal communication with the author, 2015.
20 http://muslime.tv.
21 http://ein-fremdwoerterbuch.com.
22 Jan Kuhlmann, 'Die muslimische Bloggerin Kübra Gümüsay', *Deutschlandfunk*, 16 August 2012. Available at www.deutschlandfunk.de/die-muslimische-bloggerin-Guemuesay-guemuesay.886.de.html?dram:article_id=219178 (accessed 1 December 2015).
23 Nuri Senay, personal communication with the author, 2012.
24 'Die Marktanteilsbilanz 2013', *ZDF*, 19 March 2014. Available at www.zdf.de/zdfunternehmen/zdf-erneut-marktfuehrer-die-marktanteilsbilanz-2013-100.html (accessed 1 May 2017).

25 Kübra Gümüşay, personal communication with the author, 2013.
26 *Ein Fremdwörterbuch.* Available at http://ein-fremdwoerterbuch.com/ (accessed 1 December 2015).
27 Ibid.
28 On media framing of Muslims, see Peter Morey and Amina Yaqin, *Framing Muslims: Stereotyping and Representation after 9/11* (Cambridge, MA: Harvard University Press, 2011).
29 Iris Marion Young, 'Communication and the other: Beyond deliberative democracy', in Seyla Benhabib (ed.), *Democracy and Difference: Contesting the Boundaries of the Political* (Princeton, NJ: Princeton University Press, 1996), pp. 120–35; p. 124.
30 Judith Butler, 'Merely cultural', *Social Text* 15/3–4 (1997), pp. 265–77.
31 Kübra Gümüşay, personal communication with the author, 2015.
32 Fraser, 'Rethinking the public sphere'.
33 Kübra Gümüşay, personal communication with the author, 2015.
34 Fraser, 'Rethinking the public sphere'.
35 Kübra Gümüşay, personal communication with the author, 2015.
36 Warner, *Publics and Counterpublics*.
37 'RAMSA Präsidentin Durmaz: Wir brauchen funktionierende Strukturen gegen antimuslimischen Rassismus', *Migazin*, 1 July 2015. Available at www.migazin.de/2015/07/01/ramsa-praesidentin-hatice-durmaz-wir/ (accessed 1 May 2017).
38 Saskia van Bon, Wies Dinsbach, Claudia Lechner and Mario Peucker, *Registration of Complaints about Discrimination in the Netherlands and in Germany* (Rotterdam and Bamberg: European Union Programme for Employment and Social Solidarity, 2011).
39 Lydia Nofal, 'Islamfeindlichkeit als wachsendes gesellschaftliches Phänomen', *Berliner Zustände 2012: Ein Schattenbericht über Rechtsextreminsus, Rassismus und Antisemitismus* (Berlin: Apabiz & MBR, 2013).
40 Andrea Dernbach, 'Gewalttaten gegen Muslime sollen gesondert erfasst werden', *Der Tagesspiegel*, 9 July 2014. Available at www.tagesspiegel.de/politik/islamhass-gewalttaten-gegen-muslime-sollen-gesondert-erfasst-werden/10171102.html (accessed 20 December 2014). 'Zahl der Angriffe auf Moscheen steigt deutlich', 29 July 2014. Available at www.welt.de/politik/deutschland/article130660759/Zahl-der-Angriffe-auf-Moscheen-steigt-deutlich.html (accessed 6 December 2014).
41 Kate Connolly and Jack Shenker, 'The headscarf martyr: Murder in German court sparks Egyptian fury', *Guardian*, 7 July 2009. Available at www.theguardian.com/world/2009/jul/07/german-trial-hijab-murder-egypt (accessed 9 December 2015).
42 Kübra Gümüşay, personal communication with the author, 2015.
43 Andrea T. Baumeister, 'Habermas: Discourse and cultural diversity', *Political Studies* 51 (2003), pp. 740–58.
44 Fraser, 'Rethinking the public sphere'; Warner, *Publics and Counterpublics*.

Works cited

Baumeister, Andrea T., 'Habermas: Discourse and cultural diversity', *Political Studies* 51 (2003), pp. 740–58.

Bertelsmann Stiftung, 'Religionsmonitor verstehen was verbindet: Sonderauswertung Islam 2015-Die wichtigsten Ergebnisse im Überblick', *Bertelsmann Stiftung*, 2015. Available at https://www.bertelsmann-stiftung.de/fileadmin/files/Projekte/51_Religionsmonitor/Zusammenfassung_der_Sonderauswertung.pdf (accessed 6 July 2018).

Beucker, Pascal, 'Die Konjunktur der Leitkultur', *Goethe Institut*, March 2017. Available at www.goethe.de/de/kul/ges/20721837.html (accessed 1 May 2017).

Bon, Saskia van, Wies Dinsbach, Claudia Lechner and Mario Peucker, *Registration of Complaints about Discrimination in the Netherlands and in Germany* (Rotterdam and Bamberg: European Union Programme for Employment and Social Solidarity, 2011).

Borstel, Stefan von, 'Für die meisten gehört der Islam nicht zu Deutschland', *Die Welt*, 6 October 2015. Available at www.welt.de/politik/deutschland/article147280667/Fuer-die-meisten-gehoert-der-Islam-nicht-zu-Deutschland.html (accessed 26 April 2016).

Bosse, Daniel and Eduardo Vior, *Politische Partizipation von Migranten mit muslimischem Hintergrund in Deutschland: Entwicklung und Probleme* (Magdeburg: Institut für Politikwissenschaften, 2005).

Butler, Judith, 'Merely Cultural', *Social Text* 15/3–4 (1997), pp. 265–77.

Connolly, Kate and Jack Shenker, 'The headscarf martyr: Murder in German court sparks Egyptian fury', *Guardian*, 7 July 2009. Available at www.theguardian.com/world/2009/jul/07/german-trial-hijab-murder-egypt (accessed 9 December 2015).

Çoruh, Almut S. Bruckstein, 'Wo Muslime fremd sind, sind wir es auch: Plädoyer für ein Atelier der kosmopolitischen Wissenschaftler und Künste in Berlin', *Islam.Kultur.Politik: Dossier zur Politik und Kultur* 1 (2011), pp. 21–2.

Dahlberg, Lincoln, 'The Habermasian public sphere: A specification of the idealized conditions of democratic communication', *Studies in Social and Political Thought* 10 (2004), pp. 2–18.

Dernbach, Andrea, 'Gewalttaten gegen Muslime sollen gesondert erfasst werden', *Der Tagesspiegel*, 9 July 2014. Available at www.tagesspiegel.de/politik/islamhass-gewalttaten-gegen-muslime-sollen-gesondert-erfasst-werden/10171102.html (accessed 20 December 2014).

Deutsche Welle, 'CSU denounces Merkel's refugee policy as a "mistake"', *Deutsche Welle*, 11 September 2015. Available at www.dw.com/en/csu-denounces-merkels-refugee-policy-as-a-mistake/a-18708181 (accessed 23 April 2017).

Die Welt, 'Zahl der Angriffe auf Moscheen steigt deutlich', *Die Welt*, 29 July 2014. Available at www.welt.de/politik/deutschland/article130660759/Zahl-der-Angriffe-auf-Moscheen-steigt-deutlich.html (accessed 6 December 2014).

Eckert, Stine and Kalyani Chadha, 'Muslim bloggers in Germany: An emerging counterpublic', *Media, Culture and Society* 35/8 (2013), pp. 926–42.

Fraser, Nancy, 'Rethinking the public sphere: A contribution to the critique of actually existing democracy', *Social Text* 25/26 (1990), pp. 56–80.

Göle, Nilüfer, 'Die Sichtbare Präsenz des Islam und die Grenzen der Öffentlichkeit', in Nilüfer Göle and Ludwig Ammann (eds), *Islam in Sicht: Der Auftritt von Muslimen im Öffentlichen Raum* (Bielefeld: Transcript Verlag, 2004), pp. 11–44.

Habermas, Jürgen, '*Faith and Knowledge*: Peace Prize of the German Book Trade 2001, Acceptance Speech' (2001). Available at https://www.friedenspreis-des-deutschen-buchhandels.de/sixcms/media.php/1290/2001%20Acceptance%20Speech%20 Juergen%20Habermas.pdf (accessed 6 July 2018).

Habermas, Jürgen, *The Structural Transformation of the Public Sphere: An Inquiry into a Category of Bourgeois Society* (Cambridge, MA: MIT Press, 1989).

Habermas, Jürgen, 'What is meant by a "post-secular society"? A discussion on Islam in Europe', in *Europe: The Faltering Project* (Malden, MA: Polity Press, 2009), pp. 59–77.

Habermas, Jürgen, *Zwischen Naturalismus und Religion: Philosophische Aufsätze* (Frankfurt am Main: Suhrkamp, 2009).

Kuhlmann, Jan, 'Die muslimische Bloggerin Kübra Gümüsay', *Deutschlandfunk*, 16 August 2012. Available at www.deutschlandfunk.de/die-muslimische-bloggerin-Guemuesay-guemuesay.886.de.html?dram:article_id=219178 (accessed 1 December 2015).

Migazin, 'RAMSA Präsidentin Durmaz: Wir brauchen funktionierende Strukturen gegen antimuslimischen Rassismus', *Migazin*, 1 July 2015. Available at www.migazin.de/2015/07/01/ramsa-praesidentin-hatice-durmaz-wir/ (accessed 1 May 2017).

Milioni, Dimitra, 'Probing the online counter public sphere: The case of Indymedia Athens', *Media, Culture & Society* 31/3 (2009), pp. 409–31.

Morey, Peter and Amina Yaqin, *Framing Muslims: Stereotyping and Representation after 9/11* (Cambridge, MA: Harvard University Press, 2011).

Mühe, Nina, *Muslims in the EU: Cities Report. Germany* ([n.p.]: Open Society Institute, EU Monitoring and Advocacy Program, 2007). Available at www.opensocietyfoundations.org/sites/default/files/museucitiesger_20080101_0.pdf (accessed 28 June 2016).

Nofal, Lydia, 'Islamfeindlichkeit als wachsendes gesellschaftliches Phänomen', *Berliner Zustände 2012: Ein Schattenbericht über Rechtsextreminsus, Rassismus und Antisemitismus* (Berlin: Apabiz & MBR, 2013).

Schiffauer, Werner, 'Enemies within the gates', in Tariq Modood, Anna Triandafyllidou and Ricard Zapata-Barrero (eds), *Multiculturalism, Muslims and Citizenship: A European Approach* (London: Routledge, 2006), pp. 74–116.

Wallraff, Lukas, 'Die Wiederkehr der Leitkultur-Debatte: Ein Kampfbegriff', *Deutschlandfunk* (2017). Available at www.deutschlandfunk.de/die-wiederkehr-der-leitkultur-debatte-ein-kampfbegriff.720.de.html?dram:article_id=385548 (accessed 2 May 2017) [link no longer working].

Warner, Michael, *Publics and Counterpublics* (Cambridge: Zone Books, 2002).
Wimmer, Jeffrey, 'Gegenöffentlichkeit 2.00: Formen, Nutzung und Wirkung kritischer Öffentlichkeiten im Social Web', in Ansgar Zerfaß, Martin Welker and Jan Schmidt (eds), *Kommunikation, Partizipation und Wirkungen im Social Web: Strategien und Anwendungen – Perspektiven für Wirtschaft, Politik, Publizistik* (Köln: Herbert von Halem, 2008), pp. 210–30.
Young, Iris Marion, 'Communication and the other: Beyond deliberative democracy', in Seyla Benhabib (ed.), *Democracy and Difference: Contesting the Boundaries of the Political* (Princeton, NJ: Princeton University Press, 1996), pp. 120–35.
ZDF, 'Die Marktanteilsbilanz 2013', *ZDF*, 19 March 2014. Available at www.zdf.de/zdfunternehmen/zdf-erneut-marktfuehrer-die-marktanteilsbilanz-2013-100.html (accessed 1 May 2017).

Part Four

Art beyond Islamophobia

10

Adjusting the 'Islamic' Focus: Exhibitions of Contemporary Pakistani Art in Britain in the Post-9/11 Decade

Madeline Clements

Introduction

This chapter explores how contemporary visual art from 'Islamic' Pakistan has been exhibited in Britain in the years since 9/11, and asks to what extent those artworks' potential meanings have been limited and stereotypical perspectives of Muslims and Pakistan replicated in the process. During this period, Muslim communities in the UK, of whom the greatest number are of Pakistani origin, have repeatedly been painted as a potential threat to 'the British way of life', to which they have been cast as civilizationally opposed.[1] The Islamic Republic, to whose authoritarian and patriarchal culture they are commonly assumed to remain loyal, has at the same time been posed as a dubious ally in the West-led 'War on Terror', guilty of nurturing militant groups, developing nuclear weapons, oppressing women and minorities and sympathizing with Islamic extremism.[2] Yet, at the same time, popular figures of Pakistani origin have garnered attention in Western countries as spokespeople and commentators, looked to by a curious and concerned public for explanations of (often suspect) indigenous and diasporic South Asian Islamic religious, political and cultural identities, motivations and mindsets. This is an interest that transnational anglophone writers such as Mohsin Hamid and international artists such as Imran Qureshi have, to differing degrees, entertained and addressed in works which revisit Islamophobic stereotypes and attitudes in order to problematize them.[3]

Given the extent of the gap that persists 'between representation and reality when it comes to Muslims' in Western culture, creative attempts to carve out 'space for other articulations' of experience and identity, to which Peter Morey and Amina Yaqin allude in *Framing Muslims,* and which the exhibitions I consider may exemplify, remain vital.⁴ Such ventures may re-situate acts of representation beyond a unidirectional redress to Western anxieties, or the reiteration of Orientalist and Islamophobic 'good' and 'bad' Muslim types, and even refuse the expectation of 'representativeness' itself. In so doing, these cultural acts subtly challenge paranoid, indiscriminate, anti-Muslim prejudice. Exhibitions of artworks potentially offer alternative, ambiguous and more equal grounds on which non-Muslim audiences and Muslim-background artists may come to know one another, transforming gallery spaces into sites for the refashioning of viewer–subject relationships in ways that expose the impact of contemporary Islamophobia and emphasize global shared interests and mutual vulnerability.

When it comes to support for creative arts in the UK after 9/11, funding bodies such as Arts Council England have emphasized their commitment to focusing on 'cultural diversity' in successive annual reviews.⁵ Their 2001 report, while not referring to the repercussions of the attacks on New York directly, sought to underscore the arts' capacity to bridge gaps and build understanding between diverse peoples in a 'disturbing and discordant world'. The 2002 report, however, was prefaced by excerpts from a speech by the Chief Executive, Peter Hewitt, which explicitly linked his 'aspirations for the arts' to the events of September 11th.⁶ In it, Hewitt stated that 'the important remaining boundaries in our global world are increasingly about culture, tradition, belief, religion and identity', and stressed the need for art that could 'explore and transgress' these borders; express a 'multiplicity of cultural experiences in society'; 'provide us with the depth and diversity of imaginative capital to make sense of … the complex world we live in'; and contribute to 'a more complex definition of what "we" means'.⁷ Pakistani art, whose presence had been growing in the UK through exhibitions staged in towns and cities with substantial diasporic populations since the mid-1990s, had already engaged with questions of race, faith and gender, in the process overturning stereotypes and assumptions about Muslims in South Asia and in migrant contexts.⁸ It would therefore seem well placed to fulfil the role for the arts identified by Hewitt, presenting intimate aesthetic experiences, informed by transnational, post-colonial and immigrant perspectives, which might challenge and counter Islamophobic perspectives of Muslims as violent, self-segregating, anti-cultural and misogynistic.

Such a national (and political) agenda for the arts can be both enabling and limiting for the diverse practitioners whose work it would celebrate, champion or interpret. On the one hand, Hammad Nasar suggests that Arts Council

England's policies, and those of Western art institutions in general, fall short of supporting contemporary 'artistic practices that have their roots in faith', even 'cringe ... when confronted with present day religion's visual culture'.⁹ As a result, consumable, secular perspectives on modern Muslim identity and its cultural manifestations, or on political 'hot' topics such as veiling, may be privileged to the detriment of artworks informed by deeper understandings of faith and its bearings on contemporary life. On the other hand, artwork of South Asian Muslim origin may be co-opted, as the critic Iftikhar Dadi has warned, into Western, liberal humanist 'exhibitionary regime[s]' which seek to use it 'to project a model of peaceful co-existence [and] locate and provide an appropriate model of Islam itself', rather than to facilitate the expression of more challenging aesthetic, ethical and political subjectivities.¹⁰

Bearing these caveats in mind, this chapter seeks to analyse, through close examination of the two exhibitions *Threads, Dreams, Desires: Art from Pakistan* (2002) and *Beyond the Page: Contemporary Art from Pakistan* (2006–7), how far arts organizations, curators and visual arts practitioners have attempted to work within available spaces to reset or reframe the cultural agenda regarding the depiction of Muslims in post-9/11 Britain.¹¹ They sensitively, subtly and at times critically engage the aesthetic and discursive inheritances, histories, traditions and political positions that inform contemporary understandings of the faith, while rendering palpable the individual and collective impacts of Islamophobia. In the process, they renegotiate the terms on which Muslim Pakistan, its people's faith relationships and their artistic productions are perceived and valued.

Framing Pakistani art as 'Islamic' before and after 9/11

Curatorial statements and reviews of two exhibitions often referred to in historical surveys of modern and contemporary South Asian Muslim art serve to illustrate the role that redressing Western assumptions about Muslims had in the exhibition of Pakistani art in Britain in the decade preceding 9/11.¹² *Intelligent Rebellion: Women Artists of Pakistan* (1994–5) at Bradford's Cartwright Hall Art Gallery was intended, according to its curators Salima Hashmi and Nima Poovaya-Smith, to 'overturn ... stereotypes that the West may have, about contemporary art practised in a Muslim country' and highlight women's dominance within Pakistani arts, 'belying their usual image of seclusion and subjugation'.¹³ In *A Tampered Surface: Six Artists from Pakistan* (1995–6), curated by Alnoor Mitha and Richard Hylton at Huddersfield Art Gallery and four other northern venues (Oldham, Middlesbrough, Leeds and Liverpool), 'the emergence of a significant voice which, in its challenge, counters western expectation of an "exotic" or suppressive Islamic form' might also be discerned.[14] However, the artists included seem to have been equally if not more concerned to engage with a quite specifically local dialogue around contemporary political and cultural issues pertinent to Pakistan.

Intriguingly, it is the curator Timothy Wilcox's framing of the survey show *Pakistan: Another Vision* (2000), presented by Asia House in conjunction with the journal *Arts & The Islamic World* and shown in London, Oldham, Huddersfield and Bath right at the start of the new millennium, that appears to effect the greatest distancing between contemporary Pakistani artistic practice and 'Islam' as an aesthetic and creedal influence. Wilcox's interest in this ambitious exhibition, which had a national rather than a thematic focus and brought together over fifty years of painting, sculpture and other artworks, was firm in exploring the 'Pakistani-ness' of the work included, its 'diversity of styles and techniques' and the 'wide range of attitudes to personal, social and political issues' on display.[15] Hence perhaps his keenness to shuffle off the notion of Islamic inspiration and artistic influence – ascribed a simplistic role in Western art history as functional, decorative and primitive – and to assert that modern Pakistani art is

> by no means circumscribed by Islam. It may even be true to say that Islam is not actually dominant among the five or six major traditions which are entwined in the country's present visual culture. ... In the hands of certain artists ... the arts and ideology of Islam have underpinned and sustained the creativity of an entire career. The same could not, perhaps, be said of many artists of the younger generation.[16]

It remains the case that contemporary Pakistani art is composite, informed by the visual practices of pre-Islamic civilizations and 'cultural exchange between Euramerica and Asia', as well as inflected with other cultural, ethnic, linguistic, historical and political nuances.[17] However, it would be difficult to make a convincing case about a waning interest in exploring Islamic aesthetic and ideological influences in the wake of 9/11. In this period, a generation of Pakistani artists and writers, including Aisha Khalid, Imran Qureshi, Rashid Rana, Nadeem Aslam, Mohsin Hamid and Kamila Shamsie, have become known for doing just this, and for comparing, contrasting and combining the 'Muslim' religious and cultural traditions, subjectivities and aesthetics embedded in their paintings, installations and fictional narratives with those of

Western and non-Muslim cultures. Sadia Abbas describes such a generation's work as presenting 'powerful, theologically intricate, and iconographically complex reformations of and responses to the [Pakistani] state's capture of an iconography of Islam – and to the globalization of this capture'.[18] Thus, she usefully confirms transnational and diasporic Pakistani artists' capacity to critique from both secular and religious positions both Muslim and Western manipulations of 'Islam' (as both a 'discursive site' and 'geopolitical *agon*') and the positive and negative significations with which its name is freighted.[19]

Reflecting back on the exhibitions *Intelligent Rebellion, Tampered Surface* and *Pakistan: Another Vision*, one can clearly see that it would be wrong to make a case for a crude alteration either in curatorial or in artistic practice as a result of the destruction by Islamists of New York's iconic Twin Towers. A shift in consciousness and hence political focus among a number of younger artists, however, is clear. Teacher-practitioners such as Qureshi and Khalid, for example, organized a collaborative workshop in October 2001, inaugurated in Lahore and then stretched between continents, as a means transnationally to 'work out ... reactions to the aftermath of 9/11 and the consequent US invasion of Afghanistan'.[20] It is also possible to trace the impact of an attendant rise in concern and curiosity about Muslim identities within Britain on the wider ambitions of UK-based South Asian arts organizations such as Shisha – which describes itself as 'the international agency for contemporary South Asian visual arts and crafts' – and in the more circumspect statements of the senior curators from Pakistan with whom they worked, such as Hashmi.[21]

A shift in the public reception of Pakistani art exhibited in urban European locations is also observable. Virginia Whiles notes that the political and satirical aspects of artworks shown in a Paris suburb in 2003, such as their treatments of 'war' and 'Islamicism', 'produced lively responses', surely indicative of audiences' interest in native artists' capacity to offer ironic perspectives on topical subjects relevant to Western anxieties about Muslim political and ideological affiliations in an era of 'War on Terror'.[22] Whiles also notes that viewers at a show in a commune in southern France exhibited 'an unusual demand for more information on the content' and a 'desire to decode ... mixed metaphors'.[23] This rising concern to understand the 'real' referent behind the aesthetic image may have seemed literalist in an art-historical context, but is consistent with the mainstream media's scrutiny of what images of (Pakistani) Muslim culture may teach 'us' about 'them' more broadly. Whiles attributes 'both incidences' to 'the Western media's [then] current preoccupation with Pakistan and Afghanistan', which 'wholly neglects the ongoing vitality of [the] everyday cultural life' in the country from which the artists originate, and in countries which host their artwork.[24]

The French responses she outlines, however, contrast interestingly with those of British Pakistani visitors to *It's Still Hard Being British*, which Whiles also discusses. This two-person show by Pakistan-born artists took place in 2006 at Cartwright Hall in Bradford, a city with a high Asian Muslim demographic, associated since the *Satanic Verses* protests of 1989 and the 2001 riots with 'assertive Muslim masculinities … conceptualised as deviant'. Yet the city is also populated by young Muslims from Pakistani backgrounds, particularly women, conscious of the need 'to educate people, and challenge negative stereotypes'.[25] According to Whiles, some of the viewers at the exhibition 'refus[ed] … to recognise themselves in the works' and instead asserted their contentedness with their plural Punjabi, British and Muslim identities, resisting the anxieties about belonging they felt expatriate artists were projecting upon them.[26] These contrasting ways of responding in European contexts – seeking explanations on the one hand, and negating the accuracy and authenticity of supposed representations on the other – point to potential modes of (mis-)recognition faced by individuals and organizations invested in creating and exhibiting Pakistani artworks after 9/11. This is especially true of those works that formally and thematically register their makers' reactions to a growing mistrust of Islam and the impact of the War on Terror.

Emphasizing craft: *Threads, Dreams, Desires* (2002)

In 2002, Shisha's director, Alnoor Mitha, sought to characterize ArtSouthAsia – the programme of exhibitions produced in conjunction with international curators and galleries in Britain's north-west, of which *Threads, Dreams, Desires* was part – as a cultural intervention, pitted against the stereotyping of Muslims and South Asians after 9/11 and in support of deeper reflection:

> The backlash to these dreadful attacks has included acts of physical, verbal and political violence directed at South Asian … people of 'Muslim' appearance, and the erosion of their basic human and citizenship rights. … The demonisation of 'Islam' and the 'Other' all too often obscures and distorts the long and refined traditions of Islam and its civilising influences, much of it contributing directly to the development of European cultures. *Shisha* strives, in whatever humble and modest measure, to establish a more balanced perspective.[27]

This fed into a broader endeavour to use Bangladeshi, Indian, Sri Lankan and Pakistani art to redress imbalances in the representation of migrant communities and their artistic practices, through exhibitions commissioned from 'native' curators, mounted in areas populated by high numbers of diasporic Muslim South Asians with historical links to textile industries, such as Oldham, Preston and Manchester. These aimed at exploring the 'relationships between craft and fine art' and representing that art 'as "authentically" as possible'.[28] Statements such as Mitha's may tend towards the presentation of Muslim South Asian art's alignment with 'enlightened' Western-sounding cultural values as a basis for figuring its worth. They may also risk 'iconizing' certain practices above others 'as authentically indigenous' for English audiences, thereby limiting the potential of the artworks exhibited to offer perspectives which do not fit neatly with European models of progress, inviting criticism from the local South Asian populations who, despite its commitment to an 'ideal of diversity', appear not to have been Shisha's primary target.[29] Nevertheless, as Julia Rothenberg observes, 'Works of art can be embedded in the market and sanctified by conventional cultural gatekeepers ... while at the same time acting as repositories of critical thought and complex collective emotions.'[30]

Threads, Dreams, Desires took place at the Harris Museum and Art Gallery in Preston, Lancashire, between July and September 2002, and was curated by the 'Grande Dame' of Pakistani art, Salima Hashmi. It featured contemporary works by mostly female artists, who were selected as participants in a project shaped, according to the gallery's Senior Exhibitions Officer James Green, not 'by audience development or social inclusion agendas' but by a wish to narrow the focus to 'one facet of contemporary work' and 'reflect' its Pakistani curator's 'idiosyncratic ... interests'.[31] Hashmi, born to a leftist British mother and the progressive, political Pakistani poet Faiz Ahmad Faiz, is an artist and art educator, writer and curator, and has been an activist for human and particularly women's rights. Within Pakistan she is seen as a committed teacher and patron of 'experimental, challenging and often non-commercial art', and hence as offering 'a huge support to new choices, voices and views'.[32] Her curatorial work and publications have also gained the respect of local observers – often highly critical of attempts to showcase transnational artists as 'representative' and 'authentic' – for their introduction of 'a different face/phase of Pakistan' internationally 'that is creative, contemporary and at par with other nations'. Her efforts have been recognized by British institutions for their 'consistent ... test[ing] of artistic boundaries' and extensive contribution to 'art, education, politics and society'.[33]

Secular and ecumenical in approach yet simultaneously attentive to the 'many worlds and feelings that we, as Muslims, regardless of whether we embrace that label or not, are straddling', Hashmi endeavours to support and advance Pakistani art in the region and diaspora. The perspectives of Pakistan and Islam that her curatorial work divulges are necessarily complex, and neither easily translatable nor consumable.[34]

By bringing together in *Threads* works that combined traditional embroidery and stitching techniques, henna decoration, recycled objects and miniature drawing and painting practices, Hashmi sought to identify 'strategies … evolved to question the canons of "fine art" and "craft" in Pakistan' and combine them in a 'plural … idiom'.[35] In doing so she was using her curatorial practice to unsettle and move beyond internal binaries and international prejudices. Yet in the selected artworks she also perceived a strong need on the part of the individual artists to 'speak of a multiplicity of desires, … to reinforce the vigour of irony, … probe well-worn controversies, and … forge bonds across … fissures' at a time when 'opaque … events' required interrogation.[36] It is these concerns that surface most powerfully in the works included in *Threads*, which probe not only geopolitical phenomena like the rise of the Taliban, the US-led offensive on Afghanistan and attitudes to Muslim women, but also more local political matters, such as the social containment of male and female sexuality. They offer multiple perspectives and are attuned to paradox, using subcontinentally sourced visual arts to promote more balanced views of South Asian Muslims internationally. But the multilayered fabrications of these Pakistani artists are less sensational than the references to the Taliban and culture clash might sound, and not reducible to a single interpretation, meaning or political use.

Two particular works stand out as examples of this complex approach: Ataullah and Qureshi's collaborative installation of shrouded parcels adorned with protective Qur'anic text, *Raining Presents from the Sky*; and Khalid's *Chain Stitch* (2001), a series of embroidery hoops framing plain black, red and khaki fabrics emblazoned with a single red rose.[37] The latter, resembling head-and-shoulder portraits of women in burqas familiar from Khalid's earlier miniatures of veiled women blending into patterned domestic interiors, pointed both to the negations of identity that have been perpetuated in Afghanistan under successive native and foreign military regimes and to the powerful endurance of the female. This sense was also perhaps present in Syed's minimalist sculpture *Perfect World* (2001), a pair of black knickers fabricated from off-cuts from the female body (hair, nails) and sewing needles.[38] It seemed to allude to a world in meltdown, in which seductive symbols of female sexuality transform into ambiguous and threatening images. Ataullah and Qureshi's train of sky-dropped gifts, made of metal trays covered in stained material, stuffed with rose-petals, embroidered with the protective *Hasbunallah* ('Sufficient for us is Allah') and decorated with ruptured Afghan maps and spreading trees, presented viewers with a textured combination of media and motifs, which Hashmi's accompanying catalogue text partially decodes.[39] Again, the artwork presented a sceptical perspective on the Taliban's uses of the Qur'an and the dubious benefits of American intervention, using centuries-old customs, crafts and arts to materialize within the gallery space these forces' impacts on the faith, lands and lives of local people.

In addition to works showcasing the impact of the Taliban and Western intervention, *Threads* also included other arresting works that foregrounded different concerns and interests, such as memory and mortality, and made no discernible effort to reference the violent international events, Islamophobia and abuses of Islam that so preoccupied others. Paul O'Neill reminds us that 'the curatorial constructs ideas about art', and we should question 'how and what types of knowledge and epistemologies [are] produced and enabled from within the curatorial field'.[40] Hashmi was not unconscious of this and, in concluding her catalogue text, commented intriguingly on the process of putting together the exhibition: 'Working with Shisha and … Harris … helped … achieve … a certain clarity. One sensed imperatives and ideas jostling and competing for space. … Cultural travelling has many pitfalls, and questions of representation are always contentious.'[41] *Threads*, with its expansive title, technique-based theme and heterogeneous exhibits, demonstrates a determination to avoid reducing contemporary art from Pakistan shown in Britain to something that responds only to particular events or exists to proffer insights into Muslim identities, even as it incorporates works which engage with the impacts of 9/11.

Exhibiting 'Attitude': *Beyond the Page* (2006)

There is a politics to Green and Hashmi's selection and presentation of the work of the eight artists included in *Threads* – many of whom initially trained at Lahore's prestigious National College of Arts, and subsequently at arts colleges in Europe and the United States – as witty, inquisitive, boundary-crossing and unafraid of controversy. This is in keeping with Hashmi's non-hierarchical, enquiry-driven approach.[42] A later exhibition, *Beyond the Page* (2006–7), was curated by Hammad Nasar, co-founder of the then London-based curatorial collective Green Cardamom. It involved some of the same artists, also received support from Shisha and engaged with themes similar to those explored in Hashmi's *Threads*. *Beyond the Page* differed, however, in its presentation of the exhibition as a focused enquiry into the idea of the South Asian miniature as 'an *attitude* that extend[s] beyond tradition and technique' refined in the Mughal courts, to create an 'intensity of experience', which is the effect of a 'critically and socially engaged art practice'.[43] It also took place initially in central, urban locations perhaps more likely to attract cosmopolitan audiences familiar with contemporary art and attuned to its playful provocations.[44]

As with Hashmi's exhibition, there is a notable difference between the elevated and enquiry-driven curatorial vision of Nasar – 'inspired, intrigued, [and] seduced' by contemporary Pakistani artists who were making innovative use of miniature frameworks – and the participating institutions' framings, which seem more directly attuned to the post-9/11 concerns of investors in the arts such as Hewitt.[45] The 'Foreword' to the exhibition's catalogue by Asia House's Katriana Hazell, for example, focuses less on aesthetic and investigative imperatives than on correcting historical inequalities and reflecting contemporary political and sociocultural concerns. She stresses Asia House's commitment to 'redress[ing an] imbalance' in the representation of Pakistani culture in Britain more broadly. Nasar cautions that 'in general [he] do[es] not subscribe to an idea of art being either Muslim or Pakistani', but is rather interested in how it reflects 'the idea of geographies [as] unstable constructs and histories [as] … enmeshed'. His ambition was to showcase a contemporary generation 'who live and work in a global world and respond to international issues'.[46] Hazell also speaks of a desire to use *Beyond the Page* 'to encourage discussion about Muslim cultures and modernity'.[47] Hazell thus situates the exhibition alongside other attempts to use reflective and discursive cultural practices (art, literature, memoir) to respond to what Anshuman Mondal describes as 'a genuine desire amongst many people to open themselves to different ways of thinking and being, to take on board Muslim perspectives, ideas and experiences', rather than seek the reconfirmation of Islamophobic stereotypes and prejudices.[48] This is a role to which Nasar is also attuned, despite his wariness of religious and ethnic categorizations that would occlude its complexity.[49]

Beyond the Page contained sculptures, mixed-media works and installations by eight internationally established Pakistani artists, some of whom, having felt marginalized in Western countries as a result of their pursuit of traditional South Asian creative practices and religious affiliations, continued to base themselves in Pakistan, others of whom had migrated abroad.[50] Significantly, four of the participants had previously contributed to an exhibition of collaborative miniature works entitled *Karkhana* (2003–4), also co-curated by Nasar, which grew from a project inspired by the 'fresh wave of imperialist aggression' against Muslim countries that followed 9/11, and was shaped by the 'modulation between ... individual and collective identities' in which the creative process resulted.[51] The inclusion of site-specific work in *Beyond the Page* was, according to Nasar, an attempt to extend this interest to 'a broader setting' where artists might respond to the surrounding environment and 'initiate multiple conversations', not only between themselves, their different practices and competing art histories, but also between their artworks and audiences at metropolitan British galleries.[52]

The exhibited works explored issues such as the effects of colonial encounters, the hierarchies of art history, cultural commodification, gender politics and identity construction. Yet, as in *Threads*, certain works played with Western attitudes towards Islam and Pakistan, in ways that were in some cases bolder and more provocative. These included Aisha Khalid's pointed comment on the concept of *Infinite Justice* (2001), the Bush administration's original name for its anti-Afghan offensive (Figures 10.1 and 10.2). In Khalid's mixed-media work, 'wafting cotton threads' were, in Sara Wajid's words, 'attached to hundreds of sharp needles embedded in [a] richly coloured canvass', revealing, when viewed from a distance, 'a black target ... in the middle of the soft hazy cloud'.[53] Thus

Figure 10.1 *Infinite Justice*, Aisha Khalid (2001). Image courtesy of Green Cardamom © Vipul Sangoi.

Figure 10.2 *Infinite Justice* (detail), Aisha Khalid (2001). Image courtesy of Green Cardamom © Vipul Sangoi.

Infinite Justice acted as a reminder of the pain that is inflicted on 'soft' local targets, however 'sensitively' a foreign onslaught is sanitized and repackaged by its perpetrators. The exhibition also featured later works, such as Hamra Abbas's collage *Please Do Not Touch, Stay Out and Enjoy the Show* (2004), which Nasar's catalogue may translate as 'an ode to [the artist's] Sisyphus-like attempt to secure an American visa', but which functions less as a personal diatribe than as a 'repository' for more complex, 'critical' reflection and 'collective emotion' (Figures 10.3 and 10.4).[54] For this work, Abbas arranged strips of paper printed with words 'STAY OUT' into delicate geometric Islamic patterns on the gallery wall, forming the shape of the kind of house a child draws as 'home'. A miniature painting is hung within the body of this house, but behind the admonitory paper strips, acting as a window. Thus Abbas's installation made a mockery of notions of cultural purity and preservation, whether Western or Islamic, which result in such seeming absurdities as censorship and the physical exclusion of artists, whose very raison d'être is to communicate with audiences across artificially crafted boundaries and borders.

Figure 10.3 *Please Do Not Touch, Stay Out and Enjoy the Show*, Hamra Abbas (2004). Image courtesy of Green Cardamom © Vipul Sangoi.

Figure 10.4 *Please Do Not Touch, Stay Out and Enjoy the Show* (detail), Hamra Abbas (2004). Image courtesy of Green Cardamom © Vipul Sangoi.

Figure 10.5 *Politically Incorrect*, Imran Qureshi (2006). Image courtesy of Green Cardamom © Vipul Sangoi.

Imran Qureshi's site-specific painting, *Politically Incorrect* (2006), offered a more insidious response to fears of immigrant encroachment; it featured what was by this stage his 'signature' *Basohli* leaf pattern, from the *Pahari* school of miniature painting, in pale-blue wash seeping elegantly through the gallery's air vents and creeping stain-like down its walls (Figure 10.5).[55] This was understood by one British Pakistani reviewer both to 'mirror ... the all-pervasiveness of the international policies of the world's only super-power', to which Khalid also alluded, and to 'invok[e] the macabre jihadi-glamour the remote conflict zones hold for some in the west'.[56] Qureshi's uncanny installation might more feasibly be seen as a wry reflection on matters closer to home: alarmist responses to influxes of Muslim migrants, for instance, or concerns about the impossibility of containing or eradicating strange and threateningly 'Other' Islamic traditions. It might also be taken as a reflexive comment on the colonization of British galleries by provocative Pakistani artists who push the bounds of what can be articulated. Qureshi and Abbas's aesthetic incursions at Asia House, the most impressive examples of such transgression in *Beyond the Page*, use the metropolitan gallery space to invite viewers of all faiths and none to confront the discomfort with Islamic culture's presence in the West that proliferated after 9/11 and 7/7.

Conclusions

Threads and *Beyond the Page* provided subtle forums within which aesthetic enquiries could be made into contemporary social, cultural and political issues, taking as inspiration particular technical and conceptual points of focus. These included the deployment of traditional crafts in contemporary art, thereby blurring hierarchies and distinctions, and the expression of a critical 'attitude' through adaptation of the constrained form of the Indian miniature. These were used to explore the impact of Western-led offensives on Muslim peoples in Muslim lands and the effects of Islamophobia on attitudes to Muslim migrants and aspects of Islamic culture. The exhibitions and works discussed in this chapter may be broadly in sympathy with their partner institutions' wider aims of ensuring British audiences' continued exposure to Islamic traditions, providing greater coverage within the diaspora of diverse aspects of 'authentic' Pakistani aesthetic culture and rebalancing anti-modern Muslim stereotypes. Yet the works by Ataullah, Qureshi, Khalid and Abbas examined here in particular provide composite, ambiguous reflections on the state of Islam and the status of Muslims in the West and in South Asia after 9/11, which resist co-optation as uncritical attempts to promote Muslims' inclusion in British multiculture, or identify an acceptable face for Islam as a comfortably 'moderate' counter to Islamist extremes. Yet what appears missing in these artistic investigations are ways of seeing based in faith. The transnational works of Pakistani artists appear by and large sceptical and secular in attitude and approach, and such unaffiliated positions are surely integral to the Janus-faced critiques they are able to offer. The critical endorsements of these works likewise gesture towards a secular bias within academic theory, art discourse and practice, which is uncomfortable with religious faith except in the guise of faith-based identity politics. This appears still to be the great divide which Pakistani artists and their international patrons and exhibitors might profitably begin to explore in more depth in the coming years.

Notes

1 Muslim Council of Britain, *British Muslims in Numbers: A Demographic, Socio-Economic and Health Profile of Muslims in Britain Drawing on the 2011 Census* (January 2015), p. 24. Available at www.mcb.org.uk/wp-content/uploads/2015/02/MCBCensusReport_2015.pdf (accessed 27 September 2015).
2 Tariq Ali, *The Duel* (London: Simon and Schuster, 2008), p. 4.

3 Examples include Mohsin Hamid's 'post-9/11' novel *The Reluctant Fundamentalist* (London: Penguin, 2007), in which an ambiguously 'fundamentalist' protagonist famously 'smiles' as the Twin Towers burn; and Imran Qureshi's *Side by Side 2/2: Moderate Enlightenment* (Singapore, 2009), a series of miniature paintings made in response to General Musharraf's 2002 introduction of a policy of 'Enlightened Moderation' as a means of winning US favour and tackling Islamic extremism. Featuring bearded young men in prayer caps and shalwar kameez with flowers, dumb-bells, books, camouflage bags and sneakers, these presented tongue-in-cheek performances of a 'moderate', secular Islamic identity.

4 Peter Morey and Amina Yaqin, *Framing Muslims: Stereotyping and Representation after 9/11* (Cambridge, MA: Harvard University Press, 2011), pp. 1, 17.

5 Meaning 'the full range and diversity of the culture of this country', composed of peoples of different races and ethnicities as well as those with disabilities, as defined in: Arts Council England, *Annual Review 2003* (January 2004), p. 17. Available at www.artscouncil.org.uk/arts-council-england-annual-review-2003 (accessed 28 September 2016).

6 Arts Council England, *Annual Review 2001* (October 2001), p. 2. Available at www.artscouncil.org.uk/arts-council-england-annual-review-2001; and *Annual Review 2002* (October 2002), p. 2. Available at: www.artscouncil.org.uk/arts-council-england-annual-review-2002 (both accessed 27 September 2016). Interestingly, it is not until 2010 that Islam receives specific mention. Here 'work such as Arts and Islam that seeks to examine the connections between Islam, arts practice and contemporary society' appears under 'reaching out to marginalised groups', an area of activity prioritized under the Arts Council's 2009–11 Race Equality Scheme. See Arts Council England, *Annual Review 2010/11* (2012), p. 62. Available at www.artscouncil.org.uk/arts-council-england-annual-review-201011 (accessed 28 September 2016).

7 Arts Council England, *Annual Review 2002*, p. 2.

8 John Holt and Laura Turney, 'The singular journey: South Asian visual art in Britain', in N. Ali, V. S. Kalra and S. Sayyid (eds), *A Postcolonial People: South Asians in Britain* (London: Hurst & Co., 2006), pp. 338–9.

9 Hammad Nasar, 'Art, race and religion', *Artolatry* (Spring 2007). Available at www.cosacosa.org/Artolatry-spring07.html (accessed 3 January 2017).

10 Iftikhar Dadi, *Modernism and the Art of Muslim South Asia* (Chapel Hill, NC: University of North Carolina Press, 2010), pp. 217–18.

11 This chapter will not consider *Karkhana: Contemporary Pakistani Miniatures*, an exhibition featuring twelve artworks created by six miniature painters (four of whom subsequently contributed to *Beyond the Page*), which was initially staged at Touchstones Art Gallery in Rochdale in the winter of 2003–4 and then toured to the Aldrich Contemporary Art Museum in Connecticut in 2005–6, sparked by a desire to set 'Pakistan's colonial history in a new context' following

America's invasion of Afghanistan in 2001; Jessica Hough, Hammad Nasar and Anna Sloan, 'Introduction', in Hammad Nasar (ed.), *Karkhana: A Contemporary Collaboration* (Ridgefield, CT: Aldrich Contemporary Art Museum, 2005), p. 9. The decision to exclude it was taken partly in order to ensure an even spread across the years 2001–11. However, the omission was also made because the *Karkhana* project, which was initiated outside the UK, included works which took shape virtually, as a result of a postal collaboration between artists situated in Pakistan, Australia and America, and was – according to its curators – primarily addressed to the United States as 'its unspoken but obvious audience' (ibid.). The other exhibitions focused on here, by contrast, were created specifically for British audiences.

12 See, for example, Dadi, *Modernism*, p. 219; and Holt and Turney, 'The singular journey', pp. 329–39.
13 Salima Hashmi and Nima Poovaya-Smith, quoted in Holt and Turney, 'The singular journey', pp. 338–9.
14 John Holt, 'Tampered surface', *Third Text* 10/36 (1996), p. 90.
15 Timothy Wilcox, 'Modern art in Pakistan', in T. Wilcox (ed.), *Pakistan: Another Vision – Fifty Years of Painting and Sculpture from Pakistan* (London: Arts and the Islamic World (UK), 2000), p. 9.
16 Wilcox, 'Modern art in Pakistan', p. 11.
17 Ibid.
18 Sadia Abbas, *At Freedom's Limit: Islam and the Postcolonial Predicament* (New York: Fordham University Press, 2014), pp. 6–7.
19 Abbas, *At Freedom's Limit*, p. 1. Abbas traces the genesis of Islam's current 'shape' to the ending of the Cold War in the late 1980s; Khalid, Qureshi and others first published and exhibited work on related subjects in the mid-to-late 1990s.
20 Virginia Whiles, *Art and Polemic in Pakistan* (London: I.B. Tauris, 2010), pp. 44, 149. The workshop, entitled *Darmiyan* ('in-between'), was a precursor to the *Karkhana* collaboration which resulted in the Aldrich exhibition (see above note).
21 In J. Rangasamy, J. Holt, L. Turney, A. Mitha and F. Khan (eds), *ArtSouthAsia: The First International Programme of Visual Culture from Bangladesh, India, Pakistan and Sri Lanka* (Manchester: Shisha, 2002), front pages. See also Alnoor Mitha's 'Foreword', p. 5.
22 Whiles, *Art and Polemic*, p. 214.
23 Ibid.
24 Ibid.
25 Gurchathen Sanghera and Suruchi Thapar-Björkert, '"Because I am Pakistani … and I am Muslim … I am political" – gendering political radicalism: Young femininities in Bradford', in T. Abbas (ed.), *Islamic Political Radicalism: A European Perspective* (Edinburgh: Edinburgh University Press, 2007), p. 173.

26 Whiles, *Art and Polemic*, p. 213. One wonders whether these viewers would feel themselves better represented in exhibitions such as *The Brit Pak*, curated by MICA gallery Director Reedah Al-Saie as part of Asian Art in London, and then at the Alchemy Festival, London's Southbank Centre's annual celebration of the UK's ties with subcontinental culture. Among the richly colourful figurative, abstract and calligraphic works included were those of the Pakistan-born British artist Khaver Idrees. Her eye-catching *Bohemian Rhapsody* (2008), used as the exhibition's cover image, was a motif-peppered Union Jack on which geometric star and heart patterns, a teapot and calligraphic Arabic symbols were superimposed. Idrees has stated that the layering of symbols in her paintings, some faint-edged, some distinct, 'mirror … the levels of integration' that exist in a country where she has 'never felt any conflict between … faith or lifestyle'; 'British Artist – Khaver Idrees', *Islam Awareness Week*, 2008. Available at: http://iaw.openia.com/previous/2008/british-artist-khaver-idrees (accessed 7 June 2014) [link no longer working].

27 In Rangasamy et al., *ArtSouthAsia*, p. 5 (original emphasis).

28 Ibid.

29 Bill Ashcroft, Gareth Griffiths and Helen Tiffin, *Post-Colonial Studies: The Key Concepts*, 2nd edn (London: Routledge, 2007), p. 17; Jacques Rangasamy, 'Preface', in Rangasamy et al., *ArtSouthAsia*, p. 7. The Senior Exhibitions Officer at Harris Museum and Art Gallery, Preston, which hosted *Threads*, acknowledged in his introduction to the exhibition that 'Preston does have a large South Asian population' but emphasized that 'this show is not driven by' the desire to include them and – perhaps as a result – 'will have its advocates and detractors'; James Green, 'Threads, dreams, desires', in Rangasamy et al., *ArtSouthAsia*, p. 37.

30 Julia Rothenberg, 'Art after 9/11: Critical moments in lean times', *Cultural Sociology* 6/2 (2012), p. 183.

31 Green, 'Threads', pp. 36–7.

32 'Salima Hashmi: Multiple views', *Art Now: Contemporary Art of Pakistan* (n.d.). Available at www.artnowpakistan.com/salima-hashmi-multiple-views/ (accessed 5 January 2017).

33 Art Now, 'Salima Hashmi'; 'Salima Hashmi awarded honorary doctorate at Bath Spa', *Dawn*, 8 November 2016. Available at http://images.dawn.com/news/1176547 (accessed 5 January 2017).

34 Murtaza Vali, 'Paradise found and lost: Salima Hashmi', *Art Asia Pacific* (March/April 2008). Available at http://artasiapacific.com/Magazine/57/ParadiseFoundLostSalimaHashmi (accessed 5 January 2017).

35 Salima Hashmi, 'Threads, dreams, desires: Art from Pakistan', in Rangasamy et al., *ArtSouthAsia*, p. 38.

36 Hashmi, 'Threads, dreams, desires', p. 38.

37 Photographs of these works can be seen in the exhibition catalogue (Rangasamy et al., *ArtSouthAsia*, pp. 38–40).
38 Ibid., p. 40.
39 Ibid., p. 38. Hashmi explains that the inscription 'refers to a situation where Allah's protection is sought. This refers to the tradition of going into battle, wearing verses from the Quran written on the garments under the armour and chain mail. The idea of "protection" is a loaded one in this context, since it alludes to protection from the Taliban and their brand of Islam. It also alludes to the "gifts" that rain down on a hapless people' (p. 38). While I understand Whiles's concern with a shift to 'decoding' Pakistani artworks in general after 9/11, which might negate their aesthetic intricacies and meanings, I would argue that the artworks from *Threads* under discussion, with their complex combinations of signs, do invite decryption.
40 Paul O'Neill, *The Culture of Curating and the Curating of Cultures* (Cambridge, MA: MIT Press, 2012), p. 7.
41 Hashmi, 'Threads, dreams, desires', p. 43.
42 Ibid., p. 38.
43 Hammad Nasar, '*Beyond the Page*: Curatorial notes', in Anita Dawood and Hammad Nasar (eds), *Beyond the Page: Contemporary Art from Pakistan* (London and Manchester: Asia House, Green Cardamom; Manchester City Art Gallery, Shisha, 2006), pp. 7, 10.
44 The exhibition subsequently toured to Nottingham, Birmingham and Huddersfield, cities which, like the north-western locations discussed earlier, have sizeable diasporic Pakistani and Muslim populations.
45 Aasim Zafar Khan, 'Hammad Nasar: Interview', *Newsline*, 12 May 2009. Available at http://newslinemagazine.com/magazine/interview-hammad-nasar/ (accessed 2 May 2018).
46 Katriana Hazell, in Dawood and Nasar (eds), *Beyond the Page*, p. 4. Hammad Nasar, 'Essay on the exhibition of Pakistani art in the UK' (4 December 2016). Online. Email: hammad@mac.com.
47 Hazell, in Dawood and Nasar (eds), *Beyond the Page*, p. 4. No reference is made in the catalogue to 7/7, which overtook planning for the show. However, the London bombings and related discourses around Muslims' place in multicultural Britain would have been fresh in viewers' minds.
48 Anshuman Mondal, *Young British Muslim Voices* (Oxford: Greenwood World Publishing, 2008), p. xiv.
49 Nasar, 'Art, race and religion'.
50 See Whiles, *Art and Polemic*, p. 45, for a description of Khalid's discomfort in Amsterdam in 2001.
51 Hough, Nasar and Sloan, 'Introduction', p. 9; Nasar, '*Beyond the Page*', pp. 7–8.
52 Nasar, '*Beyond the Page*', p. 8.

53 Sara Wajid, 'Beyond the Page: Contemporary art from Pakistan', *Nafas Art Magazine* (December 2006). Available at http://u-in-u.com/nafas/articles/2006/beyond-the-page/ (accessed 22 September 2016).
54 Nasar, *'Beyond the Page'*, p. 11; Rothenberg, 'Art after 9/11', p. 183.
55 Whiles, *Art and Polemic*, p. 42.
56 Wajid, 'Beyond the Page'.

Works cited

Abbas, Sadia, *At Freedom's Limit: Islam and the Postcolonial Predicament* (New York: Fordham University Press, 2014).

Ali, Tariq, *The Duel* (London: Simon and Schuster, 2008).

Art Now Pakistan, 'Salima Hashmi: Multiple views', *Art Now: Contemporary Art of Pakistan* (n.d.). Available at www.artnowpakistan.com/salima-hashmi-multiple-views/ (accessed 5 January 2017).

Arts Council England, *Annual Review 2001* (October 2001). Available at www.artscouncil.org.uk/arts-council-england-annual-review-2001 (accessed 27 September 2016).

Arts Council England, *Annual Review 2002* (October 2002). Available at: http://www.artscouncil.org.uk/arts-council-england-annual-review-2002 (accessed 27 September 2016).

Arts Council England, *Annual Review 2003* (January 2004). Available at www.artscouncil.org.uk/arts-council-england-annual-review-2003 (accessed 28 September 2016).

Arts Council England, *Annual Review 2010/11* (2012). Available at: www.artscouncil.org.uk/arts-council-england-annual-review-201011 (accessed 28 September 2016).

Ashcroft, Bill, Gareth Griffiths and Helen Tiffin, *Post-Colonial Studies: The Key Concepts*, 2nd edn (London: Routledge, 2007).

Dadi, Iftikhar, *Modernism and the Art of Muslim South Asia* (Chapel Hill, NC: University of North Carolina Press, 2010).

Dawn, 'Salima Hashmi awarded honorary doctorate at Bath Spa', *Dawn*, 8 November 2016. Available at http://images.dawn.com/news/1176547 (accessed 5 January 2017).

Green, James, 'Threads, dreams, desires', in J. Rangasamy, J. Holt, L. Turney, A. Mitha and F. Khan (eds), *ArtSouthAsia: The First International Programme of Visual Culture from Bangladesh, India, Pakistan & Sri Lanka* (Manchester: Shisha, 2002), pp. 36–7.

Hashmi, Salima, 'Threads, dreams, desires: Art from Pakistan', in J. Rangasamy, J. Holt, L. Turney, A. Mitha and F. Khan (eds), *ArtSouthAsia: The First International Programme of Visual Culture from Bangladesh, India, Pakistan & Sri Lanka* (Manchester: Shisha, 2002), pp. 38–43.

Hazell, Katriana, 'Foreword', in Anita Dawood and Hammad Nasar (eds), *Beyond the Page: Contemporary Art from Pakistan* (London and Manchester: Asia House, Green Cardamom; Manchester City Art Gallery, Shisha, 2006), p. 4.
Holt, John, 'Tampered surface', *Third Text* 10/36 (1996), pp. 87–90.
Holt, John and Laura Turney, 'The singular journey: South Asian visual art in Britain', in N. Ali, V. S. Kalra and S. Sayyid (eds), *A Postcolonial People: South Asians in Britain* (London: Hurst & Co., 2006), pp. 329–39.
Hough, Jessica, Hammad Nasar and Anna Sloan, 'Introduction', in Hammad Nasar (ed.), *Karkhana: A Contemporary Collaboration* (Ridgefield, CT: Aldrich Contemporary Art Museum, 2005), pp. 7–11.
Islam Awareness Week, 'British Artist – Khaver Idrees', *Islam Awareness Week*, 2008. Available at http://iaw.openia.com/previous/2008/british-artist-khaver-idrees (accessed 7 June 2014) [link no longer working].
Khan, Aasim Zafar, 'Interview: Hammad Nasar', *Newsline*, 12 May 2009. Available at http://newslinemagazine.com/magazine/interview-hammad-nasar/ (accessed 2 May 2018).
Mondal, Anshuman, *Young British Muslim Voices* (Oxford: Greenwood World Publishing, 2008).
Morey, Peter and Amina Yaqin, *Framing Muslims: Stereotyping and Representation after 9/11* (Cambridge, MA: Harvard University Press, 2011).
Murtaza Vali, 'Paradise found and lost: Salima Hashmi', *Art Asia Pacific* (March–April 2008). Available at http://artasiapacific.com/Magazine/57/ParadiseFoundLostSalimaHashmi (accessed 5 January 2017).
Muslim Council of Britain, *British Muslims in Numbers: A Demographic, Socio-Economic and Health Profile of Muslims in Britain Drawing on the 2011 Census* (January 2015). Available at www.mcb.org.uk/wp-content/uploads/2015/02/MCBCensusReport_2015.pdf (accessed 27 September 2015).
Nasar, Hammad, 'Art, race and religion', *Artolatry* (Spring 2007). Available at: www.cosacosa.org/Artolatry-spring07.html (accessed 3 January 2017).
Nasar, Hammad, '*Beyond the Page*: Curatorial notes', in Anita Dawood and Hammad Nasar (eds), *Beyond the Page: Contemporary Art from Pakistan* (London and Manchester: Asia House, Green Cardamom; Manchester City Art Gallery, Shisha, 2006), pp. 7–21.
O'Neill, Paul, *The Culture of Curating and the Curating of Cultures* (Cambridge, MA: MIT Press, 2012).
Rangasamy, J., J. Holt, L. Turney, A. Mitha and F. Khan (eds), *ArtSouthAsia: The First International Programme of Visual Culture from Bangladesh, India, Pakistan & Sri Lanka* (Manchester: Shisha, 2002).
Rangasamy, Jacques, 'Preface', in J. Rangasamy, J. Holt, L. Turney, A. Mitha and F. Khan (eds), *ArtSouthAsia: The First International Programme of Visual Culture from Bangladesh, India, Pakistan & Sri Lanka* (Manchester: Shisha, 2002), pp. 6–7.

Rothenberg, Julia, 'Art after 9/11: Critical moments in lean times', *Cultural Sociology* 6/2 (2012), pp. 177–200.
Sanghera, Gurchathen and Suruchi Thapar-Björkert, '"Because I am Pakistani ... and I am Muslim ... I am political" – Gendering political radicalism: Young femininities in Bradford', in T. Abbas (ed.), *Islamic Political Radicalism: A European Perspective* (Edinburgh: Edinburgh University Press, 2007), pp. 173–91.
Wajid, Sara, 'Beyond the Page: Contemporary art from Pakistan', *Nafas Art Magazine*, December 2006. Available at http://u-in-u.com/nafas/articles/2006/beyond-the-page/ (accessed 22 September 2016).
Whiles, Virginia, *Art and Polemic in Pakistan* (London: I.B. Tauris, 2010).
Wilcox, Timothy (ed.), *Pakistan: Another Vision: Fifty Years of Painting and Sculpture from Pakistan* (London: Arts and the Islamic World (UK), 2000).

11

Super Moozlim Battles Islamophobia

Leila Tarakji

While the presence of Muslims in American comics is by no means a recent phenomenon, the upsurge in the use of Islam and Muslims to shape literary plots in recent years fits within the larger trend of the heightened visibility and racialization of Muslims across Western culture after 9/11. I am interested in how contemporary depictions of Muslim superheroes in American comics reiterate or contest the demonizing and Othering effects of Islamophobia. This chapter considers how comics can serve to counter the Islamophobic attitudes that have become embedded in political and cultural discourses. I begin by reviewing the role of comics in American popular culture, particularly the potential power that is ascribed to their hybrid and iconic nature. Additionally, the ongoing tradition of the superhero as outcast – potentially problematic yet disturbingly fitting as it relates to the Muslim Other – also offers opportunities for discussion. I specifically examine how G. Willow Wilson's *Ms Marvel: No Normal* (2014), the first volume in the comic series, encounters questions of dual identity, visibility and representation while it also highlights the plurality of its protagonist's character. Ms Marvel, a title now held by the teenage Pakistani Muslim American Kamala Khan, participates in creating a space for illustrating the rich diversity, complexity and humanity of the Muslim American community. My discussion pays special attention to Kamala's superhero costume and shape-shifting abilities as well as to the various markers of difference and physical embodiments of faith that are employed. Ultimately, the significance of *Ms Marvel* extends beyond the boundaries of its text, effectively complicating the existing discourse on Muslim Americans and marking their intersectional experiences as integral to the American landscape.

Dangerous Muslim: An intervention

In *Covering Islam,* Edward Said describes how the word 'Islam' has too often 'licensed not only patent inaccuracy but also expressions of unrestrained ethnocentrism, cultural, and even racial hatred, deep yet paradoxically free-floating hostility. All this has taken place as part of what is presumed to be fair, balanced, responsible coverage of Islam.'[1] Junaid Rana affirms the deep-rootedness of this anti-Muslim hostility and Islamophobia, describing the category of 'dangerous Muslim' that is deployed via rhetoric of the state, media and popular culture. Rana contends that this rhetoric of terror, the notion of 'Islamic peril', incites racial and moral panics and is subsequently used to shape US policies and the nation's global War on Terror, thereby enforcing social control.[2]

The Muslim figure thus reveals the interwoven relationship between language, power and knowledge, between US politics, media and popular culture. Peter Morey and Amina Yaqin delineate the resurgence of Muslim stereotypes since 9/11 that 'thrust a certain type of Orientalist stereotype firmly back onto our cinema and television screens, into our news media, and into the mouths of politicians'.[3] Jack Shaheen's documentary film (based on his previously published book under the same title) *Reel Bad Arabs: How Hollywood Vilifies a People* (2006) illustrates this interrelation between Islamophobia and popular culture as he specifically highlights the link between Washington politics and Hollywood entertainment. Identifying Arabs as 'the most maligned group in the history of Hollywood', Shaheen highlights the direct correlation between Islamophobia and American foreign policy, where the image of the bad Muslim is used to engender support for the latter; he notes that Hollywood's vilification of Muslims escalated after the Second World War, particularly with the advent of the Arab–Israeli conflict, Arab oil embargo and Iranian Revolution. Shaheen demonstrates that the embracing of the mythology concerning the evil and dangerous Muslim and the prevalence of this image within our popular culture, Hollywood in particular, has played a significant role in constructing Islamophobia as a 'part of our psyche'.[4]

This discussion is interested in the potential of comics, superhero comics in particular, as a powerful means of challenging and complicating the negative and reductive representation of Muslims today. Morey and Yaqin further describe the Muslim image that is perpetuated, whereby 'behavior, the body, and dress are treated not as cultural markers but as a kind of moral index, confirming non-Muslim viewers of these images in their sense of superiority and cementing the threatening strangeness of the Muslim other'.[5] Moustafa Bayoumi expounds this idea, describing a 'new narrative [that] operates along the axis of culture' wherein 'simple acts of religious or cultural expression and the straightforward activities of Muslim daily life have become suspicious'.[6] In this 'War on Terror culture' that Bayoumi describes, Muslim Americans 'embody, quite literally, some of America's most contested political and cultural debates'.[7] Ultimately, all that is Muslim is reduced to a contentious, dangerous and monolithic Other. Wilson's *Ms Marvel*, however, presents an example that restores and embraces Muslim cultural markers of behaviour, body and dress; rather than alienate the Muslim protagonist, they enrich a subjectivity that is valuable in its intersectionality as Muslim, Pakistani, American and female. Such complex depictions serve to promote 'an understanding of Muslim connectedness, both to other Muslims and to the wider world', which Morey and Yaqin argue is necessary to counter negative portrayals of Muslims. Proposing an approach that moves beyond positive representation of Muslims, they state the following:

> Rather what is needed is a recognition of the ubiquitous cultural interpenetration that has always marked relations between Islam and the west, and an attempt to work this realization into the mainstream representational landscape, and into both cultural and political views of Muslims as something more than just a strategic problem.[8]

Ms Marvel offers such a space that recognizes this cultural interpenetration and makes Muslims – with all the markers that make them such – natural and necessary parts of the American landscape.

The casting of Kamala Khan as Ms Marvel further creates a narrative of national belonging. In *Secret Identity Crisis*, Matthew Costello specifically examines the relationship between superhero comics and national identity in a post-Cold War America. He contends the following:

> Three elements of the superhero comic render it a particularly revealing avenue for the exploration of national identity. These are the relevance of the heroic narrative to social values, the specific ideological content of the books as cultural artifacts, and the mechanism of the dual identity.[9]

While I explore the aspect of dual identity in detail below, here I will briefly address the implications of the heroic narrative for a superhero comic such as *Ms Marvel*. Costello states that 'the heroic narrative describes a story of value and virtue, defines good and evil, and offers a guide to proper action by which redemption can be achieved'.[10] A heroic narrative thus necessarily identifies the values and ideals of a society or nation and further distinguishes between good and evil, between that which is admired and feared. When the Muslim, Pakistani American Kamala Khan is depicted as a superhero – the central protagonist of the comic, no less – she is immediately granted a level of authority. In a reversal of roles, she is admired not feared, good not evil. Moreover, it is to her that we look to uphold the values of our society, to defend us and our ideals as a nation.

In addressing the subversive power of comics, Derek Parker Royal writes, 'The attitudes and prejudices of a culture can be greatly shaped by its caricatures, cartoons, and other forms of manipulated iconography.'[11] He maintains that this is particularly relevant as it applies to minority populations and groups that have been marginalized by society and history. Royal further describes comics as 'well suited to dismantle those very assumptions that problematize ethnic representation, especially as they find form in visual language. They can do this by particularizing the general, thereby undermining any attempts at subjective erasure through universalization.'[12] In the effort to 'dismantle' the assumptions and images of which Islamophobia is constituted, the potential of comics to particularize the general is critical as the perpetual possibility of terror associated with the Muslim figure is largely influenced by the homogenizing effect of Orientalism.[13] Whereas the prevalent generalization of Muslims effectively strips them of their myriad differences – which encompass a multitude of backgrounds, nationalities, languages and religious practices – the visual narratives and representations we find in comics have the potential to restore their heterogeneity and in turn their humanity. They allow readers to *see* Muslim subjects and visualize them in action as they live their daily lives, among family and friends, and as they encounter and negotiate personal challenges and struggles. Ultimately, one hopes, their familiarity as fellow human beings overcomes preconceived notions of *Otherness*.

Comic experts attribute the power of comics to their hybrid and iconic nature as well as to their unique engagement of the reader. Douglas Rushkoff describes the nature of comics and how we read them:

> This is core premise of comics, the art of sequential narrative. Our stories and their characters do not move in a line ... but through a series of windows. Frozen instants. These are the ticks of the clock, but not the spaces between each one where life actually happens or the story actually occurs. As such, a comic requires a leap of faith from its readers every time they move from one panel to the next. We move to the next panel and must absorb it before we even understand its connection to the panel before. Only then are we able to relate it to the narrative of which it is a component part. Picture, word, then connection.[14]

Thus, comics as sequential art necessitate reader participation and a 'leap of faith'. What results is an interesting dynamic between author, comic and reader. On the one hand, the gradual development of 'picture, word, then connection' offers the author the opportunity 'to instill word and image into a reader's mind before the reader has a context for this information'.[15] Rushkoff describes this as the 'tremendous power behind comics' ability to generate cultural iconography – to create modern mythology'. On the other hand, the space between windows and the 'gutter', which Rushkoff describes as the locus of life where the 'story actually occurs', constitutes gaps that must be filled in by the readers, placing them in a position of authority alongside the author.[16] The comic's narrative cannot exist without its readers, whose responsibility is to develop and articulate to themselves the connections across the sequence of windows. In the transformation of a series of 'frozen instants' into a coherent story, the readers are 'implicate[d] ... in the very telling of the story ... providing the propulsion forward'.[17] The readers become 'co-creators of their reading experience', a multisensory experience wherein they are constantly prompted to 'imaginatively "hear" sound effects and dialogue, to "smell" strong odors, or to "feel" the tactile sensations of characters'.[18]

In *Ms Marvel*, readers are first introduced to Kamala Khan via a close-up image of two 'Easy Greasy B.L.T.' sandwiches, which extends across the top of the page. The image is accompanied by the text, 'I just want to *smell* it'; this seemingly desperate desire is not yet associated with any person and may very well be our own. As we move to the next panel, we realize that the close-up perspective was offered to us through Kamala's eyes, which are focused on the sandwich with a piercing look; we see what she sees. Neither Kamala nor we can *smell* the 'delicious, delicious infidel meat' we are both eyeing. For us, as readers, the sandwich – and its smell – lies beyond our reach in the confines of the page and the Marvel Universe. We sympathize with Kamala, for whom the sandwich on display lies behind the glass window of Circle Q's 'Hot Sammiches' machine.[19] As we absorb the illustrated scene and identify with Kamala's hunger for something she cannot have, we eventually register her description of the 'infidel' meat and that it is her 'principles' (namely, the Islamic dietary law that prohibits eating pork products) that prevent her from *inhaling* the BLT sandwich and succumbing to its temptation. Thus, as readers, our sympathies and an imagined sensory experience – which is shared with Kamala – immediately place us in the midst of the comic's narrative and its subject's experiences and struggles.

Elaborating on the reading experience, experts further suggest that the reader is more easily able to identify with cartoon characters: 'the cartoon is a vacuum into which our identity and awareness are pulled, an empty shell that we inhabit' or 'become', imaginatively and metaphorically.[20] Additionally, the iconic nature of comics and our ability to perceive an author's use of symbols while also recognizing our *own* understandings and presuppositions of these symbols enable the reader to 'read the symbolic representation in his or her own context, as well as the capacity to see the symbolic representation in the context of the author, or the symbolic representation in relationship within the created world of the narrative'.[21] This allows for multiple understandings, both familiar and new, that once again create a bridge between the author and reader – and their respective ideas – via the comic. For instance, one of the first characters that *Ms Marvel* readers are introduced to is Kamala's friend 'Proud Turkish Nakia', who happens to wear hijab.[22] While public opinion often perceives the hijab as a symbol of meekness, backwardness and oppression, the fashionable Nakia presents an image of a proud and assertive woman.[23] Seeing Nakia in the world of the comic forces readers to negotiate their own presuppositions towards hijab with the very different reality illustrated by the text.[24]

Having expended considerable effort and imagination negotiating with the text and moving the narrative forward, readers naturally become increasingly invested – psychologically, emotionally and physically – in the narrative and its characters, even if the characters happen to be Muslim. Indeed, according to Said, comics 'seemed to say what couldn't otherwise be said – perhaps what wasn't permitted to be said or imagined – defying the ordinary processes of thought, which are policed, shaped, and re-shaped by all sorts of pedagogical as well as ideological pressures'.[25] Comics thus become a 'site where individuals grapple with issues of ethics, meaning, and values; ... and explore both traditional and new religious traditions'.[26] In effect, comics enable us to think outside of the traditional discourse and allow for the possibility of a Muslim figure that is *not* dangerous or evil, not Other but *human*.

Muslims in American comics

To date, American superhero comics have largely been complicit in vilifying Arabs and Muslims.[27] Rebecca Hankins defines the 'various forms of speculative fiction by Muslim and non-Muslim writers who have used Islam and Muslims as characters, plots, or colorful backgrounds' as 'fictional Islam'.[28] Within the broad collection of fictional Islam, 'Muslim characters in the forms of villains, superheroes, minor characters, and sidekicks have been depicted in American comics since at least the 1940s'.²⁹ As Hankins highlights a long history among speculative fiction writers of 'treating Islam and Muslims as backwards, evil, and intolerant', she notes that in the wake of 9/11 and the subsequent US War on Terror, they have also 'embraced the plot device of Muslims-as-terrorists'.³⁰ Fredrik Stromberg adds that there has also been a definite shift towards incorporating more positive representations of Arabs and Muslims. Nonetheless, he argues the following:

> Although such characters seem to have been created to resist stereotypical or racist configurations of Arabs and/or Muslims as terrorists, they nonetheless partake in the 'Othering' of these groups in American public discourse through stereotypes in both visual and verbal communication, and thus often unintentionally reinforce rather than counteract stereotypes of the 'Oriental Other'.³¹

Thus, whether intentionally or not, contemporary depictions of Muslim superheroes in American comics often reiterate the demonizing and Othering effects of Islamophobia and Orientalism.

The prevalence of Islam and Muslims within comics, employed as both negative and positive plot devices, echoes the tendency towards a heightened *visibility* and racialization of Muslims that has been witnessed since 9/11. Two of the largest comic distributors, DC Comics and Marvel, have both introduced a number of Muslim superheroes and heroines: Dust, for instance, is a young refugee from Afghanistan and an observant Sunni Muslim who has the power to turn into a sandstorm and wreak havoc on her enemies, ripping the skin off their bones. Dust, or Sooraya Qadir, first appeared, fully dressed in a burqa, in Marvel's *New X-Men* in 2002.³² In 'finding a place for a Muslimah heroine in the post-9/11 Marvel Universe', Julie Davis and Robert Westerfelhaus recognize the creation of Dust's character in a world that is hostile towards Islam, both in and outside of the comic book, as a courageous move. Nevertheless, they suggest that 'Dust occupies a liminal state of perpetual separation from the society she serves';³³ she remains 'in, and yet not of, the Western world she now inhabits. ... What she eats, how she dresses, and other religiously-based practices separate Dust from contemporary American culture.'³⁴ Thus, she maintains the status of outsider among her superhero and mutant peers as well as her readers.

According to Davis and Westerfelhaus, Dust's religion is viewed through the 'lens of Western civilization in general, and American culture in particular'. While normally 'religion neither shapes character depictions nor drives plotlines', Dust's character serves to highlight herself and her Muslim faith as exotic, radical and Other:

> This orientalizing impulse exploits alien aspects of the material culture and ritual practices associated with religions that differ from the Judeo-Christian tradition that has historically dominated the American mainstream. ... Highlighting Dust's religion emphasizes how Islamic identity renders her radically different from her colleagues and the culture to which they belong.[35]

The orientalizing and exotic characterization of Dust is particularly highlighted in the depiction of the religious dress that she wears. Dust repeatedly defends her modest dress, which is typically drawn as loose and flowing, saying that it protects her from the male gaze. Nevertheless, she also appears in a number of images in 'good girl' style – also described as 1940s'-style pornography – wherein 'superheroines are depicted as "wannabe centerfolds with back-arching breasts, tiny waists, and skintight costumes or extremely short skirts that reveal what's underneath whenever the heroine takes a tumble"'.[36] Ultimately, Dust remains subject to a male gaze, particularly a Western male gaze that is able to see beneath her attempts at modesty.[37]

A certain level of outward and visible difference characterizes both Dust and Kamala. As evidenced by the forbidden yet tempting bacon sandwich, the question of whether her friend Nakia wears hijab by choice or by force and whether she can or will go to a party where alcohol will be served, Kamala is grappling with her Muslim and American identities. She sees herself as different and craves normalcy: 'Why am I the only one who gets *signed out of health class*? Why do I have to bring *pakoras* to school for lunch? Why am I stuck with the *weird holidays*? Everybody else gets to be *normal*.' As she sneaks outside her bedroom window to go to the party, she asks herself, 'Why can't I?'[38] However, despite Kamala's difference and yearnings she is a relatively 'normal' teenager and more importantly a *human* character with whom readers can identify. In an interview about her character Kamala, the Muslim American author Willow Wilson comments, 'The struggles, bonds, affections and ideals that Kamala and her family share will be familiar to all readers. This is a human story, not just one about a specific minority group.'[39] Despite the universal aspects of Kamala's experiences, however, this remains *her* story, one that is very much shaped by her unique circumstances, her Muslim faith and her Pakistani roots.[40] As the title of *Ms Marvel, Volume 1: No Normal* suggests, we cannot allow notions of what is 'normal' to inhibit our selves and our actions; in order to remain true to herself, Kamala must embrace all that makes her different. In turn, readers are asked to see and appreciate both the different *and* the familiar, to find the familiar *in* the different and vice versa.

Kamala's character is distinctly different from that of Dust, whose religious-based practices alienate her from the contemporary American culture that surrounds her; Dust is unable to breach this barrier as she simply *is* different and will always remain so, isolated and alone. Conversely, Kamala is both Muslim *and* American. Moreover, her difference is one that she constantly grapples with and eventually embraces over the course of the issues. Far from being isolated by her difference, like Dust, Kamala is surrounded by family and friends, both Muslim and non-Muslim. Additionally, her infatuation with comics and superheroes reflects her inclusion or participation in American pop culture. Moreover, she has her own comic; in the male-dominated world of superheroes, this is an honour afforded to a select number of females that now includes a Muslim Pakistani American girl.

Crossroads and outcasts

Kamala's conflicted identity as a Muslim American coincides with the tradition of superheroes' dual identity. Costello observes, 'Since Superman, superheroes have generally had dual identities – they have been both civilians and superheroes.'[41] He contends that it is the most basic element of superhero comics: every superhero has a distinct story and is grappling with specific issues, in a manner that exposes readers to diverse aspects and concerns of society. The co-creator of Kamala's storyline, Sana Amanat, refers to the narrative as a Spider-Man story:

> [*Spider-Man*] was about a young teenager struggling to fit in, and the obligations that come with trying to be an adult and find yourself. The connection you have and respect you feel toward your family … . His struggles are the balance between his superhero life and his home life, and the guilt he feels about his uncle. [Khan's] are about her identity struggles. Her trying to find herself. They're told through different perspectives, but it's two very similar kind of arcs.[42]

The 'societal identity crisis' that is suggested by the tension between Kamala and other superheroes' public duty as heroes and their private role as civilians is complicated by Kamala's Muslim American identity.[43] The traditional identity crisis of heroes becomes a means of furthering our understanding of the similar crisis that afflicts Muslim Americans (particularly young people and children of immigrants). As readers, we witness the challenge of being in an environment where being Muslim means that you are in a minority; adherence to the Muslim faith makes Kamala and her Muslim family and friends *visibly* different. In the opening scene, after closely eyeing the forbidden BLT sandwich, Zoe invites Kamala and Nakia to a party on the waterfront, adding, 'If, uh, you're *allowed* to do that kind of stuff'. Nakia with her head turned, physically rejecting the idea, responds self-assuredly, 'I'm not going if there's going to be *alcohol*'. Kamala, on the other hand, appears dejected and replies, 'Yeah, I'm *not* allowed'. When Zoe pretends to compliment Nakia on her hijab or headscarf, she adds, 'But I mean ... nobody *pressured* you to start wearing it, right? Your father or somebody? Nobody's going to like *honor kill* you? I'm just *concerned*.' As Kamala peers from behind her fingers with a look of embarrassment, Nakia is unfazed by the backhanded insult and clearly unconvinced by Zoe's supposed concern; with a look of irritation, she replies, 'Actually, my dad wants me to take it off. He thinks it's a *phase*.'[44] In this revealing exchange, Nakia is proud and confident, unwavering in her beliefs and expressing clearly that it is *her* choice to wear the hijab just as it is her decision *not* to drink alcohol or attend parties where it will be served. Kamala on the other hand resents the fact that she is not *allowed* to join the party. Oblivious of Zoe's hostility, she notes, 'But she's so *nice* ... she's so adorable and *happy!*', expressing her admiration for Zoe and a desire to be 'blond and popular' like her.[45] Throughout the story, we witness Kamala continuing to struggle with the need to be accepted and the challenge of embracing the culture and beliefs that set her apart. Eventually, what is initially a source of annoyance and embarrassment becomes a source of pride and superhero strength.

Wilson observes that, like Kamala, 'all teenagers go through a period of self-definition, in which they try to decide what paths their lives will take. ... So there's an element of universality there.'[46] Kamala reaches this crossroads shortly after she attends the party – forbidden by her father – where she does indeed encounter 'strange' boys and drinking, as her father feared. After a brief time at the party, Kamala is duped into drinking a sip of orange juice mixed with vodka, and she promptly spits it out. Although she comes to the party seeking acceptance by the popular kids, she is unwilling to defy or abandon her faith; this refusal to blend in makes her unacceptable as Zoe immediately comments, 'Ugh, Kamala – no offense, but you smell like curry. I'm gonna stand somewhere else.' As Kamala and her friend Bruno walk away, in the background we can see Zoe laughing and the other 'popular' kids smiling in amusement and doing a triumphant chest bump, pleased with their prank and insults. After a brief argument with Bruno, Kamala walks away in anger, concluding to herself, 'I can never be one of them, no matter how hard I try. I'll always be poor Kamala with the weird *food rules* and the *crazy family*.'[47]

On her way home, she is intercepted by the beautiful, tall, blond, blue-eyed Captain Marvel (formerly Ms Marvel), accompanied by Captain America and Iron Man; the three classic, all-American superheroes arrive singing – in Urdu – about a yellow mustard seed and mango bud that are blooming. Kamala is at a crossroads and these three superheroes are staging an intervention; in the disapproving words of Captain America, 'You thought that if you disobeyed your parents – your culture, your religion – your classmates would *accept* you.'[48] He aptly addresses Kamala's desire for normalcy, to *not* be different, at the expense of defying her parents, culture and religion. There is a direct connection between where Kamala stands in terms of these three elements, her defiance of them and the superpowers and superhero status she is granted – arguably as a chance to reassess the decisions she is making and determine which direction she will take at this crossroads in life.

Interestingly, when Kamala questions their ability to speak Urdu, the superheroes identify themselves by declaring, 'We are *faith*. We speak all languages of beauty and hardship.'[49] This moment epitomizes the visual representation and physical embodiment of faith. Further, the scene is a manifestation of her unique desires and background, as the all-American superheroes whom Kamala idolizes come to her aid. While they appear in their traditional guise, they are also singing in Urdu and claiming to *be* faith; without tension or contradiction, they present a rich image that is filled with pride and strength. Addressing her inner conflicts, they mirror the complexity and multiplicity of her own character while suggesting the powerful potential that lies in embracing it. Notably, the moment of the three heroes' arrival is depicted as an annunciation scene, an interesting move that further explicates the sanctity and intersectionality of this moment.[50] Iron Man tells Kamala, 'You are seeing what you *need* to see.'[51] Thus, the physical, outward, visible extensions of faith become a *necessity*. In the same way that they are a necessity within the tradition of Islam itself, where we see an interesting dialectic between the interior and exterior, between an individual's inner faith in God and her outward deeds and physical acts of worship, submission to God extends to the believer's heart, mind, body and surroundings. On a foundational level, a traditionally observant Muslim believes and thus she also prays five times a day, fasts during Ramadan, pays her *zakat* and wears hijab.[52]

In the text, we see this relationship between religious faith and its visible application. After she is abruptly introduced to her supernatural powers, Kamala witnesses from a distance Zoe fall into the water; both Zoe and her boyfriend are drunk and Zoe is in danger of drowning. Kamala is processing the situation and recalls, 'There's this ayah from the *Quran* that my dad always quotes when he sees something *bad* on TV. A fire or a flood or a bombing. Whoever kills one person, it is as if he has killed all of mankind.' Then, with a look of determination on her face, 'and whoever *saves* one person, it is as if he has *saved all of mankind*.'[53] And she rushes to the rescue. In another scene, she reflects, 'Ammi and Abu taught me to always think about the *greater good*. To defend people who can't defend themselves, even if it means putting yourself at *risk*.'[54] In moments of crisis, we witness a return to elements that she had previously defied, her parents and her religion, and it is these that guide her heroic actions. Furthermore, the tensions between Kamala's public and private personas, the struggle between her Muslim and American aspects, are reconciled in a moment of overlap where one completes the other; as she assumes her American superhero role as Ms Marvel, her actions are guided by the Muslim faith that she learns to embrace. Notably, on the cover of the comic, Kamala is depicted holding three books: in the centre is *Hadith to Live By*, illustrating her commitment to Islam and the Prophetic tradition that is a primary source of guidance for Muslims after the Qur'an; *US History*, in testament to the Americanness of the trials of her character and her inherent participation in the fabric of American history and culture; and *Illustration and Design*, suggesting her individual expression of the multifaceted aspects that make up who she is, including a Muslim American, the daughter of Pakistani immigrants, a high school student and a fan fiction writer.

One of the most visible and crucial means by which Kamala comes to terms with her difference and identity as Muslim, Pakistani, American and female is through the development of her costume. This aligns with Costello's claim that costume changes mirror character development. He describes the function of the costume as a defining element: '[The] costume, representing the identity of the hero, is frequently tied to the origin of the hero's powers and thus is closely linked to the identity of the hero *as* hero.'[55] When Kamala is visited by the superheroes, she tells Captain Marvel, 'I want to be you. … Except I would wear the classic, politically incorrect costume and kick butt in giant wedge heels.'[56] And when she first transforms into Ms Marvel, she does indeed take on the tall, white, blonde image in a form-fitting, sleeveless and thigh-baring costume. It doesn't take long for her to get disenchanted with the costume: 'The hair gets in my face, the boots pinch … and this leotard is giving me an *epic wedgie*.'[57] Eventually, she makes the conscious decision to retain her natural appearance and use a burkini – her Islamic swimsuit, which her mother unearths from her closet – as her superhero costume. This physical transformation is a reflection of how she makes the title of Ms Marvel her own, rather than becoming 'a watered-down version of some other hero', as she describes.[58] Thus, her costume does indeed come to reflect critical aspects of her identity and origins.

Conclusion: Defying boundaries

Ms Marvel's physical embodiment of her identity, who *she* is, is further highlighted by the nature of her superpowers. She describes herself as 'a shape-changing, mask-wearing, sixteen year old *super "Moozlim"* from Jersey City'.[59] Willow Wilson explains the choice to make Kamala a shape-shifter:

> Shape-shifters are most often cast as bad guys and I think it reflects something telling about our society. We are very suspicious of people with multiple pieces to their identity. We really want to put people in neat little boxes and we become hostile to people who don't fit into those boxes.[60]

Thus, Kamala reclaims the identity of shape-shifters – the intersectionality and cultural interpenetration that mark Muslim Americans – as something good, admirable and desirable. The new American superhero is a female, Pakistani, American and Muslim. Multilayered and transcending boundaries that have been otherwise imposed by a racialized and Islamophobic discourse, Kamala indeed does not fit into one neat little box, and she successfully challenges the notion that we should be suspicious of her because of it. Maryanne Rhett writes in 'Orientalism and Graphic Novels: A Modern Reexamination of Popular Culture':

> A brief overview of early American comic book authors, illustrators, and publishers suggests that the comic book industry became what it is today, the voice of the voiceless, because so many of its founding figures were themselves outsiders, i.e. Jewish, communists/socialists, Avant-garde, etc. In time, the frustrations of the outcast author and artist found their way into the medium.[61]

This history of American comics highlights the *outsider* and *outcast* status of both the author-artists and their characters. Rhett continues to describe a more visible and concerted effort on behalf of outcast authors to manipulate the prevalent discourse and the knowledge of others that has hitherto been constructed:

> The modern comic book and graphic novel market, provides a newer, more attractive space for the … tradition of popular culture manipulating knowledge of 'others' as well as for adding depth to collective understandings of who and

what those others are. Even more exciting, the 'others' themselves are claiming the genre and repurposing it to meet their own needs; to tell their own story. The comic book and graphic novel industry is offering a paradigm shift.[62]

As this 'paradigm shift' is articulated, outcast authors are telling outcast stories. *Ms Marvel* represents a critical effort by Muslim Americans – namely writer Willow Wilson and Marvel editor Sana Amanat – to recast the narrative of Muslims in America in their *own* voices. It is this that makes the specificity of Kamala's character both possible and believable. 'Fans treat her like a fully realized person, one whose ethnicity is just part of the deal', writes *Village Voice* contributor Mallika Rao. She further describes *Ms Marvel* as one of Marvel's most successful series, rising to the top shortly after it was first published. Amanat elaborates, 'You get to know Kamala Khan through the fact that she really wants to eat a BLT and she would really like to have her first kiss. And then you get to know that yeah, she's a Muslim. She goes to mosque.'[63] Hence, it is Kamala's 'ordinary' Muslim American life that makes her real to her readers and gains her entry into their homes and hearts.

As evidenced in the case of *Ms Marvel*, comics present effective 'vehicles with which to engage others while also providing an avenue to facilitate a more comprehensive understanding of Islam'.[64] The powerful potential of comics and the superhero as icon was further illustrated in January 2015, when Kamala Khan literally took to the streets fighting a series of Islamophobic advertisements on San Francisco city buses that were sponsored by the anti-Muslim group the Freedom Defense Initiative (see Figures 11.1 and 11.2).

Figure 11.1 'Calling all Bigotry Busters'.

Figure 11.2 'Stamp Out Racism'.

Artists responded to this campaign by covering the advertisements with images of Ms Marvel, accompanied by messages calling out hate and bigotry: 'Calling All Bigotry Busters', 'Stamp Out Racism' and 'Free Speech Isn't a License to Spread Hate'.[65] The hybrid nature of the comic enables *Ms Marvel* to complicate the homogenizing and monolithic discourse on Muslims that exists today by extending beyond the boundaries of the text to offer a humanizing image of community and intermingling differences. Kamala's humanity, intersectionality and Muslim connectedness within the Marvel Universe make her a powerful and fitting icon in the fight for social justice *outside* of it, in the real world.

Notes

1 Edward W. Said, *Covering Islam: How the Media and the Experts Determine How We See the Rest of the World* (New York: Vintage, 1997), p. ix.
2 Junaid Rana, *Terrifying Muslims: Race and Labor in the South Asian Diaspora* (Durham, NC: Duke University Press, 2011), p. 50.
3 Peter Morey and Amina Yaqin, *Framing Muslims: Stereotyping and Representation after 9/11* (Cambridge, MA: Harvard University Press, 2011), p. 3.
4 *Reel Bad Arabs: How Hollywood Vilifies a People*, film, dir. Sut Jhally, perf. Jack Shaheen. USA: Media Education Foundation. 2006. It is important to note that, according to a 2011 study by the Pew Research Center, 'negative views about Muslims, discrimination and ignorance about Islam top the list of the problems Muslim Americans say they face' (p. 46). Additionally, 'a 55% majority of Muslim Americans

think that coverage of Islam and Muslims by American news organizations is generally unfair' (p. 51). See Pew Research Center, Muslim Americans: No Signs of Growth in Alienation or Support for Extremism (August 2011). Available at http://assets.pewresearch.org/wp-content/uploads/sites/5/legacy-pdf/Muslim%20American%20Report%2010-02-12%20fix.pdf (accessed 31 January 2015).
5   Morey and Yaqin, *Framing Muslims*, p. 3.
6   Moustafa Bayoumi, *This Muslim American Life: Dispatches from the War on Terror* (New York: New York University Press, 2015), p. 141.
7   Bayoumi, *This Muslim American Life*, p. 130.
8   Morey and Yaqin, *Framing Muslims*, p. 207.
9   Matthew Costello, *Secret Identity Crisis: Comic Books and the Unmasking of Cold War America* (New York: Continuum, 2009), p. 15.
10 Costello, *Secret Identity Crisis*, p. 15.
11 Derek Parker Royal, 'Drawing attention: Comics as a means of approaching US cultural diversity', in Lan Dong (ed.), *Teaching Comics and Graphic Narratives: Essays on Theory, Strategy and Practice* (Jefferson, NC: McFarland and Co., 2012), pp. 67–79; p. 67.
12 Royal, 'Drawing attention', p. 69.
13 Rana, *Terrifying Muslims*, pp. 63–5.
14 Douglas Rushkoff, 'Foreword: Looking for God in the gutter', in David A. Lewis and Christine Hoff Kraemer (eds), *Graven Images: Religion in Comic Books and Graphic Novels* (New York: Continuum International Publishing, 2010), p. x.
15 Rushkoff, 'Foreword', p. x.
16 Ibid.
17 Ibid.
18 Darby Orcutt, 'Comics and religion: Theoretical connections', in Lewis and Kraemer, *Graven Images*, pp. 94, 97.
19 G. Willow Wilson and Adrian Alphona, *Ms Marvel*, Vol. 1: No Normal (New York: Marvel, 2014).
20 McCloud quoted in Orcutt, 'Comics and religion', p. 95.
21 Andrew Tripp, 'Killing the graven god: Visual representations of the divine in comics', in Lewis and Kraemer, *Graven Images*, p. 117.
22 Wilson, *Ms Marvel*.
23 In science fiction literature, women in hijab are frequently characterized as 'victimized, oppressed, enslaved, abused, and/or brainwashed, and – most crucial to propelling the narrative and to engaging the western woman reader's sense of superiority – in need of liberation'. See Rebecca Hankins and Joyce Thornton, 'The influence of Muslims and Islam in science fiction, fantasy, and comics', in Iraj Omidvar and Anne R. Richards (eds), *Muslims and American Popular Culture, Vol. 2: Print Culture and Identity* (Santa Barbara, CA: Praeger 2014), p. 328.

24 As Haddad et al. point out, 'The hijab is viewed by Americans – as a symbol of cultural difference (and thus inferiority), a threat to secularity, or simply as a personal expression of religiosity – it frames the female body as an icon of the "clash of civilizations" and has far-reaching political and social implications.' See Yvonne Yasbeck Haddad, Jane I. Smith and Kathleen M. Moore, *Muslim Women in America: The Challenge of Islamic Identity Today* (New York: Oxford University Press, 2006), p. 39.
25 Edward Said, 'Introduction: Homage to Joe Sacco', in Joe Sacco, *Palestine* (Seattle, WA: Fantagraphics, 2001), pp. i–v; p. ii.
26 Lewis and Kraemer, *Graven Images*, p. 3.
27 This chapter specifically focuses on the presence of Muslims in American superhero comics. There is a significant number of superhero comics published in the Middle East, such as Naif Al-Mutawa's *The 99*, which have attained varying degrees of success in terms of countering or reifying the existing discourse on Muslims.
28 Rebecca Hankins and Joyce Thornton describe the long-standing influence and presence of Muslims and Islam in science fiction, fantasy and comics. According to the sci-fi writer Isaac Asimov, science fiction can never truly exist until 'the rationalism of science' is understood and applied in stories accordingly; thus, Hankins argues that there is a direct correlation between the wide range of advancements across the sciences that are attributed to Muslims and the 'expansion of the literary heritage of science fiction, fantasy, and speculative writing as a whole' (Rebecca Hankins and Joyce Thornton, 'The influence of Muslims and Islam in science fiction, fantasy, and comics', in Iraj Omidvar and Ann R. Richards (eds), *Muslims and American Popular Culture Vol. 2: Print Culture and Identity* (Santa Barbara, CA: Praeger, 2014), p. 74). Considering this historic Muslim influence in science fiction, it is perhaps appropriate that Muslim Americans should engage in the continued development of the field via comics by contributing their own outcast stories.
29 Hankins and Thornton, 'The influence of Muslims', p. 335.
30 Ibid., p. 331.
31 Fredrik Stromberg, '"Yo, rag-head!": Arab and Muslim superheroes in American comic books after 9/11', *Amerikastudien / American Studies* 56/4 (2011), pp. 573–601; p. 573. Available at http://www.jstor.org/stable/23509430 (accessed 6 April 2015).
32 Grant Morrison, *New X-Men*, Vol. 1, no. 133 (New York: Marvel, 2002).
33 Julie Davis and Robert Westerfelhaus, 'Finding a place for a Muslimah heroine in the post-9/11 Marvel Universe', *Feminist Media Studies* 13/5 (2013), pp. 800–9; p. 805. Available at http://dx.doi.org/10.1080/14680777.2013.838370 (accessed 5 April 2015).
34 Davis and Westerfelhaus, 'Finding a place', pp. 800–1.
35 Ibid., pp. 800–2.
36 Ibid., p. 802.
37 Jehanzeb Dar, 'Female, Muslim, and mutant: Muslim women in comic books (1)', *AltMuslimah*, 26 November 2014. Available at www.altmuslimah.com/2014/11/

female-muslim-and-mutant-muslim-women-in-comic-books-1/ (accessed 19 February 2015).
38 Wilson, *Ms Marvel*.
39 'New Marvel hero is Muslim teen', *Islamic Horizons* (January/February 2014), pp. 42–3. Available at https://issuu.com/isnacreative/docs/ih_jan-feb_14 (accessed 10 May 2015).
40 Miriam Kent notes that, while Ms Marvel highlights the intersectional experience of Kamala Khan and her unique subjectivity, critics have overlooked her specific experience of difference in favour of aspects that suggest her relatability and universality as a character. See Miriam Kent, 'Unveiling Marvels: Ms Marvel and the reception of the new Muslim superheroine', *Feminist Media Studies* 15/3 (2015), pp. 522–7.
41 Costello, *Secret Identity Crisis*, p. 18.
42 Mallika Rao, 'Ms Marvel will save you now', *Village Voice*, 5 October 2016. Available at www.villagevoice.com/2016/10/05/ms-marvel-will-save-you-now/ (accessed 2 May 2018).
43 Rao, 'Ms Marvel will save you now', p. 19.
44 Wilson, *Ms Marvel*.
45 Ibid.
46 Islamic Horizons, 'New Marvel hero'.
47 Wilson, *Ms Marvel*.
48 Ibid.
49 Ibid.
50 The Annunciation is described in the Qur'an: '[And mention] when the angels said, "O Mary, indeed Allah gives you good tidings of a word from Him, whose name will be the Messiah, Jesus, the son of Mary – distinguished in this world and the Hereafter and among those brought near [to Allah]"' (Noble Qur'an, Ali 'Imran 3.45).
51 Wilson, *Ms Marvel*.
52 'The five pillars of Islam (arkan al-Islam; also arkan al-din, "pillars of religion") comprise five official acts considered obligatory for all Muslims. The *Qur'an* presents them as a framework for worship and a sign of commitment to faith. The five pillars are the shahadah (witnessing the oneness of God and the prophethood of Muhammad), regular observance of the five prescribed daily prayers (salat), paying zakah (almsgiving), fasting (sawm; siyyam) during the month of Ramadan, and performance of the hajj (pilgrimage during the prescribed month) at least once in a lifetime'. See 'Pillars of Islam', in John L. Esposito (ed.), *The Oxford Dictionary of Islam* (Oxford: Oxford University Press, 2003). Available at http://www.oxfordislamicstudies.com/ Public/book_odi.html (accessed 9 October 2016).
53 Wilson, *Ms Marvel*.

54 Ibid.
55 Costello, *Secret Identity Crisis*, p. 19.
56 Wilson, *Ms Marvel*.
57 Ibid.
58 Ibid.
59 Ibid.
60 Jessica Holland, 'Is it a bird? Is it a plane? No – It's super Muslim', *The National: Arts and Lifestyle*, 5 February 2014. Available at www.thenational.ae/arts-culture/books/is-it-a-bird-is-it-a-plane-no-it-s-super-muslim-1.446700 (accessed 2 May 2018).
61 Maryanne Rhett, 'Orientalism and graphic novels: A modern reexamination of popular culture', in Richard Iadonisi (ed.), *Graphic History: Essays on Graphic Novels and/as History* (Cambridge: Cambridge Scholars Press, 2012), pp. 203–22; p. 207.
62 Rhett, 'Orientalism and graphic novels', p. 221.
63 Rao, 'Ms Marvel will save you now'.
64 Hankins and Thornton, 'Influence of Muslims', p. 324.
65 Andrea Letamendi, 'Meet the Muslim superhero fighting bigotry on San Francisco buses', *Guardian*, 1 February 2015. Available at https://www.theguardian.com/books/2015/feb/01/meet-the-muslim-superhero-fighting-bigotry-on-san-francisco-buses (accessed 10 October 2016).

Works cited

Bayoumi, Moustafa, *This Muslim American Life: Dispatches from the War on Terror* (New York: New York University Press, 2015).
Costello, Matthew, *Secret Identity Crisis: Comic Books and the Unmasking of Cold War America* (New York: Continuum, 2009).
Dar, Jehanzeb, 'Female, Muslim, and mutant: Muslim women in comic books (1)', *AltMuslimah*, 26 November 2014. Available at www.altmuslimah.com/2014/11/female-muslim-and-mutant-muslim-women-in-comic-books-1/ (accessed 19 February 2015).
Davis, Julie and Robert Westerfelhaus, 'Finding a place for a Muslimah heroine in the post-9/11 Marvel Universe', *Feminist Media Studies* 13/5 (2013), pp. 800–9. Available at http://dx.doi.org/10.1080/14680777.2013.838370 (accessed 5 April 2015).
Esposito, John L. (ed.), *The Oxford Dictionary of Islam* (Oxford: Oxford University Press, 2003). Available at http://www.oxfordislamicstudies.com/Public/book_odi.html (accessed 9 October 2016).
Haddad, Yvonne Yasbeck, Jane I. Smith and Kathleen M. Moore, *Muslim Women in America: The Challenge of Islamic Identity Today* (New York: Oxford University Press, 2006).

Hankins, Rebecca and Joyce Thornton, 'The influence of Muslims and Islam in science fiction, fantasy, and comics', in Iraj Omidvar and Anne R. Richards (eds), *Muslims and American Popular Culture, Vol. 2: Print Culture and Identity*(Santa Barbara, CA: Praeger, 2014), pp. 323–48.

Holland, Jessica, 'Is it a bird? Is it a plane? No – It's super Muslim', *The National: Arts and Lifestyle*, 5 February 2014. Available at www.thenational.ae/arts-culture/books/is-it-a-bird-is-it-a-plane-no-it-s-super-muslim-1.446700 (accessed 2 May 2018).

Islamic Horizons, 'New Marvel hero is Muslim teen', *Islamic Horizons* (January/February 2014), pp. 42–3. Available at https://issuu.com/isnacreative/docs/ih_jan-feb_14 (accessed 10 May 2015).

Kent, Miriam, 'Unveiling Marvels: *Ms Marvel* and the reception of the new Muslim superheroine', *Feminist Media Studies* 15/3 (2015), pp. 522–7.

Letamendi, Andrea, 'Meet the Muslim superhero fighting bigotry on San Francisco buses', *Guardian*, 1 February 2015. Available at https://www.theguardian.com/books/2015/feb/01/meet-the-muslim-superhero-fighting-bigotry-on-san-francisco-buses (accessed 10 October 2016).

Lewis, David A. and Christine Hoff Kraemer (eds), *Graven Images: Religion in Comic Books and Graphic Novels* (New York: Continuum International Publishing, 2010).

Morey, Peter and Amina Yaqin, *Framing Muslims: Stereotyping and Representation after 9/11* (Cambridge, MA: Harvard University Press, 2011).

Morrison, Grant, *New X-Men*. Vol. 1, no. 133 (New York: Marvel, 2002).

Orcutt, Darby, 'Comics and religion: Theoretical connections', in David A. Lewis and Christine Hoff Kraemer (eds), *Graven Images: Religion in Comic Books and Graphic Novels* (New York: Continuum International Publishing, 2010), pp. 93–106.

Pew Research Center, *Muslim Americans: No Signs of Growth in Alienation or Support for Extremism* (August 2011). Available at http://assets.pewresearch.org/wp-content/uploads/sites/5/legacy-pdf/Muslim%20American%20Report%2010-02-12%20fix.pdf (accessed 31 January 2015).

Rana, Junaid, *Terrifying Muslims: Race and Labor in the South Asian Diaspora* (Durham, NC: Duke University Press, 2011).

Rao, Mallika, 'Ms Marvel will save you now', *Village Voice*, 5 October 2016. Available at www.villagevoice.com/2016/10/05/ms-marvel-will-save-you-now/ (accessed 2 May 2018).

Rhett, Maryanne, 'Orientalism and graphic novels: A modern reexamination of popular culture', in Richard Iadonisi (ed.), *Graphic History: Essays on Graphic Novels and/as History* (Cambridge: Cambridge Scholars Press, 2012), pp. 203–22.

Royal, Derek Parker, 'Drawing attention: Comics as a means of approaching US cultural diversity', in Lan Dong (ed.), *Teaching Comics and Graphic Narratives: Essays on Theory, Strategy and Practice* (Jefferson, NC: McFarland and Co., 2012), pp. 67–79.

Rushkoff, Douglas, 'Foreword: Looking for God in the gutter', in David A. Lewis and Christine Hoff Kraemer (eds), *Graven Images: Religion in Comic Books and Graphic Novels* (New York: Continuum International Publishing, 2010), p. x.

Said, Edward W., *Covering Islam: How the Media and the Experts Determine How We See the Rest of the World* (New York: Vintage, 1997).

Said, Edward W. 'Introduction: Homage to Joe Sacco', in Joe Sacco, *Palestine* (Seattle, WA: Fantagraphics, 2001), pp. i–v.

Shaheen, Jack, *Reel Bad Arabs: How Hollywood Vilifies a People*, Film, dir. Sut Jhally. USA: Media Education Foundation, 2006.

Stromberg, Fredrik, '"Yo, rag-head!": Arab and Muslim superheroes in American comic books after 9/11', *Amerikastudien / American Studies* 56/4 (2011), pp. 573–601. Available at http://www.jstor.org/stable/23509430 (accessed 6 April 2015).

Tripp, Andrew, 'Killing the graven god: Visual representations of the divine in comics', in David A. Lewis and Christine Hoff Kraemer (eds), *Graven Images: Religion in Comic Books and Graphic Novels* (New York: Continuum International Publishing, 2010), pp. 107–20.

Wilson, G. Willow and Adrian Alphona, *Ms Marvel, Vol. 1: No Normal* (New York: Marvel, 2014).

12

Homegrown: The Story of a Controversy

Nadia Latif, interviewed by Peter Morey and Amina Yaqin

In 2015, the National Youth Theatre commissioned the Palestinian Turkish playwright Omar El-Khairy and the British Sudanese director Nadia Latif to devise a play about young people being drawn towards Islamist extremism in the light of the so-called 'Trojan horse' story, where radicalization of children was claimed to be taking place in Birmingham schools. Recognizing the loaded cultural assumptions in the commission, El-Khairy and Latif set about creating a complex, multifaceted in situ piece with a cast of over 100 young people aged between fourteen and eighteen, which would test some of the commonplace assumptions swirling around Muslim youth today. The play, *Homegrown*, was designed to be performed in a school, with the actors shepherding audiences from classroom to classroom to hear snippets of scenes reflecting the variety and complexity of discourse around Muslims to which young people are exposed every day.

However, two weeks before the performance was due to start its run, the National Youth Theatre pulled the play, citing a sequence of shifting reasons including safeguarding issues, police intervention, even quality concerns. Amid growing suspicion that this challenging play – which deals with a wide array of viewpoints, avoids conventional resolution and deliberately eschews any edifying 'message' – had been subject to censorship, the controversy played out in the national press.

Here, Nadia Latif describes the experiences she went through in her attempts to have the play staged and published. In the process, she reflects on the position of minority ethnic artists in an industry still dominated by white, middle-class males, and on the particular sensitivities around Islam of which *Homegrown* apparently fell foul. The fate of *Homegrown* tells us something about the limits of the framing discourse that encircles Muslims today, not least when they attempt to represent themselves. As such, it perhaps offers a lesson in the real-world cost of contesting Islamophobia.

* * *

PM and AY: Please tell us about how *Homegrown* came to be commissioned.

NL: Me and Omar were actually working on a different project, an adaptation of an Ibsen play, *Rosmersholm*, which we were going to set in Saudi Arabia in the 1960s and it was going to be about the rise of Wahhabism. And he got this email from the National Youth Theatre (NYT) saying, 'We've got an idea for a play about the radicalization of young British Muslims, specifically looking at the Birmingham Trojan Horse affair', and they wanted it to be large-scale, site-specific and, at the time, the email said (and this is brilliant), it said, 'We are looking for two writers: one British and one Muslim'. And Omar wrote back saying, 'That's all well and good, but which one am I?' And so he went in for a meeting and when he came back and I saw him the next day he was like, 'I don't think they really know what they're talking about. I think they think they can do Islam and radicalization in the same way you can do sexting or underage drug-taking, just something that's a bit contentious.' I was like, 'Well … you could turn it into something cool. The advantage of people not knowing what they're talking about is that you can be on the front foot and go, alright, I'm going to tell you what it is you should be doing.'

Anyway, the next day I got an email saying, 'Would you like to direct it?' [laughs]. And I had never worked with NYT, I had never really heard of them at that stage because I was never part of youth theatre or anything like that, not having grown up in this country. So I went in for a meeting with the NYT and I sort of said exactly the same thing as Omar said, which was like, 'In theory yes, but we need to come up with a new take on it.' Mainly that was to do with the fact that NYT is not particularly diverse. It makes all of these attempts to diversify its membership, but it's predominantly white. And so, to me, it was very difficult to square with the Trojan Horse affair where you're looking at a predominantly Muslim community in a predominantly Muslim school. Well, you can imagine them thinking, we need to find a way to tell that story that empowers white people to talk about it. Anyway, they said, 'Great, cool, fine! Why don't you guys have a couple of weeks? We'll give you some actors and you can come up with a new idea.' So we did.

PM and AY: How did you decide on your approach?

NL: At that stage we really didn't know what we were going to write [laughs]. We've just talked a big game, but we're not sure what our way into it is. But they had given us a fairly clear brief, which was, it has to be set in a school. And I said, alright. So we had this idea of a school and we were like, what do schools do? They do school plays. And so then we had this idea of a play within a play.

So we started with a formal experiment, looking at representation and who gets to speak on the behalf of people. We realized we were taking this much broader scope, which was really about understanding the new hierarchies of culture. Fifty years ago we might have a conversation about black or Irish, or black and Asian, you know what I mean, and actually when we start to move that around again, and how it intersects with LGBT communities and all of those things, and poverty, we thought actually what does the new cultural hierarchy in London in 2015, at the time, look like? And where do Muslims fit into that?

So then we had this idea, which was based on our mutual love for Spike Lee's film *Bamboozled*. I don't know if you've seen it, but it's about minstrel shows and there's this scene in it with this black actor meticulously applying whiteface makeup. I think it is one of the best scenes in cinema. And so I became really interested in taking this idea of white people speaking on behalf of Muslims and also of them playing Muslims – you see them doing it in cinema all the time – and somehow putting that in the show. And so the first four sections of the verbatims are real, that's real interviews we did with people, and the kids wrote the fake verbatim for the end, where they pretend to be Muslims in the community and transform themselves physically on stage, and it is grotesque and cartoonish and none of them know what they're doing because none of them are really comfortable with it.

Anyway, so we got the idea signed off. Started writing it. We started casting, which was a really lengthy process. I think I saw probably 400 actors and brought it down to 120. And they were great! So we started doing movement workshops. We knew we'd have ten guides shepherding the audience around the rooms and the stories would be named after the actors that were playing them.

We had an office at NYT and we would go there every day, trying to write twelve hours a day. So we went through the drafting processes and we got some notes back. Some of them are good, some of them are useless. That was a fairly standard process. And then the NYT made a season announcement and obviously our show was the jewel in the crown because it was the largest thing they'd ever attempted to do. And actually what was really unusual is that they were giving it a long run. Normally they would do it for three days and we were running for three weeks or something. Pretty impressive running a show with 120 actors for three weeks! And I also think they were sort of proud of it, they were sort of like, 'Oh, we've got this thing that we sort of don't understand.' And actually you've got to appreciate that.

PM and AY: What about the venues, because you had some difficulties with those, didn't you?

NL: Originally, NYT were like, we're going to do it at the Chelsea School of Art, but they were sort of looking at various venues and so we became involved in looking at venues too. There were schools everywhere. We saw them in Camden, in south London – I probably went to a million schools. And then we happened on a school in Bethnal Green which was perfect. It was just physically perfect. It had this really old bit, because it had something to do with the foundling movement – so this old Victorian block and then this ultra-modern, brand new block in orange and green, and these amazing bridges that linked to it. And already by then we knew we were going to have five plays running simultaneously and the audience wouldn't see each other and that you'd have to have one space that was big enough. So I said, 'It's perfect!' But then, at the same time, the three girls from Bethnal Green went to join ISIS and actually our instinct was to move, to go somewhere else because we didn't want to be ambulance chasers.

Anyway, we cast. The season press announcement came and the artistic director very ill-advisedly gave an interview to the *Guardian* at which we were not present, which is really bad practice besides anything else, where he was talking about the season, but of course all they wanted to talk about was *Homegrown*. And he really sold it hard as being about these three girls from Bethnal Green. As you know, if you read the play, the girls never even really get mentioned. It's a red herring.

Anyway, he gave this interview. You might remember it because it was published with that CCTV shot of the three Bethnal Green girls. I just rolled my eyes to the back of my head. I hate doing my own press, but I particularly hate it when other people do my own press for me. And then, the next day, I think I was in a workshop, I heard from Omar who had got a phone call from Paul Roseby, the head of NYT, saying that the Bethnal Green school had pulled out as a venue. They had been leaned on by the Tower Hamlets council. And the school just said, 'Look, there's actually no legal grounds here, but we don't want to piss off the council. That's more important to us as a relationship.' And I was like, 'Of course! My mum's a teacher. I get it, trust me!' More importantly, we were four weeks away from rehearsals and starting at that point. We were selling tickets for a show that didn't have a space, which is illegal besides anything else. The NYT didn't want to take it off sale if they could get another venue quick enough. And so they were like, 'We'll just keep it on sale and if we can't get another venue within 48 hours we'll take it off sale.'

Anyway, so we went back to our list and went to visit UCL Academy, which is up in Swiss Cottage, which was also great architecturally. We were like, 'Great, alright. Let's move here.' UCL were totally happy, 'Yeah! Let's sign. Let's do this. We love it. We know what the play is about. We think it's a great idea. We don't need to read the script. However, because of what's happened we think we should get it signed off by Camden Council.' They *did* want to see the script. That took about two weeks and all this time we're still selling tickets.

PM and AY: How, and at what point, did the police become involved?

NL: At that point, we had signed contracts so we were assuming we'd just go ahead with rehearsals and they were not going to cancel us twice. So we go into rehearsals. We were rehearsing at the new venue, UCL Academy. It's going great: I've got two associate directors and a choreographer and there's me and Omar. We are running five, six, seven rehearsal rooms simultaneously and I was sprinting in between them going, 'I like that bit, do more of that bit. That bit's rubbish. Do more of this.' Also, because it's a piece that takes place simultaneously in different classrooms, one of the hardest things is going, 'Right, if that scene happens there, I've then got to get all of the actors out of there and into the next scenes, and all of the audience out of this room without ever seeing each other, and so they don't see the other five sets of actors and audience.' So we just had all these massive war maps and matches and going, 'They're going to go that way and they're going that way and they're going to go down that staircase'.

So we had a production meeting, at the end of which there was an 'any other business' section. At that point, the producer of the NYT, who was a woman called Beth Watling, turned to me and Omar and said, 'Oh, we had a meeting with the police yesterday. And they were really lovely and they would like to read the script, so if you'd like to send us the most up to date one …' – because obviously we were adding things to it as we went along. Omar's head spun clean off his shoulders and he was like, 'What?!' Genuinely, because it was the first we'd heard of it. And it transpired that the meeting with the police had happened and that the producer had been there and members of the stage management team – which in itself was odd because you'd always have a member of the creative team there, because we're the people working with these kids. And they were suggesting a few measures which included policemen attending rehearsals, planting plain clothes police officers in the audience each night, sweeping with the bomb squad. And I'm just sitting there thinking, this is not what I left a Third World dictatorship for! And I was like, 'Well … do I have to give them the script?' And she said, 'No, no, no.' Because I was like, 'Is there an ultimatum being presented, like we won't give you your performance license or something?' 'No, not at all.' So I was like, 'Then … no! I don't want to give them the script. It's not finished and I don't want people to take things out of context.' But also I was very happy to give them this thing we call the Show Bible, which was sort of just a breakdown of everything that happens in it. So I was like, they just need to know what happens, because I know there are legitimate reasons for the police to be consulted in the policing of, say, a football match. So they might just be worried about, 'Are there any loud noises that could be misinterpreted by the neighbours?' or whatever. I'm happy to give them a list of those things in a sort of health and safety, fire safety kind of way, but I don't think they need to read what it is that we're doing. And they were like, 'OK, no problems!' And to be honest, I really don't know if they did send the script to the police because it was all in a dropbox that anyone could access. So maybe they did, I don't know.

PM and AY: How did you hear that the show had suddenly been cancelled?

NL: Well, we went back into rehearsals. And actually in all of this, what was really unusual is that the NYT had been there on the very first day of rehearsals to say, 'Hello! Welcome!' to everyone for the first hour and then they left. I think the next we saw of them was the Thursday of the second week when we had another production meeting. They had emailed that morning to say, 'Oh, can we come in this afternoon and see everything you've done so far?' And I was like, 'Yeah, welcome!'

So that Thursday afternoon we showed them everything that we'd done so far and they seemed really pleased and they gave us some really useful notes. I went home thinking, 'That was cool!' And I was at home working with my sound designer on a different show and I got a phone call from Omar – he's always the bearer of bad news – and I was like, 'Hey! What's up?' and he was like, 'Haven't you read your emails?' And I said, 'Read what?' He goes, 'Read it. Just open your emails.' So I opened them and we just simply had a group email to me, Omar and my creative team, just saying, 'We've decided to cancel the show. This does not reflect on your work.' Really? 'You'll be paid in full. Don't come to work tomorrow. We'll send you your affairs' – because all our stuff was there. 'We'll set up a meeting in a couple of weeks to debrief.' And I thought, what the fuck? Excuse me?

So, anyway, we were like, 'We're going in tomorrow because our stuff's there and I'm going to get my stuff'. Normally we would start at nine o'clock. So we thought, alright, we'll arrive there for 8.30 as usual and let them know that. When we turned up all the doors were still all locked and none of the kids were there when normally all the kids would start amassing on the steps outside quite early and then be let in at nine o'clock. None of them were there and I thought it was so weird, why aren't the kids all here? And it turns out that they'd told them to come in at ten. They didn't want to let us in, but we said, 'We're not going anywhere.' Anyway, eventually they let us in and they were sitting there with the Head of Press and the Stage Management team and I'm sitting there desperately trying not to cry and doing really badly. And then, Paul, the Artistic Director, turns up and he's like, 'Oh, why are you here?' 'Because you've fired me and I don't know why I've been fired.' And he says, 'No, we haven't fired you and it's very important for you to know we haven't fired you. The project just no longer exists.' And I was like, 'Well, it does because we wrote it! You can't … . This is like being gaslit!' It genuinely it felt like that. He said, 'I don't know what you're talking about.' And I was like, 'I've been fired. You fired me. I had a job yesterday. Today I have no job. I have been fired.' 'No, no. We're going to pay you.' 'That's not the point.'

And so then he asked if he could book us a separate meeting in a couple of weeks and I was like, 'Yeah, that would be fine, but I just need to know what's happened, so that I can not be a mad person.' At this point the kids had started turning up and they obviously knew that something was wrong because we were all sitting having a team argument. Anyway, Paul suggested we go to this separate room while he talked to the kids in the main hall. And I was like, 'Absolutely not! Not a chance. I'm not going to sit there and have you misrepresent the situation. I don't have any idea of what you're going to say. You're not going to tell me, for whatever reason, but I'm not going to let you misrepresent me to kids, some of whom I've just spent six months working with every day.'

And so all the kids were in the main hall. We go into the main hall. I've very obviously been bawling my eyes out. Omar's beard is very soggy and the kids were like, 'OK, so something's gone horribly wrong.' And so Paul says, 'Look, we've taken the decision to cancel *Homegrown*.' And his whole thing is that they had already by that point set up the replacement material. The kids had given up a certain amount of weeks and so the NYT had a sort of duty of care to fill that time, but before he even got to that bit a riot ensued. It was just screaming and shouting, 'What have we done? You came here yesterday and you thought it was all great and now you're telling us that it's not good enough. Is that what it is?' And I think also the kids were making astute points: 'You don't just get to say. … You don't just get to turn off the switch.'

So they just kept saying, 'Why? Why is this happening? What has happened?' And in the back of my head I'm going, something has happened, but he cannot tell them, so maybe he'll tell me. Maybe there's been a threat or some funding has been withdrawn, whatever it is. And so we get taken into this other room, and then they just kind of go, 'Right, so we're going to go and we're going to set up a meeting two weeks from now. And we'll have a proper debrief.' Debrief?! I want to be *briefed*! Do you know what I mean? And then they walked out, they literally walked out and I've never seen them since.

PM and AY: What happened to the subsequent meeting you were promised?

NL: They kept delaying it, cancelling it and rescheduling it and by that time everything had started playing out in the press. The board got involved and they sent us this email saying, 'Well, now it's all playing out in the press, we feel we don't need to have a meeting with you anymore'. One of my associates, who used to be a lawyer, knew very quickly that it was very important: a) to create an actual paper trail; and b) to come up with a public statement, because what NYT had told us was that they were going to email people telling them the show was no longer going on – we had already sold many tickets at this stage – and that they would be refunded in full.

This was a Saturday morning. Everything was now in the press and suddenly we get this phone call and it's from Shami Chakrabarti from Liberty. And she was like, 'I found out because I had bought a ticket and I just got this email telling me it had been cancelled and I knew that something was wrong.' She had been following it in the press and she suspected … . So we had a conversation and we ended up telling her all about it over the phone. She said, 'Right, I need to see you because I don't know what was in your play, and there are all sorts of tricky areas about inciting hatred and stuff. I need to have the legal team at Liberty look through the play to make sure that you are totally, like sort of legally clean, as it were. So just don't talk to anyone. We'll send a car to bring you to the Liberty offices.'

So we went to the Liberty offices on the Monday. Their lawyers started going over the script with a fine-tooth comb because there are all sorts of things that you could actually get in trouble for. They continued to be our legal counsellors actually for free and our press representation for free. And their thing was about how to get a statement out, working with other freedom of speech charities.

They decided to send off a load of Freedom of Information (FOI) requests to the Arts Council, Tower Hamlets Council, Camden Council, the police and the NYT. I don't know how much you know about FOI requests, but although they are technically legally binding, there is no punishment if you don't fulfil them. The only one of those that came back fulfilled was the Arts Council. Interestingly the police one came back not saying no, but saying that a FOI request is free only up to a certain number of documents – about 300 I think, I don't know what the number is – and after that you have to pay a very small fee: £15 or something. They were claiming, 'We've got more than this number of documents about said question so please give us £15', or whatever it is. Anyway, I said, 'That's a lot of documents for a show you said you had no involvement with.' And, you know, our legal team were eventually like, 'Look, you can take on the police. We will support you to take on the police, but I promise you it will get you nowhere and it will take over your life and you'll get nothing from it.'

And so I knew that was how it would end up, but I wasn't willing to be called a liar in the public sphere. Because what was happening repeatedly was that the police were going, 'We had no involvement in it. We have never met with anyone.' And I was like, 'You did because I have an email that says: "Following a meeting with the police ..."'. And at that time I knew I was going to do a Channel 4 interview, so I simply leaked them the email. Then they went back and said to the police, 'You said you didn't have meetings, so why did you send this email?' And they said, 'Oh, funny that! Turns out we did have a meeting and that police officer is now and continues to be on administrative leave!'

PM and AY: What sort of reaction did you get when news of the circumstances around the cancellation spread? And what did you do next?

NL: I mean there was a lot of, like … liberal hand-wringing – 'Oh, we've signed a public letter' – and that was all well and good. And some were real gestures of friendship, but there was a lot of mistrust. There were a lot of people who thought that actually we probably shouldn't have been doing what we were doing and it's not an appropriate subject to talk about with young people. And that was from within our own creative community, which was pretty appalling. But there were a lot of people, who I didn't know, who just came out of the woodwork: 'How can we help?'

And for a while we talked about the possibility of mounting the production, so we were talking to Secret Cinema because they were the only ones to have anything of that scope with a big performance space. In the end it just didn't work out because you can only really do a show with young people in the summer. By that point the summer was more or less over. Anyway, we managed to get a rehearsal space for two and a half weeks, which is how much rehearsal we had left, and we got the original cast back and we did evenings. We did as many hours as we could in a day just to get it finished.

So that took us to about December 2015 and at that point our original publishers were Oberon – who had published all Omar's plays before that – and they very quickly said, 'We will publish this play even though there is no production of it.' So, early in 2016 we went for a meeting with them. It was the first time we'd met with the entire publishing house – it's not a massive house, it's about twelve people, including the owners – because actually we had only been working with our editor and we were like, 'Oh, you have a boss! Actually you've got two bosses.' And we had a very uncomfortable meeting with one of them. He kept referring to 'they', which I found really problematic. You know, 'Those Muslims, what they …', whatever it was – you know, it's like when your grandfather is a bit racist. I remember because David Heinemann from Index on Censorship was at that meeting as well because we were thinking about the launch and when we left he was like, 'Who was that guy? He was the worst!' And then we got an email two days after that from the owner which said, 'Look, it's great and everything, but I don't want us to be the next *Charlie Hebdo*.'

By then we were so sick of these publishers, we were so over well-meaning white people and Omar was like, 'Dude, let's just do it on our own. Seriously, why are we working so hard to get somebody else to give us something that we can do ourselves?' And then it turned out that our designer Lorna, who did the illustrations inside the published script, her boyfriend works in publishing and he was like, 'Self-publishing is so easy! It's the easiest thing.' And so that became our absolutely clear focus. And so then Index on Censorship said, 'Well, how are you going to launch it?' We were like, 'We don't know, we haven't thought ahead.' They said, 'Well, we can take care of that.' And they did.[1]

PM and AY: In all this, did you manage to locate the actual censor: the individual or individuals who decided this might be a problem, or might contravene this or that regulation? Or was it more amorphous than that?

NL: I remember we went for a meeting at the Arts Council early on after it got cancelled and the Head of Theatre made some joke about, 'It feels as if whenever we get round to August we're always talking about censorship.' And I was like, 'Yes but let's look at the intersection of artists of colour and censorship. The people you're talking about are generally brown and black people and it's not funny!' But also, to me the problem is as much about the fact that arts funding in this country continues to fund a really antiquated sense of identity politics and actually when you get these newer forms of cultural questioning, it sort of really doesn't know what to do … . It sort of goes, 'But, but … how does this benefit the Asian community or the black community?' And you're like, 'Well, when's the black avant-garde going to rock up if we keep thinking like dinosaurs?'

And I feel that's the real problem about *Homegrown*: that the conditions for its existence are not just dependent on a cultural openness, but a creative openness that just does not exist. The avant-garde is still a reserve of the white middle classes and those sort of people weren't actually ready for it. Not that I think it's a magnum opus or anything … I just think … you know, it's a play about Muslims that does not particularly seek to educate or improve its audience, do you know what I mean? It's not a remedial piece of art in any way, it's just art for art's sake. Also, it says a lot of shit!

Ironically my best friend, who died last year, was a director called Bill Gaskill, who was responsible for taking down the Lord Chamberlain's censorship powers in the 1960s by turning the Royal Court into a members' club, which was when they put on *Saved* by Edward Bond. And I remember when it all happened with *Homegrown*, he sent me an email immediately saying, 'They will say that the play is not good enough – this is the oldest trick in the book.' But to me this whole sense of not being good enough … I could talk until I'm blue in the face about why aren't artists of colour allowed to fail. I don't know, maybe *Homegrown* is shit! I don't know, but I also essentially have a right to fail on a national scale. You've commissioned me to make a piece of art, that's how it works. I think the censor is in part the court of public opinion – that terror of what are people going to say about it. We don't know what they're going to make of it because it is not conventional, it's not remedial, it's not educational, it's not instructive or whatever … I think there's a huge amount that you can learn from it certainly, but it's not trying to be a do-gooder play.

So I think that's why, when people try and call me out on what I really think happened, I think it's like a national psyche problem. I remember when the National announced they were going to do *Another World*, which was a verbatim play about children joining ISIS, they used all of those flash words that drive me nuts, like 'brave', 'urgent'. And I was like, you're still positing this binary wherein Muslims are something to be feared, that you are essentially brave to talk about Muslims, but you are also creating a binary whereby they are not in your spaces. They do not attend your plays. Partly that is a prices issue, why there are no people of colour in the theatre, but also they don't give a shit. They don't go to your theatres, they don't care what you say in them. The fatwa against Salman Rushdie was a very specific thing that happened, but I sort of feel like its spectre hangs really heavy ... and it affects what these institutions do. Omar put it really well when he said: 'If *Homegrown* had been shut down because of crazy Muslims protesting we'd be heroes and the left would be like, look at these brave Muslims critiquing their own community.'

PM and AY: Wasn't one of the reasons you were given for the cancellation to do with safeguarding the young cast members? Did anything specific lie behind that?

NL: There was never an indication of a particular threat. I genuinely think they were safeguarding them from us. I think they were worried that they had bitten off more than they could chew and that they were exposing children to ideas that were just too big and too scary. And I'm not sure why that is because I don't think any of them ever had ... don't get me wrong, we had a lot of arguments with the kids where they were just like, 'I don't agree with this', and I was like, 'You don't have to agree with it, the point is ... '. There's a bit in it where a character says, 'I don't know why we're giving a voice to bad Muslims', and she has an argument about it and that is an argument we had. The actress herself at that point was like, 'I don't know why you don't want to represent good Muslims' and I was like, 'Aha! That's the problem!' But I guess if you look at it on the surface you can see why someone might ask, 'Why are they exposing children to a load of mad mullahs ranting about 70 virgins and all the rest of it', to which I'd reply, 'Because it's on YouTube!' It's just stuff that you can access, it's all out there in the world. I think that that sort of terrified the NYT. But I don't know why. I don't think it's anything scarier than what happens in the news.

PM and AY: Do you think the government's Prevent programme (preventing young people being drawn into violent extremism) had something to do with it?

NL: I actually think the NYT were not as conscious of Prevent when they started, but whatever conversation they had with the police made them hyper-aware of it. I genuinely think the NYT went into this just with their eyes shut. They just didn't know what they had bitten off. The hysteria of that conversation on a general cultural level is through the roof.

PM and AY: Do you think you were 'punished' for not reproducing the given agenda, providing answers to the 'Muslim problem' if you like, which was the assumption behind the commission?

NL: I think people hired us because they think that because we're Muslims we must have access to some secret answer. It's like, 'They must know why these kids go to ISIS!' And actually there's a reason the play just kind of ends without a conventional resolution. Because there isn't an answer. The play just grinds to a halt as this man who turns up and just begins to pray is like the radical force. It's as if to say, 'None of this really matters, it doesn't matter to me as a Muslim. What I care about is my faith. And my faith has nothing to do with anything that's … '. And that's what that gesture is meant to indicate. And I just felt like so much of it was just noise as well and the play is supposed to reflect that in some way: look at all this fucking noise we're just inundated with. You know and actually at the end there's just this moment of clarity: 'It's all fine … time moves forward, it's time to pray, I'm going to pray.'

So yes, I think they did expect us to come along and give them an answer and actually if you look at the play, first of all you realize that Omar and I never appear in it. The idea of having the kids as tour guides shepherding the audience around the rooms is all based on these young people: the devised scenes are all based on real YouTube footage; the verbatim dialogue is based on the people we met in Bethnal Green; and the 'fake' verbatim was written by the kids themselves. So at no point in it do you get an authentic opinion from the two of us because what we're doing is curating other people's opinions, which to us is more interesting.

It's also the thing that for us, as artists of colour, you're so often invited to critique your perceived community. So black people get to write about gun crime or knife crime, brown people get to write about honour killings, forced marriage or whatever. The expectation is that we're supposed to hang ourselves out to dry and actually for us it felt like the most avant-garde thing we could do was to critique our audience and to say: 'You … you're the problem.' It's this idea that everyone has a problematic relationship with Islam and we're going to show you how that is the case. The assumption is that the only people like that are old conservative white dudes or the EDL, that they're the only bad guys, and I'm like, 'No!' I've got as much of a problem with Naomi Wolf's white feminism and its intersection with discussions about the hijab. 'What the fuck do you know? How many hijabs have you ever worn?' Do you know what I mean? That is as problematic to me as your EDL racist: at least he waves a flag, he announces himself as a racist! And so, in all of that we don't really exist … none of these groups are us.

I think, also, we have had in this country maybe fifty years of *some* creative output from minority cultures. The question of Islam and how it can be 'a culture' is really interesting. I have a big problem with it. I was really fascinated watching the BAFTAs and I saw that Adeel Akhtar won Best Actor for *Murdered By My Father*, which unsurprisingly turns up in *Homegrown* because we hated it so much, just so much! And then think about Om Puri in *East Is East*. If you're a Muslim you can only still get rewarded for playing a violent man. We haven't really moved forward in twenty years because the only vision of Muslim masculinity is violent towards women and actually I don't care if you won a BAFTA, you're still getting rewarded for perpetrating really antiquated and damaging stereotypes. I just feel like the problem is that the people who sit on high are the same set of fusty white people and they really don't understand anything, so they go, 'You deal with it, you're a brown person, you're a black person, you can become the authority on this.' And some people genuinely believe Omar and I are authorities on radicalization. I get calls all the time from journalists who are like, 'Do you want to comment?' No! I'm an artist and I made a play and it's all in there.

Note

1   The play had an unofficial 'launch' on 6 March 2017 at Conway Hall, London, organized by Index on Censorship. Along with a panel discussion of the issues raised by the cancellation, there was an impromptu performance of some dialogue from the play delivered by cast members planted among the audience.

Index

9/11. *See also* terrorism; War on Terror
   increase in crimes against
      Muslims xvii, 37
   increase in Islamophobia xv–xvii, 71,
      190, 218
   interventionist foreign policy 36–9,
      215
   literary and artistic responses 89–99,
      205–19, 233
   perceptions of Muslims 71, 87, 187,
      207, 210, 218, 227–8, 233
   securitization 36–9, 41, 71–2,
      81, 165

Abbas, Hamra 216–19
Abbas, Sadia 133, 134, 209
Aboulela, Leila 123–5, 132–9
Abu-Lughod, Lila 108, 114–15
Afghanistan. *See also* US, foreign policy;
      War on Terror
   artistic and literary responses to
      military intervention 109,
      117–19, 209, 212, 215
   justification for military
      intervention 114–15
   opposition to military
      intervention 173
Ahmed, Leila 126
Ali, Kecia 129
Allen, Chris 4, 87–8, 166
Amanat, Sana 235, 240
Amis, Martin 88–99
Anbinder, Tyler 49–50
Annan, Kofi xvii
anti-Catholicism 18, 50, 53–4, 57–8,
   62, 63
anti-Muslim sentiment 49. *See also*
      Islamophobia
anti-Semitism. *See also* Judaism
   compared with Islamophobia 2–3,
      5–6, 30, 56–7
   contemporary xvi–xvii, 47, 55–6, 63,
      82, 98, 169, 195

European far-right politics 2–3, 10,
   60, 74
   historical 50, 54–5, 58, 60, 63
Asad, Talal 60, 127
Ataullah, Naazish 212–13, 219

Badran, Margot 127, 128
Bayoumi, Moustafa 229
Beyond the Page 207, 213–19
Buck-Morss, Susan 18
Bunzl, Matti 5–6, 10
burqa. *See* veiling
Bush, George H. W. 36.
      See also Gulf War
Bush, George W. 7, 14, 38–9, 61, 90, 114,
   215. *See also* War on Terror
Butler, Judith 127, 165–7, 171–2,
   174–6, 192

Carson, Ben 59–60
Casanova, José 47–8
censorship 17–18, 216, 248, 257–8.
      See also freedom of speech
Cincotta, Thomas 38
Cole, Juan 39
colonialism 9, 29, 75, 77, 79, 167
Conners, Joan L. 36
cooke, miriam 125, 140 n.17
Costello, Matthew 229, 235, 238
counterpublics 186–7, 192–7

Dadi, Iftikhar 207
Daesh. *See* ISIS; terrorism
Davis, Julie, and Robert
   Westerfelhaus 233–4
dehumanization of Muslims 35, 40, 71
Denmark 10, 88
Dobkowski, Michael 5, 6

Eagleton, Terry 95, 98
education
   activities for countering
      Islamophobia 152–8, 172, 175

barriers to countering
   Islamophobia   148–9
Islamic religious practices in
   schools   57, 72, 78, 81, 156, 234
Islamophobia in schools   147–8,
   158–60
no-platforming in universities   83,
   175
Prevent duty   81, 158, 165, 169–70,
   174–5
promoting inclusivity in
   schools   158–9
promoting pupil voice   150–2, 159
radicalization in schools   249–50
student activism   166, 171–6
student societies   165, 172, 174
Eisenhower, Dwight   31, 32
Elias, Jamal   131
El-Sherbini, Marwa   195
Esposito, John L.   10
Evans, Hiram W.   56

Fallaci, Oriana   9
feminism   105, 108–9, 119, 123–39, 260.
   See also gender
film   35, 107–8, 111–12, 119–20, 228,
   250, 261
Ford, Henry   55
France   2, 57–8, 72–4, 77–9, 82, 209–10
Franklin, Benjamin   50, 56
Fraser, Nancy   108, 185–7, 192–3,
   196
freedom of speech. See also censorship
   hate speech   149, 175
   purported Muslim opposition to   8,
      98, 258–9
   restricted for Muslims   17, 83, 169,
      175, 192, 255
Friedman, Uri   xix
Furnaletto, Elena   132

Gaddafi, Mu'ammar   33
Gaffney, Frank   51, 59
Game of Thrones (television series)   103,
   112, 113, 117, 118–19
gender. See also feminism; veiling
   complementarity   124, 128–30,
      135–8
   equality   115, 124, 127, 128,
      130, 135

stereotypes of Muslim men   40,
   110–12, 119, 210, 260–1
stereotypes of Muslim women   58,
   109–10, 124–6, 138–9, 172, 207,
   232
treatment of women by religion   58–9,
   124–8, 132
West 'rescuing' Muslim women   58,
   74, 109, 114–15, 126
women's rights   124, 126, 128
Germany
   emigration from   50, 53, 54
   far-right politics   xix, 82, 188
   immigration to   xix, 188
   media   xviii, 187, 189–92
   Muslim population   185–97
   nativism in   47
   perceptions of Muslims   4, 188
Gottschalk, Peter, and Gabriel
   Greenberg   8, 49
Green, James   211, 213
Gulf War   35–6, 106. See also US,
   foreign policy

Habermas, Jürgen   185, 186, 192, 196
Halliday, Fred   6, 48–9
Hamid, Mohsin   205, 208, 220 n.3
Hankins, Rebecca   232–3
Harris, Sam   96
Hashmi, Salima   207, 209, 211–14
Hassan, Waïl   133–4
hate crime   xvii, 2, 37, 81, 150, 195–6
Hazell, Katriana   214
Hewitt, Peter   206, 214
hijab. See veiling
Hitchens, Christopher   88
Hughey, Matthew W.   107–8, 112, 119
human rights
   education   149–50
   justification for military
      intervention   107, 111, 115
   legislation   149
   violations   40, 170, 210
   Western society   98, 105
Huntington, Samuel   xv–xvi, 61, 106
Hussain, Dilly   173
Hussein, Saddam   36, 39

immigration
   to France   77

to Germany   xix, 185, 188
stereotypical views of immigrants   75, 80, 152–3
threat to majority culture   xvi, 188, 216–18
to UK   xix, 3, 153, 167, 170
to US   xix, 8, 41, 49–57, 62–3, 235
India   49, 72, 74–7, 82
internet
  misinformation   3, 149–50, 155
  use by terrorists   173
  use to contest Islamophobia   11, 165, 173, 192–7
  use to spread Islamophobia   xiv, xviii, 1, 165
Iran
  American perceptions   32, 33
  hostage crisis   33, 34, 36
  Revolution   xv, 31, 34, 228
Iraq War. *See also* Gulf War; US, foreign policy; War on Terror
  human rights violations   40
  justification   36, 38–41
  literary responses   106, 109, 115, 117–19
  opposition to   173
ISIS. *See also* terrorism
  recruitment   52, 173, 176, 251, 258, 259
  refugees fleeing   2, 188
  support for   2, 170
  US foreign policy   41–2
Islam. *See also* Islamic culture and aesthetics; Qur'an; sharia; veiling
  religious practices   153–4, 193–4, 228–9, 236–7
  Sufism   124, 125, 128–32, 138
  as target of military action   40, 48
  as threat to Western values   57–62, 88–9, 91, 188, 205 (*see also* Western values)
  treatment of women   58–9, 124–8, 132
  Western perceptions   7–8, 61, 88, 131, 187–8, 205–6
Islamic culture and aesthetics   132, 207–9, 214, 216
Islamic State. *See* ISIS; terrorism
Islamophobia
  anti-Muslim groups   xviii–xix, 1, 240

  compared with other forms of racism   2–3, 5–6, 30, 56–7
  critique of term   6, 48–9, 188–9
  definition   xiv–xv, 4–7, 48–9
  history of   xiv–xvi, 29–36, 166–7
  increase in   xv, 1–4, 70–1
  influence on state policy   7, 30, 41–2, 71–2, 228
  in the media   2–3, 80–1, 149–50, 187, 189–92, 228
  as response to terrorist acts   xv, 2, 3, 165
  use of fear   xvi, 7, 30, 37, 47, 72, 228
Islamophobia: A Challenge for Us All   xiv, 5, 18, 48, 87
Israel
  anti-Israel activism   170
  Arab–Israeli conflict   6, 33, 228
  treatment of Muslims   5
  US support   7, 10, 32, 35

Jackson, Sherman   56
Judaism. *See also* anti-Semitism
  adversary of West   18, 50, 57
  Judaeo-Christian values   59–60, 63
  modernization   61

Kahf, Mohja   110, 125–6
El-Khairy, Omar   248–61
Khalid, Aisha   208, 209, 212, 215–16, 218, 219
Khan, Sadiq   1, 73
Khomeini, Ayatollah   xv, 31, 34
Ku Klux Klan   54–5, 56, 58
Kumar, Deepa   7, 31, 106, 109

Lawrence, Stephen   74, 159
Lean, Nathan   6
Le Pen, Jean-Marie   xvi, 73, 77
Le Pen, Marine   74
Lewis, Bernard   39, 106
liberalism   7–8, 12, 73–5, 119
Littman, Gisèle   88

Mahmood, Saba   126–7
Malcolm X   56
Martin, George R. R.   103–20
May, Theresa   82–3, 169
Mitha, Alnoor   207, 210–11

Modi, Narendra 13, 76–7
Mondal, Anshuman 214
Moore, Lindsey 125
Morey, Peter and Amina Yaqin,
    Framing Muslims 9–10, 166, 168, 175, 206, 228–9
multiculturalism 8, 9, 58, 73–4, 88, 219

Nasar, Hammad 206–7, 213–16
Nasser, Gamal Abdel 32–3
nativism 47–50, 54–8, 61–3. *See also* populist nationalism
neoliberalism 76–7, 81, 105
Netherlands 4, 87, 88
niqab. *See* veiling

Obama, Barack 7, 41, 48, 52, 62
O'Leary, Peter 115–16
O'Neill, Paul 213
Orientalism. *See also* Othering; stereotyping of Muslims
    Islamophobic tropes 166–7, 206
    in literature 90–9, 103–20, 123–4, 132, 227–30, 233–4
    in politics 31, 38, 42, 106
Othering 49–52, 74. *See also* Orientalism; stereotyping of Muslims

Pakistan 76–7, 139 n.9, 205–19
Pickthall, Mohammed Marmaduke 127–8
Pipes, Daniel 8, 87
populist nationalism 6, 9, 57–8, 73, 75–8. *See also* nativism
Prevent 81, 158, 165, 169–70, 174–5, 259. *See also* radicalization

Qur'an 124, 127–30, 132, 136, 213. *See also* Islam
Qureshi, Imran 205, 208, 209, 212–13, 218–19
Qutb, Sayyid 91, 94

radicalization 52, 115–17, 169–70, 173, 248–9. *See also* Prevent; terrorism
Ramadan, Tariq 74
Rana, Junaid 228
Randall, Martin 94, 95
Rao, Mallika 240

religion 59–61, 73–5, 79, 115–17. *See also* Islam; Judaism
Renton, James, and Ben Gidley 6
representations of Muslims. *See also* stereotyping of Muslims
    in comics 227–41
    in film 35, 111–12, 119–20, 228, 261
    in literature 89–99, 110, 124–6, 129–39, 208–9, 232–3
    in the media xvi–xviii, 2–3, 80–2, 149–50, 168, 187, 189–92
    on television 112, 113, 189–91, 260
    in the theatre 258
Rhett, Maryanne 239–40
Rothenburg, Julia 211
Royal, Derek Parker 230
Runnymede Trust xiv, xvii, 5, 18, 48, 87
Rushdie, Salman 89, 210, 258–9
Rushkoff, Douglas 230–1

Said, Edward xiv, 228, 232
Salih, Tayeb 133–4
Sarkozy, Nicolas 13, 77–8
Shafak, Elif 124–5, 128–32, 138–9
Shaheen, Jack 35, 111–12, 119, 228
sharia xix, 58–9, 61, 126, 132, 135, 168
Sheehi, Stephen 7
social media. *See* internet
stereotyping of Muslims. *See also* Orientalism; representations of Muslims
    challenging 148–9, 152–5, 205–7, 210, 219, 228
    dehumanizing effect 35, 40
    men 40, 110–12, 119–20, 210, 260–1
    relationship to foreign policy 7, 31–5, 38–9, 41–2, 228
    as terrorists xix, 52, 90, 93–4, 147, 152–4, 205, 233
    women 58, 109–10, 124–6, 138–9, 172, 207, 232
Stromberg, Fredrik 233
Sufism. *See under* Islam
Syed, Masooma 212–13

terrorism. *See also* ISIS; 9/11; radicalization
    Islamist attacks xv, xix–xx, 2, 165, 168, 176

justification for foreign policy   xvi, 30, 33–4, 37–41, 71–2
justification for securitization   xix, 51–3, 71–2
in literature   89–99
Muslim-as-terrorist stereotype   xix, 52, 90, 93–4, 147, 152–4, 205, 233
right-wing attacks   81, 83, 90, 154, 195
Threads, Dreams, Desires   207, 210–13, 215, 219
Tolkien, J. R. R.   103, 104, 105
Truman, Harry   31–2
Trump, Donald
 anti-Muslim rhetoric   xviii, 52–3, 58–9, 62, 88
 anti-Semitic rhetoric   55–6
 Islamophobic policies   xix, 2, 42, 51
 nativism   9, 47, 76

UK
 Brexit   2, 9, 170
 British values   71, 74, 168–9, 205
 foreign policy   xvi, 173
 history of racism   74–5, 167
 immigration to   xix, 153
 media   xvi, xviii, 2, 80, 149–50, 153, 167
 Muslim community   95, 147, 153–6, 165–6, 173, 176, 209–10, 219
 right-wing politics   2, 73
 securitization   165, 168–70 (*see also* Prevent)
US
 American values   53, 59–61, 233–5, 238
 domestic policy   xix, 2, 30, 36–9, 41–2
 elections   xviii–xix, 51–3, 61
 foreign policy   xix–xx, 7, 30–7, 39–41, 106, 213
 immigration to   49–57, 62–3
 Muslim community   52–3, 56–9, 63, 227, 229, 234–41

Vakil, AbdoolKarim   4
Veiling. *See also* Islam, religious practices

conflicts over   72, 138, 156, 189
feminist views   124, 126–7, 260
Islamophobic reactions   88, 124, 151, 155, 236
modest fashion   11, 238–9
perceptions of   125, 156, 168, 172, 232, 243 n.24
positive representations   233, 238
Western preoccupation with   110, 123, 126

Wadud, Amina   127–8, 129
Wajid, Sara   215
Warner, Michael   185–7, 194, 196
War on Terror. *See also* Afghanistan; 9/11; US, foreign policy
 artistic and literary responses to   98, 215–16, 233
 as Christian 'crusade'   48
 domestic policy   40–1, 228
 human rights violations   40
 increase of Islamophobia   12, 210, 229
 Islamophobic rhetoric   39–41, 87–90
 justification   114
 terminology   100 n.8
 use of fear   7, 72, 228
Warsi, Sayeeda   3
Western values. *See also* Islam, as threat to Western values; UK, British values; US, American values
 exporting to Muslim-majority nations   32, 75, 106
 Islam as opposed to   6–8, 10, 60, 95–9, 188, 205
 under threat   xiv–xvi, 35, 77–9, 105, 168, 216–18
Whiles, Virginia   209–10
Wilcox, Timothy   208
Wilkinson, John   105
Wilson, G. Willow   227, 229–32, 234–41

Young, Helen   105
Young, Iris   192

www.ingramcontent.com/pod-product-compliance
Lightning Source LLC
Chambersburg PA
CBHW070020010526
44117CB00011B/1649